Reciprocals and Semantic Typology

Typological Studies in Language (TSL)

A companion series to the journal *Studies in Language*. Volumes in this series are functionally and typologically oriented, covering specific topics in language by collecting together data from a wide variety of languages and language typologies.

For an overview of all books published in this series, please see
http://benjamins.com/catalog/tsl

Editor

Spike Gildea
University of Oregon

Editorial Board

Volume 98

Reciprocals and Semantic Typology
Edited by Nicholas Evans, Alice Gaby, Stephen C. Levinson and Asifa Majid

Reciprocals and Semantic Typology

Edited by

Nicholas Evans
Australian National University

Alice Gaby
University of California at Berkeley

Stephen C. Levinson

Asifa Majid
Max Planck Institute for Psycholinguistics, Nijmegen

John Benjamins Publishing Company
Amsterdam / Philadelphia

™ The paper used in this publication meets the minimum requirements of American National Standard for Information Sciences – Permanence of Paper for Printed Library Materials, ANSI z39.48-1984.

Library of Congress Cataloging-in-Publication Data

Reciprocals and semantic typology / edited by Nicholas Evans, Alice Gaby, Stephen C.
        Levinson, Asifa Majid.
        p.   cm. (Typological Studies in Language, ISSN 0167-7373 ; v. 98)
Includes bibliographical references and index.
1. Semantics. 2. Typology (Linguistics) I. Evans, Nicholas. II. Gaby, Alice. III. Levinson,
        Stephen C. IV. Majid, Asifa.
P325.R346   2011
401ʾ.43--dc22   2011013953
ISBN 978 90 272 0679 4   (Hb ; alk. paper)
ISBN 978 90 272 8662 8   (Eb)

John Benjamins Publishing Co. · P.O. Box 36224 · 1020 ME Amsterdam · The Netherlands
John Benjamins North America · P.O. Box 27519 · Philadelphia PA 19118-0519 · USA

Table of contents

Acknowledgments   VII

1. Introduction: Reciprocals and semantic typology   1
   Nicholas Evans, Stephen C. Levinson, Alice Gaby and Asifa Majid

2. The semantics of reciprocal constructions across languages:
   An extensional approach   29
   Asifa Majid, Nicholas Evans, Alice Gaby and Stephen C. Levinson

3. Semantics of Khoekhoe reciprocal constructions   61
   Christian J. Rapold

4. Reciprocal constructions in English: *Each other* and beyond   75
   Peter Hurst and Rachel Nordlinger

5. Reciprocal constructions in Indo-Pakistani Sign Language   91
   Ulrike Zeshan and Sibaji Panda

6. Mundari reciprocals   115
   Nicholas Evans and Toshiki Osada

7. Description of reciprocal situations in Lao   129
   N. J. Enfield

8. Reciprocal constructions in Mah Meri   149
   Nicole Kruspe

9. The coding of reciprocal events in Jahai   163
   Niclas Burenhult

10. Reciprocals in Yélî Dnye, the Papuan language of Rossel Island   177
    Stephen C. Levinson

11. Reciprocals in Rotokas   195
    Stuart Robinson

12. Expression of reciprocity in Savosavo   213
    Claudia Wegener

13. To have and have not: Kilivila reciprocals   225
     Gunter Senft

14. Strategies for encoding reciprocity in Mawng   233
     Ruth Singer

15. Reciprocal-marked and marked reciprocal events in Kuuk Thaayorre   251
     Alice Gaby

16. Reciprocal constructions in Olutec   265
     Roberto Zavala Maldonado

17. Reciprocal constructions in Tsafiki   277
     Connie Dickinson

18. Reciprocal constructions in Hup   315
     Patience Epps

19. Reciprocals and semantic typology: Some concluding remarks   329
     Ekkehard König

Addresses   341
Index   343

Acknowledgments

This book grew out of the project Reciprocals Across Languages, funded by the Australian Research Council (DP 37771) from 2003–6, and with substantial additional support from the Max Planck Institute for Psycholinguistics in Nijmegen. We thank both these bodies, and the University of Melbourne, School of Linguistics and Language Studies, for their financial and institutional support.

The specific design of the project we report on here was developed in informal meetings held from 2003–2004 in Melbourne and Nijmegen. Many members of the Language & Cognition and Acquisition groups participated and gave input into this stage, helping us design the video stimuli. We would also like to thank Nick Enfield who helped with the recording of the clips, and all the members of the MPI who ran around and hit and tried to delouse each other.

Data-gathering for the project, during the 2004 and 2005 field seasons, drew on the expertise of many scholars and the generous collaboration of many speakers. In addition to the scholars represented in individual chapters here, we would like to thank Dagmar Jung and Mim Corris, for obtaining data on Beaver and Barupu respectively. Specific acknowledgments to language speakers can be found in the individual chapters. We would also like to thank several other researchers whose involvement in other aspects of the project helped enrich the way we think about reciprocals, especially Leila Behrens, Robyn Loughnane, Sebastian Olcher Fedden and Volker Gast.

Presentations bringing this data together were then held at the 'Reciprocals Across Languages' workshop at MPI, Nijmegen, from April 19–21 2006, organised by the editors of this volume. We would like to thank Edith Sjoerdsma for her efficient help in organising that workshop. We thank the attendees at that workshop for their discussion and ideas, especially Martina Faller (who also reviewed some of the papers), as well as the various contributors for helping referee papers, round-robin style.

Preparation of this manuscript has benefited from the assistance of a number of MPI student assistants, who we thank here: Nan van de Meerendonk, Renske Schilte, Michelle Stapel and Kimberley den Brok for formatting, and Ludy Cilissen and Peter Nijland for help with illustrations.

Evans would additionally like to thank the Bogliasco Foundation, whose hosting of him through a Writer's Residence allowed him to write some crucial parts of the introduction.

Finally, we thank Spike Gildea for his advice as Series Editor. This book was originally proposed to the late lamented Mickey Noonan, Spike's predecessor in the Typological Studies in Language Series. Mickey was characteristically enthusiastic about the proposal, and we dedicate this book to his memory.

Nicholas Evans
Asifa Majid
Alice Gaby
Stephen C. Levinson

CHAPTER 1

Introduction

Reciprocals and semantic typology

Nicholas Evans*, Stephen C. Levinson**, Alice Gaby***
and Asifa Majid**
*Australian National University / **Max Planck Institute
for Psycholinguistics / ***Monash University

Reciprocity lies at the heart of social cognition, and with it so does the encoding of reciprocity in language via reciprocal constructions. Despite the prominence of strong universal claims about the semantics of reciprocal constructions, there is considerable descriptive literature on the semantics of reciprocals that seems to indicate variable coding and subtle cross-linguistic differences in meaning of reciprocals, both of which would make it impossible to formulate a single, essentialising definition of reciprocal semantics. These problems make it vital for studies in the semantic typology of reciprocals to employ methodologies that allow the relevant categories to emerge objectively from cross-linguistic comparison of standardised stimulus materials. We situate the rationale for the 20-language study that forms the basis for this book within this empirical approach to semantic typology, and summarise some of the findings.

1. Reciprocity in social cognition and language

子贡问曰：	A disciple of Confucius enquired:
有一言而可以终身行之乎？	"Is there one word which may guide one in
子曰：	practice throughout the whole of life?"
其恕乎！	Confucius answered,
己所不欲，勿施于人	"The word 恕 [*shù* 'reciprocity'[1]] is perhaps the word. What you do not wish others to do unto you, do not do unto them."
Confucius, Analects, Chapter 15	[Transl. Ku 1976: 138]

---

1. 'Reciprocity' is used in some translations of 恕 (e.g. http://www.yellowbridge.com/onlinelit/analects15.php), but a range of other words have also been offered: 'empathy', 'forgive, pardon'.

Reciprocity is recognised as fundamental to human society and morality by religions and ethical philosophies around the world. The evolution of complex societies in our own species – and some others – has been widely argued by evolutionary biologists to depend on reasoning about reciprocal obligations and the taking of reciprocal perspectives. Political and social theorists recognise the fundamental role of reciprocity in the social contract, as in a sentence like *And for the support of this declaration, with a firm Reliance on the Protection of divine Providence, we mutually pledge to each other our lives, our Fortunes, & our sacred Honor.*[2] In our daily lives, all sorts of interactions and escalations in social behaviour involve activities that require the reciprocally-directed activities of both parties. In fact, reciprocal activities occupy much of the narratives that interest us in novels, films and soap operas, from courtship through marriage to divorce, from meeting through exchanging gifts or gossip to fighting.

To talk and reason about such activities and principles in any accurate way we need linguistic devices to represent them. The majority of languages include special expressions for representing reciprocity, such as the *each other* construction in the English sentence cited above; more on the cross-linguistic facts below. But do these expressions always mean exactly the same thing? Do all languages have reciprocals? Do many languages have more than one reciprocal? What exactly are the meanings of the forms? How are the forms related to the meanings? These are the issues that this book is about.

1.1   Brief overview of the volume

It is the cross-linguistic comparison of how meanings are encoded within the reciprocal domain that forms the central theme of this book. In addition to hundreds of articles in the last few decades – the most important of which we will touch on as the chapter unfolds – there has been a flurry of recent books on reciprocals. The most notable of these include the massive cross-linguistic survey by Nedjalkov (2007), which brings together chapter-length descriptions of over 40 languages, each addressing a detailed questionnaire, the collections in Frajzyngier & Curl (1999) and König & Gast (2008), which cover reciprocals in dozens of languages from a range of perspectives, Kemmer's (1993) study of the middle voice, which includes substantial sections on constructions spanning the reciprocal and related meanings (especially reflexives), and the recent diachronic study of English reciprocals by Haas (2009). These works, despite their variety, all draw on the

---

2.   Declaration of Independence of the United States of America July 4, 1776.

four standard data-types used in descriptive and generative linguistics: corpora (especially the Haas book), made-up and naturally-occurring examples, and answers to typological questionnaires.

This book has a different method and a different focus. It aims to explore the semantic domain of reciprocals across languages using a fixed set of non-linguistic stimuli, which enable the relevant constructions and their semantic extension to emerge naturally during the description of the stimuli. This allows precise comparison across languages and the extraction of general patterns and outliers. It is one of the first applications of these more objective methods to a grammatical domain (though see Levinson & Meira 2003, Levinson & Wilkins 2006).

We compare a sample of 20 languages[3] spanning every continent, fifteen maximal clades (or language families),[4] and including a sign language so as to detect possible modality-specific effects.

The core of the comparison comes from speaker-descriptions of video-stimuli depicting different sorts of "reciprocal" actions (more details shortly), complemented by additional elicitation and observation. In the overall sampling, there is a skewing towards languages of the Western Pacific, which was deliberate in choice. Languages from this part of the world are poorly documented and relatively under-represented in previous surveys on reciprocals (such as Nedjalkov 2007). Our strategic inclusion of them in this volume, we hope, goes some way towards compensating for this gap in the previous literature. In fact, for most languages included here, no previous published data exists, with the obvious exception of English – included here in order to allow cross-checking of our findings and methods against the vast existing literature. Another point of comparison is with Mundari (which was represented in the 2007 Nedjalkov collection – Osada 2007). Again, its inclusion here allows the different orientations of these two projects to be compared.

In the rest of this chapter we give the typological background for the project, including the relevant semantic and structural dimensions, and our rationale for the project design. In Chapter 2, we report on an objective comparative approach

---

3. Thorough descriptions can be found in 16 of the chapters devoted to detailing the specifics of individual languages. The four remaining languages feature in the next chapter (Chapter 2), which describes the typological findings.

4. Maximal clades are the largest groupings of demonstrably related languages postulated in the literature. In the current sample, there are three major lineages from Australia (Iwaidjan, Tangkic and Pama-Nyungan). Two of our sampled languages – Iwaidja and Mawng – come from within a single clade (Iwaidjan). We also include data from three Austroasiatic languages: Mundari, from the Munda sub-branch and Jahai and Mah Meri from Aslian. All other languages in the sample are drawn from distinct maximal clades.

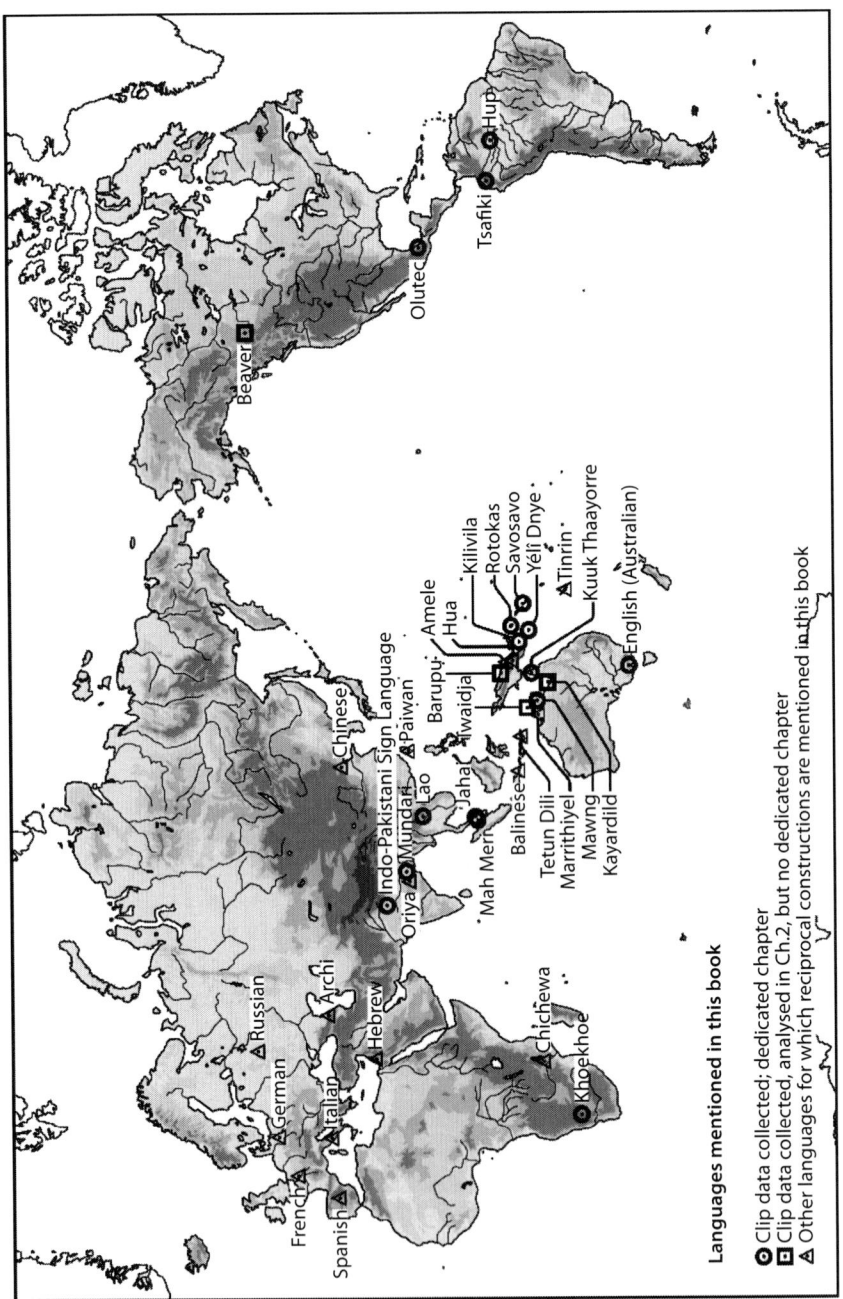

Figure 1. Languages mentioned in this book

to the data analysis using multivariate statistics. The sixteen central chapters then give details of the relevant constructions at work in individual languages. A final chapter provides a conspectus on our findings, within linguistics and beyond.

1.2   Reciprocity, morality and the translation problem

Reciprocity lies at the heart of moral reasoning and social relations, as suggested by the Confucian rule of doing to others only what one what one would like done to onself. Social reasoning about reciprocity, it is reasonable to assume, is underpinned by the interpretations and ambiguities that a given construction affords. For example, should moral injunctions like *Guests should repay each other's hospitality* or *Different generations should help each other* be interpreted as direct bilateral reciprocity, or as 'generalised reciprocity' without an exact balancing of accounts in every dyadic combination? The first interpretation would require direct repayment of hospitality to the same guest, or direct helping back of the generation that helped you, as when children look after their aging parents to repay the debt they incurred from the support the parents gave to them in youth. The second interpretation would be satisfied by A repaying the hospitality she received from B to some other guest, C, or parents helping their children, who help *their* children in turn. Kuma marriage contracts (Reay 1959) are one of many instantiations of the first interpretation. Examples of the second type are the Hindu notion of Karma – or the view of parenting given by the English word *reciprocate* in (1), and Kayardild -*thu*- in (2). The verbal suffix -*thu*- is dedicated to the marking of reciprocal relations, exemplified by (2), but can also take in chained unidirectional relations (3) that could not be expressed by the reciprocal in English, at least in this case.[5]

(1)   The parent-child, especially the mother-child relationship stands in the sharp-est contrast of all to the laws of the market. It is utterly unequal, yet there is no expectation that the sacrifice entails or requires reciprocation. On the contrary, *the only way children can reciprocate is through the love they give and the sacrifice they make for their own children*'.
                                            [Guardian Weekly Sept 24–30 2004, p. 15;
                                            Martin Jacques: The Death of Intimacy. Italics ours]

(2)   *birr-a   bala-**thu**-th*
        3du-NOM   hit-REC-ACTual
        'The two of them are hitting each other.'

---

5.   Though there are of course other verbs in English, like 'follow', which can be used of chain-ing relationships involving lines of people (*they followed each other onto the stage*) – see below.

(3) *ngada   marmirra-yarrad,*
1SG.NOM good.craftsman-other
marmirra-ntha   *mima-**thu**-tharra-nth*
good.craftsman-COMPL.OBL beget-REC-PST-COMPL.OBL
'I am a good craftsman, because I come from a lineage of good craftsmen.'
(Lit. 'because good craftsmen begot one another [in my lineage].')

(Evans 1995: 281)

So far our discussion has assumed a parallel semantics between the signs expressing reciprocity across languages, whether lexical nouns like English *reciprocity* and its counterparts, or grammatical devices like English *each other* or the
Kayardild suffix *-thu*. But there are also many languages where the formal devices
for expressing reciprocity have additional semantic possibilities, a situation which
adds further interesting ethical dimensions. Consider the following passage from
Genesis (2,25) in the Old Testament concerning Adam and Eve's state of primal
innocent nakedness unclouded by shame. In its Hebrew original it goes:

(4) *wayyihyu*   *shen-e-hem*   *'arumm-im ha='adam*
be\CR.NARR.3MPL both two-MDU=3MPL naked-MPL DEF=person
we='ish-t=o   *wa=lo=   yitboshashu*
CR=woman-FSG=3MSG   CR=NEG= be.ashamed\npst.rr.3mpl
'And they were both naked, the man and his wife, and they were not ashamed'.

(King James Version)

Now the Hebrew word *yitboshashu* is a so-called hithpael[6] form of the plural of
the triliteral root *b-o-sh* 'be ashamed'. Hithpael forms (here glossed RR for 'reflex-
ive/reciprocal') have a number of meanings, which can include reflexive, iterative,
autobenefactive and declarative/estimative[7] as well as reciprocal. This allows, in
principle, for several rather different translations: one way lies guilt, and the other
way shame.

The reflexive translation 'be ashamed of themselves' in (4) emphasises guilt as
a personal internalisation of morality and its infringement, while the reciprocal
translation 'be ashamed before each other / be ashamed in each other's presence'

---

6. More strictly, a *hithpolel*, which is the form hithpael verbs take with so-called 'hollow'
verbs, that is, verbs with a medial glide (w/y) in the root. In such cases the glide does not get
reduplicated, as it would in the paradigmatic case; rather, the *sh* is inserted. A regular hithpael
would be *yitqaddeshu*, as for the verb *q-d-sh*, but here for the verb *b-w-sh* it is *yitboshashu.*

7. I.e. 'to pretend/declare to do X' (e.g. 2 Samuel 13:5 'pretend to be ill'; Esther 8:17 'professed
to be Jews').

or even 'cause each other shame'[8], emphasises shame as something that happens in company, in other words as a social emotion. The potential ambiguity of this particular line has generated a huge amount of theological discussion, within both Jewish and Christian traditions. It has also given rise to different translations emphasising one or the other interpretation. Just consider some English versions: Young's Literal Translation (5a) favours a reflexive, the Amplified Bible (5b) and an online Torah study guide of the Jewish Bible (5c) use a reciprocal, while the King James (4) and New American Standard Bibles (5d) favour a simple verb that is mute on the question. Another, scholarly translation (Sasson 1985) favours a reciprocal causative interpretation: 'yet, they did not shame each other'.[9]

(5)   a.   *And they are both of them naked, the man and his wife, and they are not* **ashamed of themselves.**   (Young's Literal Translation)

   b.   *Now, both of them were naked, the man and his wife, but* **they felt no shame** **before each other.**   (New Jerusalem Bible)[10]

   c.   *The man and his wife were both naked, but they were not* **embarrassed by** **one another.**
       (Torah: Navigating the Bible 2. Online bar/bat mitzvah tutor. http:// bible.ort.org/books/pentd2.asp?ACTION=displaypage&BOOK=1)& CHAPTER=2)

   d.   *And the man and his wife were both naked and were not ashamed.*
                                    (New American Standard Bible)

Without taking any side in this complex hermeneutic debate, the point is that it is the grammatical ambiguity (or alternatively, semantic generality) of the hithpael construction in Hebrew, between reciprocal and reflexive readings, which opens up this interpretive space, of such great significance for Judaeo-Christian theology.

   Like the deontic modality of *should* and *ought*, reciprocity thus plays a central role in the formulation of the rules and regulations of social life. The interpretation of moral injunctions often hangs on the semantic generalities and ambiguities of these expressions, as so nicely revealed by the problems of translating ethical and legal texts.

---

8.   See Sasson (1985). Hamilton (1990).

9.   Cf. another online commentary: Le verbe yitboshashu a valeur de hitpolel, qui implique une réciprocité. D'où la traduction proposée par l'A. "ils ne se causaient mutuellement aucun embarras", sens qui convient bien à la suite du récit.". Website: cat.inist.fr/?aModele=afficheN& cpsidt=12150443.

10.   See http://en.wikipedia.org/wiki/New_Jerusalem_Bible.

2.   Reciprocals as a topic for semantic typology

The study of the matches and mismatches between the meanings of expressions drawn from different languages within a single semantic domain is the central concern of semantic typology: the systematic cross-linguistic study of meaning. Here the domain is of course reciprocity, which may be thought of independently of any particular language in terms of the logic of relations, for example as symmetrical relations defined over a set of actors (see Dalrymple et al. 1998 for the range of possible relations). The limitations of such an approach to natural language will become apparent, so a good point of departure is the meaning of English *each other* and its near-synonym *one another*.[11]

How clear is the meaning we are looking at, in fact? Once we scrutinize English sentences in detail, we find some interesting sub-types in the dimension we will call *configuration*.

(6)   *The members of this family love one another.*   [Strong]

(7)   *The people at the dinner party were married to one another.*   [Pairwise]

(8)   *The graduating students followed one another up onto the stage.*   [Chain]

(9)   *The teacher and her pupils intimidated one another.*   [Radial]

(10)   *The drunks in the pub were punching one another.*   [Melee]

(11)   *The children chased each other round in a ring.*   [Ring]

In (6) the designated relationship holds, symmetrically, between every pair of entities in the group – this is generally called a *strong reciprocal*. In (7) the group is partitioned into pairs, within each of which the relationship holds symmetrically, while outside the pairs it does not hold at all – a *pairwise reciprocal*. In (8) most of the participants will both follow and be followed (though by different people); however the first will only be followed, and the last will only follow (*reciprocal chaining*). Sentence (9) is ambiguous, but in one of its readings the teacher intimidates each of her pupils and vice versa, but no intimidation obtains between pairs of students. In (10) the pairings are more disorganised: some pairs are symmetric (pairs squaring off), some go one way, and some individuals may be left out of the action altogether (a *melee*). And in (11) each participant is both chased and a chaser, but there is no pair within which a symmetrical relation holds.[12]

---

11. Various claims about semantic differences between *each other* and *one another* have been made in the literature, though they do not stand up to scrutiny against English corpora. See Ch. 4, Section 2.1 for details and references.

12. See Langendoen (1978) and Dalrymple et al. (1998) for an even fuller set of possibilities. We concentrated our investigation on types that were most likely to received distinct treatment as garnered through pilot observations.

There are other semantic dimensions as well. Many languages use different formal means for reciprocals with two participants versus those with more, so we can propose participant *number* as a further relevant dimension. An example is the Taiwanese language Paiwan, which forms dual and plural reciprocal meanings by a different reduplication pattern: *pacun* 'look', *ma-pa-pacun* '(two) look at each other', *ma-pa-pacu-pacun* '(more than two) look at one another' (Zeitoun 2002).

A further dimension is *temporal*. Simultaneous vs sequential reciprocation – the difference between 'they looked at one another' and 'they massaged one another' – is also distinguished constructionally in some languages. Examples are the Australian language Marrithiyel (Green 1989: 120) and the Austronesian language Balinese, where simultaneous reciprocals use an intransitive construction with the prefix *ma-* (12)[13], while sequential reciprocals use a patient-focus construction filling the agent slot with the free reciprocal marker *saling* (13).

(12) *Nyoman   ma-diman   (ajak   Ketut)*
      [name]   MID-kiss   with   [name]
      'Nyoman and Ketut kissed each other.'
      'Nyoman was involved in kissing with Ketut.'

(13) *Nyoman   saling   ø-diman   (ajak   Ketut).*
      [name]   RECIP   Undergoer.Voice-kiss with   [name]
      'Nyoman and Ketut kissed each other (in turn).'
      'Nyoman was involved in kissing with Ketut.'

A further well studied dimension of variation is the *action or situation type*. Thus some English verbs (see e.g. Jespersen 1927: 325f, Lakoff & Peters 1969), will attract reciprocal interpretations when used with plural subjects even without additional marking (*they kissed, they got married*, etc.), whereas other verbs in the same syntactic frame will get reflexive interpretations (*they shaved, they washed*) and others again get joint-action but not reciprocal interpretations (*they ate, they looked*). Haiman (1983) attributes this effect to iconicity – effectively motivated by Zipfian effects on which configurations are commonest for particular event types – and points out that such constructions evoke simultaneous, stereotyped events: *John and Mary kissed* wouldn't be used, for example, if John first kisses

---

13. In fact, in Balinese simultaneous reciprocals in *ma-* are restricted to verbs denoting 'naturally reciprocal events', such as 'collide' (*ma-palu*), 'wrestle' (*ma-gulet*), 'kiss' (*ma-diman*), 'hug' (*ma-gelut*), 'bite' (*ma-gutgut*), 'meet/collide' (*ma-cantet*), 'fight' (*ma-kerah*) and 'meet in passing, e.g. on street' (*ma-papas*). Verbs for other events, such as *tebek* 'stab', need to employ the circumfix *ma-...-an* to get a reciprocal reading: *ma-tebek-an* 'stab each other, be involved in stabbing' (it is not clear whether the simultaneous / sequential contrast is then maintained with these verbs). See Arka MS for the discussion on which this is based.

Mary on the foot and then Mary kisses him on the back of the neck, whereas *John and Mary kissed each other* could be stretched to describe such an event.

Kemmer (1993) characterises the unmarked cases as 'natural reciprocal events', and shows that there is substantial convergence across languages in which events get encoded with a 'light reciprocal strategy' (unmarked in English, minimally encoded in other languages)[14]. Nonetheless, the fact that languages don't converge perfectly shows we must treat such a 'natural' class with due caution. First, there are languages where even 'natural reciprocal events' must be coded using overt reciprocal morphology; Bininj Gun-wok (Evans 2003:441) and Mundari (Chapter 6) are good examples. Secondly, the exact set of events used in such constructions varies: in Oriya one can say in effect 'they snubbed' (*apada* 'snub' used with a conjoined subject to mean 'snub each other, not be on speaking terms with each other') or in Tinrin 'they put arms on shoulders' (*rùù* 'put arms around shoulders'), used with a plural subject to mean 'put arms around each other's shoulders', (Osumi 1995). Thirdly, the set of English verbs which participate in this interpretation has changed historically: see Potter (1953) for examples of both 'love' and 'see' used in this way, e.g. *When shall we see again?* in *Cymbeline* I i.124. Was 'see' really a 'natural reciprocal event' in Shakespeare's time, as it still is in many languages today (e.g. modern Tamil *appuram paappoom* [later see:FUT:1plS] 'we will see (it/each other) later') but no longer in modern English? Such facts show that convergence across languages and historical stages in what

---

14. Kemmer (1993) adopts the strategy of distinguishing 'light' and 'heavy' reciprocal strategies since many languages oppose at least two strategies of marking reciprocal events. The strategies differ in lexical and phonological weight. The English-type conjoined-subject strategy *they kissed* is avoided in some languages, so the distinction between 'light' and 'heavy' strategies permits a more supple cross-linguistic classification: the lexical set of 'natural reciprocal events' can be investigated by seeing which verbs get reciprocal readings from the 'light' strategy, whatever it is.

In Romance languages like French, Spanish or Italian, for example, the light strategy is to use reflexive/reciprocal clitics, whereas the heavy strategy is to ramp this up by adding a binomial phrase like *l'un l'autre*, *el uno al otro*, or *l'uno l'altro* or *a vicenda*, respectively, to the basic reflexive-clitic strategy. Thus in Italian *guardarsi*, with reflexive clitic *si*, is ambiguous between reflexive readings like *guardarsi allo specchio* 'look at oneself in the mirror', and reciprocal readings like *L'amore nasce dal piacere di guardarsi, si nutre della necessità di vedersi, si conclude con l'impossibilità di separarsi* (http://www.facebook.com/note.php?note_id=156944310613; accessed 30/3/2010), i.e. 'love is born from the pleasure of looking at one another, nourished by the need to see each other, and concludes with the impossibility of separating'. Ambiguities arise, as in *mettere uno specchio per guardarsi mentre si fa l'amore* 'put a mirror to look at (yourselves/each other) while making love'. The heavy version, on the other hand, is explicitly reciprocal, as in the saying *amore non è guardarsi a vicenda: è guardare insieme nella stessa direzione*, i.e. 'love is not looking at each other, but looking together in the same direction'.

gets treated as a 'natural reciprocal event' is only partial, underlining the importance of including a varied set of situation types in one's investigations.[15]

Our own investigation began with the construction of a set of video-stimuli that depicted various events varying on the parameters identified above (Evans, Levinson, Enfield, Gaby & Majid 2004). Researchers investigating the 20 different languages took these materials to the field in order to elicit speaker descriptions which were then coded for the construction-types observed (see Chapter 2 for more details). For the stimulus set, we selected ten situation types: *chase, delouse, give, hit, hug, lean, meet, (be) next to, shake hands,* and *talk.* This selection included:

- some prima facie 'natural reciprocal events' like *hugging, meeting* and *shaking hands,*
- events like *chasing* that we might expect to exhibit more latitude in accepting reciprocals with unidirectional configurations (as in English 'the policeman and the burglar chased each other down the street'),
- events that generate social expectations of reciprocity (*giving*),
- events that tend to involve causative mutual escalation (*hitting*),
- events that are sociable but not necessarily reciprocal (*talking, delousing*),
- events that involve no human participants (*leaning, being next to*).

Two final semantic dimensions bear mention here: *initiation* and *granularity.*

Many languages distinguish reciprocal activity where both parties have equal responsibility for *initiating* or maintaining the event, from the situation where one party is the clear initiator. A nice example of this (in Examples 14 and 15 below) is the Austronesian language Tetun Dili (Williams-van-Klinken, Hajek & Nordlinger 2002:60–61). We did not explore this dimension systematically in this study but nonetheless some chapters report on constructions of this type, e.g. Chapter 16 on Olutec.

(14) *João   ho   Maria   istori   malu.*
     John   and/with   Maria   quarrel   RECIP
     'John and Maria quarrelled (no indication as to who started it).'

(15) *João   istori   malu   ho   Maria.*
     John   quarrel   RECIP   and/with   Maria
     'John quarrelled with Maria (he started it).'

---

15. We are not aware of any thorough cross-linguistic study which systematically compares a large set of predicates (numbering in e.g. the hundreds) across a diverse sample of languages, to examine the degree to which the same event types are treated as 'natural reciprocal events' in the Kemmerian sense.

Granularity has to do with how specifically the situation is being categorised. If John slaps Peter, who punches him back, we can treat this as reciprocal at a coarse level of granularity – *John and Peter hit each other* is an acceptable description – but not at a finer one, for example *John and Peter slapped each other*. Interesting discussions arose in the responses of some speakers to scenarios with fine-grained variation in event depiction. In Kruspe, Chapter 8, for example, we see how the detailed categorisation of impact verbs in the language Mah Meri means that some events which would be counted as 'hitting each other' in English run afoul of the need for reciprocity to operate at a finer level of granularity. It is likely that granularity judgments play a much greater role in the use of reciprocals than has hitherto been noted in the literature (see Evans 2008). Some unusual descriptions which are generally analysed as unidirectional (such as *The woman and the burglar chased each other down the street*), could perhaps be assimilated to bidirectional analyses if the relevant situation is not the complete event, but a subset of it – e.g. 'moving, in a way that is oriented to the other participant, such that the speed and direction of one participant is a determinant of the speed of the other'.

3.   Reciprocals as low-frequency constructions

Човек с човек се среща,
планина с планина се не среща

People meet,
mountains don't

Bulgarian proverb[16]

The pivotal role of reciprocity in social cognition and organisation should not blind us to the fact that, on grounds of frequency, it is surprising that languages bother to evolve specialised reciprocal constructions at all. Actual occurrences of these constructions in texts are remarkably low: the British National Corpus lists 103 occurrences of *each other* per million words, ten times less frequent than reflexives (1,184 of all person/numbers). Adding *one another* to *each other* moves this up a tad, to 130 words per million, i.e. roughly 1 per 10,000 words – but still about two orders of magnitude rarer than the regular pronoun *it* with 10,562 per million.

Faced with these low incidences, one might object that a crude count just based on *each other* and *one another* misses other English constructions that express reciprocal meanings in alternative ways, e.g. as a bare verb in *they kissed* or as an adjective in *of mutual benefit*. We can only pick out these other strategies

---

16. The English translation of this proverb appears in Crystal (2008); we thank Zlatka Guéntcheva for supplying us with the Bulgarian original.

by doing a hand count, reading for all ways of expressing reciprocal meanings in a stretch of text. But even this gives such low incidences as 1 occurrence every 878 words for the Jane Austen's English novel *Sense and Sensibility* or 1 every 830 words for Isabel Allende's Spanish novel *Ritrato en Sepia*. And these figures come from novels of human relationships dense with reciprocal interactions; the percentages fall by another order of magnitude in other genres like travelogues.[17] What we have with reciprocals, then, is a grammaticised category which occurs in most of the world's languages despite frequency levels far below those found for just about any other grammaticalised meaning dimension.

This low incidence means that many grammars – particularly if based on small corpora from languages with a short descriptive tradition – will not furnish sufficiently detailed exemplification to see what is going on, grammatically or semantically. Indeed, some relatively detailed grammars neglect to mention the existence of reciprocal constructions altogether.[18] Others devote frustratingly little space to exploring their syntax and semantics in detail – an average of 3.5 pages for the sample of 23 grammars surveyed in Evans (2007). Even the exemplary collection of detailed language-specific descriptions in Nedjalkov (2007) with its 85-item questionnaire (Nedjalkov & Geniušienė 2007) does not probe whether such meanings as 'chaining' and 'pairwise' reciprocals, which form a central part of the formal semantic literature on reciprocals, are encodable by the reciprocal construction. These are part of a set of meanings we explore below, and throughout this volume. Using stimulus sets enables us to upgrade the incidence of reciprocal constructions to levels where their lines of organisation become discernible.

Reciprocals are thus a unique and intriguing grammatical category which exhibit: (i) low textual frequency, (ii) high cross-linguistic incidence of grammaticisation, and (iii) centrality in the representation of social relationships. Nonetheless, some languages get away with no dedicated reciprocal construction. An example is the Kilivila language of the Trobriand Islands (Senft, Chapter 13) which despite being famed in anthropological circles for the centrality of exchange to the culture that speaks it, lacks any specialised encoding of reciprocals in its grammar (perhaps, as Senft suggests, because reciprocity can often be assumed). This raises the question of why languages bother to have reciprocal

---

17. These figures are from Evans (2007), which includes hand-count figures from English, French and Spanish.

18. For example Kibrik's detailed grammar of Archi (Kibrik 1977) does not mention any reciprocal construction in the language, but data gathered recently by Marina Chumakina using the video clips set developed in this project was able to show the existence of a very interesting type of reciprocal construction there – unfortunately this data was gathered too late to be incorporated into the present volume.

constructions at all, since reciprocal meanings can always be implicated when necessary. This is the normal strategy across the board in Kilivila, but is also widespread in English, as we saw earlier. The cancellability of the implicature in such cases is well known: in *John and Mary disagree*, the normal implicature is 'with each other'[19], but this can be cancelled in situations where it is clear that the disagreement is with a third party: *Stuart was all for going on, but John and Mary disagreed*. Although we have no ready explanation for why reciprocals so often have dedicated grammatical expression despite their infrequency, it is likely that the key role reciprocity plays in general social life is part of the answer. The infrequency may also motivate the general finding that reciprocal constructions are rarely restricted to strict symmetric, exhaustive pairings over participants – to stay in work, reciprocal constructions need to have a wider job description than the logical analysis might predict.

4.   Reciprocal constructions: Compositionality and structural variability

Equally problematic for the question of why languages should have dedicated reciprocal constructions is the complex mapping problems they raise between semantics and syntax. This strikes at the heart of Frege's principle that the meaning of complex signs can be derived from the meanings of simpler signs, along with semantically-interpreted rules of composition. This principle is so fundamental to the enterprise of semantics – particularly within the formal semantic tradition – that a key goal for semantic typology should be to examine those parts of grammars where it regularly holds and those where it doesn't.

Generative and formal semantic approaches to reciprocals have built a long and interesting tradition of investigation essentially aimed at deriving the meaning of English reciprocals by composition from the two elements *each* and *other*, through the movement or floating of the second element (Dougherty 1974, Fiengo & Lasnik 1973, Higginbotham 1980, Langendoen 1978 and Langendoen & Magloire 2003). This recapitulates, in synchronic movement analysis, a historic grammaticalisation from an earlier structure of the form 'The earls each hated the/an[20] other' or 'The earls hated one the/an other' to the merger of the two quantifying elements in *The earls hated each other / one another* (Plank 2008).

---

19. E.g. *John and Mary agree on the facts but disagree in their attitude toward the facts* [example accessed from philosophy.lander.edu/logic/posttest-02.pdf (accessed 23/3/2010)].

20. With English and German grammaticizing the indefinite-article version (*one another, einander*) and Romance languages grammaticising the definite-article version (Sp. *el uno el otro*, Fr. *l'un l'autre*, It. *l'uno l'altro* etc.).

Though a number of complex formal moves are involved, at least in languages like English, German, French, Italian and Spanish it is possible to view each element of the two-part binomial NP *each other* as mapping to a quantifier in logical form, with lambda operators achieving the correct assignment of agent/patient pairings from the participant set. This allows some semblance of iconic motivation for the English construction from the corresponding postulated meaning.

A difficulty of basing a universal account of reciprocals on *each other*-type structures is that they are far from universal. English (Hurst & Nordlinger, Chapter 4) is in fact the only language within our 20-language sample where binomial quantifier structures are the primary coding strategy for reciprocals. Three others have somewhat comparable encoding mechanisms based on reduplication of quantifiers or generic nouns – the Mah Meri *mōle mōle* construction (Kruspe, Chapter 8), the Yélî Dnye *woni-woni* construction (Levinson, Chapter 10) and the Savo-savo *mapa-mapa* construction (Wegner, Chapter 12). Another three languages have secondary strategies based on the reduplication of adverbs meaning 'return' or 'straight': Tsafiki *beko-beko*, Dickinson, Chapter 18; plus Barupu *bárubáru* and Kayardild *junkuyunku*.[21] Even on the most generous interpretation, then, substantially fewer than half the languages in our sample contain any type of binomial construction which would allow reciprocal meanings to be derived by composing two quantifiers.

Once we confront the dizzying variety of construction types used across languages, Frege's principle of compositonality becomes increasingly frayed. In fact, reciprocal constructions arguably exhibit greater structural diversity than any other grammaticised meaning (cf. Evans 2010). The means whereby they are coded take in just about every conceivable coding site – argument, predicate, auxiliary, adverb, modifier or various combinations thereof – and every grammatical level, from morpheme to word to phrase to clause to multiclausal construction. More specifically, the structural possibilities include (confining ourselves just to languages within our sample):

a. derivational verbal affixes, as in Mundari (Evans & Osada, Chapter 6), Mawng (Singer, Chapter 14), Kayardild (Evans 1995), Kuuk Thaayorre (Gaby, Chapter 15) and Hup (Epps, Chapter 18); though these are often characterised as reducing valency the effect they have is often subtle (Evans, Gaby & Nordlinger 2007).

---

21. We do not include chapter descriptions on Kayardild or Barupu here, but see Evans (1995) and Corris (2006) for descriptions of the reciprocal constructions in these languages.

b. special auxiliaries (Indo-Pakistani Sign Language (Zeshan & Panda, Chapter 5) and, diachronically, the Tsafiki *i-* and *ki-* verbal class markers (Dickinson, Chapter 17).

c. special pronominal forms, e.g. the reciprocal possessive prefix in Beaver, or the bound pronoun *gù* in Khoekhoe (Rapold, Chapter 3)

d. binomial quantifiers that function syntactically as NPs (English *each other*, Hurst & Nordlinger, Chapter 4).

e. adverbs and ideophones of various kinds (e.g. the ideophone *beko-beko* in Tsafiki, Dickinson, Chapter 17 or the reciprocal adverb *junkuyunku* in Kayardild).

f. two simultaneous clauses delivered in Sign Languages by symmetrically counterposed gestures, such as two V-shaped two finger-points moving towards each other to express 'look at each other' in Indo-Pakistani Sign Language (Zeshan & Panda, Chapter 5, Figure 5).

g. complex constructions involving more than one clause, sometimes linked through 'revolving switch-reference' as in Amele[22], sometimes juxtaposing successive distributive clauses as in the 'double distributive' construction in Mah Meri (Kruspe, Chapter 8), and sometimes employing 'reciprocal mirror constructions' that are conventiontalised chains of three clauses, as in Lao (Enfield, Chapter 7).

Some pose problems for the question of how many clauses are involved, and effectively involve one and a half clauses as in the Mawng construction discussed in Chapter 14, where one reciprocant is represented by a pronominal subject prefix while the other is represented by a contrastive subject pronoun that normally marks the 'new subject' of a different clause – but here all packed into what looks like a single clause (cf. also Evans 2010 on Iwaidja).

The exuberant range of constructional types for encoding reciprocals has drawn comment from many authors. In the preface to his massive survey, Nedjalkov (2007: xxii) wrote that 'the variety of devices used across languages to denote reciprocity and [the] variety of … types of their polysemy … are staggering'. Again, this astonishing range of formal realisations calls for explanation.

One line of argument might appeal to the complexity of the engineering demands made in overlaying two propositions onto one clause under situations of cross-coreference (to use Nedjalkov's felicitous term), with arguably a third

---

22. In Amele (Roberts 1987) and some other highlands Papuan languages like Hua (Haiman 1984: 433), switch-reference is normally anticipatory, signalling an upcoming change of subject. Just in reciprocal constructions, there is a special 'revolving subject' use, where the first switch-reference marker looks forward and the second one looks back, iconically reflecting the bidirectional activity found in reciprocal events.

proposition as well denoting joint activity or compound state (like leaning against each other). This argument would appeal to the principle that the more tasks that must be performed by a structure, the larger the number of viable design solutions. This effect is well-known in engineering and evolutionary biology (Niklas 1994, 2004)[23], and in functional linguistics normally goes under the rubric of 'competing motivations'. Unpacking this view, reciprocals simultaneously perform a number of semantic tasks, since they overlay several propositions with commuted arguments linking onto a single clause (e.g. 'John loves Mary' and 'Mary loves John' onto *John and Mary love one another*), plus a third overlaid proposition with a conjoined argument along the lines of 'John and Mary do this together'. The need for this third element comes both from further typological considerations (see Evans 2010), as well the data in this volume, particularly the discussion of the sociative meaning in Lao (Enfield, Chapter 7) and interactional meaning in Hup (Epps, Chapter 18).

A second type of explanation would assert that these very varying structures in fact express somewhat different meanings (argument variant A) or at least differences in broader semantic ranges (variant B). Wierzbicka (2009) is an example of variant A. She motivates the difference between several constructions for expressing reciprocity in English, French and Polish through meaning differences: bipartite quantifiers, as in *They are kissing each other*, contrast with the simple plural predicate, as in *They are kissing*, or the corresponding construction in Polish with a single pronominal clitic marker *się* for reflexive/reciprocal, as in *oni się całują* [they RR kiss:3pl]. Nedjalkov (2007) is an example of variant B, arguing that coding in some positions will involve 'older' constructions that have had time to accumulate a wider range of conventionalised interpretations. Either way, these are hypotheses that fall squarely within the key concerns of semantic typology, and can only be answered by methods that allow for a calibrated cross-linguistic sampling of meaning ranges for the relevant constructions – again, a central concern of this book.

5.   Different reciprocal construction types, different semantics?

The arguments of Wierzbicka and Nedjalkov, as summarised in the previous paragraph, both point to a view that structural differences in encoding reciprocity

---

23. '[E]ngineering theory shows that the number of equally efficient designs for an artifact generally is proportional to both the number and the complexity of the tasks than an artifact must perform' (Niklas 1994: 6772), and 'Morphological diversification became easier on complex as opposed to simple fitness landscapes.' (Niklas 2004: 65).

reflect semantic differences within the broader reciprocal domain. But this view is by no means uncontested. An influential paper by Dalrymple and colleagues (1994) argued that the semantics of Chicheŵa was directly comparable to that of English, even down to the ambiguities produced when embedded under belief complements in sentences like 'John and Mary think they love each other'.[24] Dalrymple et al. propose a distinct logical operator for reciprocals (represented by RECIP) which is directly associated with the relevant grammatical coding site, here the Chicheŵa reciprocal suffix or the English *each other*. This hypothesis amounts to abandoning the compositional account of the English bipartite quantifier, since there is no way to motivate the formal structure of the Chicheŵa structure – a single verb suffix.[25]

The semantics of RECIP is further explored in Dalrymple et al. (1998), where it is said to be "a single polyadic quantifier that binds two variables in its scope, both variables ranging over one set, the restricted domain of quantification". In essence RECIP builds in a range of reciprocal situations, as discussed under the dimension of *configuration* above. This allows the context to cancel inconsistent over-strong interpretations. For example, it allows *John, Mary, and Sue sit next to each other at dinner*, even though everyone only has two sides, and thus no exhaustive reciprocity is possible (barring a round table), according to the principle that a reciprocal should be read in the 'strongest way possible' consistent with the context. On this analysis, RECIP has an invariant, universal meaning that allows principled variations in context.

---

24. Standardly claimed to exhibit a triple ambiguity: (a) John thinks Mary loves him and Mary believes John loves her (b) John believes he loves Mary and Mary thinks she loves him, (c) John thinks he and Mary love each other; Mary also thinks this.

25. Even within languages that encode reciprocal situations with bipartite quantifiers, there are many problems for compositional accounts. These include (a) the fact, already pointed out by Fiengo and Lasnik (1973), that strong reciprocal interpretations are required by the unfloated construction (*Each man saw the other*) whereas binomial constructions (*The men saw each other*) have laxer semantic requirements allowing for weak reciprocity (see comments and examples based on clip data in Chapter 4, §2.2), (b) the difficulty of using movement to derive the marginal but attested English construction of the type *each…each other* (again, Chapter 4, §2.2), which should be impossible on a movement analysis, and (c) various odd properties of binomial expressions in a range of European languages, such as the fact that case choice is fixed on the first element (e.g. to nominative in Russian *drug druga*) so that while the second element varies its case in the way expected by the case frame, the first is fixed – it can't take accusative in the way that would be expected in a frame like 'I introduced John and Mary to each other'. These are all hard to explain under a compositional account but can be more readily accommodated in non-compositional ones.

How does this account hold up to the scrutiny of our broader typological sample, where detailed semantic specification is available? This question is addressed in Chapter 2, where we show that the Dalrymple et al. (1998) account fails as a universal generalization. This is for two reasons. First, it turns out that the extensional semantics of reciprocal constructions is much more variable crosslinguistically than it is portrayed by Dalrymple et al. While many constructions do share a core extensional range, significant numbers of others diverge appreciably. The main Indo-Pakistani Sign Language construction (Chapter 5), for example, does not apply to chaining events, which is exactly where the Mah Meri (Chapter 8) construction thrives. This challenges the notion of a single invariant RECIP meaning. A second problem for the generalization is that most languages have multiple, competing reciprocal constructions, each picking up part of the semantic domain of reciprocity. But if the 'strongest possible meaning' principle applied, all reciprocals would end up with identical extensions in similar contexts. That turns out not to be the case – there is a coherent division of labour between different reciprocals.

6.   The incidence of reciprocal constructions cross-linguistically

We have noted that some languages, like Kilivila (Senft, Chapter 13), do not have a reciprocal construction at all. Can we estimate what proportion of languages actually have reciprocal constructions? As should now be clear, there is no straightforward answer to this, since assessing the percentage of languages that have specialised reciprocal constructions depends on our definition. Should we, for example, confine ourselves to 'dedicated reciprocals' like *each other*? Do we include constructions with more general meanings such as reflexivity (e.g. German *sich waschen*[26]), Rotokas (Robinson, Chapter 12) or Olutec (Zavala, Chapter 16)? And do we exclude what Maslova and Nedjalkov (2005), in their WALS survey on the relation between reciprocal and reflexive constructions, call 'iconic

---

26. Heine & Miyashita (2008:210) point to the sensitivity of this ambiguous example to context, since changing the affected body part alters which interpretation, reflexive or reciprocal, is preferred: *Sie waschen sich die Hände* will normally be construed reflexively 'they wash their hands' but *sie waschen sich den Rücken* will normally be construed reciprocally as 'they wash each other's backs'. However, the possibility of a reflexive construal also with the second is shown e.g. by the existence of the following question posted on the web: *Wie waschen sich Singles eigentlich den Rücken* 'how do single people actually wash their backs?', with the reflexive construal emphasised by one posted answer *gar nicht, man läßt ihn waschen!* ('not at all, you get (someone) to wash it') [data from http://www.platinnetz.de/frage/wie-waschen-sich-singles-eigentlich-den-ruecken-313101, accessed 20/1/2010] .

reciprocals' – in these, the reciprocating actions are spread over two clauses (John likes Mary, and Mary likes John), and the reciprocal meaning appears to be simply compositional or 'iconic'? But, as argued above, in at least some languages there are specialised bi- or multiclausal constructions for expressing reciprocity, as in Amele (Roberts 1987),[27] or in a number of languages described here (e.g. the *woni-woni* construction in Yélî Dnye; Levinson, Chapter 10).

Maslova and Nedjalkov give the breakdown in Table 1 for their WALS sample of 175 languages. From these figures it appears that 90% of languages have constructions that encode reciprocity if one includes constructions that may also express reflexivity, while only 56% of languages have dedicated reciprocal-only constructions, 9% lack any special coding, while 34% (60 languages) put up with ambiguous reciprocal-reflexive coding.

Table 1. Frequencies of different types of reciprocal construction in WALS sample

Construction	N	%
only iconic reciprocal construction	16	9.1
dedicated reciprocal construction formally distinct from reflexive	99	56.6
dedicated non-reflexive reciprocal construction and a reciprocal-or-reflexive construction	16	9.1
Single Reciprocal-or-reflexive construction	44	25.1

In actual fact, however, the number of languages with dedicated reciprocal constructions is not directly recoverable from the WALS figures, since a language may have a construction that is semantically general over reciprocity and some feature other than reflexivity, e.g. distributives (see Jahai; Burenhult, Chapter 9) or interaction/joint action more generally (see Hup; Epps, Chapter 18 and Lao; Enfield, Chapter 7). This means that some of the languages counted by Maslova and Nedjalkov in their second category may actually have something more general than a 'dedicated reciprocal' meaning.

In the much smaller sample of 20 languages included in this book, 17 (or 80%) can on prima facie grounds be said to have something like a dedicated reciprocal construction: this excludes Kilivila, which has no relevant constructions at all, plus Rotokas and Olutec which each have a single construction that includes both reflexives and reciprocals. It should be emphasised, though, that (a) the sample was not constructed in order to answer the question of cross-linguistic frequency, (b) in some cases, such as Mah Meri (Kruspe, Chapter 8), Jahai (Burenhult, Chapter 9) and Tsafiki (Dickinson, Chapter 17) the dedicated reciprocal is rather

---

27. See Evans (2007:82) for arguments that the Amele construction exhibits specialised constructional properties.

a marked and rare construction, and (c) the routine applicability of the construction to some kinds of unidirectional events like giving, as in Lao and Hup, could lead us to exclude such languages from those having dedicated reciprocals.[28]

As these examples show, the question of what counts as a reciprocal construction is anything but straightforward. This in turn is part of a central and increasingly recognised problem in typology, that of comparing semantic and grammatical categories (adjective, passive, perfective, etc.) cross-linguistically – see e.g. Croft (2001, 2009), Goldberg (2006), Haspelmath (2007). One of the main goals of this book is to show that with the right explicit methods we can investigate the cross-linguistic semantics of a domain, and make meaningful typological comparisons, without having to predefine an answer to this question.

7.   Design of the present study

Given what has been said so far, any cross-linguistic study of reciprocals must:

a.   Find a way around the difficulties of prior identification of the forms of interest, since this runs the risk of simply examining the equivalents of a construction that happens to be attested in English (here: *each other / one another*) or some other reference language.

b.   Obtain detailed data in spite of the rarity of the construction type (both in texts, and in descriptions of less-well known languages). Even for a language as well explored as English, the published literature fails to deal with phenomena that crop up in this book, such as the *back-to-back* type construction or the theoretically impossible *each... each other* construction (see Hurst & Norlinger, Chapter 4). Outside English, several other chapters (e.g. Chapter 6; Evans & Osada, Mundari and Chapter 9; Burenhult, Jahai) mention construction types that had not been reported before the data elicitation for this project commenced.

c.   Produce *cross-linguistically comparable data sets* in this domain. Rarely do reference grammars, or even articles focussed on the description of reciprocals, work through all the semantic factors mentioned above: configuration, situation type, number, sequentiality/simultaneity, or animacy of participants, etc.

---

28. However, even the strictest dedicated reciprocals tend to allow some unidirectional usages, as in English *chase each other*.

d. Collect the expressive alternatives to reciprocal constructions in describing particular situations, since to understand the semantics of a domain we need to know the full set of linguistic means for describing it.[29]

Getting descriptions for a fixed set of stimuli ensures that such information is available. It can also indicate zones of expressive overlap where more than one construction are possible, and identify places where a single construction unanimously applies, versus others where the relevant construction is rivalled by others.

The study reported in this book was designed to meet constraints (a)–(d) above. Short video clips of appropriate scenes were used as stimuli – e.g. a clip of two people taking it in turns to follow one another, or of two people shaking hands, or of three people lined up so that A is delousing B, who is delousing C. The 64 clips were designed to permute the semantic factors discussed in §2 above, as well as some event-types that would not qualify as reciprocal situations in the literature, as controls.[30] A full description of the clip contents and the administration procedure appears in Chapter 2. For the purposes of cross-linguistic parity, only data coming from clip descriptions were fed into the multivariate analysis in Chapter 2, but the descriptive chapters generalize from a wider data base.

Naturally, this clip data is only a sample of linguistic behaviour, and is quite capable of failing to detect one or another construction known to exist in the language. Within each language-specific chapter, authors were asked to comment on any other known constructions for expressing meanings in this general domain, in addition to their primary focus of analysing the clip data. As an example of such a corrective, see the discussion of an interesting construction type in Olutec in Chapter 16.

---

29. This follows from the need, first articulated by Von der Gabelentz (1891) to take both a form-to-meaning (semasiological) and a meaning-to-form (onomasiological) perspective: 'form-meaning relationships of linguistic expressions can be analyzed and described from a semasiological or an onomasiological perspective; i.e. you can either investigate and describe the semantic properties of particular linguistic forms, or the various ways in which particular meanings are expressed' (Mosel 2006). This is related to the need to take both hearer-centred perspectives (what did X refer to by saying Y?) and a speaker-centred perspective (to refer to Z, what should I say?) in order to fully delineate a language's semiotic options.

30. What we were not able to do was investigate all semantic dimensions known to share polysemies with reciprocals in at least some language. This is simply because there are so many of these – reflexives, distributives, iteratives, plurals, expressions for 'friend' or 'companion', expressions for competition or random or back-and-forth motion, to name but a few – that building these factors in alongside the others we were permuting would make for an intractably large stimulus set. We hope other investigators will extend our methods to the investigation of these additional dimensions in future research.

8.   An overview of the findings

Overall, our inquiry into the reciprocal domain produces what may seem to some a paradoxical result: Coherent cross-linguistic tendencies married with linguistic idiosyncrasies. Constructions with meanings corresponding closely to those expressed by *each other* in English occur in a large number of the languages, although encoded by a wide range of structural means. But the meanings expressed are never totally identical, and in some cases diverge markedly. Family resemblance but lack of identity is in fact a result that is typical for cross-linguistic generalizations (see Evans & Levinson 2009, Levinson & Evans 2010).

In some languages (e.g. Hup, Lao) the category encoded by the best candidate for a reciprocal marker extends out to take in other forms of interactive or joint activity, in others (e.g. Jahai) it extends to other non-reciprocal types of distributive. In the other direction, there are languages (most strongly in Indo-Pakistani Sign Language, but also in Mundari and Beaver) where the extension from strong reciprocity (A does R to B, and B to A) to chained events (A does R to B, and B to C) is not permitted.

All this suggests that the particular cluster of meanings that has been focused on by researchers from Langendoen (1978) to Dalrymple et al. (1998) is not a necessarily co-occurring set, and hence not a linguistic universal requiring some special explanation. Rather, this cluster is revealed as a recurrent but not inevitable chain of polysemies. Higginbotham (1985), at the beginning of an influential paper on the semantics of reciprocals, kicks off by saying that 'theoretical questions arise in linguistics whenever we find a realm where we know far more than we are taught'. The data presented in this book show that, at least when it comes to the range of applications of reciprocals in main clauses, speakers don't know more than they are taught: they have to learn the system of each language individually. Nor can a learner bootstrap from the grammatical coding of the construction to its likely semantic range, for one result of our study is that both argument-coding and verb-coding reciprocals enjoy a wide latitude of interpretation.

Our data also points to interesting modality effects, apparently stemming from the greater codability of certain spatial relations in the four-dimensional space of Sign Languages compared to the one-dimensional stream of speech. For example, the situation where one person is running behind another – so often coded by 'they are chasing/following each other' in spoken languages – can be distinctly encoded by arraying one running figure behind another (see Zeshan & Panda, Figure 11, Chapter 5). Similarly, what might be counted as an 'iconic' production of two clauses in the linear medium of speech, becomes a dedicated reciprocal in a language that allows both clauses to be coded simultaneously on different hands. The summed modality effects of codability in Sign are probably responsible for the outlier position of Indo-Pakistani Sign Language both with respect to its overall pattern of categorisation (Chapter 2, Figure 2[31]) and its position in the constructional similarity space (Figure 8). As Zeshan and Panda point out at the end of their chapter, sign languages display significant typological variation amongst themselves, so we must await further studies of reciprocals in sign languages before we can be sure this pattern is largely due to modality-specific effects, but nonetheless the results are intriguing.

Another theme that runs through the chapters is the importance of interaction and projected shared intention to the expression of reciprocity, a theme developed in König's conspectus chapter. This is not something that comes through in the existing formal semantic literature, which has focussed on the patterning of abstract logical relationships across the participant set, abstracting away from the nature of the participants and the relationships. But it has also been neglected in much typological work – König & Kokutani (2006), for example, appeal to symmetry as the essence of reciprocity.

In designing the stimuli, we deliberately included a number of scenarios involving symmetric relations between inanimate objects, such as two objects leaning on one another. Yet in many languages, such as Rotokas (Robinson, Chapter 11), Mawng (Singer, Chapter 14) and Beaver, these were not encoded by the major construction otherwise used for encoding reciprocals. Likewise, more static relationships, such as those involving spatial layout, were often not encoded by the main reciprocal strategy, but by special constructions specialised for symmetry, such as the *back-to-back* construction in English or the symmetrical body-part construction in Jahai (Burenhult, Chapter 9, §3.4).

Our final point is a methodological one. Within semantic typology, there is growing realisation of the need to use standardised stimuli in studies of categorisation, so as to place all languages on a level playing field, rather than privileging one as the source for which translations from the others are sought. As indicated earlier in the chapter, this also provides a way of subjecting phenomena to cross-linguistic comparison without having to predefine the categories of interest in a way that may import accidental characteristics of some familiar reference language.[32]

---

31. Kilivila is the other major outlier here because it lacks reciprocal constructions altogether.

32. A valid criticism of our methodology is that, nonetheless, we defined the dimensions of our stimuli with particular issues in mind that have arisen from the consideration of the English constructions, and that, had we had taken, say, Lao or Jahai as our point of departure, we would have worked outwards in a different way. This is certainly true, and can only be ultimately resolved by adopting a 'snowballing' technique where each new set of semantic connections discovered in a particular language is added to the overall mix, gradually pushing outwards the total set of situations for which categorisation is investigated. For obvious practical reasons,

This has given rise to the approach to semantic typology that is represented by studies such as Levinson & Meira (2003), Enfield et al. (2006), Levinson & Wilkins (2006), Majid et al. (2008) and Majid & Bowerman (2007). So far, however, the emphasis within this approach has been on categories that have lain outside the main concerns of formal semantics – cutting and breaking, body-part names, spatial relations – and have historically been treated by the rather different methods used to study the semantics of the lexicon. The present study shows that these same methods can be applied to a semantic domain – reciprocity – which is generally seen as having more grammatical than lexical coding, and which has been a frequent testing ground for formal approaches.[33] This demonstrates that formal and conceptual approaches can be nicely complementary, and certainly need not be divided by primary subject matter.

Last of all, we stress that in no way does the gathering of carefully matched data stand in the way of discovering language-specific categories, since the structure of this book balances systematic multifactorial comparison (Chapter 2) with traditional language-specific analyses in Chapters 3–18. Again and again, these chapters emphasise language-particular semantic preoccupations – such as the Lao coparticipation marker *kan3*, or the Hup interactional *ʔũh*. Interestingly, these other semantic preoccupations mesh with the social motivations for an interest in reciprocity with which we began this chapter. These differences in the meaning ranges of constructions emerge from the intersection of language-internal exploration with the comparative grid made available by a set of systematic stimuli – the two approaches complement one another, together yielding more than the sum of the parts.

Abbreviations

COMPL.OBL	Complementizing Oblique	MID	Middle
FSG	Feminine Singular	MPL	Masculine Plural
MDU	Masculine Dual	RR	Reflexive/Reciprocal

---

however, only a finite set of these can be the focus of investigation at any one point of time, if we are to obtain matched data across a large set of languages.

33. Lest we be misunderstood, we are not claiming here that the approach taken here can resolve all of the issues studied by formal approaches to reciprocity – in particular the complex compositional effects resulting from the interaction of reciprocals with ambiguous syntactic structures. Rather, we are arguing that the meaning of *each other* and its congeners in simple clauses – which has in any case been a not inconsiderable part of the formal semantic literature – can be elucidated through the sorts of techniques employed here.

Acknowledgements

For the research support that made this project possible we thank the Australian Research Council (grants *Reciprocals Across Languages* and *Social cognition and language: the design resources of grammatical diversity*) and the Max Planck Society; we also thank Matthew Anstey for detailed grammatical discussion of the Hebrew passage from Genesis. Evans would also like to thank the Bogliasco Foundation for a writer's residency that enabled him to put together the initial draft of this chapter.

References

Arka, Wayan. Ms. On Balinese *ma-*: Iconicity, markedness and reflexivity.

Corris, Mim. 2006. A Grammar of Barupu: A Language of Papua New Guinea. PhD dissertation, University of Sydney.

Croft, William. 2001. *Radical Construction Grammar*. Oxford: OUP.

Croft, William. 2009. Methods for finding language universals in syntax. In *Universals of Language Today*, Sergio Scalise, Elisabetta Magni & Antonietta Bisetto (eds), 145–164. Berlin: Springer.

Crystal, David. 2008. *As They Say in Zanzibar. Proverbial Wisdom from Around the World*. Oxford: OUP.

Dalrymple, Mary, Mchombo, Sam A. & Peters, Stanley. 1994. Semantic similarities and syntactic contrasts between Chicheŵa and English reciprocals. *Linguistic Inquiry* 25(1): 145–63.

Dalrymple, Mary, Kanazawa, Makoto, Kim, Yookyung, Mchombo, Sam & Peters, Stanley. 1998. Reciprocal expressions and the concept of reciprocity. *Linguistics & Philosophy* 21(2): 159–210.

Dougherty, Ray C. 1974. The syntax and semantics of each other constructions. *Foundations of Language* 12: 1–47.

Enfield, N. J., Majid, Asifa & van Staden, Miriam (eds.). 2006. Cross-linguistic categorisation of the body: Introduction. *Language Sciences* 28(2–3): 137–147.

Evans, Nicholas. 1995. *A Grammar of Kayardild*. Berlin: Mouton de Gruyter.

Evans, Nicholas. 2003. *Bininj Gun-wok: A Pan-dialectal Grammar of Mayali, Kunwinjku and Kune*. Canberra: Pacific Linguistics.

Evans, Nicholas. 2007. Reciprocals, grammar-writing and typology. *Revue de Linguistique Roumaine* II(4): 479–506.

Evans, Nicholas. 2008. Reciprocal constructions: Towards a structural typology. In *Reciprocals and Reflexives: Cross-linguistic and Theoretical Explorations*, Ekkehard König & Volker Gast (eds), 33–104. Berlin: Mouton de Gruyter.

Evans, Nicholas. 2010. Complex events, propositional overlay and the special status of reciprocal clauses. In *Empirical and Experimental Methods in Cognitive/functional Research*, Sally Rice & John Newman (eds), 1–40. Stanford CA: CSLI.

Evans, Nicholas, Gaby, Alice & Nordlinger, Rachel. 2007. Valency mismatches and the coding of reciprocity in Australian Languages. *Linguistic Typology* 11(2): 543–599.

Evans, Nicholas & Levinson, Stephen C. 2009. The myth of language universals. *Behavioral & Brain Sciences* 32: 429–448.

Evans, Nicholas, Levinson, Stephen C., Enfield, N. J., Gaby, Alice & Majid, Asifa. 2004. Reciprocals. In *Field Manual,* Vol. 9, Asifa Majid (ed.), 25–30. Nijmegen: Max Planck Institute for Psycholinguistics, Language & Cognition Group.

Fiengo, Robert & Lasnik, Howard. 1973. The logical structure of reciprocal sentences in English. *Foundations of Language* 9: 447–68.

Frajzyngier, Zygmunt & Curl, Traci (eds). 1999. *Reciprocals: Forms and Functions.* [Typological Studies in Language 41]. Amsterdam: John Benjamins.

von der Gabelentz, Georg. 1891. *Die Sprachwissenschaft. Ihre Aufgaben, Methoden und bisherigen Ergebnisse,* 3rd edn. Tübingen: Gunter Narr.

Goldberg, Adele. 2006. *Constructions at Work: The Nature of Generalization in Language.* Oxford: OUP.

Green, Ian. 1989. Marrithiyel. A Language of the Daly River Region of Australia's Northern Territory. PhD dissertation, ANU.

Haas, Florian. 2009. *Reciprocity in English: Historical Development and Synchronic Structure.* London: Routledge.

Haiman, John. 1983. Iconic and economic motivation. *Language* 59(4): 781–819.

Haiman, John. 1984. *Hua: A Papuan language of the Eastern Highlands of New Guinea* [Studies in Language Companion Series 5]. Amsterdam: John Benjamins.

Hamilton, Victor P. 1990. *The Book of Genesis,* Chapters 1–17. Grand Rapids MI: William B. Eerdmans.

Haspelmath, Martin. 2007. Pre-established categories don't exist: Consequences for language description and typology. *Linguistic Typology* 11(1): 119–32.

Heine, Bernd & Miyashita, Hiroyuki. 2008. The intersection between reflexives and reciprocals: A grammaticalization perspective. In *Reflexivity and Reciprocity: Crosslinguistic Explorations,* Ekkehard König & Volker Gast (eds), 169–223. Berlin: Mouton de Gruyter.

Higginbotham, James. 1980. Reciprocal interpretation. *Journal of Linguistic Research* 1(3): 97–117.

Jespersen, Otto. 1927. *A Modern English Grammar on Historical Principles,* Part III, Vol. 2: *Syntax.* Heidelberg: Carl Winter.

Kemmer, Suzanne. 1993. *The Middle Voice* [Typological Studies in Language 23]. Amsterdam: John Benjamins.

Kibrik, Alexandr E. 1977. *Opyt strukturnogo opisanija arčinskogo jazyka,* Tom II: *Taksonomičeskaja grammatika.* Moscow: Isdateľstvo Moskovskogo Universiteta.

König, Ekkehard & Kokutani, Shigehiro. 2006. Towards a typology of reciprocal constructions: Focus on German and Japanese. *Linguistics* 44(2): 271–302.

König, Ekkehard & Gast, Volker. 2008. *Reciprocals and Reflexives: Theoretical and Typological Explorations.* Berlin: Mouton de Gruyter.

Lakoff, George & Peters, Stanley. 1969. Phrasal conjunction and symmetric predicates. In *Modern Studies in English,* David A. Reibel & Sanford A. Schane (eds), 113–142. Englewood Cliffs NJ: Prentice-Hall.

Langendoen, D. Terence & Magloire, Joël. 2003. The logic of reflexivity and reciprocity. In *Anaphora: A Reference Guide,* Andrew Barss (ed.). Oxford: Blackwells.

Langendoen, D. Terence. 1978. The logic of reciprocity. *Linguistic Inquiry* 9(2): 177–197.

Levinson, Stephen C. & Evans, Nicholas. 2010. Time for a sea-change in linguistics. *Lingua* 120(12): 2733–2758.

Levinson, Stephen C. & Meira, Sergio 2003. 'Natural concepts' in the spatial topological domain – adpositional meanings in crosslinguistic perspective: An exercise in semantic typology. *Language* 79(3): 484–516.

Levinson, Stephen C. & Wilkins, David P. 2006. Patterns in the data: Towards a semantic typology of spatial descriptions. In *Grammars of Space: Explorations in Cognitive Diversity*, Stephen C. Levinson & David P. Wilkins (eds.), 512–552. Cambridge: CUP.

Majid, Asifa & Bowerman, Melissa. 2007. Cutting and breaking events: A cross-linguistic perspective. Special issue of *Cognitive Linguistics* 18(2).

Majid, Asifa, Boster, James S. & Bowerman, Melissa. 2008. The cross-linguistic categorization of everyday events: A study of cutting and breaking. *Cognition* 109: 235–250.

Maslova, Elena & Nedjalkov, Vladimir P. 2005. Reciprocal constructions. In *The World Atlas of Language Structures*, Martin Haspelmath, David Gil, Bernard Comrie & Matthew Dryer (eds), 430–433. Berlin: Mouton de Gruyter.

Mosel, Ulrike. 2006. Grammaticography: The art and craft of writing grammars. In *Catching Language: The Standing Challenge of Grammar-Writing*, Felix Ameka, Alan Dench & Nicholas Evans (eds.), 41–68. Berlin: Mouton de Gruyter.

Nedjalkov, Vladimir P. & Geniušienė, Emma. 2007. Questionnaire on reciprocals. In *Reciprocal Contructions,* Vladimir P. Nedjalkov (ed.), 379–434.

Nedjalkov, Vladimir P. 2007. *Reciprocal Constructions* [Typological Studies in Language 71], 5 vols. Amsterdam: John Benjamins.

Niklas, Karl J. 1994. Morphological evolution through complex domains of fitness. *Proc. Natl. Acad. Sci USA* 91: 6772–6779.

Niklas, Karl J. 2004. Computer models of early land plant evolution. *Annual Review Earth Planet Sciences* 32: 47–66.

Osada, Toshiki. 2007. Reciprocals in Mundari. In *Reciprocal Constructions*, Vol. 4, Vladimir Nedjalkov (ed.), 1575–1592. Amsterdam: John Benjamins.

Osumi, Midori. 1995. *Tinrin grammar.* Hawaii HI: University of Hawaii Press.

Plank, Frans. 2008. Thoughts on the origin, progress, and pronominal status of reciprocal forms in Germanic, occasioned by those of Bavarian. In *Reciprocals and reflexives: cross-linguistic and theoretical explorations,* Ekkehart König & Volker Gast (eds), 169–224. Berlin: Mouton de Gruyter.

Potter, Simon. 1953. The expression of reciprocity. *English Studies* 34: 252–257.

Reay, Marie. 1959. *The Kuma.* Carlton: Melbourne University Press.

Roberts, John R. 1987. *Amele* [Croom Helm Descriptive Grammar Series]. London: Croom Helm.

Sasson, Jack M. 1985. Welo' yitbosasu (Gen 2:25) and its implications. *Bib* 66: 418–421.

Wierzbicka, Anna. 2009. Reciprocity: An NSM approach to linguistic typology and social universals. *Studies in Language* 33(1): 103–174.

Williams-van Klinken, Catharina, Hajek, John & Nordlinger, Rachel. 2002. *Tetun Dili* [Languages of the World/Materials 388], 60–61. Munich: Lincom.

Zeitoun, Elisabeth. 2002. Reciprocals in the Formosan languages: A preliminary study. Paper presented at the Ninth International Conference on Austronesian languages (9-ICAL), Canberra, 8–11 January 2002. Ms.

CHAPTER 2

The semantics of reciprocal constructions across languages

An extensional approach

Asifa Majid*, Nicholas Evans**, Alice Gaby***
and Stephen C. Levinson*

*Max Planck Institute for Psycholinguistics / **Australian National
University / ***University of California at Berkeley

How similar are reciprocal constructions in the semantic parameters they
encode? We investigate this question by using an extensional approach, which
examines similarity of meaning by examining how constructions are applied
over a set of 64 videoclips depicting reciprocal events (Evans et al. 2004). We
apply statistical modelling to descriptions from speakers of 20 languages elicited
using the videoclips. We show that there are substantial differences in meaning
between constructions of different languages.

1.   Introduction

As we saw in Chapter 1, the cross-linguistic definition of reciprocal semantics
remains controversial amongst contemporary scholars. Some investigators, such
as Dalrymple and colleagues (1998), have proposed a single universal cluster of
interpretations, independent of the means languages use to code these meanings,
whether nominal or verbal. They propose an ordered hierarchy of interpretations,
where the strongest compatible with the context wins. Other investigators, such
as Filip & Carlson (2001:417) stress that: "the interpretation of reciprocal sentences is sensitive to a rich variety of factors, both linguistic and extralinguistic,
and cannot easily be accorded any single truth-conditional meaning which per-
sists in all contexts". In a different tradition, Wierzbicka (2009) argues for four
distinct though related prototypes for reciprocity, with details differing subtly
from language to language. According to her account these meanings shade from
reciprocity to mutuality to joint and collective action, prompting her to ask how
realistic it is to lift out one of these points, essentialise it, and then assume it is 'the'
definition of reciprocal meaning cross-linguistically.

The cross-linguistic comparison of reciprocal meanings, then, runs up against the more general problem faced by any typological comparison: what reference points should one construct in the design space, in the face of the different conceptual packages evolved by different languages and in such a way that we are able to make realistic and helpful cross-linguistic comparisons while avoiding artificial 'essentialising' definitions (cf. Croft 2001, Goldberg 2009, Evans & Levinson 2009, Levinson & Evans 2010).

In the project outlined in this book we tackle this task by using an extensional set of stimuli designed to sample the denotational space for this semantic domain in a structured way that is cross-linguistically comparable. The strategy is not dissimilar to the celebrated study of colour terms by Berlin & Kay (1969), which used a fine-grained systematic set of colour chips to sample the colour space, allowing precise calibration of similarities and differences in colour terminology across languages. An advantage of this approach is that it makes minimal presuppositions about the categories in each language, thus allowing us to quantify degrees of similarity and difference on a large number of dimensions – by language, by construction type, by which situations are categorised as most similar, and so forth.

These advantages give this method great power as a tool in semantic typology. Until now, however, this method has largely been confined to areas of semantics that are the traditional domain for 'lexical semantic' approaches – lexical distinctions like 'cut' and 'break' (Majid et al. 2007, 2008), body-part terminology (Enfield et al. 2006), and spatial relations (Pederson et al. 1998). The current study is the first time this approach has been employed to strike into the heart of grammar and investigate a problem that has received thorough investigation primarily with the techniques of formal semantics.

The method by itself however naturally has limitations. It systematically explores the extensions of categories, in this case the kinds of scenes warranting the use of reciprocal constructions. Further, from responses by multiple speakers it is possible to isolate what are treated as best exemplars or 'prototypes' among the scenes, and to see how different constructions (e.g. "they talked" vs. "they talked to one another") might be applied to different sets of scenes. Nevertheless, the method clearly does not *eo ipso* deliver an analysis of the corresponding intensions of each construction (see Levinson & Meira 2003 for discussion), and thus requires supplementing by normal elicitation means, where e.g. patterns of inferences from the use of contrasting expressions can be explored. What an extensional analysis does deliver, however, is a set of precise constraints on any intensional analysis – namely the graded classes of extensions that any analysis in terms of sense must account for. In the chapters below, researchers were able to use these clues to come up with intensional definitions that might otherwise have escaped them. Intensional analysis without extensional constraints is blind, just as extensional data without intensional analysis is incomplete.

This chapter has two main goals. First, it describes the video stimuli and method of data collection used by all researchers in the "Reciprocals Across Languages" project, and introduces the sample of languages being investigated. And second, it explores the semantics of reciprocal constructions by analysing data from the entire sample with multivariate statistical techniques.

2.   Data collection for reciprocal events

2.1   The stimulus set

Our goal is to compare the extensional range of reciprocal constructions from different languages. In order to provide a basis for comparison we devised a set of videoclips that depicted a range of reciprocal events (Evans et al. 2004; these videos can be downloaded from http://fieldmanuals.mpi.nl/volumes/2004/reciprocals/). There are different ways such a set of scenes could be constructed. Ideally it might sample widely from all the different semantic fields that we know show up in constructional overlap with reciprocity, for example the reflexive, distributive, interactive, and comitative domains. But this would yield an un-manageably large set of scenes. What we have done instead is take the kind of scene – the 'canonical' reciprocal event – that has been the focus of the literature, and then explore the margins around this as widely as possible.

In the canonical reciprocal event (as in Nedjalkov 2007), such as "John and Mary hugged each other", there are just two participants (John and Mary), the subevents are simultaneous (John embraces Mary at the same time as Mary embraces John), and symmetrical (what John does to Mary, Mary does to John). These canonical reciprocal events formed the core of our stimulus set. We then varied a number of parameters in order to determine how far reciprocal coding constructions extend out to various conditions which relax the features of the canonical reciprocal situation. The crucial parameters are the number of participants, configuration, symmetry, temporal organisation, and event-type (see Table 1; Figure 1). Let's take each of these in turn.

The first parameter was the *number* of participants, which varied between two and eleven. The second parameter *configuration* comes into operation once multiple participants are involved, since then the possible permutations of who acts on whom can also vary. Where all participants act on each other symmetrically the event is fully saturated (*strong* reciprocity). For example, when four people are involved all participants could symmetrically act on all the others (*strong* in

Figure 1). But as we move away from this type, various other configurations are logically possible. A and B, and likewise C and D, could be in strong symmetrical interaction, but with no interaction between the pairs (*pairs* in Figure 1). Or A could act on B who could act on C who acts on D, resulting in a linear series of events (*chain* in Figure 1). Or A and C could each act on D who alone acts on C, etc. (*melee* in Figure 1), and so on. Figure 1 depicts some of the possible permutations of relations once we depart from full saturation (adapted from Dalrymple et al. 1998: 169, after Langendoen 1978).

The third parameter concerns whether the action is *symmetrical* or not. That is, are the participants both actors and recipients of the target event.[1] The fourth parameter is whether the subevents are *simultaneous* or sequential. This is straightforward when there are just two participants in the event, but where more than two participants are involved "both" is also a possibility, since some of the subevents could happen simultaneously but others sequentially. For example, where there are six participants in three pairs, each pairwise event could happen simultaneously, but the pairs could act on each other sequentially, i.e. first A and B act on each other, then C and D and finally E and F.

Table 1. Parameters varied in reciprocal videoclips

Number of participants	Configuration	Symmetry	Temporal organisation	Event-type
two	strong	symmetrical	simultaneous	bump
three	pair	asymmetrical	sequential	chase
four	chain		both	delouse
five	radial		(inapplicable)	follow
six	melee			give
eleven	ring			hit
	(inapplicable)*			hug
				lean
				look
				meet
				be.next.to
				shake.hand
				talk

* The "inapplicable" category under configuration and temporal organisation refers to dual asymmetrical events, i.e., where A only acts on B.

---

1.   As reported for Mah Meri in Kruspe's Chapter 8, some languages define symmetry very strictly, so that some of the scenes we had conceived of as symmetric (and which were accepted as such in most languages) did not count as symmetric in Mah Meri because distinct types of hitting were involved across subevents.

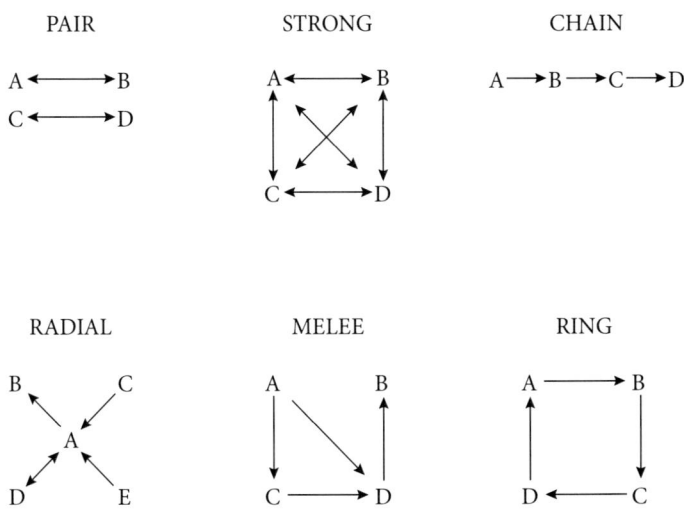

Figure 1. Configuration types manipulated in the reciprocals video stimuli

The final parameter is action or *event-type*. Since we are interested in the range of events a construction can be applied to, it is important to establish whether constraints in applicability are due to the actions being depicted, the lexical verbs involved or even to properties of morpho-syntax (e.g., phonological or argument structure constraints).

Not all combinations of all these semantic parameters could be shown to participants, since this would have meant a total of over 4000 videoclips. A representative selection of the semantic space was constructed such that each of the above parameters were depicted. Additional videoclips that depicted non-reciprocal scenarios were also included in order to establish the borders of reciprocal constructions. These all featured two participants, where only one acted on the other – e.g., one person talking with the other listening (clip #1), one person hitting another with no response (clip #17), one person giving another a watch (clip #26). In order not to exceed our participants' patience and attention, we limited the final stimulus set to 64 videoclips. A table indicating the parameter settings depicted in each clip is included in Appendix A.

2.2   The language sample

Data from 20 languages was collected using the reciprocals videoclip stimuli. Researchers elicited descriptions of the clips, and in some cases acceptability judgments in addition. Detailed descriptions of the constructions used in most of the languages can be found in independent chapters of this volume (see Table 2). The number of speakers per language for whom data was elicited varied from one to nine, with the average being three.

The languages are typologically, genetically, and geographically diverse, include languages from every continent, and sample fifteen maximal clades or language families (note that Papuan is not a language family, merely meaning 'Language spoken in Melanesia that is not Austronesian'). There is, however, an over-representation of Australian, Papuan and South-East Asian languages, partly reflecting the availability of data-gathering opportunities for project members, but also to compensate for the converse areal bias towards Eurasia and Africa in previous work (such as Nedjalkov 2007). The data were collected by language specialists in each field site as indicated in Table 2.

Table 2. Languages in sample. Specific chapter-length treatments can be found in this volume for languages marked *

Language	Affiliation	Country	Researcher
* Khoekhoe	Central Khoisan	Namibia	C. Rapold
* English (Australian)	Germanic (Indo-European)	Australia	P. Hurst & R. Nordlinger
* Indo-Pakistani Sign Language	Sign Language	India, Pakistan	U. Zeshan & S. Panda
* Mundari	Munda (Austroasiatic)	India	N. Evans & T. Osada
* Lao	Tai-Kadai	Laos	N. J. Enfield
* Mah Meri	Aslian (Austroasiatic)	Malaysia	N. Kruspe
* Jahai	Aslian (Austroasiatic)	Malaysia	N. Burenhult
* Yélî Dnye	"Papuan" Isolate	Papua New Guinea	S. C. Levinson
* Rotokas	"Papuan" Isolate	Papua New Guinea	S. Robinson
* Savosavo	"Papuan" Isolate	Solomon Islands	C. Wegener
* Kilivila	Oceanic (Austronesian)	Papua New Guinea	G. Senft
Barupu	Macro-Skou	Papua New Guinea	M. Corris
* Mawng	Iwaidjan (Australian)	Australia	R. Singer
Iwaidja	Iwaidjan (Australian)	Australia	N. Evans
Kayardⁱld	Tangkic (Australian)	Australia	N. Evans
* Kuuk Thaayorre	Pama-Nyungan (Australian)		A. Gaby
Beaver	Athabaskan (Na-Dene)	Canada	D. Jung
* Olutec	Mixe-Zoquean	Mexico	R. Zavala
* Tsafiki	Barbacoan	Ecuador	C. Dickinson
* Hup	Nadahup	Brazil	P. Epps

2.3   Procedure

For the main elicitation, the 64 videoclips were shown to the consultants in a fixed random order. The consultant viewed each clip and described what they had seen. If the consultant merely described all the subevents, the researcher probed for a compact description of the whole event. Other prompts and acceptability judgments for constructions were left to the discretion of the researcher. Descriptions were audio- or video-recorded for later transcription and coding.

Our focus in this chapter is on the spontaneously produced reciprocal constructions, and not on meta-linguistic judgments of whether constructions were applicable – though some examples of these observations appear in the language-specific chapters. Intuitive judgements of grammaticality and acceptability have been repeatedly shown to be unreliable guides to linguistic analysis (Schütze 1996, Tremblay 2005, Dąbrowska 2010) but this is especially true in semantics. In an elegant series of studies, Labov (1978) demonstrated that spontaneous descriptions of stimuli (line drawings of objects such as cups and bowls) showed a perfect series of implicational hierarchies, such that if an object could be described as a cup, then all objects lower in the scale could also be described as a cup. But, when participants were explicitly asked to judge whether an object was a cup, the implicational hierarchy collapsed, and the lawful use of terms was no longer apparent. Labov argued that participants who were explicitly asked whether an object was a cup were using a constructed definition against which they were comparing the object, whereas those who were just asked to name the object were drawing on an underlying definition which was much more systematic. He concluded "It is an unfortunate fact (for linguists) that the more people think about language, the more confused they become" (Labov 1978: 229).[2]

One other aspect of Labov's data that is pertinent here is that explicit judgments lead to more restricted application than free descriptions. Labov's participants used *cup* for fewer stimuli when they had to make a deliberative decision whether a particular stimulus was an instance of a *cup* than when they just had to describe the stimuli. Since we are interested in the range of events that a reciprocal construction can be applied to, free responses are more appropriate.

---

[2]   In addition to the recent literature on grammaticality judgements cited above, a vast literature in psychology shows that participants' reasons for *why* they produced a particular response are also prone to distortions. People often fail to report the critical factor behind their response and over-rely on a priori theories about what the causal factors ought to be (see for example Nisbett & Wilson 1977). This suggests that linguists should exercise caution in treating speaker meta-linguistic judgments as direct portals to underlying linguistic structure.

3.   Reciprocal constructions across languages

3.1   The constructions

Individual researchers, experts on the languages they study, were responsible for coding their own language data. Constructions were identified on language internal grounds, and full descriptions of the constructions can be found in the descriptive chapters in this volume. Not all constructions were "dedicated" reciprocal constructions. For example, in Jahai the main construction employed by speakers to describe videoclips was a distributive construction (Burenhult Chapter 9); in Hup an "interactional" construction predominated (Epps Chapter 18), etc. A criterion for inclusion in this statistical study was that the construction was used to describe a canonical reciprocal event – i.e. an event in which two participants acted on each other simultaneously and symmetrically. If the construction was used for any such event, then it was included in the following analyses – regardless of what its core function may be. The number of constructions included for each language varied from 0 (for Kilivila – see Senft Chapter 13) to 7 (for English – see Hurst & Nordlinger Chapter 4), with an average of 3 constructions per language. The full list of included constructions is given in Appendix B.

3.2   The coding

How similar are the semantic categories encoded by reciprocal constructions across languages? One way to address this question – and the approach we employ here – is to compare the extensional range of reciprocal constructions taken from different languages. In order to do this, we code each videoclip for which constructions were spontaneously produced by consultants. For example, if English speaker #1 used the *each other* construction to describe clip #11 which shows a man and a woman both simultaneously talking to one another, then a 1 was coded for the *each other* construction, if this construction was not used then a 0 was coded. The end result is a single matrix with language-specific constructions as columns and videoclips as rows. This basic data can be manipulated in various ways to address different questions.

4.   Overall similarity of languages in classifying reciprocal events

The question we ask to begin with is how similar are *languages* to one another in their overall strategy for encoding reciprocal events? We can address this question by comparing the overall pattern of classification presented by each language through the factor analytic methods described by Romney, Weller & Batchelder (1986; see also Majid, Boster & Bowerman 2008). The underlying assumption in this analysis is that if speakers of two languages share a common representation of what a reciprocal event is, then they will agree on which events should be encoded with a reciprocal construction, and conversely which should not. The encoding may not be identical since there may be differences in the construal of the clips, or a speaker may just not have chosen to encode that clip with a reciprocal construction on this occasion even though that clip *could* receive reciprocal encoding, or for some other reason. In a statistical analysis we can capture whether there is a common pattern of categorisation regardless of this variation and – perhaps more importantly – still be able to distinguish genuine cases of difference.

We begin with the basic matrix described above, crossing language-specific construction with videoclip matrix. This was used to create a new language-by-language matrix which indicates how similar languages are to one another as measured in terms of the extensions of their reciprocal constructions. The new matrix was constructed by counting the number of times two languages agreed that a particular event could be coded by a reciprocal construction. This count was divided by the total number of videoclips in the stimulus set to get the proportion of matches, and then corrected for chance agreement (see Romney et al. 1986 for formulae). The resulting matrix was factor analysed using principal components analysis. This is a statistical technique that reduces a large number of variables into a smaller set of factors. If there is strong similarity across languages in the extensional range of reciprocal constructions then they will correlate positively with each other and factor scores on the first factor will be positive. If languages differ in the extensional range of their constructions then they will correlate negatively and load negatively on the first factor.

Figure 2 shows how languages load on the first two factors. The x-axis depicts "consensus" – languages that load positively on this factor agree with one another on which clips are to be encoded by a reciprocal construction. From the plot it is clear that some languages do not share a strategy for encoding reciprocal events. Kilivila is the most different from the other languages, and loads the most negatively on the first factor. This is trivially the case, since Kilivila does not have any reciprocal constructions, and therefore Kilivila speakers never encoded any of the clips with a reciprocal construction. Agreement with other languages is necessarily low.

Less obviously, however, Indo-Pakistani Sign Language also correlates very little with other languages in how reciprocal events are encoded. Mah Meri and Mundari also load negatively on the first factor, indicating that the reciprocal constructions of these languages are also different in some way from the other languages. Note that Mah Meri depicts a very different pattern to Jahai, even though

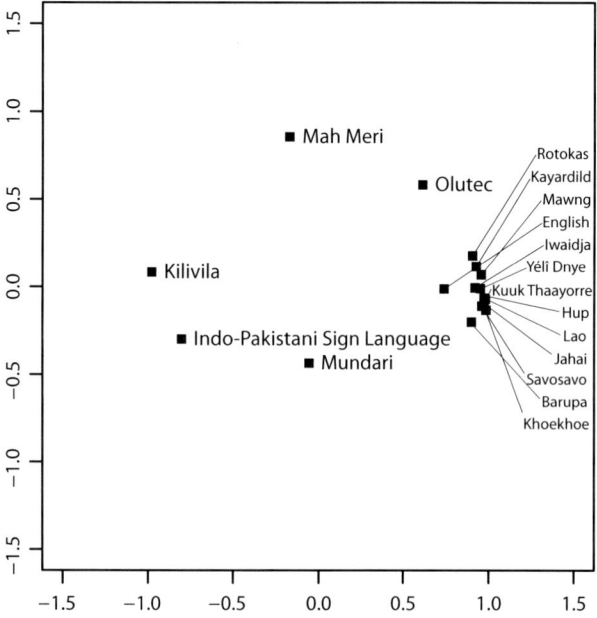

Figure 2. Factor analysis of languages according to the overall pattern of categorisation of reciprocal events

these languages are closely related. We return below to some of the reasons for the outlier status of these languages.

Another way of analysing the same data is to use cluster analysis (see Figure 4), a technique that groups together items based on the amount of agreement. Each terminal node in the figure represents a language and nodes are grouped together based on similarity, which is iconically reflected in the length of the lines before clusters join – short lines indicate more similarity, long lines less similarity. If languages all agree in which reciprocal events ought to be encoded with a reciprocal construction, that is, if there was one universal solution, we would expect to find one single large cluster (see Figure 3a). Such a constellation would be predicted by Dalrymple et al.'s (1994) analysis. If languages all disagree in which reciprocal events receive reciprocal encoding then languages would all be isolated from one another. This radical relativity constellation is depicted in Figure 3b. If, however, there are sub-groups of languages that agree with one another we would expect to see distinct clusters (see Figure 3c), as might be predicted by Wierzbicka (2009).

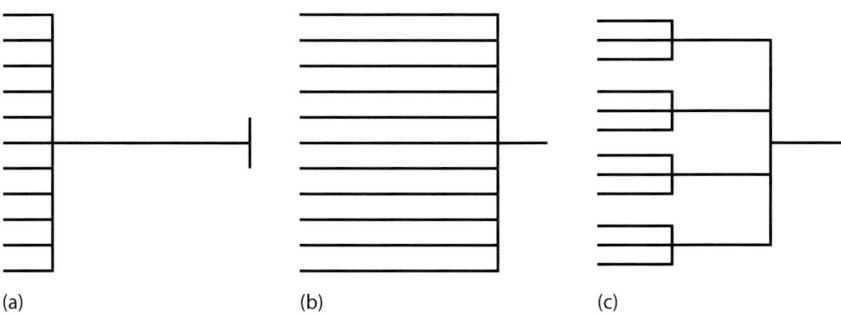

(a)   (b)   (c)

Figure 3. Hypothetical solutions to how reciprocal constructions across languages may cluster

The actual pattern – shown here in Figure 4 – is of the third type. We find two main clusters – the first subsuming most of the languages in the sample, the second grouping Kilivila and Indo-Pakistani Sign Language. The first large cluster can be considered an "agreement" cluster – these languages all roughly agree about which clips should be encoded with a reciprocal construction. Note that the shorter the lines before joining, the more agreement there is. Also, the clusters can be thought of as mobiles – they can be rotated from the arm – so the exact placement of a language name on a cluster is not meaningful; but placement within a cluster is indicative of similarity.

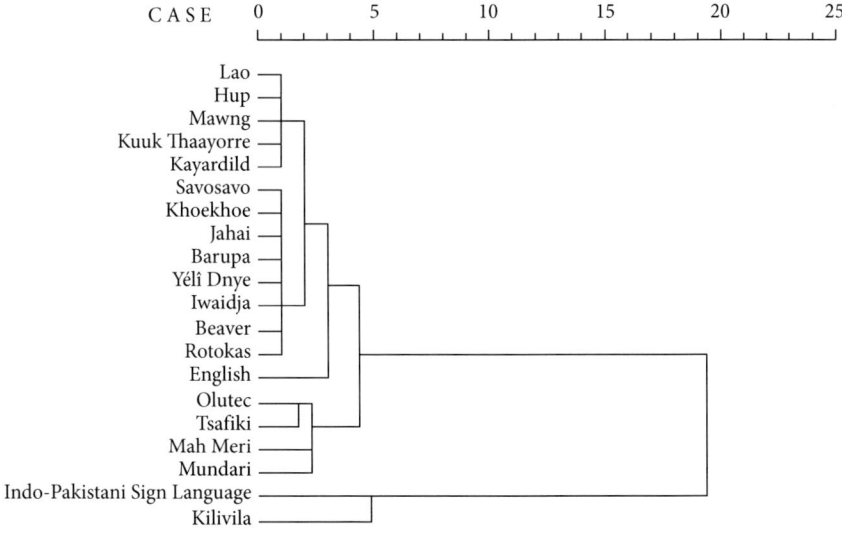

Figure 4. Cluster analysis of languages overall pattern of categorisation of reciprocal events

The big agreement cluster breaks into four subclusters. Lao, Hup, Mawng, Kuuk Thaayorre, and Kayardild, all strongly agree with one another, as does the following group starting with Savosavo and running through Rotokas. These two groups are not themselves very different, indicated by the short separation between them. English is more different again from these two groups (as indicated by the longer distance before joining with the other clusters). Olutec, Tsafiki, Mah Meri and Mundari are more different again, but still share similarities to the other languages mentioned so far, as represented by the fact that they join with the other languages into one major cluster. The major difference is between Kilivila and Indo-Pakistani Sign Language and the other languages.

Both the factor analysis and the cluster analysis indicate that Kilivila and Indo-Pakistani Sign Language are outliers. In the case of Kilivila, the reason is self-evident, since it is a language with no dedicated reciprocal, but the position of our one sign language is less so. Indo-Pakistani Sign has one construction that appears in response to canonical reciprocal events, and this construction has a very limited range of applicability, being used for only 18 videoclips. The restricted range is due to two factors (see Zeshan & Panda Chapter 5). Events where symmetry cannot be shown by parallel handshapes require a different construction altogether, a classifier-construction. This means that clips featuring chasing, following, being next-to, etc. will receive distinct coding. Furthermore, events that are asymmetric – including chaining events – do not get encoded with a reciprocal construction. Again, a separate construction is required, and this construction is not used with canonical reciprocal events that feature complete saturation. Thus Kilivila and Indo-Pakistani Sign share the property of treating all or mostly all the clips as 'non-reciprocal' events.

Mundari and Mah Meri also do not apply reciprocal constructions as widely as the other languages. In Mundari, the reciprocal infix strategy was used for strict and melee situations, but not for chaining situations. The only case where it was applied to a chaining event was when the subevents occurred simultaneously. A different construction was used for chaining events, combining the reciprocal infixation with a serialised verb whose base meaning is 'take' (see Evans & Osada Chapter 6). This construction was not included in these analyses, since it was never applied to a canonical reciprocal event. For Mah Meri, clips depicting symmetrical physical states, e.g., "be.next.to", "lean", were impossible to describe with the reciprocal construction because intransitive and stative verbs cannot enter into reciprocal constructions. Events with non-volitional or unintentional contact, e.g., "bump" likewise cannot be encoded with a reciprocal construction. Moreover, Mah Meri has a strict requirement for exact sameness of action for the reciprocal construction to apply. Impact verbs in Mah Meri have detailed semantics, and often there is no hypernym, so if two events within a clip varied in the particulars of the subevents, a concise description was not possible (Kruspe Chapter 8).

5.   Extensional range of reciprocal constructions

So far we have shown that there is considerable agreement between languages in which events should receive reciprocal encoding, but we have not investigated specific reciprocal constructions in any detail. In the above analyses, two languages can be very similar to one another, even though the first language has only one dedicated construction while the second has two, three, or more. However, even languages with multiple reciprocal encoding strategies often have a clearly identifiable main strategy with the remainder of the constructions playing a rather minor role.[3] Therefore, we concentrate on the main reciprocal encoding strategies in order to determine whether constructions share extensional range across languages. We constructed a matrix consisting of the main strategy from each language (19 columns)[4] and the videoclip stimuli (64 rows). From this basic matrix, there are at least two ways to examine how similar constructions are to one another.

The first is to determine whether constructions group and distinguish the reciprocal videoclips in the same way. Videoclips are "grouped together" when the same construction is applied to them; they are distinguished when a specific construction is applied to one but not the other. Using multidimensional scaling, we can capture the degree to which languages categorise the videoclips as semantically similar by plotting them in n-dimensional space – just as we plotted languages earlier. In such an analysis, clips that are often grouped together across language constructions will be plotted close together in space, clips that are not grouped together will be plotted further away. The extensional range of a specific construction can be indicated by use of Venn diagrams.

A second way to compare the similarity of the constructions to one another is to plot the constructions themselves, rather than the videoclips. The logic is similar to that of the analysis of the videoclips. To the extent that constructions are used over the stimulus space in similar ways, they are similar to one another and will be plotted close together in space.

---

3.   For example, many languages have a bare reciprocal construction (as in "they kissed") but it is used for only a few of the reciprocal videoclips.

4.   There is no construction for Kilivila.

5.1   Semantic space of reciprocal events

To uncover how videoclips were categorised across the constructions of different languages, we used multidimensional scaling with a binary Euclidean distance.[5] Figure 5 displays the semantic space of the videoclips. The numbers refer to specific videoclips; for convenience, configuration types for some of the clips are illustrated within the figure. Full descriptions of all the clips can be found in Appendix A. The videoclips form a dense cluster on the right hand side, with a smaller number pulled apart on the left. The stimuli on the left are the clips most likely to be excluded from the range of the reciprocal constructions we consider here. These include two-participant asymmetrical events and asymmetric radial events. Most languages clearly distinguished these events from the others.

Overall this analysis shows that across languages there is relatively little differentiation of the various reciprocal parameters built into our stimulus set. If the main reciprocal strategies of languages differed substantially in the kinds of action or 'event-types' they included in their scope then there would be much more differentiation between the clips in this plot. The relatively dense clustering of events on the right-hand side of the plot below shows that this is not the case. Note though that saturated (strong) events are among those furthest to the right, and that non-reciprocal asymmetric events are furthest to the left. Dimension 1, thus, distinguishes strong reciprocal events from asymmetric events. Chaining and melee events are separated widely on Dimension 2, with strong reciprocal events falling centrally. Thus there is structure inside this dense cluster, with canonical symmetric exchanges central, and departures of one kind or another more peripheral.

So which events do the different constructions encompass in their range? We can illustrate holding this same plot constant as a general map of the place of the clips in semantic space, and meanwhile superimpose the extensions of each language-specific construction. Figures 6–8 depict some typical extensional ranges for specific constructions in particular languages that we find in

---

5.   We used ALSCAL in SPSS to analyze the data. Multidimensional scaling (MDS) produces measures of "goodness of fit", i.e. how good the model is at capturing the data. One such measure is "stress", which measures the difference between the distances computed in MDS and the corresponding distances in the actual data. The stress of the model was quite high at .20; in MDS anything under 0.1 is considered excellent and under 0.15 acceptable. However, according to another measure of goodness of fit, the "squared correlation index", which reflects the proportion of variance accounted for by the scaled data the fit of the data was good. The RSQ for the current model was 0.85. Anything over 0.6 is considered acceptable on this measure.

our sample. The Venn diagrams indicate which videoclips a particular language construction was applied to. The broadest extensional range was exhibited by the Lao *kan3* construction and the Hup interactional (Figure 6), which were permissive in their range. These constructions are used to convey that the individuals are doing an activity together, thus including asymmetrical events such as A delousing B (#51) within their scope. Note how they nevertheless differ in whether they exclude partially symmetric chains (Hup) or radial asymmetrical exchanges (Lao).

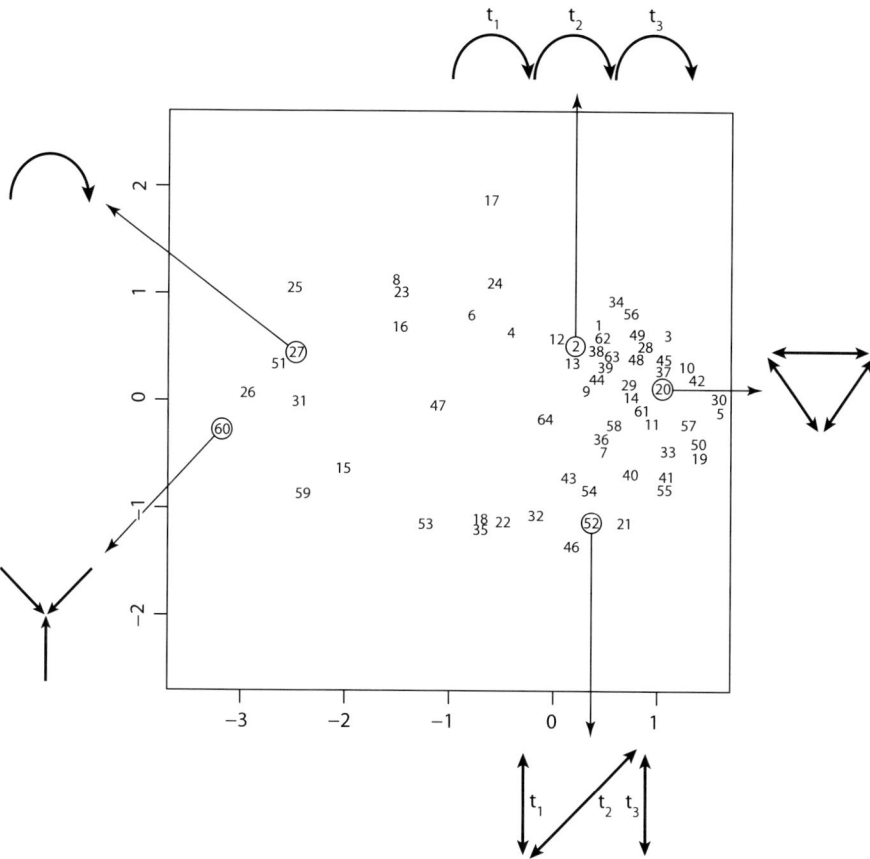

Figure 5. Multidimensional scaling solution of the videoclips as categorised across languages. Dimension 1 is on the x-axis and dimension 2 on the y-axis. The configuration type on the right-hand side is the strong reciprocal relation. Moving clock-wise, the next configuration type is melee, followed by asymmetric radial events on the bottom left-hand side, then asymmetric events, followed by chaining events at the top. The subscripts "t_1, t_2" etc. on the configuration icons indicate that the events happened sequentially

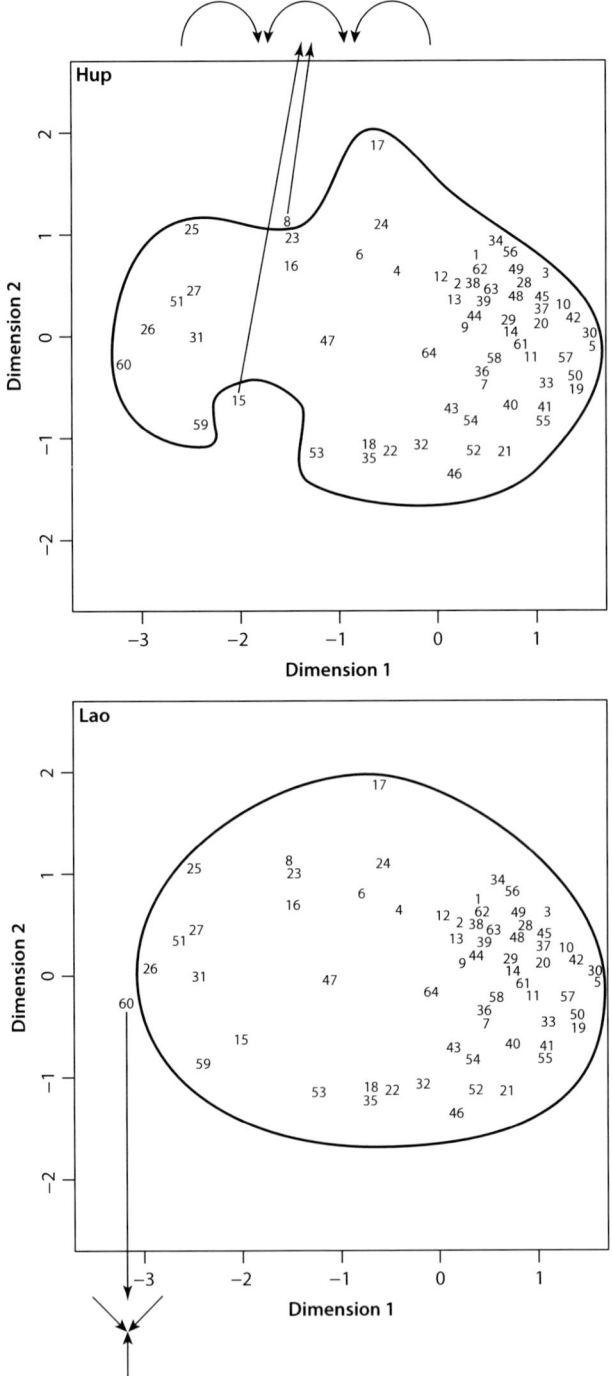

Figure 6. Extensional range for Hup (top panel) and Lao (bottom panel) constructions

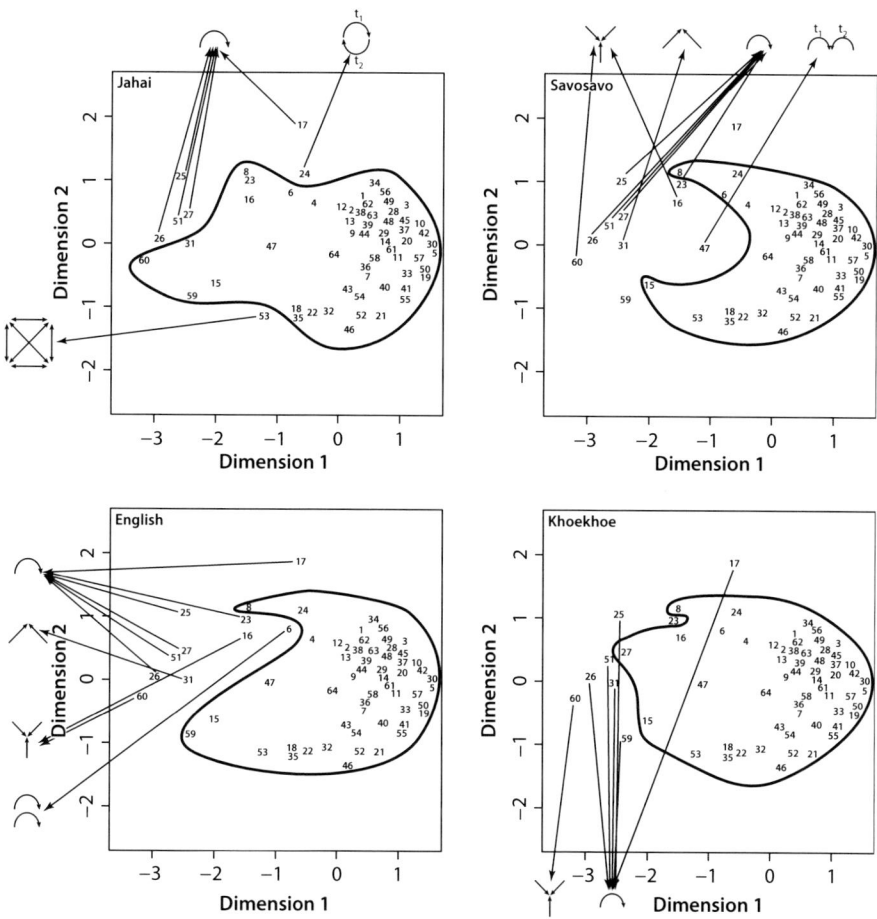

Figure 7. Extensional range for general reciprocal constructions in Jahai (top left), Savosavo (top right), English (bottom left) and Khoekhoe (bottom right)

Most of the languages did not have constructions with anything like this broadness of application. The majority of constructions analysed here excluded asymmetrical two participant events, but included the majority of the remaining clips, as exemplified by Jahai, Khoekhoe, English and Savosavo in Figure 7. Notice for example that all these languages happily include chaining and non-saturated scenes, but get picky when just two or three participants are involved in asymmetric events. The plots (setting aside Jahai for a moment) suggest why the formal semantics approach has failed to nail down reciprocal meanings – there appears to be an impressionistic filter, of the kind that legitimates general collective involvement in an exchange of actions. Jahai is the most permissive, but excludes a

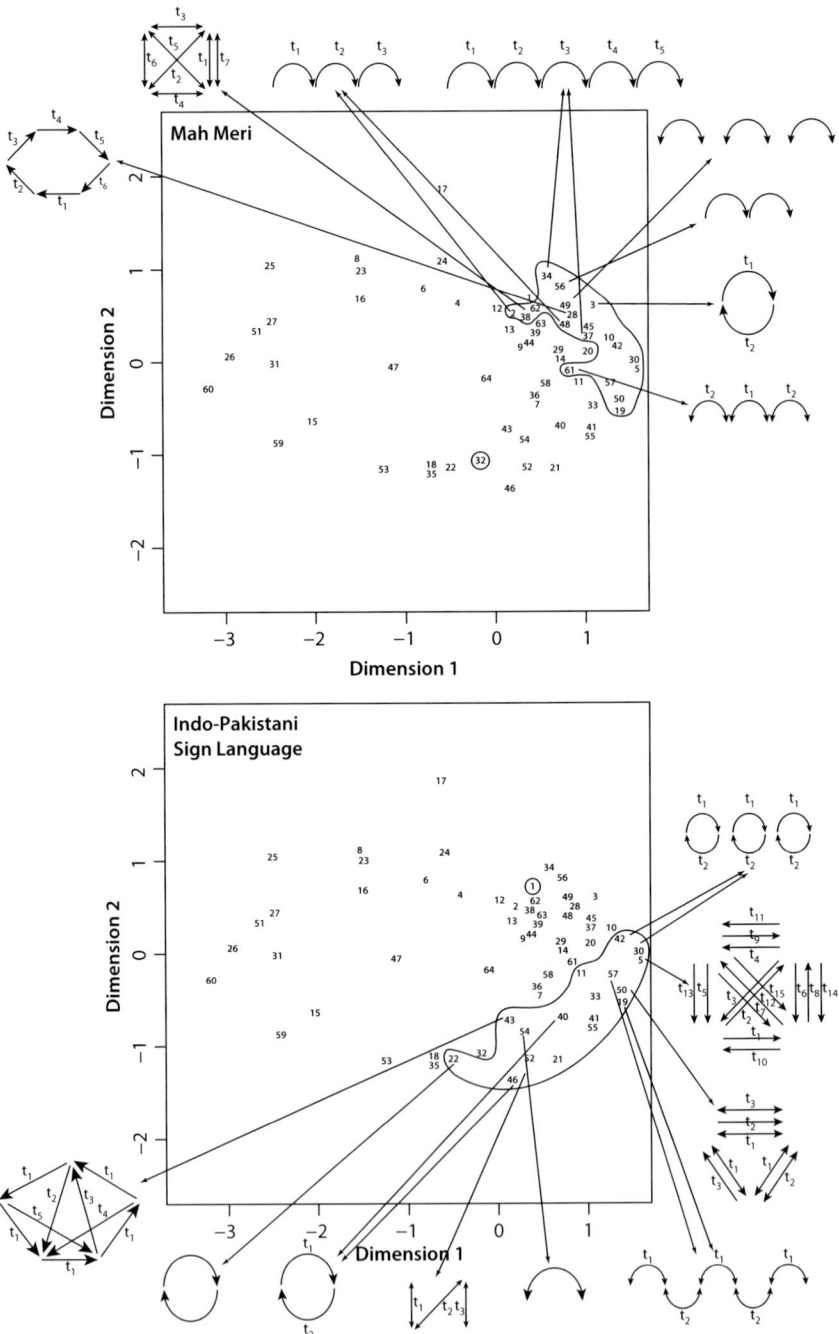

Figure 8. Extensional range for Mah Meri (top) and Indo-Pakistani Sign Language (bottom) constructions

static saturated state (four sticks leaning against each other) presumably because of the specific properties of its distributive construction.

There were, however, a few languages that had a much more restricted range. We have already noted that Indo-Pakistani Sign Language is an outlier, on the grounds of a very parsimonious use of its reciprocal construction. Figure 8 (bottom panel) shows a plot of this construction. As one can see, not only are all chaining events excluded, so are static scenes. Nevertheless the construction is not restricted to the 'canonical' saturated type, since some asymmetric melee scenes are included.[6] The Mah Meri double distributive construction also had a very restrictive application (Figure 8 top panel), but showed a complementary pattern to the Indo-Pakistani Sign construction, in that it was much more likely to be used for chaining events (Figure 8).

What these plots nicely illustrate is just how differently these language-specific constructions map onto extensional space. Although all of them are grounded in the cluster to the right of the plot, that is partly because they had to include saturated 'strong' reciprocity to qualify. Beyond that, they extend to the left or up and down to engulf quite differing regions of clip space.

5.2   Semantic similarity of constructions

Another way to see the similarity of the constructions to one another is to plot constructions, rather than clips. We ask here: to what extent are each of the reciprocal constructions used in all of the languages similar or dissimilar to one another? Constructions from unrelated languages will be grouped together to the extent that they partition the clip space in similar ways; to the extent that they partition the space in different ways, they will lie far apart from each other. Using multidimensional scaling once again,[7] but taking constructions as our unit of analysis, we can get an overview of the similarity of construction types. Figure 9 shows a plot of the main reciprocal encoding strategies. Going from right to left, constructions become progressively more restricted in how many clips they are applied to: Lao and Hup are most inclusive; Mah Meri and Indo-Pakistani Sign Language most restrictive (see Figures 6–8 to see extensional spaces). Notice, too, that many of

---

6.   The auxiliary construction was applied to clips #19 and 57, which are described as chaining events. The prototypical chaining event has an action moving sequentially along a set of participants – e.g., A hits B, B then hits C, C then hits D, etc. However, both clips #19 and 57 can also be construed as pairwise reciprocals – e.g., for clip #57 A and B, C and D, and E and F hit each other at t_1 and then B and C, and D and E hit each other at t_2.

7.   We used ALSCAL within SPSS. The stress of the model was .15, the RSQ was 0.91.

the constructions cluster at the more inclusive end of extensional space: in effect, less than a third of languages are highly selective in their application of reciprocals. This broadening of the semantics may be motivated by two factors – on the one hand, some of these constructions may have their home base off the map as it were (a matter discussed immediately below), and on the other hand, given the low textual frequencies of reciprocals in general, a broader semantics may be required if the construction is to stay alive in the language (as discussed in Chapter 1).

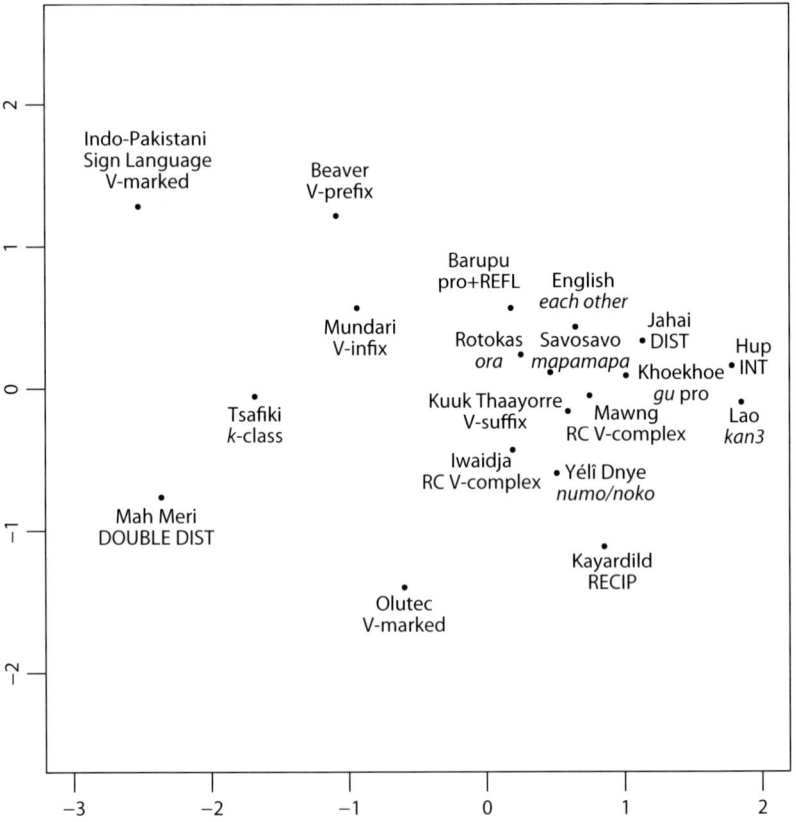

Figure 9. Constructional similarity space. The Hup and Lao constructions are the most inclusive and are plotted on the right. As we move towards the left of Dimension 1, constructions become progressively more restrictive. On Dimension 2, Indo-Pakistani Sign Language and Mah Meri are most sharply distinguished, due to their differential extension over clip space (see Figure 8)

Some quite interesting observations emerge from this analysis. One is the intriguing clue that the reciprocal extensional space has a structure somewhat independent of the particular intensions of the constructions that describe it. This we can see by considering languages where we know the intensional core is much broad-er than the reciprocal domain, and sometimes may have its home base beyond the kind of exchanges central to our study. Constructions of this type include the Jahai distributive, the Hup 'interactional' construction, and perhaps the Lao *kan3* construction of mutual interaction. The use of these constructions actually maps closer to the English 'dedicated reciprocal' *each other* construction than the use of some other dedicated reciprocals, like the Mundari verbal reciprocal.

The positive side of this observation is that it suggests the domain has an in-herent structure, so that when it is invaded by a neighbouring construction, that construction will not just nibble at the edges of the domain, but swallow the lot, as it were. The invading construction has to obey the constraints *within* the domain, even if its home-base may lie partially outside it. An analogy can perhaps be made here to the work on colour. It is well-known that some languages include in their basic colour words information about texture or succulence (Conklin 1955; see Lucy 1997), thus having a wider range of application than the hue-brightness-saturation dimensions of the Munsell colour space. Nonetheless, these colour terms obey the same restrictions in range over these three colour dimensions as do "core" colour terms (Kay & Regier 2003). The constraints on semantic range within a domain have a life of their own, and are not predictable from the wider uses and broader senses of constructions beyond it.

The more negative corollary is that – especially where constructions over-lap domains – their intensions obviously can not be read off their extensional behaviour inside a sampling of a single domain. That is yet another reason why extensional analysis must be supplemented by broader corpus studies and rich elicitation of the kind exemplified in the descriptive chapters of this volume. It is also a reason to extend analyses of this sort into the surrounding domains in ad-ditional, complementary studies.

Another interesting observation that can be extracted from this analysis is the influence of construction type on extensional range. We have already noted that dedicated reciprocal constructions themselves are not all of the same kind. We can see from Figure 9 (and more exhaustively Appendix B) that there are broad morpho-syntactic types that can be distinguished.

The prediction of Dalrymple et al. (1994) is that the meaning of reciprocal constructions should be independent of the particular construction types that ex-press it. Thus there should be no difference in the semantic ranges or reciprocals that happen to be expressed by verb-coding as opposed to nominal coding.

The contrary prediction will seem more natural to many linguists, especially where a single language deploys more than one construction, and one expects constrastive interpretations (Wierzbicka 2009). We tested whether reciprocal constructions with the same sort of marking were more similar to each other in their semantic ranges than those with different marking. That is, are recipro-cal constructions with verb-coded reciprocals (see Appendix B) more similar to other verb-coded reciprocal constructions than they are to argument-coded con-structions, in which the coding site is the NP? And, likewise, are argument-coded constructions more similar to each other than they are to verb-coded reciprocals?

We compared the distances between constructions in the similarity space in Figure 9 by comparing pairwise distances between constructions. It turns out that argument-coded constructions (such as English *each other* and Yélî Dnye *numo/noko*) are no more similar to other argument-coded constructions than they are to verb-coded ones [$t(1, 53) = .59, p = .63$]. And, in fact, verb-coded reciprocal constructions are actually more different from other verb-coded constructions than they are to argument-marking constructions [$t(1, 79) = 2.27, p < .03$]. The distances between argument-coded and verb-coded constructions is of equal size [$t(1, 44) = 1.88, p < .07$].[8] This suggests that the mode of grammatical coding does not constrain the semantic range of reciprocal meanings expressible within core reciprocal constructions. In this respect Dalrymple et al. (1994) prove to be correct. But as demonstrated in the previous sections they incorrectly predict uniform semantic ranges for reciprocal constructions.[9]

6.   Summary of results

The results of this study suggest both systematic similarities and some striking differences in the way that languages treat this domain. On the similarity side, languages carve out contiguous categories of cross-linguistic extensional space for their reciprocal constructions (see Figures 6–8). Even when they extend con-structions used elsewhere to areas of this semantic space, they do so in a sys-tematic way, so that extensionally the patterns are similar (but not identical) to those of dedicated reciprocal constructions. Most of the languages in our sample showed high agreement in the kinds of situations that reciprocal constructions

---

8.   There is a small tendency for argument-coded constructions to be closer together in se-mantic space than verb-coded constructions, but this could be due to the fact that we have only a few argument-coding constructions in our sample.

9.   We had originally predicted that participants that are not naturally in core argument posi-tions would be hard to target with a verb-coded reciprocal construction. That this prediction is largely wrong – Mundari (Chapter 6) being an exception – probably implies that there is enough syntactic machinery to move participants into core argument positions to make coding freely possible. Further investigation would be required to understand the strategies used in specific languages to achieve this.

could felicitously be applied to, as indicated by the strong agreement in the overall language comparisons.

On the other hand there are some fundamental differences between languages (Figures 2 and 4) and between the constructions (Figures 6–9) they use to cover the domain so that there are clearly no simple, strong universals in this domain, pace Dalrymple et al 1998. Some languages have no reciprocals (Kilivila in our sample), some have up to five or six distinct constructions (English, Barupu, Tsafiki). The ranges of extension vary notably. Some languages seem to use a sloppy 'general mutual involvement' criterion as in English or especially Lao, others like Mah Meri or Indo-Pakistani Sign have much more restrictive delimitation. Yet these last two differ: Indo-Pakistani sign language excludes chaining-type events from the scope of its reciprocal construction but happily includes melee-type events. Mah Meri, on the other hand, shows the opposite pattern – the reciprocal construction of this language is extended to chaining-events but shows restricted applicability to melee-type events (see Figure 8).

An interesting question is whether the diversity in meaning or extensional range could partly be an outcome of the constructional coding in the different languages. Could the differences in semantic extension, for example, be predicted from the formal coding of the constructions (as verbal, nominal, or adverbial)? The answer appears to be no. We hypothesised that reciprocal constructions coded in verb complexes might be more similar to each other than they were to argument-coded constructions, and vice versa. But our analyses show that this is not the case (see Figure 9, where e.g. both a verbal construction in Indo-Pakistani sign and an argument or nominal construction in Mah Meri are outliers to the left on dimension 1, while other languages that use either an argument-based or verbal-based strategy are clustered together to the right). Sharing the constructional mode of reciprocal coding does not seem to make two reciprocal constructions semantically more similar to each other. Overall, then, this suggests that for each language, the child language learner not only has to learn the language-specific semantic extensions of the constructions in its language, but also, independently, how they are expressed formally. The child can apparently not use the syntax to bootstrap into the semantics, or vice versa.

7.   Promises and limitations of the current approach

Finally, in the light of recent critiques of the approach employed in this chapter (see especially Wierzbicka 2009) it is worth clarifying what the approach outlined in this chapter can and cannot achieve. First, some misconceptions need to be put aside. Wierzbicka (2009: 165) makes the point that 'in human life the most important things are invisible', and that there are many 'inner' factors (intentions, desires, shared plans, etc.) which are relevant for such a socially charged category as reciprocity. She makes the criticism that the extensional approach exemplified here has an "objectivist, neo-behaviourist slant" inappropriate to the subject matter (p. 163). But the elementary fact is that there is no telepathy – mental states have to be inferred from behaviour. As psychologists have long demonstrated, people make complex intentional attributions from even the simplest of dynamic stimuli (Heider & Simmel 1944). They will do so automatically on viewing human interaction, whether in videoclips or in the real. In this study the depicted events were simple actions and participants from the different communities we investigated were able to interpret them easily (albeit with occasional puzzlement over the gender of the actors), and attributed all the intentions and desires required to make sense of them. Moreover, the very methods that Wierzbicka thinks incapable of revealing such things in fact show that she is right – reciprocity is indeed cross-linguistically anchored in intentional and social attributions. For it is noteworthy that most 'spatial-configuration' clips (depicting things next to or leaning on other things) failed to be categorised with the main cluster: all of the 'next-to' clips are outliers in Figure 5. This is something that is not predictable at all, for example, from studies of reciprocals in the logical-semantic tradition such as Langendoen (1978) and Dalrymple et al. (1998).

In addition, as we stated at the outset, we are not proposing the extensionalist multivariate approach as a substitute for the formulation of specific lexical or constructional meanings using the traditional methods of linguistic analysis. Readers are referred to the next 16 chapters for many examples of this kind of analysis. But just as any child growing up in a culture must learn the native categories of its languages from exemplifications of their use, so the analyst must use the extensional mappings of terms as the essential guide to constructing intensional categories. The extensions provide the essential constraints for the study of sense or intension.

Setting these misunderstandings aside, let us underline the two signal advantages of the methods exemplified here: comparative precision, and the way in which they do not prejudge the terms of analysis, but rather let them emerge.

First, comparative precision: Traditional methods of linguistic analysis founder given significant variation in the object of study – indeed they tend to idealise away from it. For example, there's no easy way to take ten or twenty speakers from a single language and show how their slight differences in linguistic behaviour follow from their slightly different intensional categories. Now try the same for similar numbers of speakers of twenty languages. That's the challenge, and the current methods rise to (the extensional version of) the challenge with ease. For what the approach employed here is precisely designed for is producing a measurable, precise picture of the patterning of cross-linguistic semantic variation – for answering questions like:

- How far do languages actually differ in the way they categorise events of type X?
- How important are the various potentially relevant semantic parameters in cross-linguistic categorisation? Do all languages include both semantic parameter X and parameter Y in their categorisations of this phenomenon?
- Does the conceptual patterning of the domain track geography, phylogenetic structure, typological makeup of the language, coding mechanism, culture or what?
- Which languages differ most, and which cluster together, in their categorisations?

Although the kind of method used here maps extensions not intensions, the extensional maps give an approximate guide to the intensional terrain, for the simple reason that intensional differences generally produce extensional differences (where that isn't the case, the child learner is in equal deep water with the analyst). Thus with due caution (note our remarks above about distributive, interactional and other domains neighbouring reciprocity), extensions provide a quantifiable proxy for the direct measurement of conceptual differences.

The second great advantage of the multivariate-extensional approach is that it allows the significant categories to emerge, rather than defining them prior to the study. This is a major asset, since definitional problems in a domain like reciprocity can be intractable: What counts as a reciprocal construction cross-linguistically? Exactly what situations should it include, and what should it exclude? This sort of problem bedevils just about any other kind of typological comparison, with disagreement rife on which criteria to adopt because of the relative arbitrariness of different criteria in the absence of any fixed prototype which all languages can be assumed to make reference to. Should a construction in language X be excluded as a reciprocal because it allows some asymmetric uses, or doesn't allow chaining, or takes in reflexive or sociative or distributive meanings?

These definitional decisions prove difficult or even impossible for linguists to reach consensus on. But for the approach taken here, they can simply be bypassed: the statistics are able to measure the patterning of categorisations over languages and stimuli directly, without requiring us to make a prior analytic decision on what to include. In practice, of course, there are underlying decisions in the choice of the stimuli, but these can be balanced across different expectations, so letting the data decide. There are also coding decisions to be made, but the problems here are largely language internal. In addition, for purposes of presentation or analysis we may construct a category – as we did when choosing constructions for analysis which denote at least one 'canonical reciprocal event'. But the data can be reanalysed making other decisions.

For these reasons, we believe that multivariate extensional methods have an important role in semantic typology. The data and analyses discussed in this chapter are a proof of concept that such approaches can be applied to the semantics of grammar as well as to the semantics of lexical categories, a domain in which multivariate extensional analysis has been more extensively tested.

Extending its usefulness further will require us to gradually link up other stimulus sets. As pointed out in Chapter 1, for reasons of achievable scope, we did not expand out the set of stimuli to include all the other configurations which reciprocal constructions have been reported to link to – reflexives, causatives, iteratives, distributives, sociatives, competitives, random motion and so forth. A comprehensive investigation of how far languages converge in their categorisation of this domain would need to cover those additional, neighbouring domains.

Even for the relatively constrained field covered by our data, however, it should be clear that multivariate extensional approaches can reveal an intriguing balance of similarities and differences in the cross-linguistic picture: most but by no means all languages code a good portion of extensional space rather close to what is expressed by English 'each other', but the number of nuanced variations in its patterns of extension are far greater than the literature has suggested.

Acknowledgements

Thanks to all the researchers who supplied data, analysis and interpretation that went towards this chapter. A synopsis of the study reported in this book appears in Majid, Evans, Gaby & Levinson (2011). Special thanks to Ludy Cilissen and Peter Nijland for assistance with figures.

References

Berlin, Brent & Kay, Paul. 1969. *Basic Color Terms. Their Universality and Evolution*. Berkeley CA: University of California Press.

Conklin, Harold C. 1955. Hanunóo color categories. *Southwestern Journal of Anthropology* 11(4): 339–344.

Croft, William. 2001. *Radical Construction Grammar. Syntactic Theory in Typological Perspective*. Oxford: OUP.

Dąbrowska, Ewa. 2010. Naive v. expert intuitions: An empirical study of acceptability judgments. *The Linguistic Review* 27(1): 1–23.

Dalrymple, Mary, Mchombo, Sam A. & Peters, Stanley. 1994. Semantic similarities and syntactic contrasts between Chicheŵa and English reciprocals. *Linguistic Inquiry* 25(1): 145–63.

Dalrymple, Mary, Kanazawa, Makoto, Kim, Yookyung, Mchombo, Sam & Peters, Stanley. 1998. Reciprocal expressions and the concept of reciprocity. *Linguistics & Philosophy* 21(2): 159–210.

Enfield, N. J., Majid, Asifa & van Staden, Mirjam (eds). 2006. Cross-linguistic categorisation of the body: Introduction. *Language Sciences* 28(2–3): 137–147.

Evans, Nicholas, Levinson, Stephen C., Enfield, N. J., Gaby, Alice & Majid, Asifa. 2004. Reciprocal constructions and situation type. In *Field Manual*, Vol. 9, Asifa Majid (ed.), 25–30. Nijmegen: Max Planck Institute for Psycholinguistics.

Evans, Nicholas. 2008. Reciprocal constructions: Towards a structural typology. In *Reciprocals and Reflexives: Cross-linguistic and Theoretical Explorations*, Ekkehard König & Volker Gast (eds), 33–104. Berlin: Mouton de Gruyter.

Evans, Nicholas & Levinson, Stephen C. 2009. The myth of language universals. *Behavioral & Brain Sciences* 32: 429–448.

Filip, Hana & Carlson, Gregory N. 2001. Distributivity strengthens reciprocity; collectivity weakens it. *Linguistics & Philosophy* 24: 417–466.

Goldberg, Adele. 2009. Essentialism gives way to motivation. *Behavioral and Brain Sciences* 32(5): 455–456.

Heider, Fritz & Simmel, Marianne. 1944. An experimental study of apparent behavior. *The American Journal of Psychology* 57(2): 243–259.

Kay, Paul & Regier, Terry. 2003. Resolving the question of color naming universals. *Proceedings of the National Academy of Sciences of the United States of America* 100(15): 9085–9089.

König, Ekkehard & Kokutani, Shigehiro. 2006. Towards a typology of reciprocal constructions: Focus on German and Japanese. *Linguistics* 44(2): 271–302.

Labov, William. 1978. Denotational structure. In *Papers from the Parasession on the Lexicon*, Donka Farkas, Wesley M. Jacobsen & Karol W. Todrys (eds.), 220–260. Chicago IL: Chicago Linguistics Society.

Langendoen, D. Terence. 1978. The logic of reciprocity. *Linguistic Inquiry* 9(2): 177–197.

Levinson, Stephen & Evans, Nicholas. 2010. Time for a sea-change in linguistics. Response to comments on 'The Myth of Language Universals'. *Lingua* 120(12): 2733–2758.

Levinson, Stephen C. & Meira, Sérgio. 2003. 'Natural concepts' in the spatial topological domain – adpositional meanings in crosslinguistic perspective: An exercise in semantic typology. *Language* 79(3): 485–516.

Lucy, John A. 1997. The linguistics of 'color'. In *Color Categories in Thought and Language*, Clyde L. Hardin & Luisa Maffi (eds), Cambridge: Cambridge University Press.

Majid, Asifa, Boster, James S. & Bowerman, Melissa. 2008. The cross-linguistic categorization of everyday events: A study of cutting and breaking. *Cognition* 109: 235–250.

Majid, Asifa & Bowerman, Melissa. 2007. Cutting and breaking events: A cross-linguistic perspective. Special issue of *Cognitive Linguistics* 18(2).

Majid, Asifa, Evans, Nicholas, Gaby, Alice & Levinson, Stephen C. 2011. The grammar of exchange: A comparative study of reciprocal constructions across languages. *Frontiers in Psychology* 2.

Nedjalkov, Vladimir P. (ed.). 2007. *Reciprocal Constructions* [Typological Studies in Language 71], 5 Vols. Amsterdam: John Benjamins.

Nisbett, Richard E. & Wilson, Timothy D. 1977. Telling more than we can know: Verbal reports on mental processes. *Psychological Review* 84: 231–259.

Pederson, Eric, Danziger, Eve, Wilkins, David P., Levinson, Stephen C., Kitae, Sotaro & Senft, Gunter. 1998. Semantic typology and spatial conceptualization. *Language* 74: 557–589.

Romney, A. Kimball, Weller, Susan C. & Batchelder, William H. 1986. Culture as consensus: A theory of culture and informant accuracy. *American Anthropologist* 88: 313–338.

Schütze, Carson T. 1996. *The Empirical Base of Linguistics: Grammaticality Judgments and Linguistics Methodology*. Chicago IL: The University of Chicago Press.

Tremblay, Annie. 2005. Theoretical and methodological perspectives on the use of grammaticality judgment tasks in linguistic theory. *Second Language Studies* 24: 129–167.

Wierzbicka, Anna. 2009. Reciprocity: An NSM approach to linguistic typology and social universals. *Studies in Language* 33(1): 103–174.

Appendix A.   List of videoclips with associated semantic parameters

Videoclip	Number of participants	Saturation	Symmetry	Simultaneity	Event-type
1	two	inapplicable	asymmetrical	inapplicable	talk
2	four	chain	asymmetrical	sequential	hug
3	two	strong	symmetrical	sequential	hit
4	three	strong	symmetrical	sequential	give
5	four	strong	symmetrical	sequential	hit
6	four	pair	asymmetrical	simultaneous	delouse
7	two	strong	symmetrical	simultaneous	hug
8	four	chain	symmetrical	simultaneous	next.to
9	two	strong	symmetrical	simultaneous	meet
10	two	strong	symmetrical	sequential	delouse
11	two	strong	symmetrical	sequential	talk
12	two	strong	symmetrical	simultaneous	lean
13	six	chain	asymmetrical	sequential	shake.hand
14	three	chain	asymmetrical	simultaneous	chase
15	four	chain	symmetrical	simultaneous	next.to
16	four	radial	asymmetrical	sequential	hug
17	two	inapplicable	asymmetrical	inapplicable	hit
18	two	strong	symmetrical	simultaneous	next.to
19	six	chain	symmetrical	both	give
20	three	strong	symmetrical	simultaneous	hug
21	four	melee	asymmetrical	sequential	give
22	two	strong	symmetrical	sequential	bump
23	two	inapplicable	asymmetrical	inapplicable	hug
24	two	strong	symmetrical	sequential	follow
25	two	inapplicable	asymmetrical	inapplicable	look
26	two	inapplicable	asymmetrical	inapplicable	give

Videoclip	Number of participants	Saturation	Symmetry	Simultaneity	Event-type
27	two	inapplicable	asymmetrical	inapplicable	follow
28	six	ring	asymmetrical	sequential	give
29	six	pair	symmetrical	simultaneous	hug
30	six	pair	symmetrical	sequential	give
31	three	radial	asymmetrical	simultaneous	look
32	four	radial	symmetrical	sequential	give
33	two	strong	symmetrical	simultaneous	look
34	six	chain	asymmetrical	sequential	give
35	six	pair	symmetrical	simultaneous	lean
36	two	strong	symmetrical	sequential	chase
37	six	chain	asymmetrical	sequential	give
38	four	strong	symmetrical	both	shake.hand
39	four	pair	asymmetrical	inapplicable	chase
40	two	strong	symmetrical	sequential	talk
41	two	strong	symmetrical	simultaneous	give
42	six	pair	symmetrical	sequential	hit
43	five	melee	asymmetrical	both	chase
44	four	melee	asymmetrical	sequential	hit
45	two	strong	symmetrical	simultaneous	delouse
46	two	strong	symmetrical	sequential	look
47	three	radial	asymmetrical	sequential	hug
48	four	chain	asymmetrical	sequential	hit
49	six	pair	symmetrical	simultaneous	shake.hand
50	three	strong	symmetrical	both	hit
51	two	inapplicable	asymmetrical	inapplicable	delouse
52	four	melee	symmetrical	both	hug
53	four	strong	symmetrical	simultaneous	lean
54	two	strong	symmetrical	simultaneous	hit
55	two	strong	symmetrical	simultaneous	bump
56	three	chain	asymmetrical	simultaneous	delouse
57	six	chain	symmetrical	both	hit
58	two	strong	symmetrical	sequential	hug
59	two	inapplicable	asymmetrical	inapplicable	bump
60	four	radial	asymmetrical	simultaneous	look
61	four	chain	symmetrical	both	hug
62	eleven	melee	symmetrical	both	meet
63	two	strong	symmetrical	simultaneous	shake.hand
64	two	inapplicable	asymmetrical	inapplicable	chase

Appendix B. Full list of constructions included in the comparative analyses. Key to broad-type classification: V= verb-coded, A = argument-coded (i.e. coding site is the NP), Adv = adverbial, Aux = auxiliary. Note that, in order to have large enough sets of constructions to make comparison fruitful, we adopt a coarse-grained constructional comparison with our 'broad type', close to the system used in König & Kokutani (2006) but less fine-grained than the listing in Chapter 1 or in Evans (2008). For example, the 'argument-coded' type includes both bipartite quantifier constructions of the *each other* type, but also direction prefixation of nouns with a pronominal prefix meaning 'each other('s)'

Language	Short ID	Chapter heading	Broad type	Short-hand description of constructions
Khoekhoe	c1	3.2.1		bound pronoun *gù*
	c3	3.2.4		light reciprocal (inherently reciprocal verb)
English	c1	4.2.1	A	*each other; one another*
	c2	4.2.2		*each... the other; each... each other*
	c3	4.2.3		light reciprocal, i.e. bare verb (of 'they kissed') type
	c4	4.2.4		nominal bare reciprocal
	c5	4.2.4		nominal *between*
	c6	4.2.5		*back-to-back*
IPSL	c1	5.2.1	V / Aux	verbal or auxiliary inflection
Mundari	c1	6.2.1	V	reciprocal infix <pV> to verb
Lao	c1	7.3	Adv	*kan3* construction
Mah Meri	c1	8.2.2	A	double distributive construction
	c2	8.2.1		bare conjunct construction
Jahai	c1	9.2.1	V	distributive construction
	c2	9.2.2	V	reciprocal construction
	c3	9.2.3		body part adjunct
Yélî Dnye	c1	10.2.1–2	V	*numo/noko*
	c2	10.2.3	Adv	*woni-woni*
Rotokas	c1	11.3.2		*ora* construction (sub-constructions predictable)
Savosavo	c1	12.2.1	V	*mapamapa* construction (sub-constructions predictable)
	c2	12.2.3		Bare reciprocal construction
Barupu	c1	no description	V	Pronoun plus reflexive marker *bêku*
	c2	no description	V	No pronoun, reflexive marker reduplicated *bêku-bêku*
	c3	no description	Adv	Reciprocal adverb *báru-báru* (redup-return)
	c4	no description		Bare reciprocal with dual/plural marked subject

Language	Short ID	Chapter heading	Broad type	Short-hand description of constructions
	c6	no description		Two clauses, *verb-kí* (verb-go) in the first clause and *verb-ká* (verb-come) in the second clause
Mawng	c1	14.2		RC construction
	c2	14.3.1	V	*-njili* construction
	c3	14.3.2		bare reciprocal construction
Iwaidja	c1	no description		RC construction
	c2	no description	V	*-njildin* construction
	c3	no description	Adv	bare reciprocal construction plus *ngaldaj*
Kayardild	c1	no description	V	reciprocal suffix *-(n)thu-~--nju-* to verb
	c2	no description	Adv	reciprocal adverb *junkuyunku*
	c3	no description	V	reduplicated suffix *-thunthu-* to verb
Kuuk Thaayorre	c1	15.2.1.1–2	V	reciprocal verbal suffix *-rr*
	c2	15.2.1.3	V	reflexive verbal suffix *-e*
Beaver	c1	no description	V	verbal prefix (RCP DO or RCP OO)
	c2	no description	A	possessive N prefix (RCP N)
	c3	no description	Adv	together
Olutec	c1	16.2.1	V	abs-rr-(bp-)V-pl-inv (n-n.pl)
	c2	16.2.1	V	abs-rr-(bp-)V-vclf:together-pl-inv (n-n.pl)
Tsafiki	c1	17.2.1	V	*i*-class reciprocal
	c2	17.2.1	V	*ki*-class reciprocal
	c3	17.3		*tala* 'amongst' nominal enclitic
	c4	17.6	Adv	*beko beko* 'back and forth' ideophone
	c5	no description	Adv	*manka manka* or *manchi manchi* 'one by one/each after another'
Hup	c1	18.2.1	V	verbal 'interactional' preform *ʔũh*
	c2	18.2.2	V	verbal reflexive prefix *hup-*
	c3	18.2.2	V	verbal preform *bab'-*

CHAPTER 3

Semantics of Khoekhoe
reciprocal constructions

Christian J. Rapold
Leiden University Centre for Linguistics

This paper identifies four reciprocal construction types in Khoekhoe (Central Khoisan). After a brief description of the morphosyntax of each construction, semantic factors governing their choice are explored. Besides lexical semantics, the number of participants, timing of symmetric subevents, and symmetric conceptualisation are shown to account for the distribution of the four partially competing reciprocal constructions.

1. Introduction

Khoekhoe is a Central Khoisan language spoken in Namibia, South Africa and Botswana. With around 250,000 speakers it is by far the largest Khoisan language in terms of number of speakers. Formerly known as Nama (Hottentot) or Nama/Damara, grammars of the language have appeared since the middle of the 19th century. For recent descriptions see Hagman (1977) and Böhm (1985), based on the material in Dempwolff (1934/1935). Haacke & Eiseb (2002) is a large dictionary including dialect variants.

Typological features of Khoekhoe include a flexible SOV basic constituent order, three genders and three numbers that are marked on nouns and pragmatically marked personal pronouns by portmanteau morphemes, an S/A pivot in clausal and interclausal syntax, a nominative-oblique case system with an unmarked nominative, while most semantic relations are coded by postpositions. Neither the subject nor the object are cross-referenced on the verb. Pragmatically unmarked subject pronouns are Wackernagel clitics in the second position of the clause which are formally identical with the person-number-gender markers in nouns and pragmatically marked pronouns. Object pronouns are coded as either freestanding complex pronouns or as verbal suffixes. Tense-Mood-Aspect is expressed by particles and there are verbal, nominal and other derivations. The derivational markers on the verb come before the object pronoun suffixes. Finally, the language makes extensive use of compounding and incorporation (V+V, N+V, V+N, V+Postposition, etc.).

The primary marker of reciprocity in Khoekhoe is the verbal suffix *-gù*, which has cognates with basically the same function in all Central Khoisan languages, but not in other Khoisan families. However, these other families may not be genetically related to Central Khoisan at all – see e.g. Güldemann & Vossen (2000).

2.   Reciprocal constructions in Khoekhoe

There are at least three types of reciprocal construction in Khoekhoe: A bound reciprocal pronoun (Section 2.1), bipartite quantifier NPs (Section 2.2) and a bare conjunct strategy (Section 2.3). Depending on one's theoretical point of view, a fourth, lexical strategy (Section 2.4) can be added. The reciprocal affix of the first and main strategy primarily attaches to verbs, but can also occur on certain postpositions.

2.1   Primary strategy: Bound pronoun *-gù*

The reciprocal suffix *-gù* is invariant and mainly attaches to verbs. Synchronically, the reciprocal marker is formally identical to the third person plural masculine object suffix. For the full paradigm of object pronoun suffixes traditionally given, see Haacke (1999: 182). The general template of verb morphological positions is as follows:

> Root–(Locational extension)–(Incorporated Noun / Postposition)–
> (Derivation)–(Object suffix).

Due to the formal identity of the reciprocal marker and the third person plural masculine object suffix utterances such as (1) are ambiguous without further context:

(1)   *si-da*   *ge*   *go*   *mû-gu.*[1]
      1+3-1PL.C   DECL   RECENT.PAST   see-RECP/3PL.M
      a. 'We$_{EXCL}$ saw each other.'
      b. 'We$_{EXCL}$ saw them$_{MASC}$.'

---

1.   In the current official orthography, the ambiguity is solved by writing the person-number-gender object suffixes, but not the reciprocal suffix, as separate words. For the rest, the Khoekhoe examples are represented in the official Khoekhoe orthography here, with the following minor amendments: capital letters are avoided and the glottal stop is not represented, as it is predictable from the morpheme boundaries.

This ambiguity has led some scholars to hypothesise that the reciprocal is in fact a generalised third person plural masculine object marker, a scenario that Böhm (1985:281) finds "probable". The reciprocal construction would then be the grammaticalisation product of a construction like in "they saw <u>them</u>", with a reading in which reciprocity is implicated.[2] However, according to Voßen (1997:376, cf. 346f.), the Proto-Central Khoisan etymon of the synchronic object pronoun (*-llua) is distinct from the reconstructed proto-form of the reciprocal, *-ku.[3] This means that the two forms in Khoekhoe are less likely to be diachronically related. For this reason and because the "reciprocal -gù" is invariable, we consider the reciprocal and the third person plural masculine object marker as distinct, homophonous morphemes. In the remainder of this paper, the possible non-reciprocal interpretation of the form -gù is not reflected in the glosses and translations.

According to Haacke (2001:499) the reciprocal marker -gù belongs to a set of valency changing verb derivation suffixes, along with the passive (-hĕ), applicative (-bä), reflexive (-sèn) and ventive (-xä) markers, here given with tone marks taken from Haacke and Eiseb (2002).

However, based on evidence of the Comparative test (Zec 1985) and the Coordination Test (cf. Mchombo & Ngunga 1994), we propose to analyse it as a reciprocal pronoun. These tests show that the suffix -gù does not reduce the valency of the verb it attaches to and syntactically functions like an object noun phrase (Rapold 2005). For instance, the object comparison reading (2b) of the following data would be ruled out if the reciprocal suffix were indeed a valency reducing marker, as e.g. in Chicheŵa (Dalrymple et al. 1994:155). Since the comparative noun phrase can only be interpreted as an object if there is another object in the same clause, this is evidence that the reciprocal suffix is in fact an object marker.

(2) !au-ao-n   ge   ≠gāri-ao-n   !gâ.ai   a   Inam-gu.
     hunt-man-3PL.C   DECL   breed-man-3PL.C   more.than   STAT   love-RECP
     a. 'The hunters love each other more than the farmers [love each other].'
                                                        (subject coordination)
     b. 'The hunters love each other more than [they love] the farmers.'
                                                        (object coordination)

---

2. cf. the Oceanic languages Tinrin, Sa and Mwotlap where "ordinary" pronouns can assume a reciprocal interpretation in certain contexts alongside disjunct and reflexive readings (Evans forth.:5).

3. Strictly speaking, Voßen's reconstruction of personal pronouns does not distinguish between subject and object pronouns, but since the subject and object forms of the 3rd person plural masculine are segmentally very similar in all Central Khoisan varieties for which we have the data, this conflation is negligible.

The reciprocal suffix -*gù* freely attaches to any transitive verb as long as it is semantically appropriate. It is ungrammatical on intransitive verbs. Reciprocal constructions with -*gù* can feed the periphrastic causative, and can in turn be fed by
the applicative and the three causatives (which are coded by the suffix -*i*, reduplication or periphrasis).

The antecedent of the reciprocal is commonly a dual or plural subject noun
phrase (coded by either a dual/plural NP or a conjoined NP), but in combination
with certain ditransitive verbs (3) or a periphrastic causative construction (4) the
antecedent may also be a dual or plural direct object.

(3)   *ti-ta*   *ge*   *karton-de*   *ra*   *≠gā-!nâ-gu.*
   1SG-1SG   DECL   cardboard.box-3PL.F.OBL   PROG   insert-in-RECP
   'I put the boxes into each other.'

(4)   *lgôa-n*   *ge*   *ari-ga*   *go*   *!kham-gu*   *kai.*
   child-3PL.C   DECL   dog-3PL.M.OBL   RECENT.PAST   fight-RECP   cause
   'The children made the dogs fight each other.'

Ditransitive verbs that allow a direct object antecedent of the reciprocal either involve an incorporated postposition, e.g. -*!nâ* in (3), or an incorporated transitive
verb (5). (For further details see Rapold (in prep.)).

(5)   *gao-b*   *ge*   *khoe-ga*   *ra*   *≠nau-sao-gu*
   king-3SG.M   DECL   person-3PL.M.OBL   PROG   hit-follow(tr.)-RECP
   'The king is beating the men after each other.'

As is very common for bound pronoun reciprocal strategies, the reciprocal marker -*gu* in Khoekhoe cannot function adnominally (as in 'each other's children').

Besides occurring on verbs, the reciprocal marker -*gu* may also suffix to a
few adjectives (e.g. *!kharaga-gu* 'different from each other.' (adj.), cf. *!kharaga*
'different'),[4] and is found in a few relational nouns (e.g. *khoe-!gâ-gu-n* 'siblings'
(person-brother-RECP-3pc)) and on a few postpositions (6)[5]. The occurrence of
the reciprocal marker on these non-verbs is limited to a few items and is not
productive.

---

4.   In predicative function, adjectives (and nouns) are constructed like stative verbs, but in at-
tributive function, they differ from them in that stative verbs require a relative clause to be able
to occur in a noun phrase.

5.   When hosting the reciprocal marker, these postpositions are freestanding, but their prototypical behaviour is postpositional, as e.g. in *khoe-n xō.lkhā* 'next to the people'. These postpositions may also be incorporated into the verb, to which the reciprocal pronoun is then attached.
This construction is also used by those postpositions that cannot host -*gù* when occurring as
freestanding words.

(6) *khoe-n*   *ge*   *xō.lkhā-gu*   *≠nôa.*
     person-3PL.C   DECL   next.to-RECP   sit.down.PERF
     'The people are sitting next to each other.'   (#8)

While bound reciprocal pronouns frequently exhibit reciprocal/reflexive polysemy (Evans forth.: 22), the suffix *-gù* on verbs is a strongly dedicated marker
of reciprocity. It has no polysemy with any of the following functions found in
the literature (Evans forth., Nedjalkov 2006 i.a.): reflexive, sociative, comitative,
assistive, iterative, intensive, converse, competitive, imitative. However, there
is one conventionalised case of polysemy: the suffix *-gù* can be used to convey a friendly tone in dual or plural imperatives of transitive verbs where it is
clear from the context that only one of the parties of the addressed group can
or should carry out the command. The "intended" Undergoer must be human
and be part of the same group. Pragmatically, this seems to signal that within
this group, such and such an action should occur, without directly referring to
the "intended" Actor and thereby minimising the face threat of the imperative
(Brown & Levinson 1987).

(7) *mâ.i-gu=ro*   *re!*
     stand.CAUS-RECP=2DU.F/C   OPT
     'Please just put him/her down!' (lit.: 'Put each other down!')
     (context: The addressee is holding a baby in her arms.)

(8) *tawede-gu=ro*   *re!*
     greet-RECP=2DU.F/C   OPT
     'Just greet him/her, please!' (lit.: 'Greet each other!')
     (context: The addressee forgot to greet a third person.)

In other contexts such imperatives can of course assume their literal, reciprocal
reading, and the suffix *-gù* can also be interpreted as a third plural masculine
object marker.[6] Alternatively, but not necessarily with a friendly tone, the com-
mands conveyed in (7) and (8) can be expressed by non-reciprocal imperatives
with the appropriate direct object pronouns. Those imperatives may also use the
polite V-pronoun for a single addressee (*-du*):

(7´) *mâ-i-si(=du)*   *re!*
      stand-CAUS-3SG.F(=2PL.C)   OPT
      'Put her down!' (context: The addressee is holding a baby in her arms.)

---

6. This raises the question whether the friendly use of *-gu* is really an extension of the reciprocal and not the third plural masculine use. According to our informants, however, the "friendly
-gu" has a reciprocal literal meaning.

This asymmetric use of the reciprocal marker also occurs in the declarative and interrogative in identical constellations of participants, but there the semantics of the construction is more elusive.

2.2   Supplementary strategy: Bipartite quantifier NPs

This strategy occurs with transitive verbs and consists of a bipartite quantifier noun phrase in which each of the elements is separately case-marked.

(9) *haka khoe-n   ge   nē-e   nau-e   ra   ǂnau.*
     four   person-3PL.C DECL THIS-3SG.C.OBL other-3SG.C.OBL PROG hit
     'Four people are hitting each other.'   (#5)

The first element, the demonstrative, selects the oblique case, just like lexical subjects that do not occur in clause-initial position (Haacke 1992). The second element is also in the oblique case, as all direct objects, or, if followed by certain postpositions, in the nominative (10). If both elements are in the oblique case it is still the first element that can be likened to non-clause-initial lexical subjects, because such subjects obligatorily precede other noun phrases after the declarative mood marker ge. The sequence of both elements seems to be inseparable and confined to the position after the mood marker ge, optionally preceded by the TMA marker. The two elements are usually in the third person singular of the common gender, though semantic agreement in gender and number with the clause-initial subject is possible.

(10) *khoe-n   ge   nē-e   nau-i   xō.lkha ǂnôa.*
      person-3PL.C DECL THIS-3SG.C.OBL other-3SG.C:NOM next.to sit.down.PERF
      'The people are sitting next to each other.'   (#8)

As well as having a low frequency of occurrence, this strategy is not accepted by all speakers when prompted. This strategy can in all cases be substituted by the first strategy without a discernible change in meaning (cf. (18), (6)).

2.3   Marginal strategy I: Bare conjunct strategy

The bare conjunct strategy (also less appropriately known as a "light reciprocal" construction) occurs as an alternative to the bound pronoun strategy (§2.1) with two transitive verbs, if they are to be interpreted as denoting symmetrical action. In that case they code what has been termed "naturally reciprocal events" (Kemmer 1993). Their subject must be dual or plural (whether a simple or conjunct NP) and they occur without object.

The bare conjunct strategy was found to be compatible with the following two verbs:

(11) *!kham*   'to fight'
      !gamme 'to marry'   (Haacke & Eiseb 2002)[7]

With *!gamme* 'to marry' symmetry of action is merely implicated, as evidenced by (12).

(12) *namase-b* *tsî* *mādawa-s* *tsî-ra*   *ge*   *!kharaga*
      N.-3SG.M   and   M.-3SG.F   and-3DU.F/C   DECL   different
      kuri-gu   *!nâ* *ge*   *!gamme.*
      year-3PL.M in   REM.PAST   marry
      'Namaseb(MALE PERS. NAME) and Madawas(FEM. PERS. NAME) got married in differ-
      ent years.' (i.e. to different partners)

Whether symmetry is entailed or merely implicated by *!kham* 'to fight' if used with the bare conjunct strategy is a matter for further research. Also remaining to be investigated are the semantic/pragmatic differences between the bound pronoun and the bare conjunct reciprocal strategy in combination with these verbs.

Other verbs that often select the bare conjunct strategy in other languages obligatorily take the reciprocal bound pronoun *-gù* if they are to be interpreted as denoting a symmetrical action:

(13) *‖nam* 'to embrace, hug, cuddle', *‖oa* 'kiss', *!khō-am* 'agree with' (catch-mouth),
      ≠nôa 'disagree', *mā-dawa* 'exchange', *‖goe-ū* 'have sex' (sleep-take), *xae* 'have
      sex' (vulg.), *tawede* 'greet' (all tr. verbs).

2.4   Marginal strategy II: Lexical strategy

In this strategy, symmetry of action is part of the lexical meaning of the verb; in contrast to verbs of the bare conjunct strategy, it cannot be used unidirectionally. Only three such verbs have been found in Khoekhoe so far, all of them intransitive:

(14) *‖gam*   'to talk (with one another)'
      ‖hao   'to meet, come together (temporarily), assemble, unite'
      ≠khawa 'to quarrel with, argue'

---

7. Traditionally only used with male subjects. With female subjects the passive of the same verb would be used.

(15) *khoe-gu*   *ge*   *ra*   *ǁgam.*
      person-3PL.M   DECL   PROG   talk
      'The men are talking.'   (#1)

(16) *ǀgam*   *khoe-ra*   *ge*   *ra*   *ǀhao.*
      two   person-3DU.F/C   DECL   PROG   meet
      'Two people are meeting each other.'   (#9)

If used with a singular subject, the second party is expressed by an *obligatory* postpositional phrase (x *ǀkha* 'with x') in the case of *ǀhao* 'to meet, come together (temporarily), assemble, unite', which further distinguishes this verb from one-place verbs like *ǃhoa* 'to speak, talk', where no symmetry of action is entailed.

All these verbs may occur in a compound with the verb *ū* 'to take' (*ǀhao-ū*, etc.), yielding transitive verbs that do not entail symmetry of action and that can combine with the reciprocal bound pronoun. It is not clear whether there are further semantic differences between the basic, intransitive verbs and the corresponding reciprocal-marked compounds. In the case of *ǀhao* vs. *ǀhao-ū-gu* (meet-take-RECP), one informant claimed that the latter but not the former denotes meeting upon appointment, but other people give conflicting information.

The verb *ǂkhawa* 'to quarrel with, argue' is highly exceptional in being the only intransitive verb found that can take the reciprocal suffix *-gù* for some speakers, but this was categorically rejected by others.

3.   Categories encoded in the clip data

The data for this article were collected in Mangetti West, Namibia, in September 2004, June–July 2005 and March–April 2006 from two speakers in their mid-twenties from Tsumeb and from one speaker in her early forties from Okahandja. The full set of clips (Evans et al. 2004) was used for elicitation with each of these speakers in September 2004. All of them are fluent in Afrikaans, English and Haiǁom; the one from Okahandja and one from Tsumeb also speak variants of Oshiwambo (a local Bantu language) to varying degrees. All three are primary school teachers and the elicitation posed no noteworthy problems, unlike a further recording (not included here) with a youngster from Tsumeb who provided high-resolution descriptions of subevents for most clips.

The clips fall into three groups according to the occurrence of the reciprocal strategy in the corresponding descriptions: 49 clips were coded using one of the reciprocal strategies, 8 clips were never coded with a reciprocal (nor accepted when prompted), and 7 clips could be coded with a reciprocal.[8] These groups are discussed in this order, for each of the reciprocal strategies in turn.

The 49 scenes that triggered descriptions with reciprocal strategies in all informants can be classified according to various parameters, including relative timing of the subevents (i.e. simultaneous or sequential), number of participants, mapping of the semantic macro-roles Actor and Undergoer onto participants, and conceptualisation of the main event shown. Specifically, combination of these parameters leads to the following situation types found in the coding of the 49 scenes: strong (i.e. simultaneous or sequential subevents, two participants, each being both Actor and Undergoer), chained (A > B, B > C, C > D...[9]), paired (A > B, B > A, C > D, D > C...), adjacent (participants are adjacent, typically in a row: A > B, B > A, B > C, C > B...), and melee (multiple subevents in "random" manner: e.g. A > B, B > C, C > A, D > B...). All of these scenes have in common that there are at least two participants that are both Actor and Undergoer, and this sets these clips apart from all the others. According to one informant, even *one* Actor-cum-Undergoer would be sufficient to trigger reciprocal marking with scenes such as a melee of three people engaged in hitting (e.g. A > B, C > A), though this needs to be examined in more naturally-occurring data. In any case, the single criterion of involving at least one or two Actor-cum-Undergoers is sufficient to distinguish clips in this group from all other clips, irrespective of the specific situation type.[10]

The 8 clips for which no reciprocal strategy was used nor could be used are all asymmetric situations, i.e. where *none* of the Actors involved is also Undergoer (#17, 23, 25, 26, 31, 51, 59, 60). This includes clips where the event takes place once (e.g. #23) or repeatedly (#25), and where subevents are either sequential (#25) or simultaneous (#60). Most clips in this set feature only two participants, but situations with three or four participants in simultaneous subevents also occur (#31, 60).

The *same* semantic constellations of Actor(s) and Undergoer(s) *can* be coded using a reciprocal strategy in the remaining 7 clips:

1. Asymmetric situations where one Actor is following or chasing a single Undergoer (#27, 64) can alternatively be coded by the main reciprocal strategy,

---

8. Alternative constructions were sometimes volunteered by the informants themselves, but most often we checked whether the main reciprocal strategy could be used whenever a response was given without such a strategy. The reason why we checked only the main strategy will become clear below.

9. Read as: "participant A acts on B, B on C, etc."

10. There is one exception to this, clip #39, which is discussed below.

although informants volunteer that "this is not correct and just the way some people talk" and one informant rejected a reciprocal in both cases. Similarly, clip #1, with person A talking to person B, triggered the bound reciprocal pronoun strategy and the lexical reciprocal strategy as well as no reciprocal at all. All three actions ('following', 'chasing', and 'talking') might be events that are conceptualised as typically involving a reversal of the Actor and Undergoer roles in participants within a single overall event, which may motivate the optional reciprocal coding. A further clip showing such variation is the strong, simultaneous situation in #18. Two of the respondents volunteered a construction without a reciprocal but with the adverbial /gui-b-a 'together' (17); the description by the third informant features the main reciprocal strategy (18):

(17) /gui-b-a   ǂnôa   khoe-ra   ge.
      one-3SG.M-OBL sit.down.PERF person-3DU.F/C DECL
      'They are two persons sitting together.'

(18) khoe-ra   ge ǂnû-xō./kha-gu   hâ.
      person-3DU.F/C DECL sit.down-next.to-RECP PERF
      'The two persons are sitting next to each other.'

Apparently, speakers can choose whether to conceptualise a "sitting event" with or without an Undergoer involved.

2. Slightly different macro-role constellations also *allow* reciprocal coding even though no Actor is also Undergoer (#6, 16, 47). All are expressed using the main reciprocal strategy as an alternative to no reciprocal at all. All of the situations concerned are asymmetric, with simultaneous (#6, 16) or sequential (#47) subevents. They involve three or more participants and at least two Actors. Given that most clips that never allow reciprocal coding have just two participants, this variation may suggest that the likelihood of being coded by a reciprocal strategy increases with the number of Actors/participants (and hence subevents) in a state of affairs with at least one Undegoer. This hypothesis is strengthened by the minimal pair formed by #6 and #51: Both are asymmetric situations, i.e. without any Actor-cum-Undergoer. Clip #6, with four participants, can receive reciprocal coding, while #51, with two participants, cannot. Further, the coding of #25 (featuring two participants and sequential asymmetric subevents) with no reciprocal suggests that it is the number of Actors/participants and not subevents that is crucial for the variation in the coding of the above-mentioned scenes (#6, 16, 47).

3. A third factor that causes variation is evidenced by the minimal pairs constituted by scenes #31 and #47, and #60 and #16 respectively. The first pair shows two Actors, the second three Actors, acting upon a single Undergoer.

Clips #31 and #60, with simultaneous subevents, cannot be coded using a reciprocal strategy. Clips #47 and #16, with sequential subevents, on the other hand, may be coded either without a reciprocal strategy or with the help of the main strategy. This could mean that – at least for states of affairs with a rather small number of participants that take place in quite a small space such as in #31, 47, 60 and 16 – the likelihood of being coded with a reciprocal construction increases with sequenced occurrence of the subevents.[11] It is possible that such sequences make it harder for speakers to keep track of who acts on whom and hence increases the likelihood of them assuming that at least some Actor is also Undergoer during the overall event.

To conclude, three factors increase the likelihood that an asymmetric situation is coded by the main reciprocal strategy:

- Conceptualisation of an event as (typically) involving mapping of both an Actor and an Undergoer role to at least one participant
- High number of Actors/participants, including at least one Undergoer and two Actors
- Sequenced timing of subevents

These factors can of course be combined, apparently making a reciprocal construction more likely: Clip #39 features an asymmetric situation involving an overall chasing event (factor 1), four participants, of whom two are Actors (factor 2), and sequential subevents (factor 3). This clip exclusively led to responses with the main reciprocal strategy in all three informants, and never to non-reciprocal coding. The effects of concatenation of these three factors remain to be further explored. For instance, #31 and #60 involve three or more participants and simultaneous subevents; reciprocal coding cannot be used with these clips, suggesting that number of participants is a weaker factor than sequentiality of subevents. On the other hand, repetition of a subevent by the same Actor in a clip with two participants does not allow reciprocal coding (#25).

So far, just the main reciprocal strategy has been examined. This can be used whenever any reciprocal strategy does (optionally) occur, i.e. in 49+7 out of 64 cases. The remaining reciprocal strategies are more restricted in terms of frequency of use and, in the case of the bare conjunct and lexical strategies, the semantic domain. Whenever they occur, an alternative coding with the main strategy is possible. For the bipartite quantifier strategy and bare conjunct strategy, the alternative

---

11. Whether this is a strict rule or a mere tendency cannot be decided, as there are no cases of sequential subevents coded without a reciprocal in our data. But since the database is rather small, we take a cautious stand and view it as a mere tendency.

rendering with the main strategy can use the same verb; in case of the lexical strategy the verb has to undergo compounding or a different basic verb has to be used.

Although the bipartite quantifier NPs strategy does not seem to be restricted to a specific set of verbs or semantic domain, it only occurs in responses by the speaker from Okahandja and even she only used it a single time, for clip #5. That scene was coded with the bound reciprocal pronoun by the two informants from Tsumeb. Though the speaker from Okahandja and one from Tsumeb occasionally used bipartite quantifier NPs in further elicitation sessions on reciprocals (again in contexts where other speakers use the bound pronoun strategy), the data are too scanty for generalisations about what triggers this strategy. Other people rejected sentences with bipartite quantifier NPs and even the two aforementioned informants sometimes dismissed data they had volunteered another time, which underlines the marginality of the construction.

The reason for the low frequency of the bare conjunct and lexical strategies in our data is that they are tied to specific lexical items and are not productive processes. The bare conjunct strategy was not used at all, and the lexical strategy was triggered by five clips featuring asymmetric (#1: 'talk'), strong simultaneous (#9: 'meet', 11: 'talk'), and strong sequential (#40: 'talk', 62: 'meet') situations.

4.   Conclusion

Khoekhoe has four different reciprocal constructions, of which only one is fully productive. The semantic core of reciprocal coding in Khoekhoe, as it emerges from the data discussed above, is subject to the condition that at least two participants are both Actor and Undergoer in the same state of affairs, which obtains in strong, chained, paired, adjacent and melee situations in the stimuli. In our data, where informants describe the relevant events by a single predication, reciprocal coding always occurs when this condition is met. As mentioned above, however, even one Actor-cum-Undergoer is sufficient in some cases. This condition tends to be weakened if

1.   the action in question lends itself to abstraction from the actual mapping of macro-roles onto participants to a symmetric conceptualisation (such as with 'chasing' or 'talking')
2.   there are three or more participants, including at least two Actors and one Undergoer
3.   the subevents occur in sequence

which extends the semantic domain to asymmetric situations that are optionally coded by a reciprocal strategy.

Glosses and abbreviations

C	common gender	PERF	Perfect
CAUS	causative	PROG	Progressive
DECL	declarative	RECENT	recent
DU	dual	RECP	reciprocal
EXCL	exclusive	REM	remote
F	feminine	SG	singular
M	masculine	STAT	stative
OBL	oblique case	TR	transitive
OPT	optative	/	or
PL	plural		

Acknowledgements

I wish to thank Nick Evans, Alice Gaby, Toshiki Osada and the members of the reciprocal working group at the MPI Nijmegen for useful comments on earlier versions of this article. My utmost thanks go to Mariane Kheimses, Linda Uises, Ingrid Uiras and Laurentius Davids for sharing their knowledge of Khoekhoe with me. The data for this article was collected in Mangetti West, Namibia, in 2004–2006.

References

Böhm, Gerhard. 1985. Kh?oe-kowap. *Einführung in die Sprache der Hottentotten, Nama-Dialekt* [Beiträge zur Afrikanistik 25]. Vienna: Afro-pub.

Brown, Penelope & Levinson, Stephen C. 1987. *Politeness: Some Universals in Language Usage* [Studies in Interactional Sociolinguistics 4]. Cambridge: CUP.

Dalrymple, Mary, Mchombo, Sam A. & Peters, Stanley. 1994. Semantic similarities and syntactic contrasts between Chicheŵa and English reciprocals. *Linguistic Inquiry* 25(1): 145–163.

Dempwolff, Otto. 1934/1935. Einführung in die Sprache der Nama–Hottenoten. *Zeitschrift für Eingeborenen-Sprachen* 25: 30–66, 89–134, 188–229.

Evans, Nicholas. Forthcoming. Reciprocal constructions: Towards a structural typology. In *Reciprocals and Reflexives: Cross-linguistic and Theoretical Explorations*, Ekkehard König & Volker Gast (eds), 1–57. Berlin: Mouton de Gruyter.

Evans, Nicholas, Levinson, Stephen C., Enfield, N. J., Gaby, Alice & Majid, Asifa. 2004. Reciprocal constructions and situation type. In *Field Manual*, Vol. 9, Asifa Majid (ed.), 25–30. Nijmegen: Max Planck Institute for Psycholinguistics.

Güldemann, Tom & Vossen, Rainer. 2000. Khoisan. In *African Languages: An Introduction*, Bernd Heine & Derek Nurse (eds), 99–122. Cambridge: CUP.

Haacke, Wilfrids H. G. 1992. Dislocated noun phrases in Khoekhoe (Nama/Damara): Further evidence for the sentential hypothesis. *Afrikanistische Arbeitspapiere* 29: 149–162.

Haacke, Wilfrid H. G. 1999. *The Tonology of Khoekhoe (Nama/Damara)* [Quellen zur Khoisan-Forschung 16]. Cologne: Rüdiger Köppe.

Haacke, Wilfrid H. G. 2001. Nama. In *Facts about the World's Languages: An Encyclopedia of the World's Major Languages, Past and Present,* Jane Gary & Carl Rubino (eds), 497–501. New York NY: H. W. Wilson.

Haacke, Wilfrid H. G. & Eiseb, Eliphas. 2002. *A Khoekhoegowab Dictionary with an English-Khoekhoegowab Index.* Windhoek: Gamsberg Macmillan.

Hagman, Roy S. 1977. *Nama Hottentot Grammar* [Language and Science Monographs 15]. Bloomington IN: Indiana University Press.

Kemmer, Suzanne. 1993. *The Middle Voice* [Typological Studies in Language 23]. Amsterdam: John Benjamins.

Mchombo, Sam A. & Ngunga, Armindo S. A. 1994. The syntax and semantics of the reciprocal construction in CiYao. *Linguistic Analysis* 24: 3–31.

Nedjalkov, Vladimir, P. 2006. Reciprocal constructions in Turkic languages in a typological perspective. *Turkic Languages* 10(1): 3–46.

Rapold, Christian J. 2005. Syntactic aspects of Khoekhoe reciprocals. Paper read at the 35th Colloquium on African Languages and Linguistics, Leiden, 29–31 August, 2005.

Rapold, Christian J. In preparation. Syntactic aspects of Khoekhoe reciprocals.

Voßen, Rainer. 1997. *Die Khoe-Sprachen. Ein Beitrag zur Erforschung der Sprachgeschichte Afrikas* [Quellen zur Khoisan Forschung, 12]. Cologne: Rüdiger Köppe.

Zec, Draga. 1985. Objects in Serbo-Croatian. *Proceedings of the Eleventh Annual Meeting of the Berkeley Linguistics Society*: 358–371. Berkeley CA: Berkeley Linguistics Society, University of California.

CHAPTER 4

Reciprocal constructions in English

Each other and beyond

Peter Hurst and Rachel Nordlinger
The University of Melbourne

In this paper we investigate the constructions that are used to encode reciprocal situations in English, based on responses to the 64 reciprocals videoclips developed for the *Reciprocals Across Languages* project (Evans et al. 2004). This work complements the extensive body of previous research on English reciprocals by focusing on spoken data. While our data supports the traditional view of *each other* as the primary and most common reciprocal construction in English, we find a greater degree of variation in construction types than this traditional view might suggest. Furthermore, we show that *each other* does not have the same degree of acceptability in all reciprocal situations.

1.   Introduction

In this paper we examine the encoding of reciprocals in English (Germanic, Indo-European), more specifically Australian English as spoken in Melbourne, Australia. English reciprocal constructions have been the subject of an enormous amount of literature,[1] largely based on artificially constructed examples – i.e. examples constructed for the purposes of illustrating particular syntactic and/or semantic distinctions (notable exceptions are Kjellmer 1982 and Dalrymple et al. 1998, who gather most of their data from written corpora). In this paper we complement this previous work with a discussion of the encoding of reciprocals in spoken English, based on responses to the 64 reciprocals videoclips developed

---

[1]   Including, but not limited to, Bolinger (1987), Dalrymple et al. (1994, 1998), Fiengo & Lasnik (1973), Heim, Lasnik and May (1991), Higginbotham (1980), Jørgensen (1985), Kjellmer (1982), Kruisinga & Erades (1953), Langendoen (1978), Levin (1993), Potter (1953), Stuurman (1987), Williams (1991) among many others. Note that although these studies do not discuss Australian English specifically, we have no reason to believe that the use of reciprocals by our speakers should be particularly non-standard.

for the *Reciprocals Across Languages* project (Evans et al. 2004). While our data supports the traditional view of *each other* as the primary and most common reciprocal construction in English, we find a greater degree of variation in speakers' initial responses than this traditional view might suggest. Furthermore, we show that *each other* does not have the same degree of acceptability in all reciprocal situations.[2]

2.   Reciprocal constructions in English

Compared with some languages, English has a fairly wide range of reciprocal constructions. These constructions (discussed in Section 2.1–Section 2.6) fall into the following broad categories: the reciprocal pronouns *each other* and *one another*, *each-the-other* constructions, bare reciprocal constructions, nominal reciprocal constructions, *back-to-back* constructions and reciprocal modifiers. There is also a range of other constructions that are not specifically reciprocal, but which can permit a reciprocal interpretation in different contexts; we discuss these in Section 2.7.

2.1   Reciprocal pronouns

The primary reciprocal construction in English uses the reciprocal pronoun *each other* in an NP slot, with no apparent effect on the valency of the verb.[3] *Each other* can be used in the full range of non-subject grammatical functions, including direct and indirect object, object of prepositions, and possessive phrases:

(1)   *Five people chasing each other.*   (Sarah, #43)[4]
(2)   *A group of people in a room passing items to each other.*   (Paul, #30)
(3)   *Two people sitting back to back and they lean back to touch each other's
       shoulders and take each other's weight.*   (Nick, #12)

---

2.   We follow Lichtenberk (1985) and others in distinguishing reciprocal constructions from reciprocal situations, where the latter can be (loosely) defined as a symmetric relationship between two or more participants, and the former represent the language specific ways of encoding such reciprocal semantics.

3.   Evans (2008) treats *each other* as a bipartite quantifier. While *each other* clearly involves quantifier semantics, there is evidence that syntactically it behaves more like a pronoun (Asudeh 1998) – and this is the analysis we follow here.

4.   The notation "(Speaker #x)" indicates that the preceding sentence was the speaker's description of videoclip x.

In restricted contexts it is even possible for *each other* to occur in embedded subject position, of both non-finite (4) and finite (5) clauses (at least for some speakers) (Kjellmer 1982).

(4) *They want each other to be happy.*
(5) *They know what each other wants.*

Each other always requires a semantically plural antecedent. This is usually a subject (see all of the examples above), but may have other grammatical functions, underlined in the following examples, including object (*I gave the children paintings of each other*), and possibly possessor (*?The Easter bunny left eggs at the end of the children's beds for sharing with each other*). For some speakers it is possible for the antecedent to be semantically plural, but grammatically singular, as with collective nouns (*?The English soccer crowd began to turn on each other*).

A less common variant of this construction involves the use of *one another* as the reciprocal pronoun, as in (6). *One another* appears to have the same range of grammatical possibilities as *each other*, and the two are generally held in the literature to be interchangeable (e.g. Jørgensen 1985, Dalrymple et al. 1998).

(6) *Two people take it in turns to groom one another.*   (Lee, #10)

Some other writers, however, **do** postulate a distinction between these two reciprocal pronouns. For example Potter (1953), following Kruisinga and Erades (1953) suggests that *each other* focuses more on the agents and *one another* on the shared action; Kjellmer (1982) finds support from a search on the Brown corpus for a stylistic difference, whereby *each other* is more colloquial and *one another* more literary; and Stuurman (1987) argues that *each other* is used in chained situations and *one another* in symmetric reciprocal situations. We find no support in our data for any of these distinctions. In fact, for the most part only two speakers used *one another* in our sample, suggesting that any differences may be at the level of individual speaker variation. We will have little further to say about this constructional variant.

2.2   *Each-the-other* constructions[5]

An alternative reciprocal construction in English is the *each-the-other* construction, as in (7), alongside variants like *each... everyone else's* (see (10) below).

(7) *Each man saw the other.*

---

5. In our analysis this construction includes the variant *each-everyone else* – see below for discussion.

According to Fiengo and Lasnik (1973), this construction differs from the standard *each other* construction in requiring a strong reciprocal situation type. Thus, when discussing a group of eight men, for example, (7) is only possible if it is true that the relation of 'seeing' holds bidirectionally for every possible pair in the set. *The men saw each other*, on the other hand, allows for a melee or pairwise situation type in which the reciprocal relation holds between some, but not all, possible pairings in the set (Fiengo & Lasnik 1973: 448–9).

A further difference between these two constructions, as also discussed by Fiengo and Lasnik, is that *each other* constructions "often, but not always, require that the events referred to occur simultaneously, or in the same general time span" (p. 450), whereas *each-the-other* constructions never involve such a requirement. This is demonstrated by the following examples (their (19) and (20), p. 451), where (8) is perfectly acceptable but (9) is not:

(8)   *Each of the men stared at the other: John stared at Bill for 3 hours and then Bill stared at John for 3 hours.*

(9)   **/?The men stared at each other: John stared at Bill for 3 hours and then Bill stared at John for 3 hours.*

Of the few examples in our sample of this construction, two involve the same videoclip (#38) in which there are four people each of whom systematically shake hands with all other members of the group. These examples are therefore consistent with Fiengo and Lasnik's generalisations that the *each-the-other* construction is only possible in strong reciprocal situations:

(10)   *Four people sitting in a circle, each shaking everyone else's in the circle's hands.*
        (George, #38)

Two speakers use an interesting blend of this construction which combines *each* with *each other*. This is predicted to be ungrammatical by Fiengo and Lasnik and as far as we know has not been previously reported in the literature:[6]

(11)   *Four people each shaking hands with the other.*   (Dean, #38)

(12)   *Six people each shaking hands with each other.*
        (Lee, clip #49, which shows three pairs shaking hands within the pair)

Note, however, that the variant used here looks like a combination of the *each-the-other* and the *each-other* constructions (i.e. *each-with each other*), which may

---

6.   And note the following rather similar example from the *Guardian Weekly* (10.3.06, Learning English supplement, p. 4, 'Still waiting for the bright new age', author David Graddol):

'The prisoners stand in what look like sentry booths with doors, in a raked auditorium, *each* able to see the lecturer but not *one another*.'

account for the difference in use. In the absence of further information about the possible differences between these two example types, we have treated them as variants of single construction in our analysis.

2.3 Bare reciprocal constructions[7]

A subset of English verbs such as *hug, swap* and *talk* can occur in a construction type where they have a reciprocal interpretation without overt reciprocal encoding (see Levin 1993 for detailed discussion). In this construction the participants are encoded in a single argument (the subject), and the valency of the verb is reduced by one. We refer to these constructions (exemplified in (13) and (14)) as "bare reciprocal constructions".

(13) *They are swapping things.*   (Meg, #37)
(14) *A group of people hugging.*   (Meg, #47)

Verbs found in bare reciprocal constructions can also occur in *each other* constructions, as in the following examples. Depending on the nature of the predicate, *each other* may be a direct object, or an object of a preposition in these constructions (Levin 1993):

(15) *…six people swapping things with each other.*   (Alice, #37)
(16) *Some friends hugging each other, in greeting.*   (Alice, #29)

2.4 Nominal reciprocal constructions

Some reciprocal situations can be encoded in English with a nominal reciprocal construction in which the reciprocal relation is encoded primarily through the use of a (frequently deverbal) nominal. Many of these examples involve nominalisations of verbs that allow the bare reciprocal strategy, as (17)–(19), but such constructions are possible with other types of nominals also, as in (20).

(17) *They are having an argument.*
                           (Nick, #3: Two women hit each other, one at a time.)
(18) *Two people in a conversation.*
                           (Paul, #40: Two people sitting next to each other.)
(19) *Four girls all having a group hug.*   (George, #20)
(20) *An introduction between people.*
                           (Kylie, #13: People passing a handshake down a line)

---

7. Referred to as "bare conjunct reciprocal constructions" in Evans (2008).

As reflected in the above examples, nominal reciprocals are found in a range of construction types. One common sub-construction involves the light verb *have* with the nominal forming a type of complex predicate (as in (17) and (19)). Another type of construction includes a PP headed by *between* specifying the participants in the reciprocal situation, as in (20). As far as we are aware, such nominal reciprocal constructions have not been discussed in previous literature on English reciprocals, nor in typological discussions of reciprocals cross-linguistically (e.g., Evans 2008).

2.5   *Back-to-back* constructions

In three instances our speakers made use of a reciprocal construction exemplified by (21) below:

> (21)   *Two people leaning back-to-back.*   (Dean, #12)

This construction type is highly restricted, but clearly reciprocal in its semantics. Although all instances of this construction in our data use the phrase "*back-to-back*", it appears likely that this construction can be extended to include a limited number of other body parts; chest-to-chest, face-to-face, toe-to-toe etc. and is used to describe situations involving people (or anthropomorphised entities) touching or almost touching. We have found no previous discussion of these constructions in the literature. These constructions could arguably be considered adverbial, in which case they should be treated as a variant of the reciprocal modifier construction discussed in Section 2.6.

2.6   Reciprocal modifiers

A final type of reciprocal construction in English, which was not attested in our sample, involves the use of reciprocal modifiers such as *mutual/mutually* or *reciprocal/reciprocally*. These can occur with or without the *each other* reciprocal pronoun, as in the following:

> (22)   *They are mutually compatible.*
> (23)   *They have a mutual hatred for each other.*
> (24)   *...I thought I was reciprocally linking with one (web)site...*[8]

---

8. Attested on Google 20/11/2006.

2.7   Other constructions allowing a reciprocal interpretation

Some constructions in English – usually those that encode collective and/or sequential activity – are not specifically reciprocal in their semantics, but allow for
a reciprocal interpretation when used in the appropriate context. These include
those using the adverb *together* (25), sequential constructions as in *pass X down
the line, each do X to the next* ((26)–(28)) and explicit multi-clausal statements
(29). While these are not reciprocal constructions per se, they belong to the set of
constructions which can be used to encode reciprocal situations in English.

(25) *Two men joking together.*   (Alice, #33)

(26) *Many people passing a gift or food along a line.*   (Lee, #34)

(27) *A group of people standing in a line and each one hugs the next one in line.*
                                                                                (Sarah, #2)

(28) *A group of people in a line from left to right, they shake hands with the person
      next to them.*   (Paul, #13)

(29) *Four women sitting on a couch and the middle two hug and then those two
      then turn to the person next to them and hug them.*   (Sarah, #61)

3.   Categories encoded in the videoclip data

Our study involved running the full set of *Reciprocals across Languages* videoclips with each of nine speakers of Australian English (six women, three men), all
between the ages of 30 and 38. After all their initial spontaneous responses were
recorded, speakers were then prompted with an appropriate *each other* reciprocal
construction (for the most part, regardless of whether or not one was provided
as their initial response), and asked whether it was an acceptable description of
the clip. We thus distinguish in our discussion between volunteered responses
(speakers' initial responses) and prompted responses (speakers' judgments as to
the acceptability or not of a construction of the form *They VERB each other*).

All of the constructions discussed in Section 2 above occurred in our sample, except for the reciprocal modifier constructions (Section 2.6), although with
varying degrees of frequency. While our speakers exhibited a great range of variation in the construction they volunteered for each situation type, we found no
convincing evidence for a correlation between individual reciprocal constructions and particular situation types. As expected, the *each other* construction was
the most frequent construction used to describe a reciprocal situation, and was
used across almost all reciprocal situation types. Interestingly, the situation type

with the highest percentage of non-prompted uses (100%) of *each other* was not the strong reciprocal (79% for simultaneous, 64% for sequential) but the melee – perhaps reflecting the availability of the more informative *each....the other* construction for strong reciprocal situations but not melees.

Only in the cases of pair and radial asymmetrical simultaneous situations (represented by clip #6 in which there are two pairs of people and one person delouses another, clip #31 in which two people look at a third and clip #60 in which three people watch a fourth walk past) did we receive no reciprocal responses at all in the volunteered data. The absence of reciprocal responses for these situation types may be due to the events involved ('looking at' and 'delousing'), which seem to strongly prefer symmetrical behaviour on the part of all participants for a reciprocal construction to be fully acceptable (see Section 4).

Other reciprocal construction types were scattered across the situation types: some were so small in number (e.g., nominal reciprocal constructions, *back-to-back* constructions) that it was impossible to form generalisations about their occurrence; others were more likely conditioned by the nature of the predicate, rather than the situation type (e.g. bare reciprocal constructions); and some seemed more likely due to individual speaker variation (e.g. *one another*).

Figure 1 shows the overall percentage of all reciprocal constructions (i.e., those identified in Section 2.1–Section 2.5) volunteered across the different situation types.

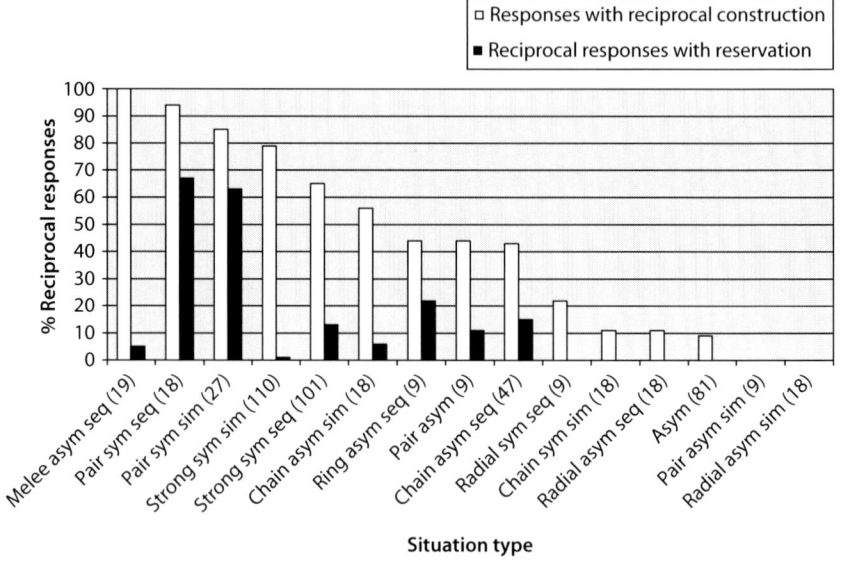

Figure 1. Percentage of reciprocal constructions produced across situation types

Figure 1 represents the relative number of reciprocal responses for each of the situation types. For example, the total number of responses to all chain asymmetric simultaneous situations was gathered together (in this case, the responses to clips #14 and #56 – two people chasing each other and delousing each other respectively). Of these 18 responses, 10 (or 56%) contained a reciprocal construction of some kind and this percentage is reflected by the white bar on the graph above *Chain Asym Sim (18)*. Of these ten reciprocal constructions, one also contained a reservation (see below). The percentage of reciprocal responses containing reservations is reflected by the black bar on the graph and is included for later reference.

As expected, our data shows that virtually all of the situation types can be encoded using a reciprocal construction. A minority of speakers were even happy to use reciprocal constructions with certain asymmetrical situations, in which we might have expected reciprocal constructions not to be possible. Following Evans (2004) we can account for these uses of the reciprocal construction as encoding the engagement of the participants in a joint activity, even if the verbal action itself is asymmetrical. For example, many of these responses involve clip #1, in which there are two people, but only one is speaking. Since the other person is actively engaged in listening (by nodding their head, watching the speaker, etc.) some speakers were happy to see the activity as shared:

(30) *Two guys having a serious conversation with one another.*   (Kylie, #1)
(31) *Person and boy talking to each other facing each other in a room.*   (Meg, #1)

Other asymmetrical situations encoded by speakers as a collective activity through the use of a reciprocal construction include the asymmetrical chasing event in clip #64 (*Two guys chasing each other down a hall*, Kylie #64), and the asymmetrical bumping event in clip #59 (*Two women knock into each other*, Alice #59). Most speakers did not use reciprocal constructions for asymmetrical situations however (see Figure 1), although some accepted them (with reservations) when prompted (see Figure 2). There also seems to be a relationship between the acceptability of a reciprocal construction in asymmetrical situation types and the type of predicate involved. Speakers were less likely to offer and accept a reciprocal construction with asymmetrical *hug*, *hit* and *look at* events than they were with *talk* and *chase* events. It seems that the use of a reciprocal construction more strongly requires symmetry of action for some events than for others. For example, some events (such as *talk* and *chase*) keep a notion of being a joint activity when asymmetrical more easily than others such as *hug* and *hit*.[9]

---

9. See Evans (2004) for further discussion on the notion of joint activity and reciprocal semantics.

As noted above, for many of the situation types, speakers volunteered a reciprocal construction but qualified it in some way. These reservations reflect a degree of discomfort with the reciprocal construction as an accurate reflection of the depicted event, and thus provide important information about speakers' understanding of the appropriateness of different reciprocal constructions to encode situation types. We therefore coded these reservations separately, as shown in Figure 1: the first bar shows the total percentage of reciprocal constructions used for that situation type (including those with reservations) and the second indicates only those reciprocal responses that included reservations, for comparative purposes. Examples of such reservations include (32) and (33) below. In most of such examples, speakers did not accept a straightforward *each other* construction even when prompted.

(32) *Two guys who are hugging each other, but they are not responsive.*   (Nick, #58
describing the clip where two men hug each other, one at a time.)

(33) *Two men who hug each other, but at different times, so one doesn't reciprocate the hug.*   (Sarah, #58)

(34) *Four people sitting on a couch, taking it in turns to punch each other in the knee down the line.*   (George, #48)

Such reservations are particularly frequent with pairwise situation types, in which speakers generally felt that the *each other* construction was unacceptable without a specification of the action being done "in pairs" or "by couples". As Figures 1 and 2 demonstrate, pairwise situations show a high proportion of reservations in both volunteered and prompted responses.[10]

(35) *Six people all in pairs and the pairs are hugging each other.*   (Dean, #29)
[Could you say *The people are hugging each other?*]
I wouldn't because it's the pairs that are hugging each other, not the six people.

(36) *A group of people sitting and two couples standing chatting and passing objects to each other.*   (George, #30)
[*They are giving each other things* rejected – need to specify that they are *couples*]

Note that the lack of a reciprocal construction in a volunteered response for a particular clip does not mean that the clip cannot be described using a reciprocal construction. In fact speakers on average would accept a reciprocal prompt, without reservation, ~30% of the time even if they did not volunteer a reciprocal construction initially.

---

10. Interestingly, these are exactly the situations in which Fiengo and Lasnik (1973) predict the *each-other* construction to be acceptable (as opposed to the *each-the-other* construction).

Figure 2 shows speaker judgments for the acceptability of a reciprocal prompt. The white bars represent the relative number of acceptable judgments for each of the situation types. For example, for the pair symmetrical sequential situation types (clips #30 and #42 in which three pairs of people give things to each other or hit each other) the speakers were asked to judge the acceptability of the prompts "The people are giving each other things / hitting each other". Of the 13 responses to these questions, 11 (i.e., 85% of the responses) agreed that the prompt was an acceptable description of the event. However, as the black bar shows, five of these responses (i.e., 38% of all the responses) added a reservation to their judgment. (Note that the total number of judgments for each situation type is included in brackets along the x-axis.)[11]

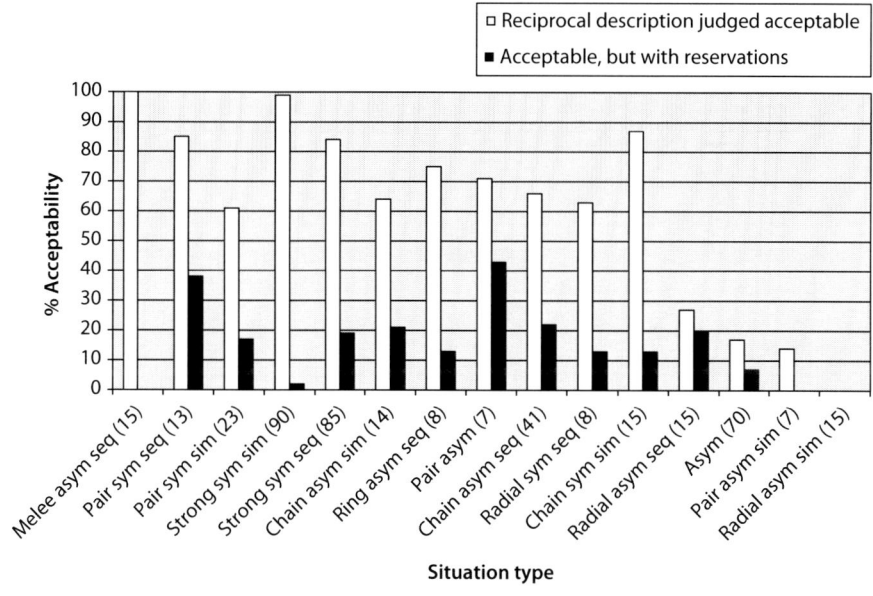

Figure 2. Acceptability of *each other* reciprocal prompts across events

As mentioned above, the prompt for clip #30 was *They are giving each other things/ stuff/gifts*. Speakers might say that the prompt was an unacceptable description of the event (e.g., Meg #30); that it was acceptable, but with a reservation (e.g., Dean #30 …*I would have described it more in terms of the pairs of people giving stuff to each other. It describes it more clearly.*); or acceptable (e.g., Lee #30).

---

11. This number is not a multiple of the number of speakers because one speaker was not prompted with reciprocal constructions at all, and on occasion some speakers' responses were missed.

Another feature of the data evident from these figures is the lower number of reciprocal constructions volunteered for chain situations when compared with melee and strong symmetric simultaneous and sequential events. Speakers were more likely to use an alternative construction to describe these events than with other situation types, usually using a construction like *doing X in turn/down the line/to the next one/to their left*, etc.

(37)   *A group of people in a line from left to right, they shake hands with the person next to them.*   (Paul, #13)

(38)   *Six people at a table, each with something in fro... an object in front of them which they pass to the person on their left, each in turn.*   (Meg, #28)

However, in contrast to the pairwise situations, speakers were more likely to accept an *each other* construction to describe chaining situations when prompted, except for clip #2 (in which four people standing in a line each turn one-by-one and hug the person next to them, without that person hugging back) for which it was felt necessary that both participants actively engage in the hug for a reciprocal construction to be acceptable.

For many speakers the prompted reciprocal construction was unacceptable in certain sequential situations involving two participants. This was particularly common with the predicates *look at* (clip #46) and *bump* (clip #22), for which speakers frequently stated that the *each other* construction could not be used because the action was not simultaneous:

(39)   *Two guys, one standing there, another one walking past and bumping him and then the second one comes along and bumps into the one that hit him first.*
                                                                         (George, #22)

        [Could you say *The men bumped into each other?*]
        No, because it's not simultaneous.

(40)   *A man and a woman sitting on seats next to each other and they at different points in time, look at each other.*   (Dean, #46)
        [Could you just say *They looked at each other?*]
        But it didn't happen concurrently, they weren't at any point both looking at each other so it sort of sounds a bit misleading.

For some speakers the acceptability of the *each other* construction with these situations was affected by the aspect of the verb, so that it was acceptable only when in the simple past (*They looked at each other*), but not in the progressive (*They are/were looking at each other*), see (41).

(41)   *A couple in a waiting room looking morose.*   (Paul, #46)
        [**They were looking at each other*, **They are looking at each other*, but *They looked at each other* – acceptable]

For other speakers such sequential situations were not acceptable with reciprocal encoding at all (e.g., Lee and Kylie #46). Interestingly, these are also the same predicates with which reciprocal constructions were often considered unacceptable in asymmetric situations (see Section 2).

4.   Conclusion

While there can be no disputing the fact that *each other* is the primary reciprocal strategy in English, and that it can be used in the full range of reciprocal situation types, the data resulting from this study revealed a number of intricacies in reciprocal encoding not discussed in the previous literature. Firstly, English has a wide range of reciprocal constructions, including nominal reciprocal constructions such as *an introduction between friends*, *back-to-back* constructions (e.g., *They are leaning back-to-back*), and related constructions that can be given a reciprocal interpretation in particular contexts (e.g., *Six people standing in a line passing on a handshake* (Meg #13)). Secondly, while *each other* is used in the full range of reciprocal situation types, it is used less frequently in chaining situations compared to other types of events and is frequently judged unacceptable in pairwise situations without additional specification as to the pairwise nature of the event.

Some intriguing connections are revealed in our data between the aspect of the clause and the acceptability of the *each other* construction, particularly with certain predicates (e.g., *hug, bump, look at*). For some speakers a sequential *look at* scenario cannot be encoded with the *each other* construction in the progressive aspect (**They are looking at each other*), but is more acceptable in the simple past (*They looked at each other*).

It is highly likely that the data in our sample has been affected by the nature of the task itself. Many speakers clearly felt that they were required to explain the videoclips as precisely as possible, and thus their responses are likely to be more specific than may be required for similar situation types in more naturalistic conversational settings. This may explain the low numbers of *each other* constructions in chaining and pairwise situation types, for example, for which speakers often felt that the *each other* construction did not adequately convey the full details of the situation (see (35) and (36) above, for example). This may also explain the difference we find between volunteered responses and prompted responses for many of these situation types. Nevertheless, the number of reservations speakers made in their judgements is an indication as to their confidence that a given situation can be described using a reciprocal construction. This technique showed that describing a pairwise situation using a reciprocal construction was far less acceptable to speakers than the equivalent melee or strong situations.

Acknowledgements

We would like to extend our deepest gratitude to our 9 respondents who kindly volunteered their time to help us with this research. Our appreciation also to Nick Evans, Asifa Majid, Alice Gaby, Elise Hurst, Christian Rapold and one anonymous referee for comments and suggestions that led to substantial improvements in our argumentation and presentation, and to audience members at the *Reciprocals across Languages* workshop at MPI, Nijmegen in April 2006 for helpful discussion. Of course, none of these people are to be held responsible for any remaining errors or infelicities. This research was funded by the *Reciprocals across Languages* project (Australian Research Council Grant DP 0343354) held at the University of Melbourne.

References

Asudeh, Ash. 1998. Anaphora and Argument Structure: Topics in the Syntax and Semantics of Reflexives and Reciprocals. MPhil. dissertation, The University of Edinburgh.

Bolinger, Dwight. 1987. Each other and its friends. In *Another Indiana University Linguistics Club, Twentieth Anniversary Volume*, 1–36. Bloomington IN: Indiana University Linguistics Club.

Dalrymple, Mary, Mchombo, Sam & Peters, Stanley. 1994. Semantic similarities and syntactic constrasts between Chichewa and English reciprocals. *Linguistic Inquiry* 25(1): 145–163.

Dalrymple, Mary, Kanazawa, Makoto, Kim, Yookyung, Mchombo, Sam & Peters, Stanley. 1998. Reciprocal expressions and the concept of reciprocity. *Linguistics and Philosophy* 21(2): 159–210.

Evans, Nicholas. 2004. Complex events, propositional overlay, and the special status of reciprocal clauses. Paper presented at the 7th Conference on Conceptual Structure, Discourse and Language (CDSL), Edmonton, 2004.

Evans, Nicholas. 2008. Reciprocal constructions: Towards a structural typology. In *Reciprocals and Reflexives: Cross-linguistic and Theoretical Explorations,* Ekkehard König & Volker Gast (eds), 33–104. Berlin: Mouton de Gruyter.

Evans, Nicholas, Levinson, Stephen C., Enfield, N. J., Gaby, Alice & Majid, Asifa. 2004. Reciprocal constructions and situation type. In *Field Manual,* Vol. 9, Asifa Majid (ed.), 25–30. Nijmegen: Max Planck Institute for Psycholinguistics.

Fiengo, Robert & Lasnik, Howard. 1973. The logical structure of reciprocal sentences in English. *Foundations of Language* 9(4): 447–468.

Heim, Irene, Lasnik, Howard & May, Robert. 1991. Reciprocity and plurality. *Linguistic Inquiry* 22(1): 63–101.

Higginbotham, James. 1980. Reciprocal interpretation. *Journal of Linguistic Research* 1: 97–117.

Jørgensen, Erik. 1985. Each other – one another. *English Studies* 66(4): 351–357.

Kjellmer, Goran. 1982. Each other and one another: On the use of the English reciprocal pronouns. *English Studies* 63(3): 231–254.

Kruisinga, Etsko & Erades, Peter A. 1953. *An English grammar.* Groningen: Noordhoff.

Langendoen, D. Terence. 1978. The logic of reciprocity. *Linguistic Inquiry* 9(2): 177–197.

Levin, Beth. 1993. *English Verb Classes and Alternations: A Preliminary Investigation*. Chicago IL: University of Chicago Press.

Lichtenberk, Frantisek. 1985. Multiple uses of reciprocal constructions. *Australian Journal of Linguistics* 5(1): 19–41.

Potter, Simeon. 1953. The expression of reciprocity. *English Studies* 34(6): 252–257.

Stuurman, Frits. 1987. Each other – one another: There will always prove to be a difference. *English Studies* 68(4): 353–360.

Williams, Edwin. 1991. Reciprocal scope. *Linguistic Inquiry* 22(1): 159–173.

CHAPTER 5

Reciprocal constructions in Indo-Pakistani Sign Language

Ulrike Zeshan and Sibaji Panda

University of Central Lancashire, Preston UK and Max Planck Institute for Psycholinguistics, Nijmegen

Indo-Pakistani Sign Language (IPSL) is the sign language used by deaf communities in a large region across India and Pakistan. This visual-gestural language has a dedicated construction for specifically expressing reciprocal relationships, which can be applied to agreement verbs and to auxiliaries. The reciprocal construction relies on a change in the movement pattern of the signs it applies to. In addition, IPSL has a number of other strategies which can have a reciprocal interpretation, and the IPSL lexicon includes a good number of inherently reciprocal signs. All reciprocal expressions can be modified in complex ways that rely on the grammatical use of the sign space. Considering grammaticalisation and lexicalisation processes linking some of these constructions is also important for a better understanding of reciprocity in IPSL.

1.   Background

1.1   Sign languages as visual-spatial languages

Sign languages are natural human languages used by deaf communities around the world. Research since the 1960's has proved beyond doubt that, far from being a loose collection of gestures and pantomime, sign languages are just as complex as spoken languages at all levels of linguistic structure (e.g. Klima & Bellugi 1979, Wilbur 1987, Boyes-Braem 1990, Sutton-Spence & Woll 1999, Sandler & Lillo-Martin 2006). However, due to their modality as visual and gestural languages, sign languages show a number of structural particularities which have no equivalent in spoken languages (cf. Emmorey 2003, Meier, Cormier & Quinto-Pozos 2002, Liddell 2003). While there are also differences between signed and spoken languages that are not due to the modality as such, we focus on modality-related characteristics in this section because this background is important for understanding the complex structures discussed in the remainder of this chapter.

Sign languages use multiple articulators in order to convey linguistic information and can be called multi-channel systems of communication. First of all, whereas speakers have only one articulatory tract at their disposal, signers have two hands which can to some extent to used independently of each other. This allows for complex constructions where the two hands may be moving in parallel, alternatingly, or in sequence, one being held in space while the other one moves. The full possibilities of this complex interplay cannot be explained in detail here (see Vermeerbergen, Leeson & Crasborn 2007 for some detailed case studies), but it is important to remember that this physical affordance of the signed modality allows for a considerable amount of simultaneity in constructions (cf. Section 2.2). Secondly, sign languages also use a large number of non-manual articulators, such as facial expressions, head movements and body postures, which adds additional layers of complexity to the manual structures. The non-manual expressions can often be compared to the role of intonation in spoken languages, though manual factors play a role here too. For the purposes of this chapter, however, non-manual articulators do not enter into the picture as an important factor.

It has often been noted that sign languages prefer simultaneous structures with respect to the organisation of their morphology as well. Given that it takes, on average, about twice as long to produce a sign than it takes to produce a word, there is a strong temporal pressure in the signing modality to compact several layers of information into a single sign (cf. Bellugi & Fischer 1972). At the same time, this is made possible by virtue use of the multiple articulators already mentioned. Simultaneous morphology in sign languages takes many different forms, not all of which are important for the purpose of this chapter. One of the most productive sub-systems occurs in the domain of aspect and aktionsart, a process originally labelled "aspectual modulation" by Klima & Bellugi 1979. The basic logic involved in this process is that various movement patterns are superimposed on a root sign, resulting in inflections for categories such as iterative, distributive, and the like. Examples of this kind of simultaneous morphology in Indian (Indo-Pakistani) Sign Language are discussed in Zeshan (2000a and 2003), and Figure 1 shows a set of example signs. The same aspectual/aktionsart process is used in Indo-Pakistani Sign Language to create reciprocal forms (see Section 2.1).

Another factor that makes sign languages different from spoken languages in principle and is extremely important in all kinds of grammatical domains is the use of the sign space. Sign languages are three-dimensional languages where the hands can be positioned and moved around freely in a conventional space surrounding the signer's torso. Use of the sign space follows grammatical conventions that differ to some extent across sign languages, although some of the basic

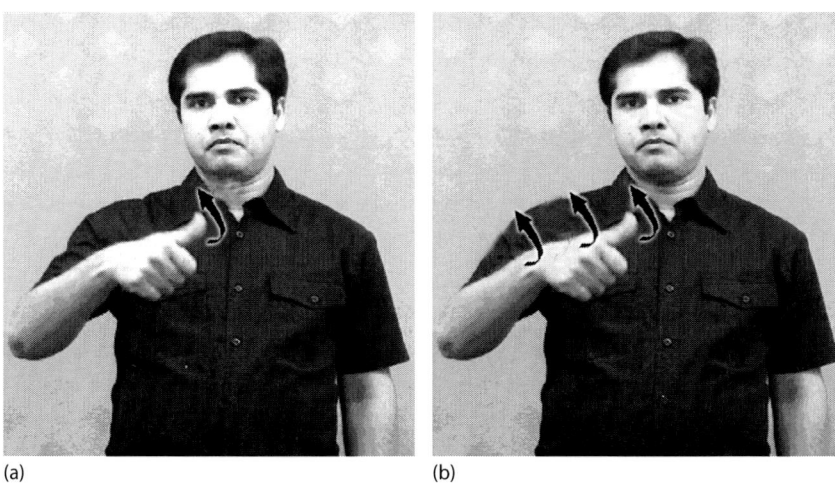

(a)   (b)

Figure 1. (a) SUCCESS 'pass, succeed', (b) SUCCESS#DISTR 'succeed in various situations; various people succeeding'

processes and construction types are commonly found. It is not possible here to elaborate on the grammatical use of the sign space in all its domains, so we focus only on those aspects that are essential for understanding the constructions discussed in the remainder of this chapter. Over the past decades, sign language linguistics has developed specialised terminologies for talking about the use of space, and since this terminology is often inaccessible to the non-specialist, the main concepts deserve a brief introduction here. We discuss the concepts of localisation, pronominal indexing, and verb agreement.

In all known sign languages, discourse referents are habitually associated with locations in the sign space. For example, a signer might mention a place name and then point to a location on the right. This location then functions as the point of reference for the place name in the subsequent discourse, so that it can be identified by pointing to the right side again, or by directing a predicate sign such as GO-TO to the right side. When a discourse referent is assigned to a location in sign space, this is called *localisation*. The point in space where the referent has been localised and which from then on can be used in a grammatical function is referred to as a *locus* (plural loci). Having localised a referent in space, the signer can refer back to the same referent simply by pointing to the same spot again with an index finger. This is equivalent to pronominal reference, and such pointing signs are called *pronominal index* points.[1] Although pronominal index pointing is

1. There are several other functions of index finger pointing in sign languages, pronominal pointing being only one of them.

iconic, pronominal systems across sign languages are not identical either in terms of the paradigm or in terms of their use in discourse.

In addition to index finger pointing or predicates being directed at a single locus, signs may also move between two loci. This is used most prominently for the purpose of spatial *verb agreement*. Agreement verbs in sign languages typically have a beginning location which is associated with the subject of the clause, and a final location which is associated with the object.[2] Thus the sign in Figure 2 has a third person subject/source (the giver) and a first person object/goal (the receiver). This is not unlike multiple person marking on verbs in some spoken languages where subject and object are marked by pronominal affixes on the verb. Verb agreement of this kind is clearly important for forming a number of reciprocal construction types, whenever a transitive or ditransitive relationship between referents is part of the meaning (e.g. 'hitting', 'giving', 'telling', etc.).

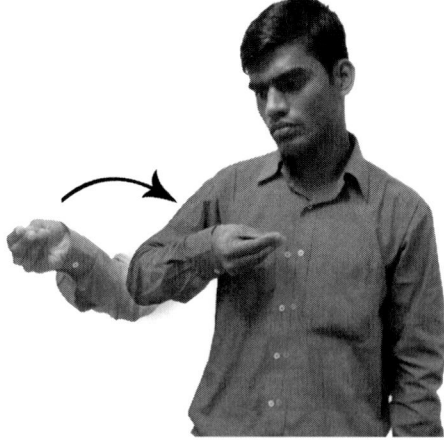

Figure 2. 3:GIVE:1 'someone gives to me'

In Indo-Pakistani Sign Language reciprocal constructions, aspectual/aktionsart morphology is relevant for assigning a reciprocal movement pattern to a basic predicate sign, and the spatial verb agreement process is relevant for assigning the beginning and end points of the movement pattern to the sign (see Section 2.1). Moreover, the reciprocal auxiliary constructions are based on pronominal index pointing (see Section 3.1).

---

2. This is an over-simplification, and there is actually considerable debate as to whether the locations represent grammatical categories, that is, subject and object, or semantic categories, that is source and goal, or spatial categories (cf. Meir 1998). There are also cases of object-only agreement and agreement in reverse order.

1.2   Indo-Pakistani Sign Language

Indo-Pakistani Sign Language (abbreviated IPSL) is the language used by deaf communities in urban centres across both India and Pakistan (cf. the map in Section 1.3). Although systematic research has not been carried out in the whole region, initial evidence suggests that the same sign language is also used in Bangladesh, and maybe in other parts of the Indian Subcontinent as well. In comparison with most Western sign languages, the community of Indo-Pakistani Sign Language users is huge, with over a million estimated users in India alone (Sethna, Vasishta & Zeshan 2004). Documented regional dialects of IPSL share a common grammar which varies little from region to region over a very large area, ranging from Pakistan in the North-West to Assam in the North-East, from Mumbai in the West to Orissa in the East, and up to the Dravidian-speaking areas with Hyderabad and Bangalore in the South (Zeshan 2006). On the other hand, lexical variation may be considerable. Several studies have documented the degree of lexical variation across several regional dialects, mostly within India (Vasishta, Woodward & Wilson 1978, Zeshan 2000b) These studies are in agreement that on average, IPSL dialects have about 75% of shared vocabulary, with about 25% of the vocabulary differing across dialects. Sociolinguistic variation in IPSL, such as gender- or age-related differences in signers, has not been studied yet.

IPSL is indigenous to the Indian Subcontinent and has not been strongly influenced by any other sign language. Although the IPSL manual alphabet that is used for fingerspelling English words is very similar to British Sign Language (BSL), there is otherwise very little evidence of BSL influence on IPSL, and the two sign languages are very different from each other in both lexicon and grammar. The age of Indo-Pakistani Sign Language is unknown, and no systematic research has been conducted into its history and origin. IPSL is not currently in close contact with other sign languages and has not been shown to belong to a larger family of sign languages. In the deaf community, the sign language is simply called SIGN, sometimes in combination with the sign for the country, as in INDIA SIGN. Indo-Pakistani Sign Language is a comparatively well-documented sign language as far as its grammatical structure is concerned. Although the language has not been officially recognised, educational programs for training sign language teachers and interpreters have been developed in India over the past five years (Sethna, Vasishta & Zeshan 2004), and there is a strong possibility that IPSL will gain official status in the near future.

While it is not necessary to provide a full typological profile of Indo-Pakistani Sign Language in this section, a few characteristics of basic IPSL clause structures can serve as additional background to the discussion of reciprocal constructions. All clauses in IPSL are predicate final, and all signs from the open lexical classes can function as predicates. Clause types (interrogative, negative, existential, imperative, etc.) are marked by obligatorily clause-final functional particles. Ellipsis is extensive, and one-word sentences are common, with the predicate the only obligatory constituent in the clause. Unlike other constituents, pronominal indexing is quite free with respect to word order, and pronouns can appear just about anywhere in the clause, often with several instances in one and the same clause. Tense is marked at the discourse level by clause-initial lexical time expressions. Example (1) exemplifies basic clause structure regularities in IPSL:

(1)   TWO+YEAR   BEFORE   INDEX:1   P-H-D   FINISH   COMPLETIVE[3]
       time expression   arguments   predicate   particle
       'I finished (my) PhD two years ago.'

As mentioned in Section 1.2, IPSL has a class of agreement verbs with spatial inflection for subject and object. However, not all semantically transitive predicates fall into this verb class. Transitive predicates that cannot be spatially inflected combine with a spatially inflected auxiliary sign which has been grammaticalised from pronominal indexing (cf. Section 3.1). The auxiliary usually follows the uninflected predicate to which it belongs immediately in the clause. However, the auxiliary can also be used together with an agreement verb, in which case there is double marking of subject and object. When complex spatial relationships are expressed in such a predicate cluster, it is also possible for the spatial inflections to be distributed over main verb and auxiliary, so that, for instance, the main verb shows subject-object agreement and the auxiliary shows the detailed spatial distribution of referents in sign space. Complex examples are discussed in Section 2.2.

1.3   Data collection for reciprocals in Indo-Pakistani Sign Language

Since the study of sign languages is a relatively new undertaking, they have not usually been considered in comparative cross-linguistic research. Thus linguistic typology is still largely a typology of spoken languages, although sign languages have much to offer in terms of the kinds of insights that can be gained from comparing their structures with the structures found in spoken languages in a

---

3.   In this chapter, IPSL examples are transcribed using the standard way of representing sign language utterances on paper, with the signs represented by glosses in capital letters. Details about the transcription conventions are listed at the end of the chapter.

particular grammatical domain. It turns out that there are indeed important particularities in the way Indo-Pakistani Sign Language expresses reciprocals, which differ from the strategies used in spoken languages.

Data collection for reciprocals in IPSL proceeded in two stages. In the first stage, the standardised elicitation procedure with video stimulus clips developed at the Max Planck Institute for Psycholinguistics was used to elicit the target structures from several deaf signers. The video clips show various people acting out situations relating to the target domain. These were shown to signers from different regions of India, that is, Uttar Pradesh, Maharashtra, Orissa, Gujarat and Andhra Pradesh. Signers viewed the clips and related in Indo-Pakistani Sign Language what they had just seen.[4] The videotaped responses were transcribed using the ELAN software, a program developed for the purpose of annotating multimedia data (see http://www.mpi.nl/tools), and then coded in a standardised way for statistical analysis.

The second stage of data collection aimed at exploring the structures that had been found in the first stage in more detail, as well as investigating their functions and semantic range in a way comparable to what is known about reciprocal constructions in spoken languages. The questionnaire developed at the University of Melbourne was used as a basis for further elicitation, and responses were videotaped from two signers, from Lucknow (Uttar Pradesh) and Indore (Madhya Pradesh). However, it proved unworkable to elicit direct translations of example sentences because this resulted in the signed utterances being influenced by English rather than being the natural way of expressing the target meaning in IPSL. We therefore used a roundabout strategy in which the meaning of events, settings and situations was explained to the subjects in IPSL, and they responded by elaborating freely on the topic. This technique was very successful and resulted in a large number of reciprocal constructions. During the elicitation session, alternative ways of expressing the same content were also explored together with the respondents. Both stages of fieldwork were carried out in Mumbai at the Ali Yavar Jung National Institute for the Hearing Handicapped, with which the

---

4. The IPSL signers responded well to these clips although a number of them were culturally strange to some degree, with unfamiliar situations being displayed. However, signers had no difficulty relating the content of the clips. The only minor difficulty was that the respondents were confused and often made errors as to who was a man and who was a woman in the film clips. This is a relevant point because the usual convention in Indo-Pakistani Sign Language is to first state the participants in a scene and then proceed to describe the events happening between them. Therefore, many of the IPSL responses begin with utterances such as "There are two men and two women…".

authors have been professionally associated. The locations of the regions where the signers come from can be seen on the map in Figure 3.[5]

Because the second author, who was also responsible for the data collection during fieldwork, is himself a native user of Indo-Pakistani Sign Language, it was possible to add a third stage of data analysis. In metalinguistic discussions about the target constructions, the available evidence from the data was evaluated and cross-checked against native signer intuitions, and further examples were added to the data corpus.

Figure 3. Regions relevant to data collection in India

---

2.   Reciprocal constructions in Indo-Pakistani Sign Language

Indo-Pakistani Sign Language has a number of strategies to express various kinds of reciprocal relationships. In this section, we make a basic distinction between a dedicated reciprocal construction, which explicitly and specifically code reciprocity on verbs or auxiliaries, and reciprocal strategies, in which reciprocity is implied but not encoded in the construction itself. Moreover, IPSL has a substantial number of inherently reciprocal predicates.

In all these constructions, the notions of simultaneous morphology and grammatical use of the sign space that were discussed in Section 1.1 are crucial for understanding the nature of the processes involved. Examples of dedicated reciprocal constructions are discussed in Section 2.1, and reciprocal strategies in Section 2.3. In addition, several of these constructions are related to one another through grammaticalisation or lexicalisation processes. These are discussed in Section 3.

2.1   Dedicated reciprocal construction

IPSL has a dedicated construction that explicitly codes reciprocal relationships and can apply to two different classes of items – agreement verbs and auxiliaries. The construction consists of a change in the movement pattern of the sign. With a limited number of signs, this change in movement pattern forms a reciprocal derivation. This morphological derivation is part of the larger family of aspect/aktionsart derivations discussed in Section 1.1. The form is always two-handed, with the movement – or sometimes the orientation – of the two hands directed towards each other. The resulting meaning is 'to X each other', where 'X' is the meaning of the basic predicate sign. Examples of this form are given in Figures 4 and 5.

Figure 4.   1:GIVE:3#RECP 'give to each other'

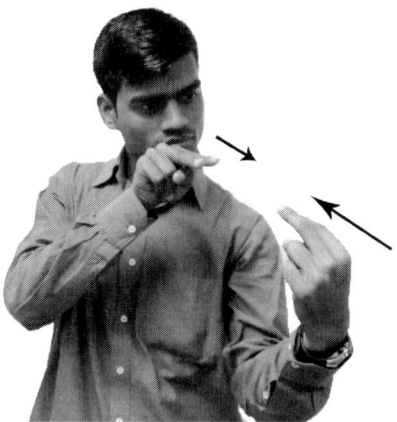

Figure 5. LOOK#RECP 'look at each other'

This derivation is frequent with some signs but is limited in applicability. For instance, the derivation cannot be applied to two-handed signs where one hand is used as the place of articulation for the other hand, such as with the sign HELP (signed with a fist placed on the palm of the second hand and moving forward). The derivation also cannot be applied to any signs that are made on the body, such as the sign FEAR (signed on the chest). Most of the signs that can take the reciprocal derivation belong to the class of agreement verbs, and therefore, they can be marked for person in addition to the reciprocal marking. An example is shown in Figure 6, where the reciprocal form of SPEAK-TO is marked for first and third person locus in the first instance ('me and s/he talked to each other'), and for two third persons in the second instance ('the two of them talked to each other').

Figure 6. 1:SPEAK-TO:3#RECP and 3a:SPEAK-TO:3b#RECP

With predicates that cannot take this morphological derivation, signers have the option of using the second relevant construction sub-type, which involves a reciprocal auxiliary meaning 'do to each other'. The auxiliary in IPSL is based on pronominal index pointing and is used in its basic form to express subject-object relationships ('me to you, s/he to him/her', etc.) with predicates that do not belong to the class of agreement verbs. Just as agreement verbs undergo a morphological derivation resulting in a reciprocal meaning, the auxiliary can also undergo the same process, and the resulting form is exactly parallel to the reciprocal verb derivation. Figure 7 shows the basic and the reciprocal form of the auxiliary.

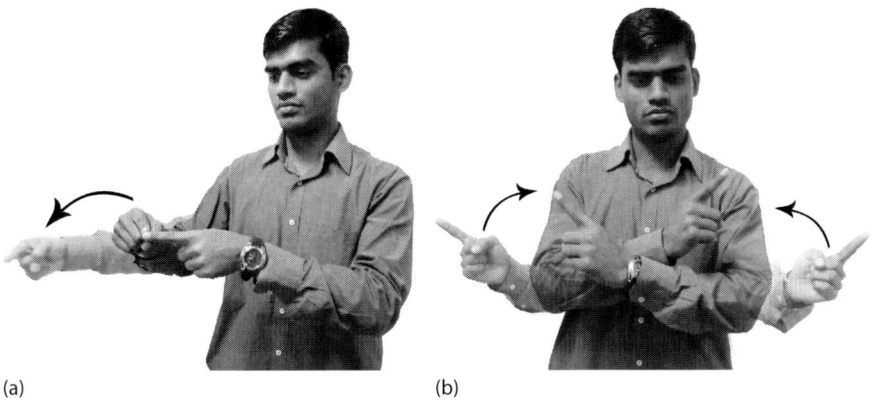

(a)   (b)

Figure 7. (a) Basic auxiliary, (b) reciprocal auxiliary

The reciprocal auxiliary is semantically empty, indicating only the relationship between its arguments – in this case, a reciprocal relationship. In the absence of a main predicate, the default meaning of the auxiliary indicates a communicative act (say, tell, talk, discuss, etc.), so that when it occurs on its own, it is often translated as 'discuss with each other'. In combination with a predicate that cannot take a reciprocal verb derivation, the auxiliary is the only carrier of the reciprocal relationship (2). However, it is also possible for a reciprocal to combine with a main verb that is already in the reciprocal derivation, in which case there is double marking of the reciprocal relationship (3).

(2)   WOMAN THREE:right WOMAN   ONE:left EMBRACE   EMBRACE
      3:AUX:3#RECP   EMBRACE   EMBRACE
      'Three women on one side and another woman opposite them embrace each
      other.'   (#52)

(3) MAN   PERSON:1 WOMAN PERSON:3   INDEX:3 /   GLASSES
     1:GIVE:3 INDEX:3   GLASSES 1:GIVE:3#RECP 1:AUX:3#RECP
     'There is a man (me) and a woman. The man gives his glasses to the woman,
     and they both give their glasses to each other.'⁶   (#41)

The parallelism between the reciprocal verb derivation and the reciprocal auxiliary is shown in Figure 8. The complete grammaticalisation channel of the reciprocal auxiliary, beginning with simple index pointing, is further explicated in
Section 3.1. Moreover, reciprocal verbs are the source of a considerable number
of inherently reciprocal predicates. This lexicalisation process is discussed in
Section 3.2.

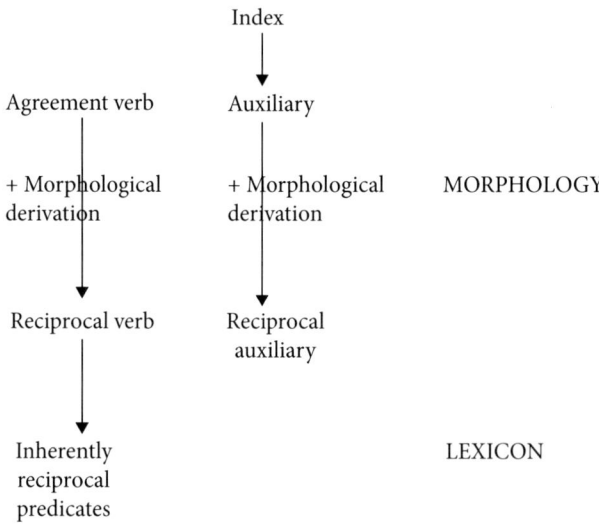

Figure 8. Reciprocal verbs and auxiliaries

The reciprocal derivation applies to both sequential and simultaneous reciprocal events, disregarding the internal temporal structure of the event. In fact, it is
sometimes impossible to express the difference between a sequential and simultaneous situation, particularly in the case of complex events. For instance, "three
pairs of people giving things to each other, all at the same time" would be signed

---

6. The signer identifies himself with one of the participants in the event, the man, and therefore signs the utterance with one of the relevant locations on/near his own body ('1' in the transcription), while the other participant is located away from the body ('3' in the transcription).
This is a common discourse strategy in IPSL.

in the same way as "three pairs of people giving things to each other, one pair at a time" (cf. Section 2.2 about complex spatial modifications). The difference in temporal sequencing would have to be expressed in a separate clause.

There are two main restrictions with respect to applicability of the dedicated reciprocal construction to event types. Firstly, events involving the movement and location of animate or inanimate entities, in terms of simply describing spatial arrays, are coded in IPSL using so-called "classifier constructions", which are available to signers as a reciprocal strategy (see Section 2.3). Therefore, events such as people approaching, chasing, following, or being next to each other, cannot be coded with a dedicated reciprocal construction, and similarly, objects in spatial arrays (next to, on top of each other, etc.) are not within the domain of reciprocals in IPSL. Secondly, the events that are described by the dedicated reciprocal construction must be symmetric, since the construction cannot be applied to asymmetric events. Asymmetric events, including chaining events, must be described with a sequence of individual – non-reciprocal – agreement verbs and/ or auxiliaries. Otherwise, the reciprocal construction can be freely used across event types. For instance, Example (2) above exemplifies a sequential melee event, whereas Example (3) is a simultaneous strong reciprocal.

2.2   Complex spatial modifications in reciprocal constructions

The reciprocal constructions described in the previous section are the simplest forms of reciprocal marking. However, both of these can be further modified in complex ways that rely on the grammatical use of the sign space. The possibilities of these secondary modifications are listed in Figure 9.

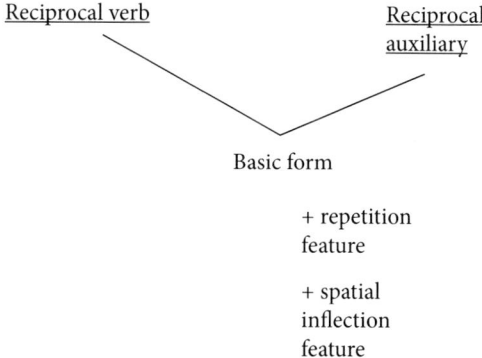

Figure 9. Secondary modifications of reciprocal constructions

The simplest secondary modification consists of adding a repetition feature, resulting in repeated movement of the sign. With the auxiliary, this results in the meaning 'do to each other repeatedly'.[7] Reciprocal verbs can similarly be repeated. Like the basic reciprocal forms, the repeated forms can also be marked for person by changing the locations involved in articulating the sign (close to the signer for first person, close to the addressee for second person, elsewhere in the sign space for third person). This spatial inflection adds additional complexity to the construction and allows for spatial settings to be reproduced in much detail in sign space through one or several complex reciprocals. Examples from the data corpus include (4) and (5), each using a different spatial array based on events of 'giving':

> [two participants; left and centre location; repeated action:]

(4)   MAN   ONE:left   WOMAN   ONE:centre   CL:LEGS
      "stand next to each other"   left:SPEAK-TO:centre#RECP   THEN
      left:GIVE:centre#RECP#ITER
      'A man and a woman stand close to each other; they talk and then exchange
      some things.'   (partial description of #30)

> [single reciprocal actions repeated at five different locations (participants indexed 3a–3j) along a semi-circular path:]

(5)   MAN   FOUR   WOMAN   TWO   WATER   TEA   3a:AUX:3b#RECP
      3c:AUX:3d#RECP   3e:AUX:3f#RECP   BANANA   3a:AUX:3b#RECP
      3c:AUX:3d#RECP   3e:AUX:3f#RECP   3g:AUX:3h#RECP   3i:AUX:3j#RECP
      'Four men and two women pass around (food and drink, like) water, tea,
      bananas, in a semi-circle, always one pair after another.'
                                                 (partial description of #19)

2.3   Other reciprocal strategies

Reciprocal meanings can be expressed by a number of other strategies in IPSL. These constructions are not explicitly reciprocal, but allow a conventional implication or inference of reciprocity. The following constructions fall into this category:

a.   Sequence of agreement verbs
b.   Sequence of auxiliaries
c.   Classifier constructions

---

7.   In another form of the auxiliary, the movement of the hands in parallel rather than directed towards each other. However, the meaning of this form does not involve reciprocity, but means 'to and fro between two locations or referents'. It is thus not a genuine reciprocal, and this analysis is supported by the fact that there is a one-handed variant of this form which has exactly the same meaning.

The first two constructions are, in a sense, the precursors to the dedicated recipro-cal constructions. They consist of a sequence of at least two agreement verbs and/ or auxiliaries, which are spatially inflected with movement from A to B in the first case and from B to A in the second case. In other words, this strategy is like saying 'I help you and you help me', 's/he to you and you to him/her', and the like. If there are more than two referents in the interaction, it is easily possible to add more verbs or auxiliaries directed at their respective locations in sign space. The following examples illustrate the range of possibilities:

(6) WOMAN   DEM:centre.down   WOMAN   CL:LEGS
right.up:COME:centre.down   SLAP:left / WOMAN   left:AUX:right
SLAP:right[8]
'There is a woman there, and (another) woman approaches and slaps her. The first woman slaps the other one in turn.'   (#3)

(7) PERSON   PERSON   SIX /   MAN   TWO   CL:LEGS
"two persons standing left"   3a:PUNCH:3b   3b:PUNCH:3a /
WOMAN   TWO   CL:LEGS   "two persons standing centre"
3c:PUNCH:3d   3d:PUNCH:3c /   WOMAN   TWO
"two persons standing right"   3e:PUNCH:3f   3f: PUNCH:3e
'There are six people. Two men (on the left) punch each other with the fist, (then) two women (in the middle) punch each other, (then) two other women (on the right) punch each other.'   (#42)

In such an utterance, a reciprocal relationship can be inferred from the fact that the movements of the individual signs are directed at each other, though this hap-pens in a sequence of separate signs rather than being expressed in a specialised reciprocal inflection.

The third reciprocal strategy, the use of classifier constructions, shows some affinity with the complex reciprocal constructions discussed in Section 2.2 in that spatial settings can be mapped accurately onto the position and movement of the hands. Classifier constructions consist of a handshape representing a certain class of referents, and movement and location features. For instance, an upright index finger can represent a person, or a curved handshape can represent a cylindrical object. The classificatory handshapes can combine with a large number of loca-tions and movements to map the spatial arrangement and movement of a scene. Inasmuch as more than one referent can be represented, a reciprocal relationship can be inherent in the complex sign formation.

---

8.   The sign SLAP only agrees with a goal/object location.

For the purpose of this chapter, we focus on the most relevant sub-type of classifier constructions, the whole-entity classifiers, where the classificatory handshape stands for a particular type of entity.[9] IPSL has two such handshapes that are mainly used for human referents. The first one PERSON (upright index finger) represents a whole upright person, the second one LEGS (index and middle finger pointing downward) represents a person by legs. In complex two-handed constructions, relationships between more than one referent can have a reciprocal interpretation depending on the exact spatial constellation. For instance, such constructions can convey the equivalent of people approaching each other, following each other, walking behind or next to each other in lines, and the like. Similarly to the sequence of agreement verbs or auxiliaries, the reciprocal relationship is inferred from the total construction rather than being explicitly realised by a separate overt morpheme. Figure 10 shows an example with the LEGS classifier, and Figure 11 with the PERSON classifier.

Figure 10. Legs classifier: 'two persons walking towards each other'

Figure 11. Person classifier: 'people running behind each other'

---

9.   Other sub-types of classifiers, used for expressing the shape or handling of objects in terms of their geometrical properties, are not discussed here. For a complete overview of all classifier constructions in various sign languages, see Emmorey (2003).

In IPSL, classifiers are outside the domain of reciprocal constructions. Even if some of them can be used to code a semantically reciprocal event, this is not coded in the classifier construction, and the "reciprocal" configuration is merely one of many other spatial configurations that simply index the movement and position of entities. In fact, descriptions of semantically reciprocal event types that use a classifier construction are incompatible with genuinely reciprocal constructions such as the reciprocal auxiliaries, and it would be impossible to add a reciprocal auxiliary to any utterance such as the ones exemplifies in Figures 10 and 11.

3.   The dynamics of reciprocal constructions

In this section, we discuss how individual signs and constructions within the domain of reciprocals develop in IPSL, using a dynamic perspective to consider both grammaticalisation and lexicalisation processes. As is often pointed out in the context of grammaticalisation theory (e.g. Hopper & Traugott 1993), these concepts can be very helpful in understanding the nature of a particular construction type or class of lexemes, and taking a dynamic, or even a diachronic, point of view often resolves theoretical puzzles where there seem to be in-between cases that are difficult to categorise in a straightforward way. Section 3.1 deals with the grammaticalisation of reciprocal auxiliaries, and Section 3.2 discusses the lexicalisation of inherently reciprocal signs.

3.1   Grammaticalisation of reciprocal auxiliaries

As mentioned above, the reciprocal auxiliary is ultimately based on pronominal index finger pointing. In this section, we trace the development by way of which more complex forms are derived from each other at every step. There is clearly a historical perspective to this discussion in the sense that the auxiliary has developed diachronically from simpler forms of pointing. However, this line of argument is not pursued in detail here, and the developmental steps can serve just as well synchronically in order to better understand the complexity of the system. The grammaticalisation of auxiliaries has also been described for other sign languages (Steinbach & Pfau 2007).

Table 1 lists the various stages of development together with their characteristics. A simple index finger pointing sign, the equivalent of a singular pronoun, is the starting point in the table. If more than one referent needs to be pointed out, sequences of two or more individual pointing signs can be produced. Thus at stage two the only difference is the number of pointing signs. Each pointing sign has its own movement feature, and thus there are two individual movements in this stage. The sequence of pointing is then further grammaticalised to form the basic auxiliary. The main formal difference that is introduced at this third stage is that there is now a single movement between the two spatial locations. The meaning is now marked for transitivity ('s/he to him/her'), and as mentioned already, a default meaning 'communicative act' is inherent in the auxiliary. At the fourth stage, this basic auxiliary receives an additional aktionsart derivation, which makes the sign two-handed. The various complex movement patterns discussed in Section 2.2 (repetition and spatial location features) can also be applied to the reciprocal auxiliary.

Table 1. Grammaticalisation of the reciprocal auxiliary

Index finger pointing		Sequence of two index points		Basic auxiliary		Reciprocal auxiliary	
personal pronoun	→	two personal pronouns (A and B)	→	+ transitivity (A to B) + default meaning 'communicative act'	→	+ reciprocal aktionsart 'to each other'	MEANING
	→	Two separate movements One hand	→	One movement A to B One hand Figure 7a	→	Complex movement patterns Two hands Figure 7b	FORM EXAMPLE

3.2   Inherently reciprocal predicates and the lexicalisation process

As mentioned above, reciprocal verbs are often the sources of inherently reciprocal signs in IPSL. It seems that the reciprocal verb derivation often leads to lexicalisation in this domain, even though not all such signs can at present be associated with related non-reciprocal source signs. All inherently reciprocal signs are two-handed, with either alternating movement or parallel movement of both hands towards each other. Not surprisingly, the meaning of these signs involves reciprocal actions such as 'meet', 'fight', 'argue', 'war', 'love', 'competition' etc. It should be noted that it can be a matter of interpretation whether a sign is inherently reciprocal or not, in particular when it is not obviously related to a non-reciprocal source sign. Therefore, we only discuss inherently reciprocal signs that clearly have a corresponding source sign.

Unlike the regular reciprocal verb derivation, inherently reciprocal signs are not entirely regular in their form and not entirely predictable in their meaning. Formally, lexicalised reciprocals often undergo shortening and assimilation compared to what would be a regular reciprocal verb derivation of the source sign. Semantically, the meanings often deviate from what a regular derivation would suggest. Table 2 gives examples of sign pairs, with the left-hand column listing the reciprocal signs and the right-hand column listing the source signs.

Table 2. Inherently reciprocal signs and their sources

Inherently reciprocal sign	Source sign
COMPETITION	SUCCESS
MEET (Indian dialects)	GO
MEET (Pakistani dialects)	PERSON
FIGHT/ARGUE	PUNCH
BUSINESS	GIVE
WAR	SHOOT
ENEMY (Karachi dialect)	SHOOT

In inherently reciprocal signs, the form of the sign has become fixed and is no longer accessible to the full range of morphological modifications. For instance, the sign BUSINESS can no longer be inflected for person, as was possible with the reciprocal source verb GIVE (cf. Figure 4 in Section 2.1), and the sign has, in fact, changed its word class. No matter whether first, second or third persons are involved in the action, the sign BUSINESS remains unchanged, and an auxiliary must be used in order to indicate these distinctions, as in Example (8):

(8) EUROPE AMERICA BUSINESS 3a:AUX:3b#ITER
'Europe and America do business with each other.'

Semantic changes are more varied than formal considerations. One type of semantic change involves generalisation of the meaning. For example, the sign FIGHT/ARGUE (based on the source sign PUNCH, see Figure 12) can refer to any kind of fight, even a purely verbal argument. Similarly, the sign WAR (based on the sign for SHOOT) does not imply a particular type of weapon and just refers to 'war' in a general sense.

Figure 12. PUNCH and FIGHT/ARGUE

Table 3 lists formal and semantic differences between some reciprocal and non-reciprocal sign pairs. As can be seen from the table, not all reciprocal signs are affected by the same degree of change in comparison to their source signs, and so it is convenient to argue that signs are lexicalised to different degrees. On a scale from the top to the bottom of the table, the sign glossed DISCUSS could still be regarded as a regular verb derivation, whereas the downmost sign are fully lexicalised. A lexicalisation continuum can thus be posited where signs enter the lexicalisation channel at one end of the continuum and emerge as fully lexicalised forms at the other end. In between, all kinds of semi-lexicalised items can be found. In this approach, it is natural that signs should show hybrid characteristics not easily classified as either a reciprocal verb derivation or an inherently reciprocal predicate. The occurrence of semi-lexicalisation is only too natural in this scenario, and thus the approach is helpful in understanding how the nature of the lexicalisation process affects the characteristics of individual signs.

Table 3. Differences between reciprocal signs and their non-reciprocal source signs

Sign pairs (reciprocal – non-reciprocal)	Change of word class	Semantic change	Shortening / assimilation	Restricted inflectional possibilities	Other formal changes
DISCUSS TELL	No	minor	No	No	Alternating movement repetition; optional loss of fixed beginning location
MEET PERSON	Yes	minor	No	No independent action of both hands; no/less morphological changes for aktionsart	No
COMPETITION SUCCESS	No	major	Loss of wrist twisting	No/less person and number distinctions	Alternating movement repetition
FIGHT/ARGUE HIT-WITH-FIST	Yes	major	Shorter movement	No/less person and number distinctions	Repeated movement
BUSINESS GIVE	Yes	major	Shorter movement	No/less person and number distinctions	Movement from the wrist
WAR SHOOT	Yes	major	No wrist action	No/less person and number distinctions	Finger wiggling

4. Conclusions

The exploration of reciprocal constructions and strategies in Indo-Pakistani Sign Language has shown that sign languages do indeed need to be considered as a separate case for the purpose of cross-linguistic comparison. Modality-specific concepts that were shown to be essential in dealing with these IPSL constructions are simultaneous morphology and the grammatical use of the sign space. Moreover, IPSL is particular in that reciprocal event types involving spatial arrays of either animate or inanimate referents are not subsumed under reciprocals constructions. It seems that rather than instantiating an abstract concept of reciprocity in these constructions, signers prefer to make optimal use of the affordances of the visual-spatial modality they operate in. This strategy blocks the applicability of genuine reciprocal constructions in these domains.

Finally, it should be noted that not all sign languages can be expected to be structured in the same way. Available literature on reciprocal constructions in sign languages is marginal at present, with only one major research paper on reciprocals in German Sign Language (Pfau & Steinbach 2003). Therefore, for a genuine comparison across sign languages themselves and across the modalities of sign and speech, it will be essential to gather data from other sign languages in order to see in how far the reciprocal constructions in these sign languages resemble the IPSL structures or are different from them.

Transcription conventions and abbrevations

Transcription conventions are:

INDEX:a	pronominal index pointing
a:SIGN:b	agreement verb with spatial movement from a to b
A-B-C	fingerspelling
XXX-XXX	single sign with multi-word English gloss
SIGN+SIGN	(simultaneous or sequential) compound
SIGN#abc	simultaneous morphological process #abc applied to a sign
/	clause break
CL: "…"	classifier sign (with meaning in quotes)
SIGN/SIGN	alternative meanings of a sign

Abbreviations are:

AUX	auxiliary	RECP	reciprocal
1	first person	ITER	iterative
3	third person	DISTR	distributive

Acknowledgements

We are very grateful to the Ali Yavar Jung National Institute for the Hearing Handi-capped (AYJNIHH) in Mumbai for supporting this research, especially with respect to the fieldwork component. In particular, we would like to thank the staff of the Indian Sign Language Cell at AJYNIHH for support during the data collection pro-cess. The German Research Council (Deutsche Forschungsgemeinschaft, DFG) has supported this research through grant no. Ze507/1–3 for the project on "Sign Lan-guage Typology – The cross-linguistic study of sign languages". Above all, we thank the Indian Sign Language users Alok Kumar Jena, Jagadish Naik, Neil Fredrick, Tushar Dave, Dharmesh Kumar, and P. Jagadeesh. They have participated in data collection and have allowed us to use their data for this research. Special thanks are due to Babloo Kumar, whose images appear in this publication along with images of one of the authors.

References

Bellugi, Ursula & Fischer, Susan. 1972. A comparison of Sign Language and spoken language: Rate and grammatical mechanisms. *Cognition: International Journal of Cognitive Psychology* 1: 173–200.

Boyes-Braem, Penny. 1990. *Einführung in die Gebärdensprache und ihre Erforschung.* (Intro-duction to sign language and its research). *Internationale Arbeiten zur Gebärdensprache und Kommunikation Gehörloser*, Bd. 11. Hamburg: Signum.

Emmorey, Karen (ed.). 2003. *Perspectives on Classifier Constructions in Sign Languages.* Mah-wah NJ: Lawrence Erlbaum Associates.

Hopper, Paul J. & Traugott, Elizabeth Closs. 1993. *Grammaticalization.* Cambridge: CUP.

Klima, Edward S. & Bellugi, Ursula. 1979. *The Signs of Language.* Cambridge MA: Harvard University Press.

Liddell, Scott K. 2003. *Grammar, Gesture and Meaning in American Sign Language.* Cambridge: CUP.

Meier, Richard, Cormier, Kearsy & Quinto-Pozos, David (eds). 2002. *Modality and Structure in Signed and Spoken Languages.* Cambridge: CUP.

Meir, Irit. 1998. *Thematic Structure and Verb Agreement in Israeli Sign Language.* PhD disserta-tion, Hebrew University of Jerusalem.

Pfau, Roland & Steinbach, Markus. 2003. Optimal reciprocals in German Sign Language. *Sign Language and Linguistics* 6(1): 3–42.

Sandler, Wendy & Lillo-Martin, Diane. 2006. *Sign Language and Linguistic Universals.* Cam-bridge: CUP.

Sethna, Meher, Vasishta, Madan & Zeshan, Ulrike. 2004. Implementation of Indian Sign Lan-guage in educational settings. *Asia Pacific Disability Rehabilitation Journal* 15(2): 15–39.

Steinbach, Markus & Pfau, Roland. 2007. Grammaticalisation of auxiliaries in sign languages. In *Visible Variation. Comparative Studies on Sign Language Structure* [Trends in Linguistics 188], Pamela Perniss, Roland Pfau & Markus Steinbach (eds). Berlin: Mouton de Gruyter.

Sutton-Spence, Rachel & Woll, Bencie. 1999. *The Linguistics of British Sign Language*. Cambridge: CUP.

Vasishta, Madan, Woodward, James & Wilson, Kirk L. 1978. Sign language in India: Regional variations within the deaf population. *Journal of Applied Linguistics* 4(2): 66–74.

Vermeerbergen, Myriam, Leeson, Lorraine & Crasborn, Onno. 2007. *Simultaneity in Signed Languages* [Current Issues in Linguistic Theory 281]. Amsterdam: John Benjamins.

Wilbur, Ronnie B. 1987. *American Sign Language. Liguistic and Applied Dimensions*. Boston MA: College-Hill Press.

Zeshan, Ulrike. 2000a. *Sign Language in Indopakistan: A Description of a Signed Language*. Amsterdam: John Benjamins.

Zeshan, Ulrike. 2000b. *Gebärdensprachen des indischen Subkontinents* (Sign languages of the Indian subcontinent). Munich: Lincom.

Zeshan, Ulrike. 2003. Indo-Pakistani Sign Language grammar: A typological outline. *Sign Language Studies* 3(2): 157–212.

Zeshan, Ulrike. 2006. Regional variation in Indo-Pakistani Sign Language – Evidence from content questions and negatives. In *Interrogative and Negative Constructions in Sign Languages* [Sign Language Typology Series 1], Ulrike Zeshan (ed.). Nijmegen: Ishara Press.

CHAPTER 6

Mundari reciprocals

Nicholas Evans and Toshiki Osada

Australian National University / Research Institute for Humanity and Nature Kyoto, Japan

This paper investigates the semantics of reciprocal constructions in Mundari, an Austro-Asiatic language of northern India. Two grammatical constructions express reciprocity: a basic construction, which infixes ‹pV› to verb roots, and a serialised construction adding -idi 'take' to the basic reciprocal. The reciprocal construction is limited to subject-object coreference and cannot be fed by affixal derivational processes like applicatives or causatives, though it can be fed by zero conversion from other word classes; it may itself feed the causative. From a semantic perspective, the most unusual feature of Mundari reciprocals is the existence of a specialised construction for expressing sequential chaining situations, namely the serialised construction with -idi 'take'; the basic reciprocal construction is not acceptable for sequential chaining situations.

1. Introduction

Mundari belongs to the Munda branch of Austroasiatic. It is spoken in northern India by around three quarters of a million people, primarily in the state of Jharkand. There are four dialects – Hasadaq, Naguri, TamaRia and Keraq – of which the first is used for the data in this paper.[1] For materials on the language see Hoffmann and van Emelen's (1930–1979) massive encyclopaedic dictionary, and Hoffmann (1903), Cook (1965), Langendoen (1967) and Osada (1992, 2008) for grammatical descriptions, and Osada (2007) for additional details on Munda reciprocals.

There is only a distant genetic and typological relationship between the Munda languages and the other, Mon-Khmer, branch of Austroasiatic, represented in this volume by the papers on Mah Meri by Kruspe and on Jahai by Burenhult.

---

1. Some scholars (e.g. Pinnow 1959:2) argue that Ho should also be considered a dialect of Mundari, though its speakers regard it as a distinct language and themselves as a distinct ethnic unit.

Though it has sometimes been asserted that Mundari is a 'fluid' word-class language without distinct word-classes, it is more accurate to say that it does in fact have distinct word-classes (noun, verb, adjective), with liberal (but not unlimited) possibilities for zero-conversion between them (Evans & Osada 2005). A point of resemblance the Munda languages share with most Austroasiatic languages (and even with relatively isolating languages like Cambodian) is their use of infixation. Though more recently grammaticalised morphemes are invariably suffixes (under Indo-Aryan and Dravidian influence), there are many traces of a rich original system combining prefixes and infixes.

As we shall see, the primary marker of reciprocity in Mundari is the use of an infixed ‹pV› after the first syllable of verbs. Although this has some cognates more widely in Austroasiatic, their functions vary rather widely. And while several other Munda languages (Santali, Korku, Remo) make use of infixation to express reciprocity, others employ prefixes only (Sora, Kharia and Juang). Zide & Anderson (2001:519) suggest that proto-Munda made use of a combination of prefix + infix to express reciprocity, and that, moreover 'The infixed element of the reciprocal in Proto-Munda is likely an intrusion from another infix, possibly one originally used with nouns'. We are still far from fully understanding the diachronic source of the Mundari reciprocal infix, but it appears likely that while the overall strategy of employing infixes goes back at least to proto-Austroasiatic,[2] the use of an infix ‹pV› to express reciprocity is a relatively late development within north Munda branch.[3]

Mundari has SOV word-order, complex verbal suffixing for voice, a benefactive applicative, up to three agreement positions and a rich set of TAM categories (Munda 1971, Osada 1992). Subjects are cross-referenced by an enclitic to whichever constituent precedes the verb (1); note that, as with *pusikoking* in (1), this can produce a sequence of a number suffix to the word itself (here *-ko*, marking its host 'cats' as plural) plus a (person and number) clitic indexing the subject (here =*king*, indexing the subject *seta-king* 'two dogs'). Third person dual and plural

---

2.   And see Reid (1994) for arguments that it goes back even further to proto-Austric, the putative common ancestor of Austroasiatic and Austronesian – in fact, the presence of apparently cognate infixes in both these families is a central piece of evidence for Reid's lumping argument.

3.   On the other hand, South Munda prefixes descending from an original form *kaR-/kɔR- have likely cognates in Mon-Khmer, e.g. Bahnar *kə-*: cf. *dah* 'kick'; *kə-dah* 'kick each other') (Banker 1964:107–9). For Munda and Kherwari ‹pV›, Pinnow (1966:184–5) suggests cognacy with a Mon-Khmer infix expressing abstracts and/or pluralisation, as in Khmer *rien* 'to learn', *ropien* 'to study' but the exact semantic pathway remains unclear. He is almost certainly correct, however, in seeing the reciprocal meaning as a secondary development.

subject clitics are formally identical with the corresponding number suffixes on nouns, and with the object suffixes on verbs (like *-ko* in *huakedkoa*) but can be distinguished by their position.

(1) *seta-king   pusi-ko=king   hua-ke-d-ko-a.*
     dog-DU   cat-PL=3duSBJ   bite-COMPL-TR-3plOBJ-IND
     'The two dogs bit the cats.'

When no preverbal element is present for the subject pronoun to attach to, it encliticises to the verb itself (2).

(2) *hua-ke-d-ko-a=king.*
     bite-COMPL-TR-3plOBJ-IND=3duSBJ
     'The two of them bit them.'

2. Reciprocal constructions in Mundari

Reciprocity is normally expressed in Mundari by infixation of ‹pV› (Section 2.1). For chaining situations, which are of course not prototypical reciprocals, a variant of this is used: ‹pV› infixation is supplemented by serialisation with the verb *idi* 'take' or *au* 'bring' (Section 2.2). With some intransitive verbs it is possible to make simple use of an intransitive verb with a plural subject, as discussed in Section 2.3, though we do not consider this a dedicated reciprocal construction since other interpretations are available.

2.1 Primary strategy: Infixation of ‹pV› to the verb

The primary strategy for encoding reciprocity in Mundari involves the infixation of a morpheme ‹pV› after the first syllable of verb[4] roots, where V is a copy of

---

4. The statement of this restriction to verbs is complicated by the generous zero-conversion possibilities open to Mundari, which convert many nouns into verbs without overt marking, e.g. *buru* 'mountain' (n.); 'heap up' (v.t.) (see Evans & Osada 2005). If ‹pV› then occurs on a root of basic nominal meaning, how do we know if it has attached to the noun or the verb? If we consider the semantics, however, the most economical explanation is to see it as a verbal derivation in all cases: in *bu‹pu›ru* 'heap each other up', for example, the reciprocal interpretation, is clearly composed by taking the verbal meaning as input. An infixed reciprocal form exists for one locational noun (*japaq* 'near', *japapaq* 'near each other', which might lead one to think that relational nouns can be productively reciprocalised, but the couple of kinship nouns attested with an appropriate form have rather idiosyncratic meanings, while the formally identical infix found with adjectives has an intensive meaning: *marang* 'large', *maparang* 'very large'.

the first-syllable vowel.[5] Examples are *lepel* 'see‹RECP›' (< *lel*), *jopoar* 'greet‹RECP›' (< *joar*), *jupuTid* 'touch‹RECP›' (< *juTid*), *hapambud* 'embrace‹RECP›', (< *hambud*), and *tapabiRi* 'slap‹RECP›' (< *tabiRi*). This is the overwhelmingly most common way of describing the scenes in the stimulus set.[6]

The reciprocating participants are represented by a conjoined NP or a pronoun denoting the whole reciprocant set, and an intransitive version of the verb is substituted for the transitive found in the corresponding unidirectional construction. The intransitive verb differs in two ways from the corresponding transitive: it lacks a suffix in the object slot, and it replaces the transitive suffix *-d~-q* with the intransitive suffix *-n*. The points of structural contrast are bolded in Examples (3)–(4).

(3) *Soma=ñ*   *lel-ki-q-i-a*[7]
     Soma=1sgSBJ   see-COMPL-TR-3sgOBJ-IND
     'I saw Soma.'

(4) a. *Soma   ad   añ   do=**ling**   le‹pe›l-ke-**n**-a.*
         Soma   and   I   TOP=1EXCL.duSBJ   see‹RECP›-COMPL-INTR-IND
         'Soma and I saw each other.'

     b. *le‹pe›l-ke-**n**-a=**ling***
         see-COMPL-TR-3sgOBJ-IND=1EXCL.duSBJ
         'We (two, exclusive) saw each other.'

With ditransitive verbs in Mundari the object slot can represent either the theme or the recipient, as shown by the ambiguity of (5a). In the corresponding reciprocal constructions, however, the argument coreferential with the subject must be interpreted as the recipient, never the theme (5b). Note that with reciprocalised ditransitive verbs the intransitive verbal suffix is used and the object slot is empty, even though the NP representing the theme argument looks like an object, from its position and its lack of postpositional marking.

(5) a. *Soma   seta-ko   hon-ko=eq*   *om-ke-d-ko-a.*
         Soma   dog-PL   child-PL=3sgSBJ   give-COMPL-TR-3plOBJ-IND
         i. 'Soma gave the dogs to/for the children.'
         ii. 'Soma gave the children to/for the dogs.'

---

5. Except that for words with a series of nasal vowels, only vowels right of the infix retain nasalisation after infixation; the vowel in the infix is optionally nasalised: cf. *dāRā* 'search' but *da‹pa›Rā* 'search for each other', but also *dapāRātana*.

6. Maki Purti, in spontaneous speech, occasionally uses a double infix on monosyllabic roots in cases of interacting groups, e.g. *sapapab* ‹*sab*› 'catch each other (of groups of children involved in playing)'. This phenomenon deserves further investigation but did not appear in the clip data.

7. Underlying this is *lel-ke-d-iq-a*, but the sequence *kediqia* regularly becomes *kiqia*.

b. *hon-ko   seta-ko=ko   o‹po›m-ke-n-a.*
child-PL   dog-PL=3plSBJ   give‹RECP›-COMPL-INTR-IND
'The children gave the dogs to each other.'
(*'The children gave each other to the dogs.')

There are strict constraints on the two grammatical roles occupied by reciprocants, which largely limit this construction to cases where the corresponding unidirectional description involves action of a subject upon an object. For example, it is not possible to feed a benefactive argument (added by the benefactive applicative suffix *-a*) into the reciprocal construction, nor can it normally be used for cases where one participant is a possessor (e.g. 'Soma and his child cut each other's paper'). Nor is it possible to have the reciprocal relation holding between two non-subjects as in English examples like 'I introduced Soma and Maki to each other', except for the special case of causativised reciprocals described below.

The only exception to this 'subject-object coreference constraint' is for intimate possession or location, where the object is either a body-part of the reciprocants (e.g. 'Soma and his child have cut each other's hair', in (6)), or a closely-associated entity like lice. Note that many languages treat lice equivalently to body-parts, e.g. Bininj Gun-wok (Evans 2003).

(6) *[Soma ay-aq   hon-loq]ₛᵤᵦⱼ [ub] ₒᵦⱼ =king la‹pa›Tab-ja-n-a.*
Soma   he-POSS   child-with   hair=3dusSBJ   cut‹RECP›-INGR-INTR-IND
'Soma and his child have cut each other's hair.'

(7) *[siku] ₒᵦⱼ =ko da‹pā›Rā-ta-n-a.*
lice=3plSBJ   search-PROG-INTR-IND
'They are searching for lice on each other, they are searching each other for lice.'   (#56)[8]

The reciprocal may feed the passive (8), or causative (9) formations, each of which is coded by a suffix to the verb; the passive is somewhat rare and unnatural.

(8) *a‹pa›d-oq-ta-n-a=le*
miss‹RECP›-PASS-PROG-INTR-IND=1pl.EXCL.SBJ
'We were almost missed by each other.' (Because of some outside cause, e.g. the fog.)

(9) *hon-ko   hora-re   seta-king=ko*
child-PL   street-LOC   dog-du=3plSBJ
go‹po›y-rika-ke-d-king-a.
kill‹RECP›-CAUS-COMPL-TR-3duOBJ-IND
'The children caused two dogs to fight each other on the street.'

---

8. Throughout this chapter examples identified as '#N' refer to descriptions of the appropriately numbered videoclip.

Apart from the object body-part construction, we can summarise these constraints by saying that reciprocal formation

i.   must involve strict subject–object coreference
ii. the reciprocal must be the first operation as one composes the clause, if there are several diathesis-changing affixes.

In other words, it may feed other diathesis changes such as reflexive, passive and causative, but it may not be fed by them (e.g. by the benefactive).[9] Further, even though the language regularly permits causativisation by zero-conversion of base intransitives (e.g. *goy* 'die (v.i.); kill (v.t.)'), and transitives derived by such zero-converted causativisation may be reciprocalised (e.g. *go‹po›y* 'kill each other'), reciprocalised forms may not feed causativising zero-conversion.[10]

2.2   Supplementary strategy: Reciprocal infix plus serialisation

Mundari uses two types of verb serialisation – left-headed and equipollent – to express a wide range of meanings. In left-headed serialisations, the first verb retains its literal meaning, while the second takes on a special construction-specific meaning, and in such cases will be capitalised in glosses: cf. *nam-jom* [get-EAT] 'get for oneself', *rasika-goy* [rejoice-DIE] 'rejoice excessively', *lel-ruRa* [see-RETURN] 'see again'. In equipollent serialisations there is simply a coordinate meaning, e.g. *jom-nu* [eat-drink] 'eat and drink', *maq-goy* [cut_with_axe-kill] 'kill with an axe'.

Reciprocal infixation forms one test for distinguishing these two types. With the coordinative type, each conjoined verb is separately infixed for the reciprocal ((10), (11)), whereas with left-headed serialisations only the head verb receives such infixation (12). In the case of serialisations whose second element is *laq* 'compete', it is also possible to infix just the second element, with the meaning 'compete in V-ing', e.g. *nir-lapaq* [run-compete‹RECP›] 'compete in running', *jom-lapaq* [eat-compete‹RECP›] 'compete in eating'.

---

9.   This contrasts interestingly with languages like Bininj Gun-wok (Evans 2003) or many Bantu languages (Mchombo 1991, Hyman 2003), where benefactives and other applicatives may feed reciprocals. Significantly, in these languages both applicatives and reciprocals are encoded by prefixes or suffixes rather than infixes, and it may be that there is a morphological constraint preventing infixes from having semantic scope over suffixes.

10.   In the closely related Santali, however, reciprocal verbs may be zero-causativised: Bodding (1929) gives the example *ne‹pe›l-ket'-kin-a=ko* [see‹RECP›-COMPL.TR-3duOBJ-PRD=3plSBJ] 'They made them (two) see each other.'

(10) *hoRo-ko*   *piRi-re=ko*   *ma‹pa›q-go‹po›y-ta-n-a.*
      person-PL   field-LOC=3plSBJ   cut_with_axe‹RECP›-kill‹RECP›-PROG-INTR
      'The people are killing each other with axes in the field.'

(11) *ni‹pi›r-la‹pa›q-ta-n-a=kin*
      run‹RECP›-compete‹RECP›-PROG-INTR-IND=3duSBJ
      'They are chasing each other.'   (#36)

(12) *hoRo-ko=ko*   *le‹pe›l-ruRa-ke-n-a*
      person-PL=3plSBJ   see‹RECP›-RETURN-COMPL-INTR-IND
      'The people saw each other again.'

One such left-headed serialisation, though not previously described in the literature on Mundari reciprocals, appears a number of times in our reciprocals data.
The verb *idi* 'take' may be used in serialised constructions to describe motion
onward or away, or continuation (Osada 1992: 112), e.g. *nir-idi* [run-TAKE] 'run
away', *kuli-idi* [ask-take] 'go on asking a question'. In our data this verb is combined with reciprocal verbs in a number of examples involving 'chained reciprocal' action (A > B > C); an example is (13). See Section 3 for further discussion of
the precise examples involved.

(13) *o‹po›m-idi-ta-n-a=ko*
      give‹RECP›-TAKE-PROG-INTR-IND=3plSBJ
      'They give it on to one another (away from me).'   (#28)

A further type of serialisation involves the verb *au* 'bring'. This normally specifies
that the motion is towards the speaker, e.g. *nir-au* [run-BRING] 'to come running
this way', *jom-au* 'to go for taking food and then come back'. However, when serialised with the reciprocal verb *o‹po›m* 'exchange' it adds the meaning 'carry out
(recip. action) repeatedly or customarily', as in (14). This construction, however,
did not occur as a response to the clip data.

(14) *sida-ate=le*   *o‹po›m-au-ta-n-a*
      previous-from=1pEXCL.SBJ   give‹RECP›-BRING-PROG-INTR-IND
      'We have been exchanging with one another for a long time.'

2.3   Plural subjects with intransitive verbs, with no reciprocal marking

There are several examples in the data where a verb or other predicate is simply
used with a plural subject, without infixation with ‹pV›, to describe situations that
are reasonably construed as reciprocal. An example with *jagar* 'talk' is (15):

(15) *kulgiya=kin*   *jagar-ta-n-a*
      husband&wife=3duSBJ   talk-PROG-INTR-IND
      'They two, man and wife, are talking.'   (#11)

In (15) reciprocal action is implicated but not entailed. It may mean 'they two, husband and wife, are talking to each other', but it may also mean 'they two, husband and wife, are talking to a third party or an audience'.

This verb is characterised by an atypical range of argument structures, in addition to its basic intransitive use. Unusually, the person being talked to may be coded either by a suffix in the direct object slot (as in *jagar-ke-d-ko-a=ñ* 'I talked to them', where *ko* is the third person plural object marker), or by a suffix in the indirect object slot after the benefactive applicative *-a*: *jagar-a-ko-ta-n-a=ñ* [talk-BEN-3pl. IO-PROG-INTR-IND=1sgSBJ] 'I am talking to them'. The first of these structures may also feed reciprocal formation, as in (16); the resultant reciprocal stem *japagar* has also been lexicalised, via zero-conversion to a noun, with the meaning 'negotiation'.

> (16) *ja‹pa›gar-ta-n-a=kin.*
>   talk‹RECP›-PROG-INTR-IND=3duSBJ
>   'The two of them are talking to each other.'   (#9)

A tricky analytic problem, in the case of plural-subject verbs without reciprocal marking such as (15), is whether these should be treated as a distinct 'conjunct strategy', comparable to the formation employed with English constructions like 'John and Mary kissed', or whether they merely predicate joint activity, as their plural subjects suggest, with reciprocity being inferred by implicature alongside other, non-reciprocal readings, as in (15) above.

A straightforward example of plural intransitives used to denote joint activity is (17), in which there is no overt expression of reciprocity: the plural subject simply implicates joint activity.

> (17) *panti-re=ko*   *dub-ta-n-a*
>   row-LOC=3plSBJ   sit-PROG-INTR-IND
>   'They are sitting in a row.'   (#15)

In the case of English the reasons for considering reciprocals with conjoined subjects as a particular construction include the clear lexical restriction on which verbs are involved, the fact that reciprocal readings are entailed rather than implicated with certain verbs,[11] and the existence of specific characterising sets of alternative constructions (see Lakoff & Peters 1969, Kemmer 1993, and Levin 1993, *inter alia*). There is no comparable evidence in Mundari. In contrast to English, this construction cannot be used for such canonical reciprocal activities as 'meet',

---

11. The classic illustration of this is that some verbs, used in this construction, entail reciprocity (*John and Mary met -> John and Mary met one another*) whereas others only implicate it (though *John and Mary disagreed* implicates 'with one another' this implicature can be defeated, as in *Tony thought George's decision was correct, but John and Mary disagreed*).

'fight', 'quarrel' or 'make love', all of which would be coded with the reciprocal infix in Mundari – so we do not analyse it as a distinct reciprocal construction here.

There are thus just two construction types dedicated to the expression of reciprocity: the reciprocal infix (with accompanying valency change and use of the intransitive marker), and the reciprocal infix combined with serialised *idi* 'take' or *au* 'bring'.

3.   Categories encoded in the clip data

Complete data was obtained from a single speaker – Sugundas Hasapurti, around 65 years old – and more restricted data from his daughter Maki Purti (age 42). Both these sessions were recorded by Evans in Kyoto with Maki Purti, who resides there, in June 2004, and with Sugundas Hasapurti in June 2005 during a visit to his daughter. Sugundas speaks Mundari and Hindi; Maki Purti speaks Mundari, Hindi, English and Japanese, and assisted in the translation of the Sugundas data.[12]

The basic reciprocal construction was the main strategy employed – Sugundas used it for 33 out of 64 clips. For strict and melee situations, whether simultaneous or sequential, the basic infixed construction was the description of choice. Examples are:

(18)   *joa-re=ko*   *ta‹pa›biRi-ta-n-a.*
        cheek-LOC=3plSBJ   slap‹RECP›-PROG-INTR-IND
        'They are slapping each other on the cheek.'   (#5) (hit, strict sequential)

(19)   *dulaRa-te=king*   *ha‹pa›mbud-ta-n-a*
        affection-LOC=3duSBJ   hug‹RECP›-PROG-INTR-IND
        'They two are hugging.'   (#7, strict simultaneous)

(20)   *ta‹pa›biRi-ta-n-a=ko*
        slap-PROG-INTR-IND=3plSBJ
        'They are slapping one another.'   (#44) (melee, sequential)

This construction was only used once for a chaining situation – (7), which was the only chaining example exhibiting simultaneity (#56, with A delousing B, while B simultaneously delouses C).[13] For all other chained events in the data the basic reciprocal construction was not used. Instead, the serialised construction with 'take' was used ((13), (21), (22)), or the reciprocal construction was avoided altogether.

---

12. We did not discern any influence of the other languages they know on the data collected here, except in the case of the verb for 'shake hands' discussed below.

13. For #2, a chained sequential hugging scene involving four people, Sugundas first offered a regular reciprocal (*hapambudtanako*), then corrected it to the serialised form in (21); Maki Purti only gave, and would only accept, the form with *-idi* given in (21).

(21) *ha‹pa›mbud-idi-ta-n-a=ko*
      hug-TAKE-PROG-INTR-IND=3plSBJ
      'They are hugging one another.'
                              (#2) (4, chain, sequential – alternative description)

(22) *panti-re   dub-aka-n=ci*
      row-LOC   sit-INIT.PROG-INTR=CONJ
      gi‹pi›l-idi-ta-n-a=ko
      punch‹RECP›-TAKE-PROG-INTR-IND=3plSBJ
      'They are sitting in a row and punching each other down the line.'   (#48)

Overall, the serialised construction was used for three of the chained situations
(scenes 2, 28 and 48), all non-simultaneous. The failure to use any reciprocal coding with #6, where six people in a chain sequentially shake hands, was probably
due to the general unavailability of reciprocal marking with this verb, considered
a foreign (Hindi) word for a foreign activity. But in the case of two further chained
scenes (#34, #37), which both used the verb 'give', this explanation is not available,
since the relevant verb occurs elsewhere both in the basic reciprocal construction and with the compounded construction. It is possible that the semantically
complex nature of these scenes, in which different objects were being given, is the
reason why neither reciprocal construction could be used here. Be that as it may,
there is overall a clear dispreference for using the basic reciprocal construction
for chained situations, and a clear preference for the serialised construction which
specifically encodes chained, sequential situations. Maki Purti, in particular, is
quite vehement in rejecting the acceptability of the basic reciprocal construction
with any sequential chained situation.

4.   Conclusion

Mundari reciprocal constructions are interesting in several ways. Formally they
are unusual in employing infixation as the main marker of reciprocity. If we assume that the semantic effects of infixation are restricted to the morpheme it applies to, this would explain why reciprocal formation cannot be fed by any other
valency-rearranging process (causativisation or applicatives) even though it may
feed them (passive, causative). Mundari reciprocals are also unusually strict in being limited to cases where the coreference is between subject and object positions.
The inability of applicatives to feed the reciprocal means there is no dedicated
means for expressing reciprocity with other types of argument structure.
     Semantically, Mundari reciprocals are cross-lingusitically unusual in pro-
viding a dedicated construction type for sequential chaining situations, which
are preferentially described by a construction combining reciprocal infixation

with a serialised verb whose base meaning is 'take', and which elsewhere adds meanings like 'motion onward or away', or continuation, to the head verb of the construction. With this construction available for sequential chaining situations – and required wherever the situation departs doubly from the prototypical 'simultaneous symmetric' situation by being both sequential and non-symmetric in the sense of involving chaining – the basic reciprocal construction has a more limited semantic range, and is normally only used for strict and melee situations. The Mundari data thus suggest that it was empirically premature for Dalrymple et al. (1994, 1998) to claim that reciprocal constructions in all languages have a comparably broad semantic range, which takes in chaining situations besides the more prototypical conditions of strict reciprocity, and that this claim was flawed by being based on too narrow a sample of the world's languages. However, our data on the chained-reciprocal construction in Mundari so far comes only from the clip descriptions elicited for this project – in fact, the construction had not even been identified in previous studies of Mundari. The next step in research on Mundari reciprocals will be to examine its use in more naturally-occurring data.

Orthography and abbreviations

Various methods have been used for writing Mundari. Here we employ a practical orthography using the following special symbols or digraphs: capital letters for retroflex consonants (thus T = /ʈ/, R = /ɽ/), ñ for the palatal nasal /ɲ/, ng for the velar nasal /ŋ/, and q for the glottal stop /ʔ/. The 'checked' realisation of word-final stops, where the voicing contrast is neutralised, is realised phonetically as pre-glottalisation plus a subsequent nasal release. Since this is phonemically predictable we do not show it here, simply writing them with the appropriate voiced stop symbol, e.g. *sab* 'catch' for [saʔp$^{(m)}$]. In Hoffmann's works this word would be written with a wedge under the b: [saḅ].

We employ the following non-obvious abbreviations:

CAUS	causative	OBJ	object
COMPL	completive aspect	PASS	passive
CONJ	conjunction	POSS	possessive
EXCL	exclusive	PROG	progressive oriented
IND	indicative	RECP	reciprocal
INGR	ingressive	SBJ	subject
INIT.PROG	initiated progressive	TOP	topic
INTR	intransitive	TR	transitive
LOC	locative		

The nominal number suffixes are written upper-case (DU(al), PL(ural)) to distinguish them from the (person plus) number enclitics and verbal suffixes with which they are homophonous.

Acknowledgements

It is a pleasure to thank Maki Purti and Sugundas Hasapurti for providing the Mundari data, Steve Levinson, Niclas Burenhult and Alice Gaby for critical comments on an earlier draft, Asifa Majid for discussion of coding, and the audience at the Nijmegen reciprocals workshop (April, 2006) for their questions. The research reported on here was supported by the Australian Research Council Discovery Project 'Reciprocals Across Languages' (DP 0343354), and we gratefully acknowledge their assistance.

References

Banker, Elizabeth M. 1964. Bahnar affixation. *Mon-Khmer Studies* 1: 99–118.
Bodding, Paul O. 1929. *Materials for a Santali grammar* II. Dumka: The Santal Mission of the Northern Church.
Cook, Walter A. 1965. A Descriptive Analysis of Mundari: A Study of the Structure of the Mundari Language According to the Methods of Linguistic Science. PhD dissertation, Georgetown University.
Dalrymple, Mary, Kanazawa, Makoto, Kim, Yookyung, Mchombo, Sam & Peters, Stanley. 1998. Reciprocal expressions and the concept of reciprocity. *Linguistics and Philosophy* 21: 159–210.
Dalrymple, Mary, Mchombo, Sam & Peters, Stanley. 1994. Semantic similarities and syntactic contrasts between Chicheŵa and English reciprocals. *Linguistic Inquiry* 25(1): 145–163.
Evans, Nicholas & Osada, Toshiki. 2005. Mundari: The myth of a language without word classes. *Linguistic Typology* 9(3): 351–390.
Evans, Nicholas. 2003. *Bininj Gun-wok: A Pan-dialectal Grammar of Mayali, Kunwinjku and Kune*. Canberra: Pacific Linguistics.
Hoffmann, John. 1903. *Mundari Grammar*. Calcutta: The Secretariat Press.
Hoffmann, John & van Emelen, Arthur. 1930–1979. *Encyclopaedia Mundarica*, XVI vols. Patna: Bihar.
Hyman, Larry. 2003. Suffix ordering in Bantu: A morphocentric approach. In *Yearbook of Morphology*, Geert Booij & Jaap van Marle (eds.), 245–281. Dordrecht: Kluwer.
Kemmer, Suzanne. 1993. *The Middle Voice* [Typological Studies in Language 23]. Amsterdam: John Benjamins.
Lakoff, George & Peters, Stanley. 1969. Phrasal conjunction and symmetric predicates. In *Modern Studies in English*, David A. Reibel & Sanford A. Schane (eds), 113–142. Englewood Cliffs NJ: Prentice Hall.
Langendoen, Terence D. 1967. Mundari verb conjugation. *Linguistics* 32: 39–57.

Levin, Beth. 1993. *English Verb Classes and Alternations. A Preliminary Investigation.* Chicago IL: The University of Chicago Press.

Mchombo, Sam A. 1991. Reciprocalization in Chichewa: A lexical account. *Linguistic Analysis* 21: 3–22.

Munda, Ramdayal D. 1971. Aspect of the Mundari verb. *Indian Linguistics* 32: 27–49.

Osada, Toshiki. 1992. *A Reference Grammar of Mundari.* Tokyo: Institute for the Languages and Cultures of Asia and Africa.

Osada, Toshiki. 2007. Reciprocals in Mundari. In *Reciprocal Constructions,* Vol. 4. [Typological Studies in Language 21], Vladimir Nedjalkov (ed.), 1575–1592. Amsterdam: John Benjamins.

Osada, Toshiki. 2008. Mundari. In *The Munda Languages*, Gregory Anderson (ed.), 99–164. London: Routledge.

Pinnow, Heinz-Jürgen. 1959. *Versuch einer historischen Lautlehre der Kharia-Sprache.* Wiesbaden: Otto Harassowitz.

Pinnow, Heinz-Jürgen. 1966. A comparative study of the verb in the Munda languages. In *Studies on Comparative Austroasiatic Linguistics*, Norman H. Zide (ed.), 96–123. The Hague: Mouton.

Reid, Lawrence. 1994. Morphological evidence for Austric. *Oceanic Linguistics* 33(2): 323–344.

Zide, Norman & Anderson, Gregory. 2001. The proto-Munda verb system and some connections with Mon-Khmer. In *The Yearbook of South Asian Languages and Linguistics 2001*, Peri Bhaskararao & Karumuri V. Subbarao (eds), 517–540. New Delhi: Sage.

CHAPTER 7

Description of reciprocal situations in Lao

N. J. Enfield

Max Planck Institute for Psycholinguistics and Radboud University Nijmegen

This chapter describes the grammatical resources available to speakers of Lao for describing situations that can be described broadly as 'reciprocal'. The analysis is based on complementary methods: elicitation by means of non-linguistic stimuli, exploratory consultation with native speakers, and investigation of corpora of spontaneous language use. Typically, reciprocal situations are described using a semantically general 'collaborative' marker on an action verb. The resultant meaning is that some set of people participate in a situation 'together', broadly construed. The collaborative marker is found in two distinct syntactic constructions, which differ in terms of their information structural contexts of use. The chapter first explores in detail the semantic range of the collaborative marker as it occurs in the more common 'Type 1' construction, and then discusses a special pragmatic context for the 'Type 2' construction. There is some methodological discussion concerning the results of elicitation via video stimuli. The chapter also discusses two specialised constructions dedicated to the expression of strict reciprocity.

1. Introduction

Reciprocal situations – as in *They gave each other diamonds* – are among those situation types whose description is handled less straightforwardly by the world's grammars than more canonical types like simple transitives ('see', 'hit') and intransitives ('sneeze', 'walk'). In describing less canonical situation types, grammars go for work-around solutions, more complex and sometimes less obvious ways of structuring the description of events and other states of affairs. Examples include situations with three or more participants (Hudson 1992, Newman 1996, 1997, Narasimhan et al. 2007), with unusual configurations of transitivity parameters (Hopper & Thompson 1980), and with actor and undergoer arguments that do not show the standard asymmetrical alignment, as in reflexives (where actor and undergoer are one and the same entity; Frajzyngier & Curl 1999a, Kemmer 1993, Geniušienė 1987) or reciprocals (where distinct entities map onto multiple semantic roles; Dalrymple et al. 1998, Frajzyngier & Curl 1999b).

The present volume is partly about the range of ways in which languages distinguish the grammatical encoding of reciprocal situations from the encoding of other types of situation. Each language should have a formal way of distinguishing the description of symmetrically reiterated events like *They saw each other* from asymmetrical ones like *He saw her*. A second issue is cross-linguistic variation in the (extensional and intensional) semantics of constructions which may be used for the description of canonical reciprocal events. The broader theoretical issues concerning comparative research on how languages cope with the non-canonical argument structure configurations that reciprocal situations give rise to are dealt with in the introduction to this volume (cf. also Frajzyngier & Curl 1999b, Dalrymple et al. 1998). This chapter contributes to the comparative project described in the introduction, with an account of the lexico-grammatical resources which Lao speakers possess for the description of reciprocal situations, as well as the broader expressive functionality of those resources.

To preview the descriptive content of the chapter, Lao speakers have two main lexico-grammatical resources for describing reciprocal situations. One of these is a narrowly specialised, relatively seldom occurring construction, which I call the reciprocal mirror construction. It has the structure 'I V_α you, you V_α me', typically appended to a differently worded description of the event. The reciprocal mirror construction is confined to the description of events that are strictly reciprocal; that is, where for some predicate for which A and B are participants, A acts upon B *and* B acts upon A (see Section 4.2, below). The other of the two main constructional means for describing reciprocal situations in Lao is far more common and is the main focus in this chapter. This construction, featuring the nominal particle *kan3* occupying an (erstwhile) object slot in the verb phrase, is more general in meaning than strict reciprocity of action or orientation. The *kan3* construction is used for the description of a range of situation types in which multiple participants map onto multiple roles of a single predicate. This covers reciprocal situations (*They saw each other*) as well as situations in which people carry out some activity together (*They celebrated together*), or are inherently or properly complementary in action or orientation (*One gives while the other receives, One is a clone of the other*). The data are consistent with an analysis of the *kan3* construction as having a single, general meaning applying across this range of situations (as opposed to a polysemy account whereby *kan3* would entail strict reciprocity in some cases and something else in other cases).

The findings are the combined result of two distinct complementary procedures of data collection and analysis: (1) showing prepared, focused stimuli to consultants for description, and eliciting a set of linguistic types which target the description of these tokens (a set of videoclips; see introduction to this volume for a description of these stimuli); (2) searching existing texts (narratives, conversations collected for general grammatical description) for the range of token situations in which the target types are used (the target type being the particle *kan3*). These are complemented by interviews with native-speaker consultants in a fieldwork setting, probing possible descriptions of possible situations (to test hypotheses suggested by 1 and 2). This combination of multiple methods is the ideal approach to semantic typology (Enfield, Majid & Van Staden 2006:138–139). Each method can shed light on the problem which the others may not.[1] In the context of this volume, procedure 1 forms a basis for comparison across languages, and contributes to the formation of hypotheses of language-specific meaning. Procedure 2 and the interviews with consultants target the intensional analysis of language-specific types.

2.   Lao

Lao is a Southwestern Tai language, spoken in Laos, Thailand, and Cambodia. It is the national language of Laos (Enfield 1999, 2007). It is closely related to Thai (Iwasaki & Horie 2005) in all structural respects. Lao is isolating and analytic in morphological organisation, with no case-marking, and no cross-referencing or verbal agreement. Grammatical relations in a transitive clause are canonically signaled by constituent order (SV/AVO):

(1) *dèèng3   cuup5/phop1   sèèng3*
     Deng   kiss/meet   Seng
     'Deng kissed/met Seng.'

Widespread zero anaphora (almost any contextually retrievable argument can be ellipsed) along with heavy topic prominence (fronting) and common post-placement of arguments means that surface constituent order varies a lot. This, combined with the fact that there is no morphological marking of grammatical relations (whether on clausal heads or dependents), results in significant context-dependence for mapping of arguments onto semantic roles. These morphosyntactic features are highly characteristic of languages of the immediate mainland South East Asia area (Enfield 2005).

---

1. The methodological critique leveled at an earlier draft of this chapter in an otherwise useful article by Wierzbicka (2009:162–4) misrepresents my view (and misquotes it; the draft was not final), implying that I and colleagues privilege 'objectivist' and 'neo-behaviourist' stimulus-based elicitation methods, thereby failing to tap into the native concepts under study. This is baffling, as I am at pains in this chapter to stress the opposite, namely that while stimulus-based techniques are a useful comparative tool, they alone are not sufficient for semantic analysis (the 'Nijmegen School' has never proposed otherwise), hence my heavy reliance on non-elicited examples, and my attention to methodological limitations (see Sections 3.3.4 and 3.4).

3.   'Reciprocal' marking with *kan3*

The key resource in Lao for describing the kinds of situations included under the reciprocal rubric is the particle *kan3*.[2] I refer to it as a collaborative marker (glossed COLL), since its meaning is more general than 'reciprocal'. This is an independent word and does not belong in a larger form class. It appears in an object slot, typically immediately after a verb (though there are some occasions in which it may appear after a noun, for example when the noun is incorporated; cf. Examples (5), (22), below).

Verbs with inherently reciprocal meanings require explicit marking using *kan3*. Thus, while English has reciprocal readings of objectless strings like *John and Mary met (Ø) at the park* and *They kissed (Ø)*, these zero objects in Lao are taken to be contextually retrievable, tracked arguments. Example (2) is interpreted as having an ellipsed object argument whose referent is not (included in) the plural subject *khacaw4*:

(2)   *khacaw4*   *cuup5/phop1*
      3PL.P   kiss/meet
      'They kissed/met him/her/them.' (NOT: 'They kissed/met each other.')

For the reciprocal reading, *kan3* is required:

(3)   *khacaw4*   *cuup5/phop1*   *kan3*
      3PL.P   kiss/meet   COLL
      'They kissed/met each other.'

The marker *kan3* conveys a general idea that a predicate is true of multiple individuals 'together', covering not only actions done *to* each other but also those done *with* each other, and even entirely asymmetrical relations (where one of the participants does not correspond to the actor role of the verb at all), as long as the people involved are consensually or otherwise rightfully playing their part in the activity or state of affairs as a whole.

There are two main types of *kan3* construction, which I shall call Type 1 and Type 2.

---

2.   There is a complex variant *sùng1 kan3 lèq1 kan3*, made up of *sùng1* a relative marker 'which', and two instances of the reciprocal marker *kan3*, in coordination marked by *lèq1* 'and' (see Example (46) in this chapter). It is a stylistically high form of expression, suitable for writing and for more formal speech such as in traditional narratives. There is a homonym, the verb *kan3* 'hold back, constrain, resist, block'. In the closely related language Thai, there is an 'intimate' third person pronoun *kan3* (presumably cognate).

3.1   Type 1 *kan3* construction: 'A and B V *kan3*'

The most common type of *kan3* construction involves (a) a single subject argument whose meaning is plural (either inherently plural like the plural pronoun *khacaw4* in Example (3), or a compound of more than one noun conjoined by *kap2* 'with/and' as in Example (4)), (b) a main verb, and (c) *kan3* in postverbal position:

(4) *dèèng3   kap2   sèèng3   hên3/vaw4/tii3/khaa5   kan3*
    Deng   with   Seng   see/speak/hit/kill   COLL
    'Deng and Seng saw/spoke-to/hit/killed each other.'

If an incorporated object of the verb is expressed (usually a body part such as *naa5* 'face' in the following example, see also Example (22), below),[3] it comes in the immediate postverbal slot, with *kan3* in the main object slot:

(5) *dèèng3   kap2   sèèng3   hên3   naa5   kan3*
    Deng   with   Seng   see   face   COLL
    'Deng and Seng saw each other's faces.'

Of the four example verbs shown in the Type 1 construction in (4), *vaw4* 'speak' is intransitive and does not allow another human participant as a direct complement in a transitive construction (cf. (1), above):

(6) *dèèng3   hên3/khaa5/tii3   sèèng3*
    Deng   see/kill/hit   Seng
    'Deng saw/killed/hit Seng.'

(7) **dèèng3   vaw4   sèèng3*
    Deng   speak   Seng
    'Deng spoke Seng.'

For *vaw4* 'speak' in a regular two-place expression, the second argument is marked by *kap2* 'with':

(8) *dèèng3   vaw4   kap2   sèèng3*
    Deng   speak   with   Seng
    'Deng spoke with Seng.'

---

3.   On the status of the post verbal body part term as incorporated and thus distinct from a regular, full object noun phrase, see Enfield (2006: 195, 2007: 356ff).

3.2   Type 2 *kan3* construction: 'A V *kan3* with B'

A second type of *kan3* construction features separation of otherwise conjoined subject arguments, where the second of the two – marked by *kap2* 'with/and', as in the subject of Example (4), above – is moved into a postposed, peripheral position. The key difference between the two types of *kan3* construction is the separation of the noun phrase conjuncts. The verb remains marked by *kan3*:

(9)   *dèèng3   vaw4/tii3   kan3   kap2   sèèng3*
      Deng   speak/hit   COLL   with   Seng
      'Deng spoke-to/fought each other with Seng.'

(10)   **dèèng3   hên3/khaa5   kan3   kap2   sèèng3*
       Deng   see/kill   COLL   with   Seng
       'Deng saw/killed each other with Seng.'

Most discussion in this chapter concerns the more common Type 1 construction. The Type 2 construction is treated separately, in Section 3.4, below. It is more restricted in scope, partly because it does not allow most transitive verbs. Those verbs that may occur in the Type 2 construction can all also occur in the Type 1 (compare *vaw4* 'speak' and *tii3* 'hit, fight (with)' in Examples (4) and (9)). More significantly, the alternation between the two constructions is associated with different information structure construals (see Section 3.4, below).

3.3   Semantic range of the Type 1 *kan3* construction

The particle *kan3* has a strikingly wide range of use over situation types. This is revealed both by observation of its range of occurrence in natural texts, and by its very liberal use across video stimulus materials developed for the comparative field research documented in this volume. As the chapters of this volume show, it is typical for a grammatical resource which is used to describe a canonical reciprocal situation to also be extended to refer to other types of situation which are not literally reciprocal in a strong sense, but which relax certain defining components (cf. Langendoen 1978, Dalrymple et al. 1998, introduction to this volume). For the purpose of organising the Lao data in this section, I use the following informal categories of situation type associated with the use of *kan3*:

(11)   a.   Strict reciprocal (e.g. *They hugged each other*, *They gave each other diamonds*): where for some multiple of participants, *all* map onto *both* actor and undergoer roles of the predicate (with some logical variations depending on quantitative and temporal relations between multiplied events, etc.).

b. Loose reciprocal (e.g. *The dogs ate each other, The plates were stacked on top of each other*): where for some multiple of participants, multiple participants map onto the actor role and multiple participants map onto the undergoer role, but strict reciprocity does not apply.
c. Collective (e.g. *They celebrated together, They ate dinner together*): where for some multiple of participants, all map onto the same role of the predicate.
d. Complementary (yet asymmetric) (e.g. *She gave him a watch, One of them is a clone of the other*): where for some multiple of participants, some participant maps onto one role, and the other maps onto a complementary role. The respective roles are not the same, but they properly complement each other to make the situation complete.

In the rest of this section, I describe the range of application of the Type 1 *kan3* construction (for the more restricted Type 2 *kan3* construction, and the reciprocal mirror construction, see Section 3.4 and Section 4.2, below).

To give an idea of how surprisingly broad the extension of *kan3* is, in three speakers' descriptions of the full set of 64 reciprocal stimulus clips (Evans et al. 2004), there was only one clip whose target situation was unanimously described without using *kan3*. In this clip (#60), three people who are sitting side by side watch a fourth person walk by. For only a few other clips did one or more speakers omit *kan3* from the description. For example, in describing a clip in which one actor walks along and bumps into another, one speaker omitted *kan3*. The others described it as 'people bumping into each other' (although they acknowledged that only one actor bumps into the other; i.e., they would not break it down into two events, A bumped B and B bumped A). Most clips in the full stimulus set were spontaneously coded by all three speakers using a Type 1 *kan3* construction.

3.3.1 *Strict reciprocal*

The *kan3* marker may be used for describing situations which are strictly reciprocal, in the sense defined in (11a), above. Here are two text examples:[4]

(12)   *qaw3*   *hua3*   *laan4*   *son2*   *kan3*
        take   head   bald   butt   COLL
        '(They'd) butt each other with (their) bald heads.'

(13)   *jaan4*   *pajø*   *phop1*   *kan3*   *kòòn1*
        afraid   DIR.ABL   meet   COLL   before
        '(We're) afraid (they'll) meet each other before (the appointed time).'

---

4. These cases are types of multi-verb constructions (Enfield 2007: 337ff), which act effectively like single verbs for the purposes of the syntax of *kan3* – that is, *kan3* is placed in the object slot of the whole verb complex.

Kan3 is also applicable where the reciprocated actions are separated in time. The following text example refers to two schools whose students would occasionally make visits to the other school – that is, at one time, students of School A would visit School B, at another time, students of School B would visit School A:

(14) nakø-hian2   tòò1   nakø-hian2   naø   pajø   jaam3 kan3
      CT.AGT-study connect CT.AGT-study TOP.PERIPH DIR.ABL visit   COLL
      'Student to student, (they'd) go (and) visit each other.'

Verbs of interpersonal communication and social relations are expressed using *kan3*, as in the following text examples:

(15) ngùk1   hua3 saj1 kan3 lèkaø   lèèw4
      toss.head head put   COLL C.LNK   finish
      '(We'd) toss our heads at/towards each other, and that'd be it.'

(16) tèè1 vaa1 mii2   ñang3   kaø   lom2
      but   COMP there.is   INDEF.INAN T.LNK talk
      kan3 paj3 daj4 juu1
      COLL go   can   FAC.WEAK
      'But whatever the (problems), (we) could talk (to) each other (about them).'

(17) man2 mak1 duu3-thuuk5   kan3 lùang1   saa3sanaa3
      3.B   tend look.down.on   COLL concerning religion
      'They tend to look down on each other concerning religion.'

(18) hêt1   siaw1   kan3
      make   best.friend COLL
      '(We) became best friends (with) each other.'

Verbs of exchange encode a reciprocation of transfer. If *She and John exchanged diamonds*, then she transferred diamonds to John and John transferred diamonds to her.[5] Events of this kind of reciprocal exchange such as the compound *lèèk4-pian1* in the following example, are expressed using *kan3*:

(19) khaa5 maa2 lèkaø   maø   lèèk4- pian1   kan3
      kill   come C.LNK   DIR.ALL   exchange-change   COLL
      '(We'd) kill (the cattle) and then (we and the other villagers would) exchange (the food) with each other.'

---

5. Verbs of exchange are therefore distinct from verbs of transfer such as *haj5* 'give' in Example (40), below, which encode a one-way event. If *She gave John diamonds*, only she corresponds to the actor role of the predicate 'give': Unlike in *They exchanged diamonds*, it doesn't mean that John gave her diamonds in return.

3.3.2 *Loose reciprocal*

Events which are loosely reciprocal in the sense defined in (11b), above, are readily described with *kan3*, as in these two examples from texts:

(20) *phuak4 daj3   kaø   hum4   kan3   qaw3   vaj4   bòø   fang2*
      group   INDEF T.LNK cover COLL   take   keep   NEG   listen
      'They were all on top of each other, unrestrainable.'

(21) *bòòk5 haj5   huu4   kan3   thua1   thang2   mùang2*
      tell   give   know   COLL   all   whole   city
      '(They) told each other all across the city....'

The following example (overheard in context by the author) was shouted by an adult to a group of children playing boisterously with long sharp sticks. The speaker warns that someone could get their eye pierced. Despite the asymmetry of the situation described, *kan3* is used. The speaker is not saying that A will pierce B's eye *and* B will pierce A's eye. It doesn't matter which of the multiple participants would be actor and which would be undergoer, it could be any of them:

(22) *lavang2   suat5   taa3   kan3   dee4*
      watch.out pierce eye   COLL   FAC.ONRCD
      'Watch out for piercing each other's eyes, y'hear!'

A chaining type reciprocal relation (cf. *They followed each other in to the room*) may also be described by *kan3*:

(23) *saam3 sop2   lian2   kan3*
      three corpse be.in.a.row   COLL
      '(I saw) three corpses (lying) in a row.'

In a sub-category of this type, the subject is a singular noun, and the use of *kan3* coerces a plural reading of the subject participant, where multiple *parts* of the participant are in loose reciprocal relationship:

(24) *sùak4   kòòng3   kan3*
      string heaped   COLL
      'The string is heaped on itself.' (From a director-matcher task, describing a mess of twine)

3.3.3 *Collective*

Kan3 may convey the sense that each participant performs the denoted action or situational role in the same way, quite distinct from any sense of reciprocity (as per (11c), above):

(25) *khacaw4   salòòng3   kan3*
3PL.P   celebrate   COLL
'They celebrated (together).' (overheard by author)

(26) *phanan2   kan3   kaø   lêkø-lêk1   nòjø-nòòj4*
gamble   COLL   T.LNK   RDP.A-little   RDP.A-small
'(They) gamble (with each other) a little here and there.'

(27) *pan3   kan3   kin3*
divide   COLL   eat
'(They) divide (the goat meat amongst each other) to eat.'
(overheard by author)

(28) *hoom2   ngen2   kan3   phuu5   lêkø-lêk1   nòjø-nòòj4*
assemble   money   COLL   person   RDP.A-little   RDP.A-small
'(They'd) pool their money together, a little each.'

Similarly, *kan3* marks togetherness in spatial orientation:

(29) *kaj1   phùùn4-mùang2   man2   ñèè5   kan3   kaø   daj4*
chicken   traditional   3.B   stuff   COLL   T.LNK   can
'Free range chickens, it's okay for them to be stuffed in together
(in their pens).'

(30) *mii2   thahaan3   laaw2   thahaan3   falang1   pon3   kan3*
there.is   soldier   Lao   soldier   French   mix   COLL
'There were Lao soldiers (and) French soldiers mixed together.'

(31) *taw4-hoom2   kan3*
converge-assemble   COLL
'to assemble (together)'

(32) *phuak4   qaaj4   pòk2   qaaj4   ñang3   nang1   kan3*
group   eBr   Pok   eBr   INDEF   sit   COLL
'(Brother) Pok and company sat together.'

Relatedly, a verb marked by *kan3* can serve as an adverbial adjunct referring to actions or qualities being somehow the same, done equally, at the same time, or together:

(33) *man2   ñòòn4   man2   khaj1   phòòm4   kan3*
3.B   because   3.B   lay.eggs   be.simultaneous   COLL
'It's because they lay eggs at the same time.'

(34) *haj5   dùng3   khêng1   samee3   kan3*
give   pull   be.tight   be.equal   COLL
'Pull (the ropes) equally tight.'

Similar adverbial expressions with *kan3* can appear in preverbal position:[6]

(35) phaa2   kan3   khùn5
lead.along COLL ascend
'(They) went up (the bank) together.' (lit. 'led each other up')

(36) khaw3 ñaat4 kan3 kin3 khaw5
3PL.B snatch COLL eat rice
'They fought with each other to eat the meal.'

In the next examples, *kan3* denotes a kind of general applicability of the predicate's meaning across a collective of individuals:

(37) bòø   phòò2   kan3   kin3
NEG be.enough COLL eat
'(It's) not enough (for everyone) to eat.'

(38) khòòng3 man2 niñom2   kan3 nèèw2   nan4 dêj2
owing.to 3.B   be.popular COLL manner DEM FAC.NEWS
'Since that sort of thing was popular (with everyone), you know.'

(39) kaan3 nap1 khanèèn2 caø nap1 kan3 bèèp5   nan4
NMLZ count score   IRR count COLL manner DEM
'(In the Lao sport *katòò*), regarding the counting of scores, (everyone) counts like that.'

3.3.4 *Complementary (yet asymmetric)*

So far we have encountered descriptions of situations in which multiple participants (or some coerced equivalent, such as the multiple *parts* of a single participant; Example (24), above) are participating in the same way. By contrast, in the next class of cases, *kan3* describes situations in which participants contribute in unalike yet complementary ways (as per (11d), above). Consider this description of a simple transfer scene: a videoclip in which one actor gives another actor a watch:

(40) qaw3 moong2 haj5 kan3
take watch give COLL
'(They're) giving "each other" a watch.'

Only one actor gives. The other only receives. While the receiver does in a sense do something which rightfully contributes to the event as a whole (i.e., receive the gift), the two participants play distinct roles with respect to the predicate *haj5*

---

6. These cases are not distinct *kan3* constructions, but incorporate verb+*kan3* units in adverbial functions; see Enfield (2007: 477).

'give'. What this *kan3*-marked description of an unequivocally asymmetrical event seems to have in common with the categories we have examined so far is that it conveys the idea that the participants are taking part together in the event. Giving is an event type which lends itself well to this construal, since there is a rightful complementary action: receiving.

While the responses to video stimuli clearly show that *kan3* may unproblematically mark events of non-reciprocated giving, this kind of response is more common in the stimulus descriptions than in natural texts. Perhaps the decontextualised nature of the watch-giving scene (the videoclip is only a few seconds long) makes the event look like it is part of a game the actors are playing. If informants surmise that there is no purpose to the depicted act of giving other than its being acted out for the camera, or more importantly that this moment of action is not embedded in a trajectory of narrative action, perhaps it doesn't matter who actually gave and who received (cf. Example (22), above). One way of putting it is that together the two actors engage in a joint activity of giving a watch – the 'together' notion licensing a *kan3* construction in describing the videoclip.

Following are examples from spontaneous language use where *kan3* is used in description of clips in which a true reciprocal meaning is clearly not intended, nor is the idea that the participants each perform the same action or contribute to the situation in the same way. Rather, in these cases, they 'together' take part in a situation defined by the action of a single participant, where the other's contribution is complementary.

Here is an example from a description of an accident on a wide country road in which a truck flattens a motorcycle (and the motorcycle does not flatten the truck in any sense):

(41) *khaw3 kaø   ñang2 pajø   jiap5   kan3   daj4*
      3PL.B   T.LNK still   DIR.ABL flatten COLL   can
      '(The road was 15 metres wide, and) they were still able to flatten each other.'

Next, the single defining action is telling a story. This activity is rightfully complemented by a consenting listening audience:

(42) *haw2 caø   ñok1   qaw3   nithaan2 siang2-miang5 maø   law1   kan3*
      1.FA   IRR   raise take   tale   Siang Miang   DIR.ALL tell   COLL
      'I'm going to offer the story of Siang Miang to tell "each other".'

The next example (overheard by the author) describes a situation in which a movie actor is extracting the someone's sore tooth with pliers, and the two are rolling around, tussling. While the action is distinctly asymmetrical, the tooth-pulling activity rightfully involves a consenting jaw:

(43) *lok1*   *khèèw5*   *kan3*
     pull.out   tooth   COLL
     '(They're) pulling each other's teeth out.'

One evening in Vientiane, I telephoned B's house, trying to locate a friend A, who was visiting the city, and who I knew was dining with B that evening. A third person answered the phone. I asked for A, and was told he had already left. Then I asked for B, and was told this:

(44) *khacaw4* *paj3* *song1*   *kan3*
     3PL.P   go   send.home   COLL
     'They're sending "each other" home.'

While the predicated action *song1* 'to send somebody (home)' is clearly asymmetrical – only one sends the other home – the two are equally collaborating in the overall event.

In the next example, a Lao speaker was watching a movie in which one of the characters had been cloned. Having missed the beginning of the film, and puzzled for a while as to why the same actor was playing two characters on the screen at the same time, the speaker realised what was going on and said:

(45) *qoo4* *khacaw4* *khloon2*   *kan3*
     INTJ   3PL.P   to.clone   COLL
     'Oh, they're clones of each other.'

One is the real character, the other is the clone. They are not literally clones of each other. Yet they are in a rightfully complementary relationship. Note that this asymmetrical situation is also readily described with a reciprocal marker in English, as shown in the translation of (45).

Finally, a cow is accosted by a tiger, and agrees for the tiger to eat it, but asks that it first be allowed to go home and bid farewell to its calf. Its resignation to the inevitability of being eaten is accompanied with this remark:

(46) *sùa3* *kap2* *ngua2* *man2* *pên3* *qaahaan3* *sùng1* *kan3* *lèq1* *kan3*
     tiger   with   cow   3.B   COP   food   REL   COLL   and   COLL
     'The tiger and the cow are food for each other.'

The relation predicated here is portrayed as rightful, the way of the world – the cow and the tiger are in a symbiotic relationship defined by the cow's being food for the tiger. In a sense, they each play an equal part.

3.4   Type 2 *kan3* construction, and its information structure properties

The Type 2 *kan3* construction is less common in texts than Type 1, and significantly, was never once produced as a description of the video stimulus materials (despite *kan3* being used in describing all but one of the 64 stimulus videoclips). This appears to be due to an information structure difference between the constructions. In the Type 1 construction, the relevant participants are packaged into a single noun phrase either as an inherently plural noun or pronoun (including coerced plurals such as the multiple-parts reading of 'string' in Example (24), above), or a conjunct noun phrase. Irrespective of internal complexity of the subject argument, in the Type 1 *kan3* construction the members of this set of participants are expressed as a single information-structural unit. Members of the set therefore share a single discourse status (focused/presupposed, given/new, topical, etc). This type of information packaging is fitting for description of the stimulus videoclips, which run for just a few seconds, and which are devoid of any contextually framing trajectory or narrative action. Each clip is designed such that nothing in the situation, beyond any inherent asymmetry of respective roles in the behaviour taking place, encourages differential treatment of the participants with respect to discourse-level information structure. The reason the stimulus clips never elicited the Type 2 construction is because the Type 2 construction codes the participants in separate noun phrases and thereby construes the participants as distinct from each other in information status terms (e.g. with respect to reference-tracking).

In the text examples of the Type 2 *kan3* construction, half were in descriptions of events of interpersonal communication:

(47)   *phit2*   *kan3 jaang1 ñaj1   kap2   cêk2*
     disagree   COLL   way   big   with   Chinaman
     '(He) disagreed in a big way with the Chinaman.'

(48)   *haw2   kaø   vaw4   kan3   kap2   phòò1-baan4*
     1.FA   T.LNK   speak   COLL   with   father-village
     'I spoke with the village chief.'

Other examples of the Type 2 *kan3* construction involved *khùù2* 'to be like', expressing the notion of "like", "same as":

(49)   *còq2   ngaa2   saj1   khùù2   kan3   kap2   tum4-paa3-khaaw3*
     insert   tusk   put   be.like   COLL   with   "white fish basket trap"
     'Tusks are inserted (in this type of trap) like (in a) "white fish basket trap".'
     (From a video-recorded interview about fish traps.)

(50)   *suung3   khùù2   kan3   kap2   naaj2*
     tall   be.like   COLL   with   boss
     '(She's) tall like (her) boss.'

In each case, the subject (i.e. the noun phrase that appears before the verb) is a distinct, tracked participant in the discourse. Its reference is accessible, old, topical information relative to the other participant.

To summarise, there is one essential difference between the Type 1 and Type 2 *kan3* constructions: Type 1 refers to the multiple participants with a single, continuous noun phrase, while Type 2 splits them up. In this way, Type 1 treats the participants as a single unit for information structure purposes (e.g. focus, reference-tracking), while Type 2 treats them as distinct units. The need for this information-structural distinctness arises naturally in discourse, where a distinct narrative trajectory can impose differential values for otherwise equivalently involved entities.

4. Ways to express strict reciprocity in Lao

The previous section established that the *kan3* construction does not entail reciprocity. Its meaning is more general, covering a broader range of situations, yet compatible with reciprocal situations. Reciprocal situations are aptly described by the *kan3* construction because they fit the general description of being situations in which multiple participants map onto multiple roles (and mostly, when each argument maps onto the actor role of the predicate, though not necessarily onto an undergoer role). When it is necessary to be more specific and unequivocally depict the situation as strictly reciprocal there are also a couple of ways to do this in Lao. Both ways involve the combination of a *kan3* construction with another type of construction.

4.1 The *suu1 NP suu1 VP* construction

The following text example illustrates the *suu1 NP suu1 VP* construction, meaning 'Each and every NP VP-ed':

(51) *suu1   khon2   suu1   maw2*
     each   person   each   intoxicated
     'Each and every person was drunk.'

(52) *suu1   hùan2   suu1   mii2   nam4-saang5*
     each   house   each   have   water-well
     'Each and every house has a water well.'

This construction can combine with the Type 1 *kan3* construction to unequivocally express strictly reciprocal situations. Thus, a videoclip in which two actors hug each other (A hugs B and B hugs A; #7) can be described with a simple Type 1 *kan3* construction (*kòòt5 kan3* 'hug COLL'), and can also be combined with the *suu1 NP suu1 VP* construction:

(53) *suu1   khon2   suu1   kòòt5   kan3*
      each   person   each   hug   COLL
      'Each person hugged each other.'

The meaning of the combination of these constructions, illustrated in (53), is that for the set of actors, each acts upon the other in the way specified in the predicate. That is, each participant maps onto *both* the actor and undergoer roles of the predicate (regardless of whether the events are simultaneous or sequential). Thus, while examples like a videoclip in which A hugs B but B doesn't hug A may be described with a simple *kan3* expression (i.e. *kòòt5 kan3* "hug COLL"), the combined expression with *suu1* in (53) would be inapplicable. The *kan3*-plus-*suu1* construction cannot be used for any of the many less-than-strictly-reciprocal situations to which *kan3* alone may readily apply (see Sections 3.3.2–3.3.4, above).[7]

4.2   The reciprocal mirror construction: 'I V_α you, you V_α me'

In describing the reciprocal video stimulus clips, speakers would occasionally add to a simple *kan3* construction an explicit spelling-out of the reciprocal relation, using 1st and 2nd person pronouns (though where these do not necessarily refer to the speech-act participants). Here is a description of a videoclip (#3) in which A hits B and B hits A (sequentiality or simultaneity is irrelevant to the expression's applicability):

(54) *khacaw4   tii3   kan3 – khòòj5   tii3   caw4   caw4   tii3   khòòj5*
      3PL.P   hit   COLL   1SG.P   hit   2SG.P   2SG.P   hit   1SG.P
      'They hit each other – I hit you, you hit me.'

As noted already, some clips which are not strictly reciprocal can nevertheless be described using a *kan3* construction, as in the following description of an asymmetrical scene (#51) in which one actor is delousing the hair of another:

(55) *khacaw4   haa3   haw3   haj5   kan3*
      3PL.P   seek   louse   give   COLL
      'They're seeking lice for each other.'

---

7. To be clear, it is the *combination* of the *suu1* construction and the *kan3* construction that narrows the reading to strict reciprocity. It is not that the *suu1* construction is used when *kan3* has a more strictly reciprocal meaning, since I have argued that *kan3* is general with respect to symmetry of participation, and is compatible with stricter and looser senses of reciprocity.

If the mirror construction were added here, it could not describe the same event, but would only felicitously describe an event in which A delouses B's hair *and* B delouses A's hair. The next example describes a clip in which each acts upon the other, but it cannot describe a clip in which one participant is passive:

(56) *khacaw4   haa3   haw3   haj5   kan3*
       3PL.P   seek   louse   give   COLL
       khòòj5 haa3 haw3   haj5 caw4   caw4   haa3 haw3   haj5   khòòj5
       1SG.P   seek louse give 2SG.P 2SG.P seek louse give   1SG.P
       'They're seeking lice for each other – you seek lice for me, I seek lice for you.'

The mirror construction is a dedicated constructional strategy for expressing reciprocal event relations. Its meaning is not derived from simple composition of distinct parts. This is clear from the fact that the pronouns meaning 'I' and 'you' do not refer to speech event participants, as they normally would.

5.   Conclusion

The particle *kan3* is the standard tool for describing reciprocal situations in Lao, but it is not a dedicated marker of reciprocality. Events and situations which may be felicitously described by *kan3* feature a multiplicity of participants in some event, possibly by acting equally upon each other as in strictly reciprocal type events, possibly by doing the same action or being in the same state together (collectively or at the same time), or even just by co-participating in a situation in which the participants are equally committed or rightfully co-participating, despite a distinct asymmetry. These are not separate meanings of *kan3*, rather the meaning of *kan3* is general across these types of situation. When it is necessary to be more specific and encode a situation as strictly reciprocal, Lao speakers can do this by using further resources in combination with a *kan3* construction.

The semantic typology methodology adopted here has featured the complementary data collection tasks of (a) eliciting descriptions of a set of stimuli, a collection of token instantiations of distinct areas of the semantic space under consideration (in this case, situations depicted in short videoclips), and (b) drawing examples of the target forms from corpora of natural language use and discussing what they refer to, complemented by (c) focused consultation with native speakers, exploring the limits of extensional applicability of the descriptive types. It is a two-way street, from token referents to type descriptions *and* from type descriptions to token referents (onomasiology meets semasiology; Geeraerts 1997). The combined approach supplies both an anchor for comparative work and a route to language-specific facts. In the case of the description of reciprocal events in Lao, the set of videoclip stimuli helped to establish that the meaning of Lao *kan3* has a meaning more general than 'reciprocal', and subsequent consultation of spontaneous texts fleshed out the reach of the particle's broader, naturally occurring distribution. All components of the procedure played a role in discovery of the facts reported.

Abbreviations

The transliteration of Lao used here follows IPA standard except for the following: *e* = schwa; *ê* = high-mid front vowel; *è* = low front vowel; *ò* = low back vowel; *ù* = high back unrounded vowel; *ng* = velar nasal; *ñ* = palatal nasal; *q* = glottal stop. Lexical tone is indicated by syllable-final numeral, as follows: 1 = mid level (33); 2 = high rising (35); 3 = low rising (13); 4 = high falling (51); 5 = low falling (31); ø = unstressed/ atonal. Abbreviations are:

1/2/3	1st/2nd/3rd person	INDEF	indefinite pronoun
ABL	ablative	INTJ	interjection
ALL	allative	IRR	irrealis
AGT	agent	NEG	negation
B	bare	NEWS	new information
C.LNK	clause linker	NMLZ	nominaliser
COLL	collaborative	ONRCD	on record
COMP	complementiser	PERIPH	peripheral
COP	copula	RDP	reduplication
CT	class term	P	polite
DEM	demonstrative	PL	plural
DIR	directional particle	REL	relativiser
eBr	elder brother	SG	singular
FA	familiar	T.LNK	topic linker
FAC	factive particle	TOP	topic
FOC	focus	WEAK	weakening position

Acknowledgements

Thanks to Steve Levinson, Nick Evans, Asifa Majid, and an anonymous reviewer for helpful comments on a draft of this chapter. I gratefully acknowledge the research and fieldwork support of the Max Planck Institute for Psycholinguistics, Nijmegen.

References

Dalrymple, Mary, Kanazawa, Makoto, Kim, Yookyung, Mchombo, Sam & Peters, Stanley. 1998. Reciprocal expressions and the concept of reciprocity. *Linguistics And Philosophy* 21(2): 159–210.

Enfield, N. J. 1999. Lao as a national Language. *Laos: Culture and Society*, Grant Evans (ed.), 258–90. Chiang Mai: Silkworm Books.

Enfield, N. J. 2005. Areal linguistics and mainland Southeast Asia. *Annual Review of Anthropology* 34: 181–206.

Enfield, N. J. 2006. Lao body part terms. *Language Sciences* 28(2–3): 181–200.

Enfield, N. J. 2007. *A Grammar of Lao*. Berlin: Mouton.

Enfield, N. J., Majid, Asifa & van Staden, Miriam. 2006. Cross-linguistic categorization of the body: Introduction. *Language Sciences* 28(2–3): 137–147.

Evans, Nicholas, Levinson, Stephen C., Enfield, N. J., Gaby, Alice & Majid, Asifa. 2004. Reciprocal constructions and situation type. In *Field Manual*, Vol. 9, Asifa Majid (ed.), 25–30. Nijmegen: Max Planck Institute for Psycholinguistics.

Frajzyngier, Zygmunt & Curl, Traci S. 1999a. *Reflexives: Forms and Functions* [Typological Studies in Language 40]. Amsterdam: John Benjamins.

Frajzyngier, Zygmunt & Curl, Traci S. 1999b. *Reciprocals: Forms and Functions* [Typological Studies in Language 41]. Amsterdam: John Benjamins.

Geeraerts, Dirk. 1997. *Diachronic Prototype Semantics: A Contribution to Historical Lexicology*. Oxford: Clarendon Press.

Geniušienė, Emma. 1987. *The Typology of Reflexives*. Berlin: Mouton de Gruyter.

Hopper, Paul J. & Thompson, Sandra A. 1980. Transitivity in grammar and discourse. *Language* 56(2): 251–299.

Hudson, Richard A. 1992. So-called 'double objects' and grammatical relations. *Language* 68: 251–276.

Iwasaki, Shoichi & Horie, Inkapiromu P. 2005. *A Reference Grammar of Thai*. Cambridge: CUP.

Kemmer, Suzanne. 1993. *The Middle Voice* [Typological Studies in Language 23]. Amsterdam: John Benjamins.

Langendoen, D. Terence. 1978. The logic of reciprocity. *Linguistic Inquiry* 9(2): 177–197.

Narasimhan, Bhuvana, Eisenbeiss, Sonja & Brown, Penelope. 2007. *The Linguistic Encoding of Multiple-participant Events*. Special issue of *Linguistics* 45(3).

Newman, John. 1996. *Give: A Cognitive Linguistic Study*. Berlin: Mouton de Gruyter.

Newman, John. 1997. *The Linguistics of Giving* [Typological Studies in Language 36] Amsterdam: John Benjamins.

Wierzbicka, Anna. 2009. Reciprocity: An NSM approach to linguistic typology and social universals. *Studies in Language* 33(1): 103–174.

CHAPTER 8

Reciprocal constructions in Mah Meri

Nicole Kruspe

This paper provides an account of reciprocal constructions in Mah Meri, an Aslian (Austroasiatic) language spoken in peninsular Malaysia. A brief outline of the relevant grammatical points is provided before turning to examine the two constructions identified. The 'bare conjunct' construction centres on a small class of 'naturally reciprocal' verbs where the participants are encoded as a single NP. The typologically unique 'double distributive' construction is used with all other semantically appropriate verbs and encodes the two participants separately, but with the same form. It emerges that in Mah Meri reciprocal constructions are only used for situations of strict reciprocity where the event is symmetrical, constant, and saturated.

1.   Introduction

Mah Meri[1] belongs to the Aslian branch of Mon-Khmer (Austroasiatic), and is spoken in pockets along an 80 km stretch of the southwestern coast of Selangor, Malaysia. The total Mah Meri population is around 2,896. The language is related to Northern Aslian Jahai (Burenhult, this volume, 2005) and distantly related to Munda (Evans & Osada this volume).

Lexical materials, and texts were published in the colonial era (Skeat 1896, Skeat & Blagden 1906). There is no grammatical description (see Kruspe 2010, Kruspe in prep. a).

The variety described here is spoken at Kampung Orang Asli Bukit Bangkong, Sepang, a village of approximately 600 people. The language is highly endangered;

---

1.   Mah Meri has no written tradition. For the sake of consistency Mah Meri (*hmaʔ mbəri*) (person forest) is used here in the received orthography of the authorities. In ethnographic writing, the Mah Meri are also known as Besisi (Skeat 1896; Skeat & Blagden 1906), and Ma' Betisek (Wazir 1981) and Hma' Btsisi' (Nowak 1986) in particular with reference to communities on Carey Island. The community at Bukit Bangkong refer to themselves simply as *hmaʔ hɛ* (person 1PL) 'our people'. They do not identify with the term Besisi or any of its variants.

the Mah Meri, originally animistic swidden horticulturalists and shore-line foragers are increasingly assimilating into mainstream society, seeking employment in the rural and urban sectors and adopting mainstream religions.

1.1   Typological characteristics relevant to reciprocals

Mah Meri is one of four languages constituting the Southern branch of Aslian (Benjamin 1976; Diffloth 1975). The language bears little resemblance to immediately related languages and is well along the road to transforming into an isolating type, more typical of its distant Mon-Khmer relatives, e.g., Vietnamese or Minor Mlabri (Rischel 1995), and the languages of the wider mainland Southeast Asian *Sprachbund*. For example, unlike the related Aslian languages Semelai (Kruspe 2004) or Jahai (Burenhult 2005), Mah Meri has a small inventory of productive derivational processes (e.g., there are no productive valence increasing processes) and there is no morphosyntactic marking of core arguments, as shown in the intransitive and transitive clauses in Examples (1) and (2) respectively. The change in type has perhaps resulted from the influences of *koiné* varieties of colloquial Malay (Gil 2002: 241–2) which have long provided the means of inter-ethnic communication with the Mah Meri's neighbours – speakers of various Chinese dialects, the Austronesian languages Javanese, Malay and Temuan, and various Dravidian languages.

(1) ʔaʔạt   nimbol   bawaw   nɔŋ.
     1SG   come.from   sea   PST:PROX
     'I came from the sea just now.'[2]

(2) hŋkiʔ   tomboʔ   ləmɔl   ke.
     3   punch   man   that
     'He punched that man.'   (#5[3])

Constituent order at the clause level is not fixed and a range of possible permutations occurs. In the intransitive clause in Example (1) above ordering is SV, Example (3) below shows that VS is also possible.

(3) lɛp   do   haʔ   tạk.
     enter   water   LOC   ear
     'Water got into (my) ear.'

---

2. The orthographic system used in this paper is phonemic, differing from the standard IPA only with regard to /j/ and /ɟ/ which are represented here as /y/ and /j/ respectively.

3. The numerals marked with a hash refer to the videoclips from the Reciprocal stimuli task (Evans et al. 2004).

The 'basic' order in the transitive clause is AVO as in (2) above. This is the more frequent pattern in the responses to the Reciprocals stimuli task, however in texts VAO order is more common, as in (4). The verb form is unchanged, and there is no overt morphosyntactic coding of either of the post-verbal arguments. Given the right context the ordering in the last clause in (4) could also be interpreted as VOA 'I saw him'.

(4) *ləpas ke   nɔŋ,   ʔəʔət kədeʔ, kaye hŋkiʔ ʔəʔət.*
     after that PST:PROX 1SG   hide   see   3   1SG
     'After that, I hid, (lest) he see me.'

Zero representation of arguments is common as shown in Example (5).

(5) *bəlah,   kəbəs nancọk.*
     cut.open die   immediately
     '(They) cut (them) open, (and) (they) died straight away.'

Mah Meri exhibits a limited set of distinctions in its pronominal paradigm. There is no inclusive/exclusive distinction made for first person, and no number distinction in second and third person (Table 1).

Table 1. Mah Meri personal pronouns

Person	SG	PL
1	*ʔəʔət ~ ʔəʔəc*	*hɛ*
2	*hiʔ*	
3	*hŋkiʔ*	

Synthetic dual and trial pronouns are formed by compounding a pronoun and a numeral classifier, e.g., *papeʔ* (CLF:person:three) 'three persons' as in trial *hŋkiʔ papeʔ* (3 CLF:person:three) 'they three' and the dual form shown in (6).

(6) *ʔəʔət baba   ləpas.*
     1SG   CLF:person:two escape
     'We two (exclusive) escaped.'

There is a third person possessive pronoun *han* '3POSS', e.g., *yeʔ han* (elder.brother 3POSS) 'his/their elder brother'. As with Aslian languages in general, there are neither reflexive nor reciprocal pronouns.

2.   Reciprocals in Mah Meri

In Mah Meri there are two dedicated constructions for conveying reciprocity: the use of a 'naturally' reciprocal verb in a 'bare conjunct' construction, and the 'double distributive' construction. It is also possible to employ conjoined NPs in a construction (NP) *sama?* NP ((NP) same as NP), however this is not specifically a reciprocal construction, but rather implies that the two participants acted in unison. It is not discussed further here.

Both of these constructions are highly constrained, being restricted to situations of strict reciprocity, and only available to transitive verbs.

2.1   Bare conjunct construction

'Naturally' reciprocal verbs are a class of verbs which describe 'naturally' reciprocal events (see Kemmer 1993:102). Although Kemmer uses the term to label an event type, it is adopted here to label a subclass of verbs.

The 'naturally' reciprocal verbs describe a prototypical reciprocal situation where two animate participants engage in an act of reciprocity. The clause does not require any overt reciprocal marking to express a reciprocal situation. Like English verbs of this type, the Mah Meri verbs may also be used in a reciprocal construction, see Examples (20)–(21) Section 2.2 below.

'Naturally' reciprocal verbs form a small class of exclusively transitive verbs, including: *kahɔn* 'to kiss', *nɔhɔn* (*nɔ-hɔn* DTR-kiss) 'to kiss passionately', *sɔroh* 'to meet', *bwal* 'to converse' from Malay *bual* 'to converse', *salap̣* 'to greet' from Malay *salam* 'to greet', *pəloʔ* 'to hug' from Malay *peluk* 'to hug', *ŋaheʔ* 'to quarrel, argue, fight' from Malay *kelahir* 'to squabble', *tuka* (*barạk*) 'to exchange (things) ' from Malay *tukar (barang)* 'to exchange (things)'.

In a basic clause with two participants, the situation is a normal 'unidirectional' type where A acts upon B, V(A, B) as in Example (2) above. When a 'naturally' reciprocal verb is used in a 'unidirectional' construction, it expresses a converse relationship between the two participants where V(A,B) and V(B,A).

(7) *hŋkiʔ sɔroh   kawạt=han.*
     3   meet   friend=3POSS
     'He is meeting his friends.'   (#29)

Participant A may be construed as the initiator as in Example (7) above, but overall it expresses a symmetrical situation where B reciprocates A. Importantly, A may be substituted with B and vice versa without a change in the overall meaning.

This class of verbs allows for a specialised construction, the 'bare conjunct' construction (Evans 2008: 43) where the reciprocants are encoded as a single NP with plural reference (the 'conjunct'). The minimal number of reciprocants is two, but any number is permissible, see Examples (8)–(9) below.

(8) *hŋkiʔ ŋaheʔ.*
      3   argue
      'They are arguing (with each other).'   (#11)

(9) *hŋkiʔ papeʔ   pɔloʔ.*
      3   CLF:person:three hug
      'They three are hugging (each other).'   (#20)

The A in Example (8) may be interpreted as singular, in which case the clause means 'He is arguing (with someone)', where the O is not expressed.

The question of the valence of this construction type is problematic and remains unresolved. While the clause has a single argument, there is no evidence to conclude either way that, (a) the clause remains transitive, or (b) zero-conversion produces an intransitive clause. However in general, zero conversion is not a feature of Mah Meri grammar.

A reciprocal reading is not available to non-'naturally' reciprocal verbs used in this construction. Instead, the construction expresses joint or collective activity as shown in Example (10), a unidirectional clause with zero representation of the O, as shown by the acceptable free translation, and the speakers' unanimous rejection of a reciprocal interpretation for this clause.

(10) *hŋkiʔ papeʔ   halaw.*
       3   CLF:person:three chase
       'They three are chasing (them).'
       *'They three are chasing (each other).'   (#14)

The relations that exist between the reciprocants in the bare conjunct construction must be cancelled in order to obtain a strictly unidirectional reading, e.g., placing the adverbial *gǝna* 'alone' after the verb to show that only one participant was involved, as in Example (11). In the absence of the adverb, (11) would be understood as either a 'bare conjunct' reciprocal 'Those people are conversing', or 'That person is talking (to someone)' with the O unexpressed, similar to (8) above.

(11) *hmaʔ ke   bwal   gǝna.*
       person that converse   alone
       'That person is conversing alone / (with) (him)self.'   (#1)

The class of 'naturally' reciprocal verbs is not unique to Mah Meri; both Semelai (Kruspe 2004) and Ceq Wong (Kruspe in prep. b) also have classes of these verbs which behave in a similar manner, e.g., Ceq Wong *teʔ salam* (3DU greet) 'They two greet (each other)', see Section 3.

To summarise, the class of 'naturally' reciprocal verbs has a dedicated construction, the 'bare conjunct construction', to express the symmetric situation type where the reciprocants are encoded as a single NP. This interpretation is not available to other verbs. When non-'naturally' reciprocal verbs are used in this construction, the situation type described is asymmetrical and a symmetrical situation cannot be derived from it.

2.2   Double distributive construction

The 'double distributive' construction is used to describe strict reciprocal situations. This type is not mentioned in Evans' typology (Evans 2008). In this highly iconic construction type the reciprocants are encoded individually, but with an identical form *mole* 'DISTR', in a construction *mole* V *mole* (DISTR V DISTR) underlining the inverse relationship that holds between the participants.

> (12)   *mole*   *cawɛ*   *mole*
>   DISTR   slap.downward   DISTR
>   'They are slapping each other with a downward motion.'   (#5, modified)

The lexeme *mole* 'DISTR'[4], which can only take an animate entity as its referent, is provisionally classified as a member of the nominal class on distributional grounds (Kruspe in prep. a), and given the provisional gloss 'DISTR'. It is roughly translatable as 'each one' or 'each/the other'. *mole* 'DISTR' is also used in the 'single distributive' construction to express distributive situation types and is discussed briefly below.

The double distributive construction is used with any semantically appropriate transitive verb, and in the present task co-occurred with verbs such as *pɛt* 'to hit', *pəgək* 'to hold' (from Malay *pegang* 'to grasp'), *tampa* 'to slap' (from Malay *tampar* 'to slap'), *baci* (*sup/koy*) (go through (hair/head)) 'to go through (s.o's hair)', *talɔk ci* (seek louse) 'to seek lice/delouse', *jɔt* 'to give', *buruʔ* 'to chase' (from Malay *buru* 'to hunt'). Naturally reciprocal verbs also occur in this construction, (see Examples (20)–(21) in Section 3).

---

4.   Skeat and Blagden record *mulih* 'each (man)' (1906:586 E3). The etymology of *mole* is uncertain. It may be bimorphemic where *mo-* is a reduction of Mah Meri *muy* 'one', and *le* is cognate with an indefinite deictic as in Semai *ki-liːʔ* '(an)other', or Khmer *ʔəi-ləu* 'what/when' (G. Diffloth 2006 p.c.).

Unlike the basic transitive construction neither of the NPs representing the reciprocants in this construction type can have zero representation, and the constituent order of the clause is fixed.

The argument structure of the clause remains unclear. The clause appears to have AVO ordering, where the A and O are each represented separately by *mole*. However, in some instances there appear to be three constituents in a two participant clause, with NPs which are an integral part of the event, e.g., body part nouns as in (14)–(15), or the theme of exchange verbs as in (21) below, immediately following the verb [*mole* V N *mole*]. Although the intonation pattern might suggest that post-verbal *mole* is the possessor of this noun [N *mole*$_{POSS}$] and would thus form a single constituent, consultants rejected this interpretation. An alternative analysis is that the post-verbal noun is incorporated into the verbs which is consistent with the fixed constituent order, the inseparability of the verb and NP, and the inability to modify the NP. Noun incorporation is not a general feature of Mah Meri grammar and appears to be confined to this construction.

(13) *mole   suwe   sup   mole.*
      DISTR   look.through   hair   DISTR
      'They are looking through each other's hair.'   (#10, #45)

(14) *mole   pɛt   bahoʔ   mole.*
      DISTR   hit   shoulder   DISTR
      'They are hitting each other's shoulders.'   (#50)

The double distributive construction can be negated when the event is not perceived as fulfilling the requirements of reciprocity as in (16).

(15) *hmaʔ   ke,   hmba   hmba   cakạp.   mole   cakap   mole   ŋgɔt.*
      person   that   two   two   speak   DISTR   speak   DISTR   NEG
      'Those people, both are speaking. They are not speaking to each other.' (#11)

Before summarising the double distributive construction, we will briefly examine *mole* 'DISTR' as it is used in single distributive constructions.

2.2.1 *Distributor S/A construction*

In this construction the focus is on the distributor. *mole* 'DISTR' replaces the S or A of the clause. It expresses a unidirectional event repeated in succession by individual members of a group or set[5].

In the intransitive clause in Example (16) *mole* is associated with the S of the clause, and may occur in either pre- or post-verbal position.

---

5. Simultaneous collective activity is expressed by the post-verbal nominal *ganan* 'COLL'.

(16) *mole   yot   dah,   tiba?   mole   mbo!*
     DISTR return PRF   arrive DISTR EMPH
     'One went home, *another* one arrived!'

When *mole* 'DISTR' is associated with the A of the transitive clause, a distributive reading also obtains, however note that A has a fixed pre-verbal position as in (17).

(17) *mole   ca,   mole   ca;   tʰac   dəke   ɰa?.*
     DISTR eat   DISTR eat   polished.off like.that just
     'One eats, another one eats (and so on); (it's) polished off just like that.'

2.2.2 *Distributee O construction*

mole 'DISTR' occurs in a fixed post-verbal position in the transitive clause replacing the O, to express an action directed at a series of individuals, or 'distributees'.

(18) *hŋki?   tampa   mole.*
     3   slap   DISTR
     'He slapped each one.'

Post-verbal *mole* 'DISTR' typically co-occurs with verbs of giving or sharing, e.g., *jət* 'to give' or *hageh* 'to share out', where *mole* 'DISTR' is associated with the recipient of the activity: *jət* [NP]$_O$ [*ha?* NP]$_{REC}$ → *jət* [NP]$_O$ [*mole*]$_{REC}$ (recalling that *ha?* 'LOC' is a locative preposition).

(19) *hŋki?   jət   muntɛ̃t   mole.*
     3   give   little   DISTR
     'He gave a little (to) each one.'

In unidirectional clauses *mole* 'DISTR' may replace a single pre-or post-verbal NP to express the distributive. When used in both pre- and post-verbal slots of a basic transitive clause, the resulting construction describes a symmetrical relationship between the two participants. This is summarised in Table 2.

Table 2. Summary of *mole* constructions

Position of *mole*	Substituted constituent	Function
Pre-verbal	S/A	Distributive
Post-verbal	S/O	Distributive
Pre- and post-verbal	A and O	Reciprocal

In this section it has been shown that Mah Meri only encodes reciprocals of the strict symmetrical situation type, and only using inherently transitive verbs. 'Naturally' reciprocal verbs have a single argument construction, the bare conjunct construction, available only to this class of verbs. The double distributive construction, which encodes the reciprocants as separate arguments but identical in form, is used for all other semantically appropriate verbs.

3.   Categories encoded in the data clips

Four consultants provided linguistic descriptions to the videoclips. Data was collected in individual sessions, in 2005 at Kampung Orang Asli Bukit Bangkong, Malaysia. The four closely related participants whose ages ranged from mid twenties to early fifties, have all spent their entire lives in the village, are bilingual in the local *koiné* variety of Malay, and have either a passive or limited knowledge of the national language *Bahasa Melayu*.

The resulting responses exhibited considerable variation, sometimes reflecting personal preference in choice of expression, at other times reflecting the consultant's individual perception of the scenario presented in the videoclip.

Thirty-six of the clips failed to generate a reciprocal construction in the response. These ranged from strict sequential clips as in #4, #24, #36, #46, #58, strict simultaneous clips as in #12, #33, #41, #52–54, melee sequential clips as in #32, #43–44, asymmetrical (paired) sequential clips as depicted in #6, #16, #25–27, #31, #51, #59, #64, and asymmetrical simultaneous clips as in #60. Chained sequential clips such as #13–14 elicited a reciprocal construction for the sub-event, but not the macro event.

A further nine clips only generated a reciprocal response from one of the four consultants. This varied amongst consultants from clip to clip, so the variation is attributed to differences in individual perceptions of the scene. This group of clips included the asymmetrical sequential events in #1 and #23, the chained sequential situation types in #34, the chained simultaneous as in #56, the strong and melee sequential situations #3 and #21 respectively.

Uniform, or near uniform responses involving one of the reciprocal construction types were provided for nine of the clips (strict sequential #10, #38, and #62, strict simultaneous clips #20 and #45, pairwise simultaneous #29 and #49, pairwise sequential clip #30, and chain sequential clip #37.

There were a number of inherent problems in the videoclips relating specifically to the depiction of events. Two main problems were identified. In the first case, the action was not held constant across all components of an event preventing the elicitation of a unified description, and therefore failing to meet the required criteria for a reciprocal construction in Mah Meri. Lexical items in Mah Meri often exhibit detailed semantics, with no corresponding generic verb. An example of this was encountered with the "hitting" scenes, where each participant "hit" in a different manner, either with a different degree of force, or making contact with a different part of the body, and so forth. In response, consultants produced blow-by-blow multiclausal descriptions of the event (as with #42, where three pairs hit each other). Once this problem was identified, responses were prompted on the basis of the actions being constant, generally resulting in a double distributive construction as shown with '#5, modified' in Example (12) above.

Secondly, the complexity of the events often confounded the consultants. Factors included the poor depiction of the target event, as in scenes depicting 'chase', 'look', and 'follow'. Consultants failed to comprehend the target activity, prompting one speaker to remark that if the acting hadn't been so sloppy, he could have done the task properly!

The task provided some interesting observations which had not emerged from other methods of investigation. As reported in the section on reciprocal construction types (Section 2), intransitive and stative verbs do not enter into reciprocal constructions, thus clips which depicted physical proximity, e.g., 'next to' (#8 people sitting next to each other), or 'leaning' (#35 sticks leaning together) in the stimuli set caused consultants great difficulty in responding at all. It also emerged that some activities like non-volitional or unintentional physical contact (*laŋa* 'to bump' from Malay *langgar* 'to collide') are incompatible with reciprocity in Mah Meri.

Similar trends also emerged when the task was run with Semelai and Ceq Wong consultants, suggesting that while Mah Meri may be divergent in some areas, the conceptualisation and encoding of reciprocal situation types retains common features with related languages.

Turning back to the constructions described in Section 2, the following trends were noted in their use during the stimuli task.

3.1   Bare conjunct construction

Many of the situations depicted in the videoclips were of "naturally" reciprocal events, so constructions involving "naturally" reciprocal verbs featured strongly in response to the stimuli. They were used for strict situation types, both simultaneous and sequential. The choice of construction type, either encoding the reciprocants in separate NPs, or as a single NP (the bare conjunct construction) appeared to be dictated by the consultants' perception of the event. Only the latter are considered in this account.

"Naturally" reciprocal verbs were also frequently used in the double distributive construction, as in (20), to express less prototypical cases of reciprocity, such as chain sequential situations (#14, #28), adjacent simultaneous situations (#19, #61), and pairwise sequential situations like #30 (Example (21)), providing elaboration of the prototypically reciprocal sub-event. In the first clause the speaker uses a "naturally" reciprocal verb in the bare conjunct construction.

(20) *mole   salạp   mole.*
      DISTR   greet   DISTR
      'They are greeting each other.'   (#38, #49)

(21) *hmaʔ   ke   tuka   barạk;   mole   tuka   barạk   mole.*
      person that exchange thing   DISTR exchange thing   DISTR
      'Those people are exchanging things; each one exchanges something with the other.'

When the reciprocal relation was not depicted, consultants consistently employed constructions which cancelled the relation in order to encode the asymmetry of the situation. Amongst strategies employed were coding the non-reciprocating participant as an oblique with the locative preposition *haʔ* 'LOC' as in (22); using a multiclausal depiction in Example (23) where the second clause shows that reciprocity does not obtain, or preventing a plural interpretation of the subject NP and making explicit that only one participant is involved as in Example (11), Section 2.1.

(22) *hŋkiʔ   papeʔ   pəloʔ   haʔ   ləmɔl.*
      3   CLF:person:three hug   LOC   man
      'They three hug the guy.'   (#16)

(23) *kawạt   hŋkiʔ   pəloʔ   hŋkiʔ,   hŋkiʔ   hŋɔc   ɰaʔ.*
      friend   3   hug   3   3   be.still   just
      'His friends hug him, (but) he's just motionless.'   (#16)

The spontaneous responses in (22)–(23) were provided for clip #16 where a man does not reciprocate the hug but stands stiffly his hands by his side.[6] The structure in (22) would also be used if someone hugged an individual or entity incapable of reciprocating.

---

6. Clips #1 and #16 drew almost parallel constructions in Ceq Wong and Semelai which also have "naturally" reciprocal verbs. Compare the Ceq Wong clauses: *gən kaⁱbɔt* (3PL hug‹PROG›) 'They are hugging', and *gən kəbɔt kaʔ ʔuh* (3PL hug LOC 3SG) 'They hug him (but he doesn't reciprocate)' (Kruspe field notes 2006) for (#16), and the Mah Meri Example (22) above.

3.2   The double distributive construction

The double distributive construction was used in strict symmetrical reciprocal situations involving two or more participants where the activity was held constant (i.e., all sub-events were identical), and saturation obtained. This construction was not compatible with mêlée-type events where the action takes place back and forth to different people as depicted in #21 and #43–44.

The consultants maintain that the double distributive construction is equivalent to a multiclausal construction providing a blow-by-blow account of the component sub-events where V(A,B) and V(B,A), and the reciprocal construction is a more precise or more economical way of expressing it, especially in relation to simultaneous events. This appears to allow for it to be used to express the sub-events of chain situation types. In certain chain sequences, the construction is used to depict the strict reciprocal sub-events of the macro event e.g., as in #37, Example (24).

(24) *nam ʔɔrᾳk   tə‹la›jik,   mole   jᾳt   mole.*
      six   CLF:person be.standing‹DISTR› DISTR give DISTR
      'Six people are standing about (and) each one gives (something) to the other.'

In general, the double distributive construction used in this manner required clarification of the number of participants as in responses to #14, #20, #30 and #39, showing that it was not being used to describe the prototypical strict reciprocal situation. In (25) the consultant shows that each sub-event involves a different set of reciprocants.

(25) *mole   buruʔ   mole,   mole   buruʔ   mole.   samaʔ   ŋgɔt.*
      DISTR pursue DISTR DISTR pursue DISTR same.as NEG
      'They're pursuing each other, (and) they're pursuing each other. (But they are) not (all pursuing each other) together.'   (#14)

4.   Conclusion

Although I have amassed a substantial body of spontaneous Mah Meri data in a range of genres, reciprocal constructions were virtually nonexistent. Whilst I was aware of the "naturally" reciprocal verbs, I had not been able to elicit a reciprocal construction for other verbs (the results were always a calque on the Malay construction)[7] and I had only ever heard the double distributive construction uttered spontaneously on a couple of occasions.

---

7. Calques on Malay did not occur when running the stimuli.

The results that emerged from running this task revealed two patterns: (a) a set of verbs with "naturally" reciprocal implicature which are used in the bare conjunct construction, and (b) the double distributive construction, derived from a distributive semantic base. The former encodes the reciprocants as a single argument, the 'conjunct', whilst the latter encodes the reciprocants separately, but in an identical form, *mole* 'DISTR'. This double distributive construction also features a unique case of noun incorporation not found elsewhere in the language.

Mah Meri resembles other Aslian languages, such as Semelai (Kruspe 2004) and Semaq Beri (Kruspe field notes 2010), also Southern Aslian languages, and Jahai (see Burenhult this volume, 2005) and Ceq Wong (Kruspe in prep. b) both Northern Aslian languages, where reciprocal constructions are elusive, and different strategies are available rather than one clear reciprocal construction. The results of this task warrant further research into general verbal semantics and clausal syntax of Mah Meri especially with respect to valence and argument structure, and in particular with respect to the "naturally" reciprocal verbs.

Abbreviations

All abbreviations follow the standard Leipzig glossing rules with the following additions:

COLL	collective
DTR	detransitive
EMPH	emphatic
REC	recipient
~	in free variation with
‹ ›	morpheme boundary for infixes

Acknowledgements

Research into Mah Meri was funded by the MPI-EVA, Leipzig (1999–2001) and the Hans Rausing Endangered Languages Documentation Programme, SOAS, London (2005–2007). Funding was also provided by the Australian Research Council Discovery Grant 'Reciprocals Across Languages' (Project ID DP0343354). Special thanks go to the four consultants – Fauziah Zainal, Azman Zainal, Menuh Simbi and Zamzuri Zamzam – along with the wider community at Kampung Orang Asli, Bukit Bangkong. Thanks also go to Prof. Datuk Dr. Shamsul Amri Baharuddin, Universiti Kebangsaan Malaysia, and to the Prime Minister's Department, Putrajaya and the

JHEOA (Department of Aboriginal Affairs), Kuala Lumpur for providing permission to undertake research in Malaysia.

I would also like to thank Niclas Burenhult, Gerard Diffloth, Patience Epps, Nicholas Evans, Stephen Levinson, and participants at the Reciprocals workshops at the University of Melbourne, 2005, and at MPI, Nijmegen, 2006 for comments on earlier drafts.

References

Benjamin, Geoffrey. 1976. Austroasiatic subgroupings and prehistory in the Malay Peninsula. In *Austroasiatic Studies,* Part I, Philip N. Jenner, Laurence C. Thompson & Stanley Starosta (eds.), 37–128. Honolulu HI: University of Hawai'i Press.

Burenhult, Niclas. 2005. *A Grammar of Jahai.* Canberra: Pacific Linguistics.

Diffloth, Gérard. 1975. Les langues mon-khmer du Malaisie: Classification historique et innovations. *Asie du sud-est et monde insulinde* 6(4): 1–19

Evans, Nicholas. 2008. Reciprocal constructions: Towards a structural typology. In *Reciprocals and Reflexives: Cross-linguistic and Theoretical Explorations*, Ekkehard König & Volker Gast (eds), Berlin: Mouton de Gruyter.

Evans, Nicholas, Levinson, Stephen C., Enfield, N. J., Gaby, Alice & Majid, Asifa. 2004. Reciprocal constructions and situation type. In *Field Manual*, Vol. 9, Asifa Majid (ed.), 25–30. Nijmegen: Max Planck Institute for Psycholinguistics.

Gil, David. 2002. The prefixes *di-* and *N-* in Malay/Indonesian dialects. In *The History and Typology of Western Austronesian Voice System,* Fay Wouk & Malcolm Ross (eds), 241–83. Canberra: Pacific Linguistics, Research School of Pacific and Asian Studies, Australian National University.

Kemmer, Suzanne. 1993. *The Middle Voice* [Typological Studies in Language 23]. Amsterdam: John Benjamins.

Kruspe, Nicole. 2004. *A Grammar of Semelai.* Cambridge: CUP.

Kruspe, Nicole. 2010. *A Dictionary of Mah Meri, as spoken at Bukit Bangkong* [Oceanic Linguistics Special Publication 36]. Honolulu HI: University of Hawai'i Press.

Kruspe, Nicole. In preparation a. *A Grammar of Mah Meri.*

Kruspe, Nicole. In preparation b. *A Grammar of Ceq Wong.*

Nowak, Barbara. 1986. Marriage and Household: Btsisi' Responses to a Changing World. PhD dissertation, State University of New York at Buffalo.

Rischel, Jørgen. 1995. *Minor Mlabri. A Hunter-gatherer Language of Northern Indochina.* Copenhagen: Museum Tusculanum Press.

Skeat, Walter W. 1896. Besisi word list. *Selangor Journal* 5.

Skeat, Walter W. & Blagden, Charles O. 1906. *Pagan Races of the Malay Peninsula.* London: Macmillan Press.

Wazir, Jahan Karim. 1981. *Ma' Betisék concepts of living things.* London: Athlone Press [London School of Economics, Social Anthropology 54].

CHAPTER 9

The coding of reciprocal events in Jahai

Niclas Burenhult

Max Planck Institute for Psycholinguistics and Lund University

This work explores the linguistic encoding of reciprocal events in Jahai (Aslian, Mon-Khmer, Malay Peninsula) on the basis of linguistic descriptions of the video stimuli of the 'Reciprocal constructions and situation type' task (Evans et al. 2004). Reciprocal situation types find expression in three different constructions: distributive verb forms, reciprocal verb forms, and adjunct phrases containing a body part noun. Distributives represent the dominant strategy, reciprocal forms and body part adjuncts being highly restricted across event types and consultants. The distributive and reciprocal morphemes manifest intricate morphological processes typical of Aslian languages. The paper also addresses some analytical problems raised by the data, such as structural ambiguity and restrictions on derivation, as well as individual variation.

1. Introduction

Jahai is an Aslian (Mon-Khmer) language spoken in a mountainous area of northern Peninsular Malaysia and southernmost Thailand. Its speakers are traditionally mobile foragers and number approximately 1000. Like other Aslian languages, Jahai is characterised by a large set of vowel phonemes, elaborate pronominal and demonstrative systems, and rich and productive paradigms of verbal and nominal derivation employing intricate morphological processes of affixation (prefixes and infixes) and partial reduplication. The basic word order is SVO. Ellipsis of arguments is prevalent. Jahai shows evidence of substantial lexical borrowing from Malay, the Austronesian majority language of the peninsula. Jahai is fairly closely related to Mah Meri (see Kruspe this volume) and distantly to Mundari (see Evans & Osada this volume). For a comprehensive account of the language, readers are referred to Burenhult (2005).

This paper explores reciprocity in Jahai on the basis of linguistic descriptions of the video stimuli of the 'Reciprocal constructions and situation type' task (Evans et al. 2004). Reciprocals and reflexives have been elusive in previous grammatical work on Jahai (Burenhult 2005) due to difficulties in isolating specific categories dedicated to such situations. Thanks to the stimuli task, the present work provides interesting new insights into the coding of reciprocal events in Jahai.

2.   Constructions

Reciprocal situation types tend to find expression in three different constructions: distributive forms of verbs (Section 2.1), reciprocal forms of verbs (Section 2.2), and an adjunct phrase containing a body part noun (Section 2.3).

2.1   The distributive

The most common strategy is the distributive form of verbs. The Jahai distributive is a derivational *Aktionsart*[1] category expressed with a reduplicative verbal affix. Its general semantic function is to signal that the state or action designated by the verb is distributed over more than one person, object or location, typically but not necessarily more or less simultaneously. This may involve the salient distribution of the state or action over multiple, often spatially distinct, subjects, as in Examples (1)–(4).

(1)   *kritəh-kritəh   yapēh   biw-bəw*
      DP-car   1PL.EXCL   DISTR-big
      'Our cars are big.'

(2)   *heʔ   ya=jik-jok   haden*
      1PL.INCL   IRR=DISTR-to.move   tomorrow
      'We will move [in different directions] tomorrow.'

(3)   *wih   rih-rɔh   slay*
      3DU   DISTR-to.clear   swidden
      'They cleared [different parts of] a swidden.'

(4)   *gin   ʔik-ʔɛk   rotih*
      3PL   DISTR-to.give   cookie
      'They are giving cookies to each other.' or 'They are distributing cookies.'

It may also express that a singular subject is involved in an action, or characterised by a state, which is distributed over multiple locations or multiple participants acted upon, as in Examples (5)–(6):

---

1.   The term *Aktionsart* is used here unconventionally for categories of verbal derivation which encode non-temporal meanings expressing the inherent spatial or participant constituency of the state or event designated by the verb (Burenhult 2005: 93–94).

(5) *mnraʔ ʔoʔ **hit-hũt**   cn=jlmɔl*
     person 3SG DISTR-to.reveal.oneself SOURCE=mountain
     'The person revealed himself [here and there] on the mountain.'

(6) *ʔoʔ **ʔik-ʔɛk**   sɛc   ton*
     3SG DISTR-to.give   meat   DEM
     'He distributed the meat.'

The distributive affix is made up of a prespecified vowel *i* and underspecified consonants whose slots are filled by copies of the consonants of the verb base. There are two allomorphs, determined by the syllabic structure of the base. One allomorph, associated with monosyllabic CVC bases, is a syllable /CiC/ which is prefixed to the base. The two consonant slots of the affix are filled by copies of the onset and coda of the CVC base. The distributive forms in (1)–(6) above all exemplify this allomorph. The second allomorph, associated with sesquisyllabic[2] and disyllabic verb bases, is a sequence /iC/ which is infixed before the final CVC syllable of the base. The consonant slot of the affix is filled by a copy of the coda of this final CVC syllable. Examples include *s<ir>yɔr* (from *syɔr* 'to swim'), *k<iŋ>riŋ* (from *kriŋ* 'to be dry'), *b<il>dil* (from *bdil* 'to shoot'), and *t<im>nɛm* (from *tanɛm* 'to plant').[3] The last example is one of few involving a disyllabic base; consultants often reject distributive derivation of disyllabic verbs.

It is not clear whether distributive verb forms are associated with any reduction in valence, as any such patterns are obscured by the argument ellipsis typical of the language. Intransitive uses are the most common, but this applies to most non-derived verbs as well.

2.2   The reciprocal

A more rare strategy is a verb form tentatively called 'reciprocal' in Burenhult (2005: 104). Like the distributive, it is a derivational category expressed with a verbal affix. Previous elicited data suggest its semantic function is to signal joint action or reciprocity, but its paucity in natural language data has so far precluded further analysis. An example is given in (7); see further examples in Section 3.3.

---

2.   The term 'sesquisyllable', originally coined by Matisoff (1973: 86), literally means 'one-and-a-half syllable'. It refers to forms which are phonetically disyllabic, but in which the vowel of the first syllable is epenthetic and predictable (and therefore usually omitted in phonemic orthographies like the one employed here).

3.   Such processes of consonant copying are typical of Aslian morphology (see Kruspe 2004; Burenhult 2005). However, their employment for distributive derivation has so far only been documented in Jahai and its close relative Menriq (Burenhult, field notes).

(7) *gin   ma-mɛy*
     3PL RECP-to.delouse
     'They are delousing each other.'   (#6)

The reciprocal affix has two allomorphs, again determined by the syllabic structure of the base. One is associated with monosyllabic CVC bases and consists of a
syllable /Ca/, with an underspecified consonant onset and a prespecified vowel *a*.
This is prefixed to the base. The consonant slot of the affix is filled by a copy of the
onset of the CVC base, producing forms like *ca-cɔl* (from *cɔl* 'to tell'), *ga-gey* (from
gey 'to eat'), and *ʔa-ʔɛl* (from *ʔɛl* 'to look'). The second allomorph, associated with
sesquisyllabic verb bases, is simply the vowel *a*. This is infixed before the final CVC
syllable of the base. Examples include *s<a>mɛɲ* (from *smɛɲ* 'to ask'), *b<a>dil* (from
bdil 'to shoot'), and *ʔ<a>nay* (from *ʔnay* 'to bathe'). The reciprocal morpheme has
not been documented in connection with disyllabic verbs. Its pattern of consonant
copying is foreign to Jahai in that it associates its consonant left-to-right rather than
right-to-left, leading to the marked process of first copying the onset of the final
syllable rather than its coda (Burenhult 2005: 57–58). Given that a morphophone-
mically identical /a/ morpheme is the preferred marker of reciprocity in Semnam
(Burenhult, field notes) and Temiar (Benjamin in press), two neighbouring Central
Aslian languages, it could be suggested that it is borrowed.[4]

So far the reciprocal morpheme has been found to attach only to dynamic
verbs, not stative ones. Unlike the distributive, it seems to occur only on verbs
with non-singular subjects. Argument ellipsis again makes it difficult to determine its valence properties; most instances in the data are not accompanied by a
direct object. Both distributive and reciprocal forms feed further derivational affixation (e.g. progressive and iterative aspect, as well as nominalisation) but they
do not feed each other. Thus, structurally, the two are mutually exclusive.

2.3   Body part adjuncts

The third type of construction is a post-verbal adjunct phrase consisting of a body
part noun and a preceding word *samɛʔ*, e.g. *samɛʔ krɔʔ* 'back-to-back'. A typical
example is given in (8); see further examples in Section 3.4.

(8) *wih   ŋɔk   samɛʔ   krɔʔ*
     3DU to.sit SYMM back
     'They were seated back-to-back.'

---

4. In both Semnam and Temiar, reciprocal forms usually involve the combined marking of the
/a/ morpheme and a progressive prefix *b-* or *bə-*, as in Semnam *b-ha-hɔɔh* 'to follow each other'
(Burenhult, field notes) and Temiar *b-s<a>maaɲ* 'to ask each other' (Benjamin in press).

Body part nouns documented in this construction include *krɔʔ* 'back', *mit* 'eye', *cyas* 'hand', *dadaʔ* 'chest', and *hɛ̃ɲ* 'teeth'. The word *samɛʔ* is a borrowing of Malay *sama* 'same', 'like'. It is not clear from the structural behaviour of Jahai *samɛʔ* whether it is best interpreted here as an adverb, preposition or relational noun. However, it conveys a sense of symmetry and the body part adjuncts are readily translatable into English manner adverbials like *back-to-back, eye-to-eye* etc. with a clear meaning of bodily symmetry between two participants (see also Hurst & Nordlinger this volume).[5]

Body part adjuncts form a supplementary strategy which has been found to occur occasionally in some reciprocal situation types together with unmarked or distributive verb forms, but not with reciprocal verb forms.

3.   The clip data

This section describes the Jahai linguistic data from the 'Reciprocal constructions and situation type' video elicitation task. The data was collected in the field by the author in 2004, and consists of descriptions of the full set of videoclips by four consultants. The consultants are all male native speakers of Jahai aged between 20 and 40, and they reside in the resettlement village of Sungai Banun, in Hulu Perak district, Perak state, Peninsular Malaysia. All four are proficient in Malay, and they also have some knowledge of Temiar, a neighbouring Central Aslian language. The consultants were shown the videoclips and asked to describe the events taking place in them. They were also encouraged to provide alternative descriptions. In addition, the researcher frequently produced alternative descriptions for judgement of acceptability. Section 3.1 considers some factors which complicate the analysis. Sections 3.2–3.4 describe the behaviour and distribution of the three types of construction outlined in Section 2.

3.1   Problematic issues

The data raise some interesting problems which will be addressed first.

3.1.1   *Syllable structure and Malay loans*
As mentioned in Sections 2.1 and 2.2, reciprocal affixation has not previously been documented to occur with disyllabic verbs, and distributive affixation only marginally so. This is because the pre-final syllable of disyllabic words is already

---

5.   For an account of the various functions of *sama* in one Malay dialect, including its function as a marker of participant symmetry, see Gil (2004).

saturated with a phonemic vowel and sometimes a consonant coda. Infixation rules would require this V(C) sequence to be deleted before the distributive and reciprocal (and other) affixes can be added (it does happen, but only marginally, see below). Thus, the syllabic structure of words places formal (albeit not absolute) restrictions on distributive and reciprocal derivation. This is particularly apparent in borrowed Malay verbs which, unlike most indigenous Jahai verbs, are almost invariably di- or trisyllabic.

This restriction is very apparent in the data. In fact, disyllabicity in verbs (mostly of Malay origin) is the best predictor of non-derivation. The target events affected include bumping (Jahai *laɲah* 'to collide', from Malay *langgar*), chasing (Jahai *tampɛŋ*), hitting (Jahai *tampəh* 'to slap', from Malay *tampar*), and shaking hands (Jahai *jabat* 'to grasp hand', from Malay *jabat*). The structural rather than semantic nature of this restriction is further evidenced by alternative verb forms used occasionally by consultants for some of the target events in question. For example, one consultant differs from the others in that he did not use the borrowed underived verb *laɲah* to describe bumping events but *k<iŋ>niŋ*, which is the distributive form of an indigenous sesquisyllabic verb *kniŋ* 'to collide'. Another consultant differs from the others in that he did not use borrowed Malay terms for describing hand-shaking but instead *cip-cɛp*, the distributive form of an indigenous monosyllabic verb *cɛp* 'to grasp'.

There are occasional exceptions to the restriction. On one occasion one consultant spontaneously used the distributive form *h<it>mat*, from the disyllabic Malay loan *hamat* 'to chase' (Malay *hambat*). Another consultant used the distributive form *tiʔmoʔ*, from *tumoʔ* 'to hit' (Malay *tumbuk*). And two consultants accepted a distributive derivation *sl<it>mat* of the Malay loan *slamat* 'to greet' (Malay *selamat*).

To conclude, the relative paucity of derived verb forms (perhaps distributives in particular) in the Jahai descriptions of bumping, chasing, hitting, and hand-shaking events results from a structural restriction of the language, not a semantic one. Indeed, the evidence of the alternative indigenous verbs suggests that some of the events in question would have been described with distributive verb forms had the structural circumstances allowed it (that is, had the informants more consistently used indigenous rather than borrowed verbs).

3.1.2 *Distributive-imperfective homophony*
A problem of categorial ambiguity applies to some verb forms encountered in the data. Jahai imperfectives, a derivational category not dealt with here, are formed according to morphophonemic processes very similar to those of distributives (Burenhult 2005: 94–95). The consonants of the final syllable of the verb base are copied and affixed in the same way. The only difference is that the imperfective

morpheme does not contain a prespecified vowel *i*, but instead an underspecified epenthetic vowel usually realised as schwa [ə]. The auditory distinction between distributives and imperfectives is therefore normally straightforward.

However, Jahai realisation rules for epenthetic vowels in affixed forms require such vowels to be realised as [i] if preceding a copied palatal consonant. For example, the imperfective forms *gy-gey* (from *gey* 'to eat') and *l<c>wec* (from *lwec* 'to climb') are realised phonetically as [giygey] and [licwec] respectively. This means that, in all verbs ending with a palatal consonant (including the stop *c*, the nasal *ɲ*, the fricative *s*, and the approximant *y*), the distributive and imperfective forms will be homophonous (see Burenhult 2005: 36, 102). Unfortunately there is no apparent way of structurally disambiguating the two, e.g. through further affixation.[6]

This phonetically rooted problem of categorial ambiguity applies to two Jahai verbs which occur rather frequently in the clip data: *mɛy* 'to delouse' and *hay* 'to follow', both of which end with the palatal approximant. We therefore cannot be absolutely sure that their derived forms encountered in the data are distributives. However, imperfective verb forms are almost totally absent elsewhere in the data (where they would be easily identified), so it is probably safe to assume that spontaneous occurrences of the ambiguous forms are indeed distributives. But there is reason to be cautious about those elicited examples of distributive *mɛy* and *hay* where the researcher produced the forms for prompted speaker judgement. Consultants could easily interpret these as imperfectives, in which case they are likely to accept them as correct since, given the right pragmatic circumstances, imperfectives can be used to describe most situations.

3.1.3   *Individual variation*

Another complicating factor is individual variation in consultants' descriptions and judgements. Individual participants are of course likely to take different perspectives on the task and the stimuli. Further, the Northern Aslian speech communities display significant idiolectal variation, not least at the lexical level. This is due to the great social-geographical mobility of their speakers (Benjamin 1976: 76, 1985: 234–235; Burenhult 2005: 6–7). Dialectal variation between the four consultants may also be a factor: two of them originate from the area they now all inhabit, while the other two originate from fairly distant eastern and southern parts of the Jahai territory. In the clip data, individual variation has at least three manifestations:

---

6.   Other Aslian languages also display examples of reduplicative processes which result in morphological ambiguities. For examples in Semai (Central Aslian), see Diffloth (1972).

1. Choice of verb – Different consultants sometimes used different verbs to describe the same target event. As described in Section 3.1.1, this affects the data to the extent that some verbs are structurally available to derivation while others are not.

2. Presence or absence of reciprocal forms – While the spontaneous use of distributives was rather similar across consultants, their use of reciprocals shows considerable individual variation. One consultant neither produced nor accepted any reciprocal forms. Another consultant produced one description with the reciprocal form but did not accept it for other events. A third consultant produced three such descriptions but similarly did not accept it for other events. The fourth consultant spontaneously produced five, and accepted them for a large number of other events (see 3 below).

3. Degree of willingness to provide and accept alternative verb forms – Three consultants only sparingly produced alternative verb derivations in addition to their initial descriptions of clips, and they seldom accepted additional verb forms proposed by the researcher. The fourth consultant, however, fairly consistently produced spontaneous alternative verb forms, and was much more inclined to accept forms proposed by the researcher. The main consequence of this is that the reciprocal form of verbs is considerably more well-represented in the fourth consultant than in the others.

The individual variation in consultants' approach to the task calls for some caution in interpreting the data, especially in relation to judgements of acceptability. The subsequent analysis will therefore maintain a distinction between preferred descriptions (typically the spontaneous ones) and acceptable/accepted descriptions.

3.2   The distributive

Distributive forms pervade the data. Disregarding those target events which were described with disyllabic verbs (see Section 3.1.1), distributive derivation comes out as the overall dominant strategy. For two consultants it was the most common construction in spontaneous descriptions. For the other two, non-derived verbs were slightly more common. It was frequently given or accepted as a possible alternative to non-derived verbs. Considering that many of the events described with non-derived disyllabic verbs are also likely to have attracted distributive marking had syllabic structure permitted, it is probably fair to say that the distributive description is possible across most of the situation types. For example, spontaneous as well accepted distributives frequently describe the strong, chaining, adjacent, pairwise as well as melée situation types. Some examples:

(9) *gin ʔik-ʔɛk   bukuʔ*
     3PL DISTR-to.give book
     'They are giving each other a book.'   (#4)[7]

(10) *wih dwaʔ nn-kɛn   wih miy-mɛy   ciʔ*
     3DU two   UNIT-CLF 3DU DISTR-to.delouse louse
     'Those two are delousing.'   (#6)

(11) *wih t<ih>bɔh*
     3DU to.hit<DISTR>
     'They are hitting (each other).'   (#54)

However, there are some illuminating gaps. Distributive forms were dispreferred in favour of non-derived ones for asymmetrical situation types. This applies especially to the dual asymmetrical events, e.g. delousing (#51), following (#27), giving (#26), hitting (#17), and looking (#25), which completely lack distributive descriptions (spontaneous as well as accepted ones), as well as hugging (#23), where only one consultant provided a distributive description. The equivalent event of talking (#1) attracted the distributive from three consultants, but it is easy to see how this event can be interpreted as symmetrical rather than asymmetrical (the listener is nodding in reply to the speaker). Indeed, the consultant who gave a non-derived description picked this out and used a third person singular subject with the 'talk' verb (*ʔoʔ cɔl*). The others used a third person dual subject with the distributive form of the same verb (*wih cil-cɔl*).

The situation is less clear with non-dual asymmetrical events. Two events involving asymmetrical looking (#31, #60) do seem to associate primarily with non-derivation, but two events of hugging (#16, #47) elicited distributive description from at least one consultant. In this case it is likely that plural actors prompted this usage. One asymmetrical event of delousing (two participants pairwise delousing two others, #6, see Example (9)) elicited distributive descriptions from all consultants. In this case, distribution of the event across two asymmetrical pairs clearly overrides asymmetry as such. This shows that distributive marking does not associate with strong symmetry *per se* – its function is to signal distribution of the event over (in this case) multiple actors, be it a reciprocal event or not (see Sections 2.1 and 4).

Another gap is to be found in clip #24. This is a following event with strong but sequential dual symmetry, where one person follows another and then the roles reverse. No consultant provided a distributive description here. Apparently, the one shift of roles between two participants inhibits the distributive in this

---

7. Full descriptions of the videoclips can be found in the appendix to the introduction of this volume.

case. The act of following takes place only once for each participant, and there is not even partial temporal overlapping of the act over participants. The event is therefore primarily interpretable as distributed in time rather than over person or space.[8] A similar explanation is possible for clip #46, a looking event with similarly strong sequential dual symmetry with only one shift of roles, where non-derivation was the first choice for three consultants.

3.3   The reciprocal

As mentioned in Section 3.1.3, there were considerable individual differences in reciprocal usage. One consultant never used it, the other three produced it occasionally. One of the latter also accepted the reciprocal for quite a few additional scenes. We will begin by looking only at the spontaneous (first choice) instances of the reciprocal, of which there are nine. They occur with clips #4, #6, #10, #19, #21, #45, and #56. Of these, #10 and #45 each received spontaneous reciprocal description from two consultants, the others only from one.

These nine instances cannot be clearly linked to any of the parameters of cardinality, temporality or saturation (cf. Evans et al. 2004). They describe events involving two, three, four or six participants. Some of them describe sequential events, others simultaneous ones. While sporadically describing events of adjacency, asymmetry, chaining, and melée, there appears to be some connection to highly symmetrical (strongly saturated) situations (five instances).

However, the best predictor is which verb was used to describe the event. Six of the instances describe delousing events and all involve the reciprocal form *ma-mɛy*, from *mɛy* 'delouse'. Two consultants used the reciprocal *only* for delousing events, and for one of these consultants it was the main strategy of describing these events (in three out of the five delousing situations). The remaining three instances, produced by a single consultant, all describe situations of giving and involve the reciprocal form *ʔa-ʔɛk*, from *ʔɛk* 'to give'. One might speculate that this restriction of spontaneously produced reciprocals to situations of delousing and giving indicates that reciprocal usage is associated with benefactive reciprocity (in the sense of 'for each other'). Reciprocals do not occur spontaneously with the less benefactive situations of following, hugging, looking, and talking, for example. Note that the disyllabic verbs used to describe situations of bumping, chasing, hitting, and hand-shaking may conceal informative patterns here (see Section 3.1.1).

---

8.   Recall that the Jahai distributive does not encode temporal distribution (see Section 2.1). Such distribution is instead expressed with a separate aspectual morpheme, the iterative. Iterative forms of verbs feed distributive derivation, producing forms which encode spatial or participant distribution over multiple points in time (Burenhult 2005: 99–100, 102–104).

One consultant accepted prompted reciprocal descriptions of an additional 15 clips. Seven of these instances describe delousing and giving situations, six describe hugging situations, and two describe looking situations.

The scarcity of examples and the evident individual differences make it difficult to draw conclusions about the reciprocal. Clearly it is a strategy which was not available to every speaker, and, between speakers who used it, there were considerable differences in degree. Possibly the reciprocal morpheme is not fully productive for all speakers and dialects. This could explain its individual skewing in usage. A low degree of productivity could also explain its clear connection to certain verbs.

In almost all the situation types where a reciprocal description is possible (spontaneous as well as prompted), distributive description is also possible. So while the two constructions are mutually exclusive at the structural level (recall that the two types of derivation do not feed each other), they do overlap semantically.

Examples of reciprocal descriptions are given below.

(12) *wih* **ma**-*mɛy*   *kuy*
      3DU RECP-to.delouse head
      'They are delousing each other's head.'   (#10)

(13) *gin* *ʔa*-*ʔɛk*
      3PL RECP-to.give
      'They are giving each other [X].'   (#21)

3.4   The body part adjuncts

Body part adjuncts were used by all consultants but rarely and to varying degrees. The number of clips for which they were used by each consultant was eight, five, two, and one, respectively. The adjuncts occur as optional supplements to either non-derived verbs or distributive forms of verbs, never to reciprocal verb forms. In relation to the reciprocal parameters, body part adjuncts show a clear preference to associate with duality, simultaneity, and strong saturation. Event types with which they occur include bumping, hugging, leaning, looking, hand-shaking, and talking. Several body part nouns are represented, including *krɔʔ* 'back' (for leaning events #12 and #35 and bumping event #22), *dadaʔ* 'chest' (for bumping event #55 and hugging events #7 and #16), *cyas* 'hand' (for hand-shaking events #38, #49 and #63), *mit* 'eye' (for looking event #33), and *hɛ̃ɲ* 'teeth' (for talking event #11). Examples are given in (13) and (14).

(14) *wih* *ʔɛl*   *samɛʔ* *mit*
      3DU to.look SYMM eye
      'They are looking into each other's eyes.' (lit. 'They look eye-to-eye.')   (#33)

(15) *wih ʔim-ʔəm*   *samɛʔ dadaʔ*
      3DU DISTR-to.hug SYMM chest
      'They are hugging (chest-to-chest).'   (#7)

4.   Conclusion

The 'Reciprocal constructions and situation type' task provides new insights into the Jahai linguistic coding of reciprocal situations. It attracts three construction types: distributive verb forms, reciprocal verb forms, and body part adjunct phrases.

Distributive forms abound in the data, and it is clear that distributive marking has a close association with many reciprocal events. As has been shown, however, distributives are not restricted to such situations but signal any form of salient distribution of a state or event across participants and/or locations. The reciprocal events form a subcategory of such distributed situations, and reciprocity may simply be a contextual reading of the distributive in some situations (cf. Davies 2000; Filip & Carlson 2001; and Faller 2007). Importantly, events in which the action is not distributed over more than one actor tend not to attract distributive marking.

The failure of the task to systematically attract reciprocal forms of verbs calls for a re-assessment of the reciprocal morpheme. Its restricted distribution indicates that it is currently not a dedicated marker of general reciprocity. This may be connected to low productivity of the morpheme. Possibly it represents an archaic reciprocal still associated with some verbs but gradually replaced by distributive marking. Perhaps even more likely, it is a recent introduction which has not yet got a foothold in the language. Such interpretations find some support in the fact that distributive forms are acceptable for the same situations and that the two do not feed each other morphologically. Recall the foreign pattern of consonant copying of the reciprocal affix and its possible Central Aslian origin (see Section 2.2). It is noteworthy that the one consultant who was most inclined to use and accept the reciprocal originates in the southern part of the territory which borders the Temiar language area. Conversely, the one consultant who never used it originates in an eastern part of the territory which is not adjacent to the Temiar area.

Furthermore, we cannot yet exclude the possibility that reciprocal marking can associate with situations other than reciprocal ones. In such a case, the reciprocal could be similar to the distributive in not encoding reciprocity *per se* but being invasive to some extent of reciprocal situations. Only additional research can shed further light on this, and the association between this affix and the notion of 'benefit' may be worth pursuing.

The body part adjuncts, unlike distributives and reciprocals, pattern rather well within the prototypical reciprocal parameters of duality, simultaneity, and strong saturation. They seem dedicated to expressing marked bodily symmetry. Like reciprocal forms of verbs, however, they are infrequent in the data, forming a peripheral and optional strategy.

Orthography and abbreviations

The phonemic inventory of Jahai has 20 consonant phonemes and 16 vowel phonemes, 9 oral vowels contrasting with a slightly smaller set of nasal counterparts. The orthography employed in this paper is phonemically based and largely conforms to the IPA. It departs from the standard IPA and from the orthography used in Burenhult (2005) in that the voiced palatal stop is symbolised by *j* and the palatal approximant by *y*. The phonemic rendering of forms requires that epenthetic vowels are omitted, which frequently results in complex consonant clusters. For information on syllabification patterns and the phonetic realisation of epenthetic vowels in Jahai, see Burenhult (2005: 33–38).

The following abbreviations are used:

1	first person	INCL	inclusive
3	third person	IRR	irrealis
CLF	classifier	PL	plural
DU	dual	RECP	reciprocal
DEM	demonstrative	SG	singular
DISTR	distributive	SOURCE	source
DP	diverse plural	SYMM	symmetrical
EXCL	exclusive	UNIT	unitiser

Acknowledgements

I wish to express my acknowledgements to the Economic Planning Unit, Putrajaya; the Department of Aboriginal Affairs, Kuala Lumpur; the Department of Speech and Hearing Sciences, National University of Malaysia, Kuala Lumpur; and the Jahai community of Sungai Banun, Hulu Perak. I am grateful to Michael Dunn, Alice Gaby, Nick Evans, Nicole Kruspe, Asifa Majid, and Ruth Singer for their helpful input. This work was carried out with the support of the Max Planck Society, a European Community Marie Curie Fellowship, and a Volkswagen Foundation DoBeS grant. The author is solely responsible for information communicated and the European Commission is not responsible for any views or results expressed.

References

Benjamin, Geoffrey. 1976. Austroasiatic subgroupings and prehistory in the Malay Peninsula. In *Austroasiatic Studies,* Part I, Philip N. Jenner, Lawrence C. Thompson & Stanley Starosta (eds), 37–128. Honolulu HI: The University Press of Hawaii.

Benjamin, Geoffrey. 1985. In the long term: Three themes in Malayan cultural ecology. In *Cultural Values and Human Ecology in Southeast Asia*, Karl L. Hutterer, A. Terry Rambo & George Lovelace (eds), 219–278. Ann Arbor MI: Center for South and Southeast Asian Studies, University of Michigan.

Benjamin, Geoffrey. In press. Deponent verbs and middle-voice nouns in Temiar. Mon-Khmer Studies.

Burenhult, Niclas. 2005. *A Grammar of Jahai*. Canberra: Pacific Linguistics.

Davies, William D. 2000. Events in Madurese reciprocals. *Oceanic Linguistics* 39(1): 123–143.

Diffloth, Gérard. 1972. Ambiguïté morphologique en semai. In *Langues et techniques, nature et société*, 1: *Approche linguistique*, Jacqueline M. C. Thomas & Lucien Bernot (eds), 91–93. Paris: Klincksieck.

Evans, Nicholas, Levinson, Stephen C., Enfield, N. J., Gaby, Alice & Majid, Asifa. 2004. Reciprocal constructions and situation type. In *Field Manual,* Vol. 9, Asifa Majid (ed.), 25–30. Nijmegen: Max Planck Institute for Psycholinguistics.

Faller, Martina. 2007. Reciprocity without reciprocals: A case study of Cusco Quechua. In *Proceedings of SULA 3: The Semantics of Under-Represented Languages in the Americas*, Michael Becker & Andrew Mckenzie (eds), 35–52. Amherst MA: GLSA.

Filip, Hana & Carlson, Gregory N. 2001. Distributivity strengthens reciprocity; collectivity weakens it. *Linguistics and Philosophy* 24: 417–466.

Gil, David. 2004. Riau Indonesian *sama*: Explorations in macrofunctionality. In *Coordinating Constructions* [Typological Studies in Language 58], Martin Haspelmath (ed.), 371–424. Amsterdam: John Benjamins.

Kruspe, Nicole. 2004. *A Grammar of Semelai*. Cambridge: CUP.

Matisoff, James A. 1973. Tonogenesis in Southeast Asia. In *Consonant Types and Tone*, Larry M. Hyman (ed.), 71–95. Los Angeles CA: University of Southern California.

CHAPTER 10

Reciprocals in Yélî Dnye, the Papuan language of Rossel Island

Stephen C. Levinson

Max Planck Institute for Psycholinguistics and Radboud University Nijmegen

Yélî Dnye has two discernable dedicated constructions for reciprocal marking. The first and main construction uses a dedicated reciprocal pronoun *numo*, somewhat like English *each other*. We can recognise two subconstructions. First, the '*numo*-construction', where the reciprocal pronoun is a patient of the verb, and where the invariant pronoun *numo* is obligatorily incorporated, triggering intransitivisation (e.g. A-NPs become absolutive). This subconstruction has complexities, for example in the punctual aspect only, the verb is inflected like a transitive, but with enclitics mismatching actual person/number. In the second variant or subconstruction, the '*noko*-construction', the same reciprocal pronoun (sometimes case-marked as *noko*) occurs but now in oblique positions with either transitive or intransitive verbs. The reciprocal element here has some peculiar binding properties. Finally, the second independent construction is a dedicated periphrastic (or *woni...woni*) construction, glossing 'the one did X to the other, and the other did X to the one'. It is one of the rare *cross-serial dependencies* that show that natural languages cannot be modelled by context-free phrase-structure grammars. Finally, the usage of these two distinct constructions is discussed.

1.   Background

Rossel Island (154.14 E, 11.22 S), lying c. 450 km offshore to the east from New Guinea is the easternmost landfall of the Louiseade archipelago. It is a 'high' island, roughly equidistant between the Solomons and New Guinea, and belongs territorially to Papua New Guinea, although there is little commerce with the mainland. Four thousand souls live on Rossel, all primarily (or only) speakers of Yélî Dnye, a so-called 'Papuan' (i.e. non-Austronesian) language. The language is an isolate, with no known connections to any other extant language (various speculations by Wurm 1982 and others notwithstanding). Latest bioinformatic methods applied to structural properties still leave the matter unresolved (Dunn et al. 2005). Earlier materials are confined to a sketch grammar detailing phonology and verbal inflection and a 3000 word dictionary (Henderson 1995, Henderson & Henderson 1999), but a full grammar and many detailed papers have been prepared by the present author (see references in the bibliography).

The language has many unusual properties. It has a huge phoneme inventory (90 phonemes by traditional criteria), with some segments unique to phonetic science (Maddieson & Levinson, in prep.). Verb agreement is exhibited through (a) an immense arrays of proclitics (over 1000), which are portmanteau morphs expressing negation, tense, aspect, person/number of subject, deixis, evidentiality, associated motion, counterfactuality – potentially all in one monosyllable, (b) a somewhat smaller set of enclitics which code for both subject and object properties, transitivity, and all the tense/aspect/person/number features, but using a classification which cross-cuts the proclitic categories. One aspect of this cross-classification, relevant below, is the collapse of the 9 person/number categories of the proclitics into 2 categories for most of the enclitics:

Table 1. Monofocal/Polyfocal distinction as a cross-classification of the nine person-number distinctions in enclitics

	Singular	Dual	Plural
1st person			
2nd person	MONOFOCAL		
3rd person		POLYFOCAL	

Most verbs supplete, especially on tense, mood and aspect, but sometimes on other features (like person) too. Morphological derivation is however pretty restricted. Syntactic structure is flat; both the NP and the immediate verbal complex (verb and its clitics) are highly structured (although there is no VP), but the order of major phrases is free (although typically verb final).

Relevant for the present topic is the fact that the language is strongly ergative. Noun phrases are case-marked on an ergative-absolutive basis (the absolutive being unmarked), and there is a full range of other cases, including an experiencer case. All NPs, including pronominals, can be ergative case-marked, and only personal pronouns (not e.g. relative pronouns or Wh-pronouns) can in certain circumstances be subjects of transitive clauses and unmarked as ergative. While the agreement proclitics on the verb are 'nominative' in character, in the sense that they are indifferent to transitive vs. intransitive subjects, there are partially redundant enclitics on the verb that treat subjects of transitive vs. intransitive clauses entirely differently – they look more 'ergative' in character (see Levinson, in prep. a). Many aspects of the grammar – e.g. argument structure alternations, nominalisations, quantifier floating – hinge on the distinction between ergative vs. absolutive noun phrases, and in this sense the language can be said to be syntactically ergative (Levinson, in prep. a).

Another aspect of the grammar pertinent to the present topic is the formation of reflexives. Reflexives are formed with a special reflexive/emphatic nominal, *chóóchóó*. Where the reflexive pronoun is in patient role (i.e. can be interpreted as the object of a transitive verb), the verb is inflected like a normal transitive and the reflexive is in unmarked (presumably absolutive) case bound by an ergative subject.[1] Because the element *chóóchóó* is also an emphatic, there is a general ambiguity in interpretation of these structures:

(1) *Weta ngê chóóchóó dê*   *vy:a Ø*
     Weta ERG 3.self   3SBJ.ImmPast hit   MonofocalsBJ.3SG.OBJ.PROX.tense
     i.   'Weta killed himself.'
     ii. 'Weta himself killed (that animate entity).'

This construction contrasts with the corresponding reciprocal pronoun constructions (specifically the *numo* subconstruction, described below) in systematic ways. The subject of reflexives is in ergative case, while that of the corresponding reciprocal must be in the absolutive (unmarked) case; the reflexive pronoun has nine variants for person/number, while the reciprocal pronoun is indeclinable; the reflexive pronoun acts like a normal O-argument in absolutive case, while the reciprocal pronoun is obligatorily incorporated. (The one thing they have in common is that agreement marked in transitive enclitics is neutralised to 3rd person object regardless of actual subject person, but this is optional for reflexives and obligatory for reciprocals). Moreover, there does not seem to be any semantic overlap which would allow the same scene to be coded either reflexively or reciprocally.

2.   Reciprocal coding

Reciprocal events are coded using one of the constructions in the following table, each of which is explained in one of the following sections. As mentioned, the *numo* and *noko* subconstructions are treated as subtypes of a single major dedicated reciprocal construction, somewhat similar to *each other* constructions in

---

1.   The reflexive pronoun is never directly case-marked. It can occur in the subject position of e.g. nominal clauses, and it can occur coreferential with an explicit object – the complexities lie beyond the current essay (see Levinson, in prep. b).

English. However, the constructional details of the two variants are sufficiently specialised to warrant separate description below.

Table 2. The reciprocal constructions

	Reciprocal pronoun construction			Periphrastic construction
Properties	(i) *numo*-subconstruction	(ii) *noko*-subconstruction		*woni-woni* construction
		Oblique	possessive	
Case of subject	absolutive	ergative, absolutive	ergative, absolutive, experiencer	ergative
Transitive enclitics	+ in punctual aspect – in continuous aspect	+/–	+	+
Deviant agreement	+	–	–	–

2.1   The *numo* subconstruction – reciprocal pronouns as patients of transitive verbs

Let us concentrate first on the *numo* subconstruction. *Numo* is a dedicated reciprocal pronoun, unlike most other pronouns invariant for number/person (but presupposing dual or plural). In the eponymous construction, *numo* can be understood to be a kind of object of the verb, which must be a transitive root (all verbs are transitive or intransitive, and there are few valence-changing operations). However, *numo* in this construction is obligatorily incorporated and the subject of the verb must be in the absolutive case.[2] Compare the following normal transitive (a) with its corresponding reciprocal (b):

> (2) a. *Kakan ngê Nganapwe-Ø   wunê   kp:anê   Ø*
> Kakan ERG Nganapwe-ABS 3HAB.CI chasing MFS.3SG.OBJ.PROX.TR
> 'Kakan habitually chases Nganapwe.'

---

2. There is regular incorporation in this language, but as we will see this construction has irregular transitivity features. Example (a) shows a transitive sentence, and (b) its regular incorporated counterpart:

   (a) *tpile   nyimo*   *ghêêghêê té*
   thing 2SG/1dualImmFut.CI+Motion washing pl.OBJ.MF.SBJ.TR
   'We 2 are going to wash the dishes (things).'
   (b) *nyimo*   *tpile ghêêghêê mo*
   2SG/1dualImmFutCI+Motion thing washing dualSBJ.PROX.INTR
   'We two are going dishes-washing.'

b. *Kakan-* Ø *Nganapwe-* Ø *wunê* *numo*
Kakan-ABS Nganapwe-ABS 3HAB.CI each.other
kp:anê *mo*
chasing 3DualSBJ.PROX.INTR.CI
'Kakan and Nganapwe habitually chase each other.'

Note that in (b), in addition to the loss of ergative case on the subject, *numo* now appears between the verbal proclitic (here *wunê*) and verb (*kp:anê*) – a position only open to incorporated objects.[3] Note also that the verbal enclitic *mo* at the end of the sentence marks the clause as intransitive. As a second illustration, the following shows a pair of sentences in the habitual mood (without overt NPs, as is typical) – they differ only in that the second is reciprocal and behaves like an intransitive:

(3) a. *a* *vye* *dumo*
3HABContPROX hitting PFsubject3DualObjectHABContPROX.TR
'They-Dual$_1$ are habitually hitting them-Dual$_2$.'
(i.e. those two guys are habitually hitting those other two guys)

b. *a* *numo* *vyee* *nódó*
3HABContPROX each.other hitting HABContPROX.DualSubject.INTR
'They two are habitually hitting each other.'

Although the ergative marking of the subject is always lost and *numo is* always incorporated in this reciprocal subconstruction, the marking of transitivity in the enclitic is complex and variable, according to aspect. Just in case the aspect is continuous (in either the indicative or habitual mood),[4] the verbal enclitics are fully intransitive (in the sense that they are drawn from a distinct set restricted to intransitive verbs). In all other cases, the enclitics are transitive, despite the fact that the subject is in absolute case and the object (the reciprocal pronoun *numo*) is incorporated. But these transitive clitics are deviant in the sense that they have frozen person/number values – they always encode a Monofocal subject (that is, a singular *or* 1st person subject) and a 3rd person object – despite the fact that a reciprocal sentence must logically have a dual or plural subject and an object

---

3. There is evidence that *numo* is not an ordinary incorporated nominal, because another nominal can be incorporated with it as in:

ka *numo* *mbodo* *l:âmol:âmo* *mo*
Cert3SG.CI each.other head fixing DualSBJ.INTR
'They are fixing each other's heads (delousing).'

However, Yélî Dnye does allow phrasal incorporation in other cases too.

4. For language internal reasons, habitual must be interpreted as a mood and not an aspect.

matching in person/number. The following sentences, each constituted by just a verb and its clitics (+/− *numo*), illustrate these different values of the enclitics.

(4) a. **proclitic**   **verb**   **enclitic**
       nmî   *vy:a*   *té*
       1PL.ImmPast.Punct   hit.PROX   Monfocal.SBJ.3PL.OBJ.ImmPast
       'We3 hit them3 today.'

   b. *nmî*   *numo*   *vy:a*   *té*
       1PL.ImmPast.Punct   each.other   hit.PROX   Monfocal.SBJ.3PL.OBJ.ImmPast
       'We3 hit each other today.'

   c. *dê*   *vy:a*   *t:oo*
       3.ImmPast.Punct   hit.PROX   Polyfocal.SBJ.3PL.OBJ.ImmPast
       'They3 hit them3 today.'

   d. *dê*   *numo*   *vy:a*   *té*
       3.ImmPast.Punct   each.other   hit.PROX   Monfocal.SBJ.3PL.OBJ.ImmPast
       'They3 hit each other.'

Sentence (a) shows a normal transitive, with an enclitic encoding a monofocal (here 1st person plural) subject and a 3rd person plural object. Note how the reciprocal counterpart in (b) happens to have the same enclitic as (a), even though the object is now actually 1st person. If we take a normal transitive clause with a 3rd person subject as in (c), we see that it takes a different enclitic, *t:oo*, coding a Polyfocal subject (2nd or 3rd person dual or plural) and a 3rd plural object. The reciprocal counterpart of this sentence given in (d) has an enclitic marking Monofocal subject even though the subject is actually Polyfocal. In this way, whenever the intransitivised verb peculiarly takes transitive enclitics, it does so in a deviant manner.

Thus, although Yélî Dnye has productive incorporation with concomitant intransitivisation (A-role subject becomes absolutive, verb inflects as intransitive), this construction is special because (a) the incorporation is obligatory, (b) intransitivisation is partial in the punctual aspect, (c) verbal agreement is deviant in the punctual aspect.

To summarise, here is how to cook the *numo* subconstruction:

1. Encode the A-argument in absolutive case;
2. Add *numo* inside the verbal proclitics in the slot reserved for incorporated objects;
3. If the aspect is punctual, make the verbal enclitic inflect like a transitive – but use deviant agreement in the verbal enclitic, which must code *as if* for a 3rd person object and *as if* for a Monofocal Subject, as appropriate for the tense;

4. If the aspect is continuous, make the verb intransitive – use the dual or plural verbal enclitic appropriate to the actual subject number (dual, plural) and the tense.

Thus, only verbs in the continuous aspect trigger the full marking of intransitivity, as in Table 3:

Table 3. Special properties of the numo subconstruction

Aspect	Punctual	Continuous
A-NPs Absolutive	+	+
Incorporated *numo*	+	+
Intransitive inflection	–	+
Transitive inflection as if singular subject and 3rd person object	+	–

A point worth emphasing is that, although the fully intransitivising pattern in the continuous aspect is parallel to other cases of object incorporation, the punctual pattern is entirely unique to this construction: there are no other constructions in the language where an incorporated object triggers transitive enclitics, and no other cases where the agreement system is systematically shifted to the singular (Monofocal) for a necessarily plural subject. That makes it a unique subconstruction.

2.2 The *noko* subconstruction – reciprocals in oblique and possessive positions

Just like the English reciprocal *each other*, the Yélî Dnye reciprocal pronoun can occur outside the object slot of a transitive verb, in oblique adjuncts and possessive phrases (cf. *They bumped against each other, They like each other's friends*). In these other slots, the reciprocal pronoun is liberated from the special constructional correlates seen in the prior section.

I will call this variant of the reciprocal pronoun construction the *noko* subconstruction, after its typical exponent element, *noko*, which is the same reciprocal pronoun as in the prior section, but here in dative/allative form (it is possible to substitute this suppletive dative form with the non-suppletive *numo ka*, 'to each other'). Unlike the *numo* subconstruction, the *noko* subconstruction has no constraints on the subject, which can be ergative or absolutive, or on the verb which can be transitive or intransitive, or on the inflectional system which just agrees as usual (with a wrinkle mentioned below). *Noko* or its equivalents can occur wherever a pronoun can occur in oblique or possessive phrases (even, it seems, when not bound by a higher NP). Unlike almost every other pronoun in the language,[5] which has its own nine-cell paradigm (3 persons, singular/dual/plural), *noko/numo* is invariant.

Noko can thus occur in transitive clauses with ergative subjects, both implicit and explicit:

(5) a. *kópu   dê   noko   dnye   dy:ââ*
       message two to.each.other 1DualImmPastPI send
       'We2 sent 2 messages to each other (today).'

   b. *Pikwe Lamonga y:oo   Mutros noko   dê   y:ee*
       Pikwe Lamonga ERG+PL tobacco to.each.other 3ImmPastPI gave
       ngmê
       PFS_3SG.OBJ.PROX(tvPostN)
       'Pikwe and Lamonga gave the tobacco to each other.'

Note that in (b) a Polyfocal subject receives Polyfocal marking in the enclitic, unlike in the *numo* construction. Further, fully intransitive clauses with intransitive verbs can host *noko*:

(6) a. *yoo   noko   ka   kwopwepe té*
       people to.each.other Def3PRS.CI quarrel   PL.SBJ.PROX.INTR
       'The people (3+) are quarreling with each other.'

   b. *yoo   numo   ka (=noko) ka   dnyepéli   té*
       people each.other DAT   Def3PRS.CI squabbling PL.SBJ.PROX.INTR
       'The people are squabbling with each other.'

   c. *Teacher yoo   noko   ka   mbumu té*
       Teacher plural to.each.other Def3PRS.CI talking PL.SBJ.PROX.INTR
       'The teachers are talking to each other.'

Many oblique positions are introduced by postpositions, and *numo* (not *noko* in this case) can occur as the complement of many other postpositions, in both transitive and intransitive clauses.

(7) a. *Kakan Ghalyu y:oo   nté   numo u l:êê   dîy:o dê   ch:ee*
       Kakan Ghalyu ERG+PL food each its reason 3ImmPast cook
       ngmê
       PFS_3SG.OBJ.PROX(tvPostN)
       'Kakan and Ghalyu cooked for each other' (lit. 'on account of each other').

---

5. The relative pronoun *n:ii* and the interrogative pronoun *n:uu* seem to be the only other invariant personal pronouns. Most pronouns have, in addition to their 9-cell array, suppletive variants for various cases (as with *noko*).

b. *tp:ee dmââdî numo   'nuwo   ka   nt:uu   mo*
    boy   girl   each.other nose+LOC 3PRS.CI kiss/salivate SBJ.DU
    'The boy and girl are kissing each other on the nose.'
    lit. 'salivating/kissing on each other's noses' (putting noses together is
    sign of affection)

Just as in English, this subconstruction can extend to a fairly loose sense of reciprocity of a chaining sort (cf. the familiar 'sit next to/kiss/be on top of/be touching
each other'):

(8) a. *Yidika Mwolâ numo chedê ka   tóó mo*
         Yidika Mwolâ each   near   3PRS.CI sit DualCI.PROX.INTR
         'Yidika and Mwolâ are sitting next to each other.'
     b. *Yidika Mwolâ Pikuwa numo   chedê ka   pyede*
         Yidika Mwolâ Pikuwa each.other near   3PRS.CI sit.PL
         té
         DualCI.PROX.INTR
         'Yidika, Mwolâ and Pikuwa are sitting next to each other.'
     c. *pileti dyuu numo   u   pwopwo a   wee*
         plate   pile each.other 3sGPoss top   3PRS.CI stand.PL
         'The pile of plates are standing on top of each other.'
     d. *keeme kîgha numo   p:uu   ka   pyede*
         mango fruit each.other on/against 3PRS.CI sit.PL
         'The mangos are touching each other.'
     e. *tiini dyuu numo   u kwo kwo a   wee*
         tin   pile each.other inside inside 3PRS.CI stand.PL
         'The pile of tins are stacked inside one another.'

There is a distinct subtype of *noko*-construction which involves the reciprocal
pronoun acting as the possessor of a core, non-oblique argument:

(9) *kî   yéli   y:oo   numo   kóó dmi kêdê*
     these people ERG.PL each.other hand CL   CERT3sGImmPastPI
     mgîmî   ngmê
     grab   PolysBJ.F3SG.OBJ
     'These people grabbed each other's hands.'

Notice that this contrasts with possessives inside sometimes covert oblique phrases as in (7b), and that the fact that the head noun is not the reciprocal blocks
the incorporated *numo*-construction. *Numo* here is a mere possessive modifier
within an NP.

   Although the *noko*-construction as a whole seems familiar enough from
its English counterpart (a similar invariant reciprocal pronoun of fairly free

occurrence), there are a couple of interesting properties. First, the binding constraints are unclear. For example, the language has experiencer 'subjects' marked
with the dative or a special experiencer case. The reciprocal pronoun can be such
an experiencer 'subject' bound by a possessive in another NP as in (a) below, but
equally it can occur in such a possessive NP and be bound by such an experiencer
subject as in (b):

> (10)   a.   *yi   yi   dê   noko   a   kwo   mo*
>   their desire Dual to.each.other 3CI   standing 3DualSBJ.INTR
>   'They want/need each other.'
>   lit. 'Their two desires are standing to each other.'
>   b.   *Yidika Pikwe numo   nee   dê   u   yi   dê*
>   Yidika Pikwe each.other's canoe Dual 3SG.POSS   desire Dual
>   *y:e   a   kwo   mo*
>   DualEXP 3CI stand DualSBJ
>   'Yidika and Pikwe each want the other's canoes.'
>   lit. 'Yidika and Pikwe each other's two canoes its two desires are stand-
>   ing to them.'

In the (a) case the dual desires are the surface subject, as reflected in the verb inflection, and the dative-case reciprocal *noko* is the experiencer 'subject' bound by
the possessive *yi* in the Absolutive NP (surface subject). In the (b) sentence, the
possessive *numo* reciprocal is bound by the Experiencer-case-marked resumptive
pronoun (*y:e*) (referring to Yidika and Pikwe). So here the Experiencer subject
binds the possessive in the Absolutive NP. This suggests that the binding is determined by degrees of obliqueness or embeddedness:

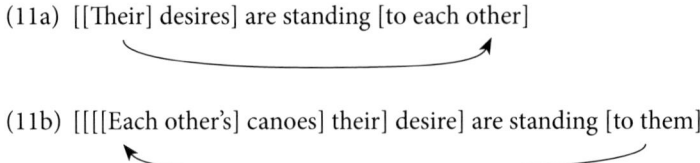

(11a) [[Their] desires] are standing [to each other]

(11b) [[[[Each other's] canoes] their] desire] are standing [to them]

In general, the binding properties of reciprocals and reflexives may help us to
understand the as yet unresolved questions about the syntactic status of Yélî Dnye
arguments. Note that in the first, *numo*-subconstruction, we saw that an ergative NP may not bind the incorporated absolutive O-NP (*numo*) – this is a constraint that holds across the board, although ergative NPs can bind reciprocal
pronouns in oblique or possessive constructions. On the other hand, absolutive
NPs can bind incorporated reciprocals or oblique ones. Now we have just seen
that possessors may bind, or may be bound by, experiencer NPs. Very tentatively
these facts jointly suggest a binder hierarchy like the following:

$$\text{Absolutive} > \text{Ergative} > \text{Oblique} > \left\{ \begin{array}{l} \text{Possessive} \\ \\ \text{Experiencer} \end{array} \right.$$

where each can only bind an NP lower or equal on the hierarchy. Such a hierarchy would be in line with the fact that Yélî Dnye shows other evidence of being a syntactically ergative language (Levinson, in prep. a). Note that a simpler solution, whereby the verbal clitics are actually the binders, won't work given the experiencer sentences where the inflections agree with the surface absolutive (e.g. in (8b) the experiencer binds the reciprocal, but the verb agrees with the absolutive 'desire' nominal).

Finally, a curious phenomenon occurs with verbs of giving, which supplete on person of recipient. We earlier noted that in the *numo*-subconstruction in the punctual aspect where transitive agreement clitics occur, these enclitics encode a singular (actually Monofocal) subject and 3rd person object regardless of actual person/number. Now in the one case where oblique reciprocals can control 'agreement', this too is 3rd person. This case is the verb 'to give' which has different forms for 'give to 3rd person' and 'give to 1st/2nd person', thus 'agreeing' with the person of the recipient, as in (a) below:

(12) a.   *u.kwo*   *ngmêda*   *y:oo,*   *a*   *ka*
           him.DAT   INDEF.1SGImmPast give.to.3rd(non-followed)   1SG   DAT
           ngmêda   *kê*
           INDEFetc.   give.to.1/2
           'I gave him one book, and he gave me/you one.'
      b.   *puku dmi*   *dê*   *noko*   *dnye*   *y:ee*
           book bundle   two   to.each.other   1Dual.ImmPast.PI   give.to3rdPerson
           dê
           MFS.3DualOBJ.PROX
           'We2 gave each other the two books.'

Now notice that in (b) despite the reciprocal 1st/2nd person reciprocation, *y:ee* 'give-to-3rd-person' is used instead of the expected *kê* 'give-to-1st/2nd-person'.[6] Thus there is something quite systematic in this 3rd person agreement with reciprocals.

---

6.   The verb forms *y:oo* and *y:ee* are the same verb – the forms alternate according to whether there is a non-zero enclitic (followed form) or a zero one (non-followed form).

2.3   The periphrastic *woni...woni* construction

There is a totally unrelated construction that can have a systematic reciprocal interpretation. This is based on the pronoun *woni*: a sequence *woni...woni* has the interpretation 'the one ... the other':

(13)   *kî   pini   wonî   ngê   woni   da   mgoko*
       That   man   the.one   ERG   the.other   3ImmPast+CLOSE   hug
       'The one man hugged the other.'

When however two such *woni...woni* sequences occur they have an unambiguously reciprocal interpretation:

(14)   *kî   pini   wonî   ngê   woni   da   mgoko,*
       That   man   the.one   ERG   the.other   3ImmPast+CLOSE   hug

       wonî   ngê   woni   myedê   mgoko
       the.other   ERG   the.one   also.3ImmPast   hug
       'The one man₁ hugged the other₂, and also the other₂ hugged the one₁,'
       (i.e. They hugged each other one by one)

The *woni...woni* construction seems to be used, in preference to the *numo* or *noko* constructions, for reciprocal actions which are not simultaneous, but which can rather be thought about as two separate events. The reciprocal use of the construction has some theoretical interest: it is one of the rare *cross-serial dependencies* that show that natural languages cannot be modelled by context-free phrase-structure grammars (of the GPSG type, see Partee, ter Meulen & Wall 1990: 503ff). For the *intensional* (as opposed to *extensional*) dependencies in question are of the following sort, where the second *woni ngê* (*woni* + ERG) depends for its interpretation on its contrast to the first *woni ngê* (the second 'the other' means 'not the prior one in the same syntactic role'), and similarly for the two instances of *woni* in the unmarked Absolutive case:

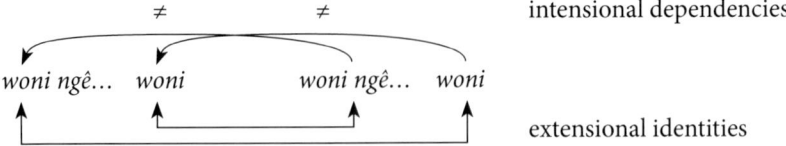

Summarising this section, we have three distinct constructions, each with their own complexities. Interest now turns to how they are actually deployed.

3. Semantics and usage patterns

3.1 General remarks

On the basis of systematic elicitation data (MPI Field Manual 2003, Reciprocals Questionnaire; Evans & Nordlinger 2004), a number of general observations can be made.

It was noted at the beginning of this paper that usage of reciprocals does not overlap with reflexives. Nor does it overlap with distributives, which are expressed with two different constructions – the first involving *ntémwintémwi* as in (a) entails that the predicate holds for each subject, and the second involving reduplicated numerals as in (b) entails 'n-at-a-time' (batch application of the predicate):

(15)   a.   *Mwonî Yidika Chris k:ii nt:uu   ntémwintémwi ka pîpî   ngmê*
            Mwonî Yidika Chris banana fruit each   3CI eating PFS3SG.OBJ
            'Mwonî, Yidika and Chris are each eating a banana.'7

      b.   *Mwonî ngê dee w:uu miyó miyó ka nt:ene*
            Mwonî ERG yam seeds two   two 3CI planting
            'Mwonî is planting yams two-by-two (two in each hole).'

Despite this lack of overlap with reflexivity or distributivity, usage of the reciprocal is quite broad. For example, where an event occurs in which each party does a distinct but complementary action (as in giving~receiving), the reciprocal is sometimes employed:

(16)   a.   *pini n:ii dê y:oo tuu noko   dê   y:ee*
            man who two ERG axe to.each.other 3ImmPast give.to3
            ngmê,   kê   vyîlo
            PFS3SG.OBJ that the.one
            'The two men who gave each other an axe, those two.'

      b.   *pini n:ii dê y:oo tuu dê   noko   dê   y:ee*
            man who two ERG axe Dual to.each.other 3ImmPast give.to3
            d:oo,   kê   vyîlo dê
            PFS3SG.OBJ that the.one Dual
            'The two men who gave each other the two axes, those ones.'

The (a) sentence is easily read as describing a single axe-giving event. Although the (b) sentence has the natural interpretation of an exchange of axes, it can also

---

7.   The ergative marker may be dispensed with in a list of three or more names.

be read as one man gave the other two axes! Other asymmetrical relations expressed with the reciprocal include chasing, following, etc.:

(17) a. *Yidika Lamonga numo   kuwó   ka   paa   mo*
          Yidika Lamonga each.other behind 3CI walk DualSBJ
          'Yidika and Lamonga are walking behind one another.'

      b. *mbêpê   pyu   yoo wunê   numo   kp:anê té*
          running doers PL 3HAB.PROX+CLOSE each.other chase PL.SBJ
          'The runners are chasing each other (round the track).'

There appear to be a number of non-obvious grammatical constraints that emerged from this elicitation. Speakers do not like more than one PP in a sentence, and so a spatial PP will block a reciprocal PP, and vice versa:

(18) a. *Yidika Mwolâ numo   chedê ka   tóó mo*
          Yidika Mwolâ each.other near 3PRS.CI sit DualCI.PROX.INTR
          'Yidika and Mwolâ are sitting next to each other.'

      b. *Yidika Mwolâ siit   mbêmê ka   tóó mo*
          Yidika Mwolâ bench on   3PRS.CI sit DualCI.PROX.INTR
          'Yidika and Mwolâ are sitting on a bench.'

Although verbs like 'speak to' and 'hug' usually presuppose reciprocal actions and so don't require overt reciprocals, they can happily occur with them. On the other hand, there are some verbs that do seem to require reciprocals, notably verbs of quarreling:

(19) a. *yoo **noko**   ka   dnyepéli té*
          PL   RECIP.DAT CERT3CI quarrel PL.INTR
          'They are arguing with each other.'

      b. *yoo **noko**   ka   kwopwepe té*
          PL   RECIP.DAT CERT3CI quarrel PL.INTR
          'They are quarrelling with each other.'

Other facts about usage emerge from the description of a systematic set of video-clips, to which we now turn.

3.2   Description of video stimuli

The clips in the MPI 2004 Field Manual (Evans et al. 2004) oppose such features of reciprocal actions as whether they are simultaneous vs. sequential, symmetrical vs. asymmetrical, chained vs. melee, etc. The distribution of the constructions

over the 64 clips (as used by just one consultant)[8] was examined to see if there
was a clear restriction of one construction to a restricted class of types of scene.
What one might expect is that the less prototypical or more marginal a reciprocal
scene is, the less likely it is to receive a core reciprocal construction. Twelve scenes
were described without using one of our three reciprocal constructions, i.e. in
non-reciprocal terms. Of these, 9 scenes had indeed no reciprocation of actions,
two were 'melee', and one involved sequential chaining without reciprocation. It
is clear in all these cases why a reciprocal was avoided: for example in one of the
melee scenes (scene 32) a single girl gives to each of three other girls a present and
gets one from each in exchange – this could not be coded accurately using one
reciprocal clause, it would take three.

Similarly, the periphrastic *woni...woni* construction might have been expected on Gricean grounds to pick up less stereotypical reciprocal scenarios. There
were just six usages – four of them were indeed on sequential or delayed reciprocal actions (scene 2, 22, 46, 58), but two (scenes 41, 54) were prototypical simultaneous acts of giving or slapping between two protagonists.[9]

At the other end of the constructional range, it might be expected that the
incorporated *numo* subconstruction might be more restricted in use than the
oblique *noko* subconstruction, since incorporation often carries stereotypical
connotations. There were fourteen uses of the *numo* subconstruction, and of
these five (scenes 23, 42, 44, 48, 64) lacked simultaneous pairwise reciprocation.
Of these five, three scenes involved hitting, of which two involved non-simultaneous reciprocation of action, while one scene (48) involved non-reciprocation
(a chain of actors, with the first hitting the second, the second the third, etc.).
Scene 23 involved one active hugging participant and one passive – this was described using the strong reciprocal by other consultants too. Scene 64 (one way
chasing) shows the potentially broad application of this construction.

---

8. Three other consultants' descriptions were collected and transcribed but not yet analysed.
The frequency of constructions used by the informant is shown in the following table (in 12
cases no reciprocal was used):

	Reciprocal pronoun construction			Periphrastic construction
	(i) *numo*-subconstruction	(ii) *noko*-subconstruction		*woni-woni* construction
		oblique	possessive	
Frequency	14	25	5	6

9. Perhaps the prediction was wrong – the *woni-woni* construction is both more verbose and
actually more precise than the others, which permit a greater latitude for asymmetrical event
description.

Finally, we turn to the *noko*-construction, using the reciprocal pronoun in oblique or possessive constructions. A prediction here was that the possessive version, as in 'They hit each other's shoulders', might code more prototypical reciprocal events compared to the oblique PP version as in 'they hit on each other's shoulders'. There were just six of this possessive type, and four of them involved all parties pairwise reciprocating (5, 38, 62, 63), while the other two involved simultaneous pairwise reciprocation, without cross-pair reciprocation (13, 49). The oblique *noko* construction appeared fairly unconstrained in use, being happily applied to sequential (non-immediate) reciprocation, and to four asymmetrical scenes (1, 17, 25, 39) without reciprocation (involving one way talking, hitting, looking and chasing).

The results suggest that the four options – avoiding a reciprocal, using the *woni-woni*, *numo* or *noko* constructions – are systematically deployed, with the *numo* and possessive *noko* constructions being most constrained to prototypical reciprocal scenes. Since there were overlaps in distribution (e.g. *woni-woni* being used to code prototypical scenes), it seems unlikely that the coding is entirely due to semantic factors. More likely is that where a range of constructions can be employed, the use of one rather than another is motivated by Gricean pragmatic factors. Suppose, for example, that the use of the *numo* construction I-implicates (Levinson 2000) stereotypical scenarios – then avoidance of use of this form may suggest that the scene is less than prototypically reciprocal. Similarly, use of a verbose form like the *woni-woni* construction may suggest (by M-implicature, Levinson 2000) that a more direct reciprocal would be misleading. A pragmatic analysis of the oppositions here would predict some of the flexibility of actual usage.

4. Conclusions

This language isolate clearly has two dedicated reciprocal constructions, one of which has well defined subtypes, which thus treat reciprocity as a distinct semantic domain, not overlapping with e.g. distributive or reflexive situations. The main construction, with its three subtypes, is built on an indeclinable reciprocal pronoun. Linguistically most interesting is the incorporated *numo*-subconstruction, which shows varied degrees of intransitivisation under aspect alternation. This construction, along with a possessive reciprocal construction, seems generally restricted to prototype reciprocal scenes, even though it semantically extends to one-way actions of giving, chasing and the like.

Abbreviations

(Where space permits, these abbreviations are spelt out for ease of reading.)

1, 2, 3	grammatical person	MFS	Monofocal Subject
ABS	absolutive case	OBJ	Object
CERT	'certain' (epistemic modifier)	pl/PL	Plural
		PF	Polyfocal (2nd, 3rd person dual or plural)
CI	continuous indicative		
CONT	continuous aspect	PFS	Polyfocal Subject
+CLOSE	deictic 'hither'	PI	punctual indicative
DAT	Dative	POSS	possessive
DU	Dual	PRS	present tense
ERG	ergative case	PROX	proximate tense (3 tenses closest to coding time)
EXP	experiencer case		
HAB	Habitual	PUNCT	punctual aspect
ImmFut	immediate future tense	SG	Singular
ImmPast	immediate past tense	SBJ	subject
INTR	intransitive	TR	transitive
MF	Monofocal (singular or 1st person)		

References

Dunn, Michael, Terrill, Angela, Reesink, Ger, Foley, Robert A. & Levinson, Stephen C. 2005. Structural phylogenetics and the reconstruction of ancient language history. *Science* 309(5743): 2072–2075.

Evans, Nicholas, Levinson, Stephen C., Enfield, N. J., Gaby, Alice & Majid, Asifa. 2004. Reciprocal constructions and situation type. In *Field Manual,* Vol. 9, Asifa Majid (ed.), 25–30. Nijmegen: Max Planck Institute for Psycholinguistics.

Evans, Nicholas & Nordlinger, Rachel. 2004. Reciprocals across languages. Field questionnaire materials. <http://www.linguistics.unimelb.edu.au/research/projects/reciprocals/papers/recips.questionnaire.sept.pdf>.

Henderson, James E. 1995. Phonology and grammar of Yele: Papua New Guinea. *Pacific Linguistics Series* B-112: 1–110.

Henderson, James E. & Henderson, Anne. 1999. *Nt:u k'opu dyuu u puku dmi* (Rossel-English Dictionary), 2nd edn. Ukarumpa: SIL Printroom.

Levinson, Stephen C. 2000. *Presumptive Meanings: The Theory of Generalized Conversational Implicature.* Cambridge MA: The MIT Press.

Levinson, Stephen C. In preparation a. Syntactic ergativity in Yélî Dnye, the Papuan language of Rossel Island, and its implications for typology. *Linguistic Typology.*

Levinson, Stephen C. In preparation b. *A Grammar of Yélî Dnye.*

Maddieson, Ian & Levinson, Stephen C. In preparation c. The phonetics of Yélî Dnye, the language of Rossel Island.

Partee, Barbara H., ter Meulen, Alice & Wall, Robert E. 1990. *Mathematical Methods in Linguistics.* Dordrecht: Kluwer.

Wurm, Stephen A. 1982. *Papuan Languages of Oceania.* Tübingen: Narr.

CHAPTER 11

Reciprocals in Rotokas

Stuart Robinson

Max Planck Institute for Psycholinguistics

This paper describes the syntax and semantics of reciprocity in the Central dialect of Rotokas, a non-Austronesian (Papuan) language spoken in Bougainville, Papua New Guinea. In Central Rotokas, there are three main reciprocal construction types, which differ formally according to where the reflexive/reciprocal marker (*ora-*) occurs in the clause: on the verb, on a pronominal argument or adjunct, or on a body part noun. The choice of construction type is determined by two considerations: the valency of the verb (i.e., whether it has one or two core arguments) and whether the reciprocal action is performed on a body part. The construction types are compatible with a wide range of the logical subtypes of reciprocity (strong, melee, chaining, etc.).

1.   Introduction

Rotokas is a non-Austronesian (Papuan) language with approximately 4000 speakers in central Bougainville, Papua New Guinea (Allen & Hurd 1963; Tryon 2005). There are four main dialects of the language: Central, Aita, Pipipaia, and Atsilima.[1] This paper describes reciprocals in the Central dialect of the language, which is the only dialect described in any detail (though see Robinson 2006a on the Aita dialect). For prior descriptions of Central Rotokas, see Firchow and Firchow (1969) on its phonology and Firchow (1971, 1977, 1987) on its morphosyntax.[2]

---

1.   The status of Atsilima as a dialect is questionable. Allen and Hurd (1963) describe it as a "sublanguage" of Rotokas while many Rotokas speakers describe it as a "mix" of Rotokas and Kereaka.

2.   Some primary materials (in Rotokas) are available from the Summer Institute of Linguistics: a vocabulary (Firchow 1973), a collection of stories (mostly folk tales) (Firchow and Akoitai 1974), and descriptions of Rotokas customs (Firchow 1974).

On the basis of lexicostatistics, Allen and Hurd (1963:20) claim that Rotokas belongs to the Kunua-Keriaka-Rotokas-Eivo stock and to the Rotokas-Eivo family.[3] Although the lexicostatistical methodology used by Allen and Hurd (1963) is questionable, comparative evidence from pronouns supports a similar high-level grouping (Ross 2001, 2005). Wurm (1972, 1975) claims that the Rotokas Family belongs to the East Papuan phylum, but this larger grouping is not widely accepted (Ross 2001, 2005; Dunn et al. 2002, 2005).

2. Grammatical background

Rotokas is an agglutinating language, in the sense that words may (and often do) consist of multiple morphemes, but these morphemes are reasonably invariant in form, making their identification straightforward.[4]

The basic constituent order of Rotokas can be characterised as AOV/SV (using Dixon (1994)'s primitives S, A; and O), as in (2a). O occupies a fixed position and cannot be freely elided; S and A (the subject) can be freely elided and can also occur postverbally when realised as a pronoun or full NP. Postverbal subjects give rise to OVA/VS constituent order, as in (1b) and (2b). The symbols α and β will be explained shortly.

(1) a. *(oira-to)*   *uusi-pa-ro-i*
         man-SG.M sleep-CONT-3SG.M$_\beta$-PRS$_\alpha$
         'The man is sleeping.'

     b. *uusi-pa-ro-i*   *(oira-to)*
         sleep-CONT-3SG.M$_\beta$-PRS$_\alpha$ man-SG.M
         'The man is sleeping.'

(2) a. *(oira-to)*   *koie upo-pa-re-voi*
         man-SG.M pig hit-CONT-3SG.M$_\beta$-PRS$_\beta$
         'The man is hitting the pig.'

     b. *koie upo-pa-re-voi*   *(oira-to)*
         pig hit-CONT-3SG.M$_\beta$-PRS$_\beta$ man-SG.M
         'The man is hitting the pig.'

---

3. Allen and Hurd (1963) define a stock as languages sharing 12% to 28% cognate vocabulary and a family as languages sharing 28% to 81% cognate vocabulary: Eivo (35% shared cognates), Keriaka (30%), and Kunua (22%).

4. The main exception to this generalisation are the tense/mood markers on the verb and the various pronominal paradigms (personal, relative, possessive, and demonstrative), where segmentation is not entirely straightforward.

Rotokas is head-marking (Nichols, 1986), with considerable verbal morphology, including markers for tense, aspect, mood as well as the person, number, and gender of the subject. Verbal inflection falls into two mutually exclusive classes, α and β: α agreement is illustrated in (1) and β inflection in (2). Most verb roots can take either α or β inflection but not both.[5] The full paradigm is provided in Table 1. (Note that the distinction between α and β subject agreement is neutralised for some configurations of person, number, and gender.)

Table 1. Verbal inflection for subject agreement

Person	Number	Gender	α	β
1st person	Singular		-ra	-a
	Dual		-ve	
	Plural Inclusive		-vio	
	Plural Exclusive		-io	
	Singular		-u	-ri
2nd person	Dual	M	-si	
		F	-ere	
	Plural		-ta	
	Singular	M	-ro	-re
		F	-o	-e
3rd person	Dual	M	-si	
		F	-ere	
	Plural		-a	-i

The situation with tense/mood marking is somewhat more complicated. While the suffixes in the realis mood paradigm are sensitive to the distinction between α and β verbal inflection, the suffixes in the irrealis mood paradigm are sensitive to the gender of the subject: one set occurs on verbs with neuter subjects while the other occurs on verbs with non-neuter subjects (i.e., masculine or feminine). The various tense categories and their markers are provided in Table 2.[6]

---

5. A minority of verb roots are labile, in the sense that they can show either α or β inflection. These labile roots are of both the S = A and S = O type; they show α inflection when they function as intransitive verbs and β inflection when they function as transitive verbs.

6. Additional segmentation of the tense/mood markers is possible, but raises analytical issues that go beyond the scope of this paper and are irrelevant to the issue of reciprocity.

Table 2. Tense/mood categories

		Verb class	
Realis		α	β
Past	Remote	-epa	-va
	Distant	-erao	-vorao
	Near	-era	-vora
	Immediate	-e	-vo
Present		-ei	-voi

		Gender of subject	
Irrealis		N	M/F
Simple		-pe	-ve
Habitual		-peira	-veira
Future	Near	-pere	-vere
	Distant	-perea	-verea

The contrast between α and β verbal inflection can be seen clearly in (3). Although both verbs have a third person masculine singular subject and occur in the remote past tense, they take distinct forms of subject agreement and tense marking: *kopii* 'die' shows α inflection whereas *gau* 'cry' shows β inflection.

(3) a.   *Siovisa tavara-to   uva araoko-to   kopii-ro-epa*
          Siovisa twin-SG.M   and brother-SG.M   die-3SG.M$_α$-RP$_α$
          'Siovisa is a twin and his brother died.'

     b.   *uva kakae-to   gau-pa-re-va   ovusia gau ovi*
          and child-SG.M   cry-CONT-3SG.M$_β$-RP$_β$ while cry CLF
          kovekove-pa-epa   kakate   siovara Iare
          fall.RDP-CONT-RP$_α$ bamboo   inside   POST
          'The boy cried as the tears fell down inside of the bamboo.'

Although the verbs in (3) are both intransitive, they take distinct forms of verbal inflection because Rotokas has a system of split intransitivity: transitive verbs consistently show β agreement while intransitive verbs are split between the two patterns of agreement. Some intransitive verbs show α inflection, such as *uusi* 'sleep' in (1) or *kopii* 'die' in (3a), while others show β inflection, such as *gau* 'cry' in (3b). Semi-transitive verbs taking a second, oblique argument are likewise split between α-agreement (e.g., *reasi* 'dislike') and β-agreement (e.g., *tara* 'look for').

Rotokas has a number of valency-changing derivations which affect the form of verbal inflection taken by a derived stem: morphological causative, reflexive/

reciprocal, and object incorporation.[7] These valency-changing derivations have a systematic effect on verbal inflection: valency-increasing derivations show β inflection while valency-decreasing derivations show α inflection. For example, the intransitive verb root *uriri* 'be scared' normally shows α inflection, as in (4a), but the transitive verb stem derived from it with the morphological causative suffix *-pie* shows β inflection, as in (4b).

(4) a. *uva* *rei-vira* *uriri-ra-epa*
  so large-ADV be_scared-1SG$_α$-RP$_α$
  'I was really scared.' (Firchow and Akoitai 1974:35)

  b. *rera* *uriri-pie-re-va* *aue=ia* *kuuvu-va rakoru*
  PRO.3SG.M be-scared-CAUS-3SG.M$_β$-RP$_β$ DUM=ABL fake-F.SG snake
  'He frightened him with a pretend snake.' (Reader, Ahu)

Noun incorporation is a valency-decreasing derivation recognisable primarily on the basis of a change in verbal inflection (and by the absence of nominal morphology on the patient/theme). For example, the verb root *tara* 'look for/seek' normally shows β agreement and selects oblique marking in the form of the enclitic *=re* for its patient/theme, as in (5a), but when the patient/theme is incorporated, it shows α agreement and the patient/theme is a bare noun root, as in (5b).

(5) a. *opita* *isi=re* *tara-pa-a-voi*
  coconut CLF=ALL seek-CONT-1.SG$_β$-PRS$_β$
  'I'm looking for a coconut.'

  b. *opita* *tara-pa-ra-i*
  coconut seek-CONT-1.SG$_α$-PRS$_α$
  'I'm looking for coconuts.'

3. Reciprocals in Rotokas

3.1 General information

There is no clear formal distinction between reflexives and reciprocals in Rotokas, both of which are marked by the prefix *ora-*. This appears to be true for all construction types that will be discussed in Section 3.2, and is illustrated in (6), where

---

7. There is another derivation, marked by *-viro* or *-piro*, which probably best qualifies as a resultative construction (although it is labelled "completive" by Firchow (1987) on the basis of its sensitivity to telicity). It might also be analysed as a valency-changing derivation, but its status as such is less certain.

the the prefix marker *ora-* derives a reflexive/reciprocal verb from the causative verb stem *kopiipie* 'kill' (in turn derived from *kopii* 'die'). It is ambiguous between a reflexive and a reciprocal reading, as the free translation suggests.

(6)   *ora-kopii-pie-pa-a-i*
      RR-die-CAUS-CONT-3PL$_\alpha$-PRS$_\alpha$
      'They are killing themselves. / They are killing each other.'

Although context typically disambiguates, the only explicit means of distinguishing between the two possible readings is through use of the adverb *oisiaropavira* (for some speakers, simply *oisiopavira*), which means 'mutually' or 'reciprocally'.[8]

(7)   *oisiaropavira   ora-kopii-pie-pa-a-i*
      reciprocally   RR-die-CAUS-CONT-3PL$_\alpha$-PRS$_\alpha$
      'They are killing each other.' (≠ 'They are killing themselves.')

3.2   Reciprocal construction types

There are three main reciprocal constructions in Rotokas, which differ formally according to where the prefix *ora-* occurs in the clause. These construction types are listed below in Table 3.

Table 3. Reciprocal construction types in Rotokas

Construction type	Description
1 Verb marking	*ora-* occurs on the verb
2 Pronoun marking	*ora-* occurs on a pronoun
3 Noun marking	*ora-* occurs on a body part noun

3.2.1 *Construction 1: Verb marking*
The primary reciprocal construction in Rotokas involves the prefixation of *ora-* to the verb stem. By way of illustration, compare the transitive sentence in (8a) with the reciprocal sentence in (8b).

(8)   a.   *oira kakae-ro   riako   kakae-ro   tario-pa-i-voi*
          male child-CLF.PL   female   child-CLF.PL   chase-CONT-3PL$_\beta$-PRS$_\beta$
          'The little boys are chasing the little girls.'

---

8. The reciprocal adverb *oisiaropavira* is morphologically complex and consists of three morphemes: the base form *oisio* or *oisiaro*, which appears to be related to the complementizer for comparisons of manner; the derivational suffix *-pa*; and the adverbial suffix *-vira*.

   b.   *oira   kakae-ro   ora riako   kakae-ro   ora-tario-pa-a-i*
      male child-CLF.PL and female child-CLF.PL RR-chase-CONT-3PL$_α$-PRS$_α$
      'The little boys and little girls are chasing each other.'

This reciprocal construction is intransitive (with α subject agreement) and can be characterised as a valency-decreasing derivation to the extent that it is available for all transitive verbs (i.e., verbs with two core arguments, a subject and a direct object). Ditransitive verbs are also capable of entering into the verb marking reciprocal construction. For example, the ditransitive verb *vate* 'give' appears in an indirect object construction (where the theme is O) in (9a) and as a verb marking reciprocal in (9b). Note that the theme in (9b) has been demoted to an oblique argument. This can be understood as a consequence of the fact that the reciprocal construction is intransitive and permits only one core argument, forcing any others into the periphery.

(9)   a.   *rotokasi-pa-irara aita-pa-irara=pa aasi-ara   vate-pa-i-voi*
        Rotokas-DV-PL   Aita-DV-PL=BEN betel_nut-PL.N give-CONT-3PL$_β$-PRS$_β$
        'The Rotokas men are giving betel nut to the Aita men.'
     b.   *rotokasi-pa-irara   ora aita-pa-irara*
        Rotokas-DV-PL   and Aita-DV-PL
        ora-vatevate-pa-a-i   aasi-ara=ia
        RR-give.RDP-CONT-3PL$_α$-PRS$_α$ betel_nut-PL.N=ABL
        'The Rotokas and Aita men are giving each other betel nut.'

There are also a number of intransitive verb stems that appear in the verb-marking reciprocal construction. These verbs can occur with or without the reflexive/reciprocal prefix *ora-* with no obvious change in meaning or valency. For example, the verb stem *tupetupereo* 'line up' can occur with or without *ora-*, as in (10) (where parentheses indicate optionality).

(10) *balusi-ara   (ora)-tupetupereo-pa-i rere-pa-oro*
      plane-PL.N   RR-line_up-CONT-PRS$_α$ descend-CONT-DEP.SIM
      rasi-toa=ia
      ground-3.SG.M=ABL
      'The planes lined up as they landed.'

A number of verb stems of this type are listed below in Table 4.[9] Note that most of these verbs would qualify as "natural reciprocals" to the extent that they are "symmetric predicates" (Haiman 1985; Langendoen 1992).

---

9. This list is not exhaustive and simply lists those verbs stems that were readily identifiable in an electronic lexical database of Rotokas under development by the author.

Table 4. Intransitive verb roots capable of taking *ora*

Verb stem	Gloss	Notes
paupau	'race'	fossilized reduplication?
pekapekara	'line up'	reduplication of *pekara* 'miss narrowly'
riga	'spread, scattered'	
sekari	'shake hands'	Tok Pisin loan
takato	'argue'	
topogo	'be reckless/careless'	
(tupe)tupereo	'in pairs'	optional reduplication
uugaa	'kiss'	
virato	'segregated, refined'	

3.2.2 *Construction 2: Pronoun marking*

There is a second reciprocal construction type that differs from the first to the extent that the prefix *ora-* occurs on an oblique pronoun (rather than on the verb itself) which agrees with the subject in terms of person, number, and gender. For example, in (11a), reciprocal marking does not occur on the verb root *reasi* 'dislike', and prefixation of *ora-* to this verb root is in fact ungrammatical, as shown in (11b). Instead, reciprocal marking in (11a) occurs on the third person plural masculine pronoun.

(11) a. *oira kakae-ro   ora riako kakae-ro   ora-voea=pa*
          male child-CLF.PL and female child-CLF.PL RR-PRO.3PL.M=BEN
          reasi-pa-a-i
          dislike-CONT-3PL$_\alpha$-PRS$_\alpha$
          'Little boys and little girls dislike each other.'

  b. **oira kakae-ro   ora riako kakae-ro   ora-reasi-pa-a-i*
          male child-CLF.PL and female child-CLF.PL RR-dislike-CONT-3PL$_\alpha$-PRS$_\alpha$
          'Little boys and little girls dislike each other.'

The difference between verb and pronoun marking reciprocal constructions has to do with the distinction between core and oblique argument (Andrews 1985). The prefix *ora-* occurs on the verb when a verb has two core arguments (transitive); it appears on a pronoun when a verb takes only an oblique argument (semi-transitive).

The noun-marking construction is found with verbs taking an oblique argument regardless of what type of oblique marking they select or whether they normally show α or β agreement. For example, the verb *tara* 'look for' takes an oblique argument but shows β agreement, as illustrated in (12a), and reciprocals based on it are also pronoun marking, as can be seen in (12b).

(12) a. *oira-ra riako-ra=re   tara-pa-i-voi*
      man-PL woman-PL=ALL seek-CONT-3PL$_\beta$-PRS$_\beta$
      'The men are looking for the women.'

    b. *oirara ora riakora   ora-voea=re   tara-pa-a-i*
      men   and women RR-PRO.3PL.M=ALL seek-CONT-3PL$_\alpha$-PRS$_\alpha$
      'The men and women are looking for each other.'

Finally, the reciprocal/reflexive prefix *ora-* also occurs with pronouns that function as adjuncts (as opposed to core or oblique arguments), as in (13) and (14).

(13) *vo-vokiaro   uva oisoa   ora-vaiterei   ruvara=ia uusi-pa-si*
     SPEC-night and always RR-PRO.2DU.M near=ABL sleep-CONT-3DU.M
     'During the night they slept next to each other.'

(14) *oira-ra   sopore-re-va   Reitae ora-rera   iava*
     man-PL.HUM enlighten-3SG.M-RP$_\beta$ Reitae RR-PRO.3SG.M POST
     'Reitae enlightened the people about himself.'

3.2.3 *Construction 3: Noun marking*

Whereas the difference between the two previous constructions has to do with the
distinction between core and oblique arguments, this third reciprocal construction type is semantically restricted. It is only found when a reflexive or reciprocal
action is performed on body parts, as illustrated in (15) and (16).

(15) *Riku rere   tou=ia   ora-kokoto-aro   roo-ro-e*
     Riku bamboo CLF=ABL RR-cut.RDP-POSS cut-3SG.M-IP$_\alpha$
     'Riku cut his own leg on small bamboo shoots.'   (Robinson 2006b)

(16) *uva ora-vavae-aro   tapatapa-pa-si-ei*
     and RR-hand-POSS   hit.RDP-CONT-3DU.M-PRS$_\alpha$
     'And (they) hit each other's hands.'   (#54, TT)

Given the presence of the prefix *ora-* and the use of α inflection with verb roots
that normally function transitively and show β inflection, it may appear that this
construction involves the incorporation of a body part term into the verbal complex, akin to noun incorporation (see (5)). There are, however, good reasons to
reject such an analysis. First, in the canonical incorporating construction, incorporated objects occur as bare stems, without postpositional enclitics or syntactic modifiers such as classifiers, as shown by the contrast between the transitive
clause (17a) and its counterpart with object incorporation in (17b).

(17) a. *ragai   opita   isi-re   tara-pa-a-voi*
      PRO.1SG coconut CLF=ALL seek-CONT-1SG$_\beta$-PRS$_\beta$
      'I'm looking for a coconut.'

b. *ragai* *opita* *tara-pa-ra-i*
 PRO.1SG coconut seek-CONT-1SG$_\alpha$-PRS$_\alpha$
 'I'm looking for coconuts.'

However, in the noun marking reciprocal constructions, body part nouns take possessive morphology (*-aro*), as already seen in (15).

 Second, whereas noun-incorporated bare clauses consistently show α-inflection, the noun-marking reflexive/reciprocal construction is variable, as it is capable of occurring with either α or β agreement, as in (18).

(18) *ora-kagave-aro* *upo-pa-si-ei/voi*
  RR-face-POSS hit-CONT-3DU.M-PRS$_\alpha$/PRS$_\beta$
  'They are hitting each other in the face.'

There is no readily identifiable difference associated with the choice of α or β inflection in this construction and it is therefore assumed to be free variation. The form of inflection is not dependent on the particular verb root, however, since the same variability is found with verb roots other than *upo* 'hit', such as *kotukotu* 'bite (reduplicated)', which occurs with the prefix *ora-* in (19) but nevertheless shows β agreement.

(19) *Rupeiri ora-reuri-aro* *kotukotu-pa-re-voi*
  Rupeiri RR-tooth-POSS bite.RDP-CONT$_\beta$ 3SG.M-PRS$_\beta$
  'Rupeiri is biting his own teeth.'

Third, whereas adverbials cannot intervene between an incorporated noun and the incorporating verb stem, no such constraint operates with body-part reciprocals. For example, the adverb *ikauvira* 'quickly' cannot intervene between the verb and its incorporated object in (20).

(20) a. *ikau-vira* *opita-kuri-pa-ra-i*
   run-ADV coconut-scrape-CONT-1SG$_\alpha$-PRS$_\alpha$
   'I am quickly coconut-scraping.'
  b. **opita ikau-vira kuri-pa-ra-i*
   coconut run-ADV scrape-CONT-1SG$_\alpha$-PRS$_\alpha$
   'I am quickly coconut-scraping.'

However, the adverb *oisiaropavira* 'reciprocally' is free to occur between the verb and the body part marked by *ora-*, as illustrated in (21).

(21) a. *oisiaropavira ora-kagave-aro* *upo-pa-si-ei*
   reciprocally RR-face-POSS hit-CONT-3DU.M-PRS$_\alpha$
   'They are hitting each other in the face.'

b. *ora-kagave-aro oisiaropavira upo-pa-si-ei*
RR-face-POSS   reciprocally   hit-CONT-3DU.M-PRS$_\alpha$
'They are hitting each other in the face.'

4. Semantics of reciprocity

In order to study the extensional semantics of reciprocal constructions in Roto-kas, the video stimuli of Evans et al. (2004) were run with five native speakers of Rotokas. The spontaneous verbal descriptions of these clips provided by consul-tants were recorded by the author and transcribed by a native-speaker of Rotokas, Timothy Taureviri, and then translated into Tok Pisin by another native speaker, Sera Mon. Both native speaker consultants are adults (roughly in their fifties) who were raised in a Rotokas-speaking environment and now reside in the Wakunai District. Both consultants are bilingual in Tok Pisin (Neo-Melanesian) and Rotokas.

The transcribed description of the stimuli were coded for construction type and analysis of the coded transcriptions reveals that the three construction types fill out a wide range of semantic subtypes of reciprocity. Nearly all of the clips were described using a reciprocal construction by at least one subject and most by more than one. The main exception to this rule were the asymmetrical situations, which were not typically described using a reflexive/reciprocal construction.

In general, reciprocal scenes that were not described using a reflexive/recri-procal construction were either misinterpreted by consultants or depicted situa-tions that were described as a series of events rather than as a single macro-event. This chunking into subevents is more commonly the case when the element of simultaneity is lacking. For example, a video clip where a number of individuals give one another books is described as two separate events using two conjoined clauses in (22).

(22) a. *riako-va   vuku-a   vate-e-voi   oira-toarei osa*
woman-SG.F book-SG.N give-3SG.F$_\beta$-PRS$_\beta$ man-DU.M as
pau-pa-si-ei
sit-CONT-3DU.M-PRS$_\alpha$
'A woman gives the book to two men as the two of them sit down.'

b. *uva va=ia   ora-vatevate-a-i*
and PRO.3SG.N=LOC RR-give.RDP-3PL-PRS$_\alpha$
'and they give it to each other.'   (#4, AM)

Situations of strong reciprocity – where each individual involved in the situation plays the role of actor as well as undergoer in every possible pairing – are proto-typical reciprocal situations and not surprisingly are generally described using reciprocal constructions, as illustrated in (23).

(23) *ora-tautau-aro   tapatapa-pa-a-i*   *viovoko-irara vairei*
      RR-cheeks-POSS hit.RDP-CONT-3PL$_\alpha$-PRS$_\alpha$ teenager-PL PRO.3F.DU
      riako-rirei   ari vaiterei   oira-toarei
      woman-F.DU   but PRO.2M.DU   man-M.DU
      'The teenagers – two males and two female – are hitting each other's cheeks.'
                                                          (#5, LR)

Other less prototypical reciprocal situation types were also described using the
reflexive/reciprocal construction. For example, melee situations – which differ
from strong reciprocity by not insisting on reciprocity across every possible pairing of individuals – are also generally described using reciprocal constructions,
as illustrated in (24).

(24) *o-resiura-vu   tore-pa-a-i*   *uva ora-rau-a-i*
      SPEC-four-ALT stand-CONT-3PL$_\alpha$-PRS$_\alpha$ and RR-hug-3PL$_\alpha$-PRS$_\alpha$
      ora-agesi-pie-oro
      RR-laugh-CAUS-DEP.SIM
      'These four are standing and hugging each other laughing.'   (#52, AM)

Situations of adjacency – where there is strong reciprocity between immediately
adjacent pairs of individuals, but not across the entire set of indivduals – are also
described using the reflexive/reciprocal construction, as illustrated by (25), which
depicts a situation where each individual in a line hits, and is hit by, the person
immediately next to him or her.

(25) *oea-vu   tore-pa-a-i*
      PRO.3PL.M-ALT stand-CONT-3PL$_\alpha$-PRS$_\alpha$
      uva ora-tapatapa-a-i   voea   rutu
      and RR-hit.RDP-3PL$_\alpha$-PRS$_\alpha$ PRO.3PL.M very
      'They are standing and they are all hitting each other.'   (#57, AM)

Pairwise situations – where strong reciprocity obtains within but not across pairings of indivduals – are also described using the reflexive/reciprocal construction,
as in (26), which describes two pairs of individuals where the roles played by the
members of the pair are not exchanged (one is actor and the other undergoer, but
not vice-versa).

(26) *o-resiura-vu   ora-voea=ia   iru   tara-pa-a-i*
      SPEC-four-ALT RR-PRO.3PL.M=ABL louse seek-CONT-3PL$_\alpha$-PRS$_\alpha$
      'The four of them are looking for lice on each other.'   (#6, LR)

The reciprocal construction is also used in situations that are weakly reciprocal in the sense that actors do not also play the role of undergoers in any of the potential pairings of individuals. These are chaining situations, which can be described using the reflexive/reciprocal construction, as illustrated in (27).

(27) *airoa-vu*   *vairoo*   *airoa*   *ora-iru-pa-a-i*
  PRO.3PL.F-ALT   DEM.PROX.PL.F   PRO.3PL.F   RR-delouse-CONT-3PL$_\alpha$-PRS$_\alpha$
  'These other women are delousing one another.'   (#56, SM)

A further example of a chaining situation described using the reflexive/reciprocal construction is provided in (28), where the verb root meaning 'to line up in pairs' is used to describe the situation of a large number of men dying one after another from illness.

(28) *ora-tupereo-iraoirao-pa-a-i*   *oira-ra*
  RR-follow-INTENS.RDP-CONT-3PL$_\alpha$-PRS$_\alpha$ men-PL.M
  kopii-pa-oro   *vao=ia*   *riro-a*   *upi-a*
  die-CONT-DEP.SIM   DEM.PROX.3SG.N=INSTR   big-N.SG   sick-SG.N
  'The men really follow right after each other dying from this big sickness.'
                                                      (Robinson 2006b)

Asymmetric situations are generally not described using the reflexive/reciprocal construction. The only example obtained using the video stimuli is (29), which describes a situation where one woman hugs another, who stands stiffly and does not reciprocate the hug.[10]

(29) *vairei*   *tou-pa-ere-voi*   *riako-rirei*   *tore-vira*
  PRO.3DU.F   be-CONT-3DU.F-PRS$_\beta$ woman-F.DU   stand-ADV
  uva *ora-rau-ere-i-ei*
  so   RR-hug-3DU.F-EPEN-PRS$_\alpha$
  'Two women are standing and hugging one another.'   (#23, AM)

Asymmetric situations are not incompatible with the reflexive/reciprocal construction, as can be seen from (30), which comes from a text concerning traditional burial customs and describes the asymmetric situation of the living burying

---

10. Although this is meant to represent an asymmetrical situation, and probably would be perceived as such by many Westerners, it is unclear how it was perceived by the Rotokas consultants, who were unsure of how to interpret the situation, probably in large measure because hugging is not a common practice among the Rotokas but also in part because they did not know how to interpret the hugged woman's unresponsiveness.

the dead. This is an interesting case of asymmetry, given that it is one where the undergoer is not even a potential actor.[11]

(30) *uva oisio eisi osia oisioa ora-tova-pa-a-ve   voari tuariri*
      so   like ABL as always RR-bury-CONT-3PL-SUB long ago
      'And so just like that they would always bury one another long ago.'
                                                                (Firchow 1974)

5.   Conclusion

The distribution of reciprocal construction types in Rotokas is predicted by a combination of factors. Unless the reciprocal action in the clause is performed on a body part, in which case the noun marking construction will be found, the general rule is: a reciprocal situation described by a verb with two core arguments will be verb marking whereas one described by a verb with a single core argument will be pronoun marking. However, there are exceptions to the general rule. For example, the verb *reo* 'talk' is an intransitive verb of speaking which takes α subject agreement and encodes the addressee as an oblique argument, as in (31) or (32).[12]

(31) *pisipisia-vira   Rarasiori   reo-pa-ro-e   kakae vure=re*
      different-ADV Robinson talk-CONT-3SG.M$_\alpha$ -IP$_\alpha$ child FP=ALL
      'Robinson spoke differently to the children.'

(32) *teapi ragai=va   voroko-pa-u   osia vii=re*
      PROH PRO.1SG=COM arrogant-CONT-2SG as   PRO.2SG=ALL
      reoreo-pa-ra
      talk.RDP-CONT-1SG
      'Don't be arrogant towards me as I'm talking to you.'

Although we would expect the prefix *ora-* to occur on a pronominal oblique argument, this is not in fact what happens, as can be seen from (33) and (34).

(33) *vaiterei   oira-to-arei   ora-reo-pa-si-ei*
      PRO.3.DU.M man-SG.DU.M RR-talk-CONT-3DU.M-PRS$_\alpha$
      'The two men are talking to one another.'   (#1, AM)

---

11. The undergoer (the dead) could *in theory* be potential agents, say, in a supernatural situation where the dead arise to bury their descendants (alive or dead)! But no such belief is described in the text from which (30) is taken (or anywhere else, for that matter).

12. Note that *reo* is reduplicated in (32). Reduplication does not mark reciprocity in and of itself, but it is nevertheless strongly associated with reciprocity given that it marks iterativity and many reciprocal situations involved iterated action.

(34) *Sive kakae vure auau-pa-e-vo   uvare   riro-vira*
      Sive child FP   quiet-CONT-3SG.F$_\beta$-IP$_\beta$ because big-ADV
      ora-reo-pa-a-e
      RR-talk-CONT-3PL$_\alpha$-IP$_\alpha$
      'Sive quieted the children because they were talking loudly amongst
      themselves.'

This could be treated as a lexical idiosyncracy (by treating *reo* as one of the
intransitive verbs from Table 4 that indifferently take the prefix *ora-*), thereby
preserving the general rule; however, this raises some questions concerning the
nature of the difference between verb marking and pronoun marking reciprocals. It may prove to be the case that a grammatical generalisation couched in
terms of the distinction between core and oblique can be derived from lexical
semantics through a more sophisticated linking algorithm (Davis 2001; Levin
& Hovav 2006; Van Valin 2006). A full account of this mapping might better
explain the distribution of construction types as well as other aspects of the
language's argument structure (e.g., its split intransitivity). Whatever the final
analysis proves to be, these considerations underscore the challenges reciprocals pose for an account of transitivity and argument structure not just in Rotokas but also cross-linguistically (Evans et al. 2005).

As far the semantics of reciprocity in Rotokas is concerned, the three construction types in Rotokas are quite broad in their interpretation. They appear
to be compatible with all of the major logical subtypes of reciprocity (including
even asymmetrical situations in some cases), although some logical subtypes of
reciprocity (e.g., strong) are more likely to be encoded using a dedicated reciprocal construction than others (e.g., asymmetrical).

The diachronic origins of the Rotokas reciprocal system also merits attention. The formal resemblance between the reflexive/reciprocal marker and the
conjunction *ora* is striking and suggests that the reflexive/reciprocal construction
may have arisen through the reanalysis of a conjunction; however, phonological similarity must be interpreted cautiously in Rotokas, given that the language
has an unusually small phoneme inventory, which increases the probability of
accidental similarity, and is known to have arisen by collapsing a voicing/nasal-
ity distinction (Robinson 2006a), which may have obscured distinct diachronic
sources for the two morphemes. Speculation concerning the diachronic origins
of the construction must await the identification of cognate forms in related languages. Unfortunately, comparative work is not possible at present given that the
languages most closely related to Rotokas (Eivo, Kereaka, and Konua) are almost
entirely undocumented (Tryon 2005).

Abbreviations

The following abbreviations are used in morphemic glossing:

ADV	adverbial	INSTR	instrumental
ABL	ablative	IP	immediate past
ALL	allative	M	masculine
ALT	alternate	N	neuter
BEN	benefactive	PL	plural
CAUS	causative	POSS	possessive
CLF	classifier	POST	postposition
CONT	continuous	PRS	present
DEM	demonstrative	PRO	pronominal
DEP	dependent	PROG	progressive
DV	derivational	PROX	proximate
DU	dual	RDP	reduplication
DUM	dummy pronoun	RP	remote past
EPEN	epenthetic	RR	reflexive/reciprocal
F	feminine	SG	singular
FP	free pluraliser	SIM	simultaneous
HUM	human	SUB	subjunctive
INTENS	intensifier	SPEC	specifier

References

Allen, Jerry & Hurd, Conrad. 1963. *Languages of the Bougainville District*. Ukarumpa: Summer Institute of Linguistics.

Andrews, Avery. 1985. The major functions of the noun phrase. In *Language Typology and Syntactic Description,* Vol. I: *Clause Structure*, Timothy Shopen (ed.), 62–154. Cambridge: CUP.

Davis, Anthony R. 2001. *Linking by Types in the Hierarchical Lexicon*. Stanford CA: CSLI.

Dixon, R. M. W. 1994. *Ergativity*. Cambridge: CUP.

Dunn, Michael, Reesink, Ger & Terrill, Angela. 2002. The East Papuan languages: A preliminary typological appraisal. *Oceanic Linguistics* 41(1): 28–62.

Dunn, Michael, Terrill, Angela, Reesink, Ger, Foley, Robert A. & Levinson, Stephen C. 2005. Structural phylogenetics and the reconstruction of ancient language history. *Science* 309(5743): 2072–2075.

Evans, Nicholas & Osada, Toshiki. 2005. Mundari: The myth of a language without word classes. *Linguistic Typology* 9(3): 351–90.

Evans, Nicholas, Levinson, Stephen C., Enfield, N. J., Gaby, Alice & Majid, Asifa. 2004. Reciprocals. In *Field Manual,* Vol. 9, Asifa Majid (ed.), 25–30. Nijmegen: Max Planck Institute for Psycholinguistics, Language & Cognition Group.

Firchow, Irwin B. 1971. Rotokas referentials. *Kivung* 4: 175–186.

Firchow, Irwin B. 1973. *A Vocabulary of Rotokas*. Ukarumpa: Summer Institute of Linguistics.

Firchow, Irwin B. (ed.). 1974. *Rotokasipairara Pitupituaro / Rotokas Customs*. Ukarumpa: Summer Institute of Linguistics.

Firchow, Irwin B. 1977. Some functions of Rotokas referentials. In *Proceedings of the S.I.L. Consultants Seminar, Ukarumpa, 1976* [Workpapers in Papua New Guinea Languages 20], Richard Loving & David Thomas (eds), 133–42. Ukarumpa: Summer Institute of Linguistics.

Firchow, Irwin B. 1987. Form and function of Rotokas words. *Language and Linguistics in Melanesia* 15: 5–111.

Firchow, Irwin B. & Akoitai, David (eds.). 1974. *Rotokas Reo Vo Siposiporoaro Vo Toupai / Rotokas Stories*. Ukarumpa: Summer Institute of Linguistics.

Firchow, Irwin B. & Firchow, Jacqueline. 1969. An abbreviated phoneme inventory. *Anthropological Linguistics* 11: 271–276.

Haiman, John (ed.). 1985. *Natural Syntax: Iconicity or Erosion*. Cambridge: CUP.

Langendoen, D. Terence. 1992. Symmetric relations. In *The Joy of Grammar: A Festschrift in Honor of James D. McCawley*, Diane Brentari, Gary Larson & Lynn MacLeod (eds), 199–212. Amsterdam: John Benjamins.

Levin, Beth & Rappaport Hovav, Malka. 2006. *Argument Realization*. Cambridge: CUP.

Nichols, Johanna. 1986. Head-marking and dependent-marking grammar. *Language* 62: 56–119.

Robinson, Stuart. 2006a. The phoneme inventory of the Aita dialect of Rotokas. *Oceanic Linguistics* 45(1): 206–209.

Robinson, Stuart. 2006b. Rotokas dictionary, Shoebox format.

Ross, Malcolm. 2001. Is there an East Papuan phylum? Evidence from pronouns. In *The Boy from Bundaberg: Studies in Melanesian linguistics in honour of Tom Dutton*, Andrew Pawley, Malcolm Ross & Darrell Tryon (eds), 301–321. Canberra: Pacific Linguistics.

Ross, Malcolm. 2005. Pronouns as a preliminary diagnostic for grouping Papuan languages. In *Papuan Pasts*, Andrew Pawley, Robert Attenborough, Robin Hide & Jack Golson (eds), 15–66. Canberra: Pacific Linguistics.

Tryon, Darrell. 2005. The languages of Bougainville. In *Bougainville Before the Conflict*, Anthony J. Regan & Helga M. Griffin (eds), 31–46. Canberra: Pandanus Books.

Van Valin, Robert D. 2006. *Exploring the Syntax-Semantics Interface*. Cambridge: CUP.

Wurm, Stephen A. 1972. The classification of Papuan languages and its problems. *Linguistic Communications* 6: 118–178.

Wurm, Stephen A. 1975. The East Papuan Phylum in general. In *New Guinea Area Languages and Language Study,* Vol. 1: *Papuan Languages and the New Guinea Linguistic Scene*, Stephen A. Wurm (ed.), 783–804. Canberra: Pacific Linguistics [C 38].

CHAPTER 12

Expression of reciprocity in Savosavo

Claudia Wegener

Karl-Franzens-Universität Graz and Max Planck Institute
for Psycholinguistics

This paper describes how reciprocity is expressed in the Papuan (i.e. non-Austronesian) language Savosavo, spoken in the Solomon Islands. The main strategy is to use the reciprocal nominal *mapamapa*, which can occur in different NP positions and always triggers default third person singular masculine agreement, regardless of the number and gender of the referents. After a description of this as well as another strategy that is occasionally used (the 'joint activity construction'), the paper will provide a detailed analysis of data elicited with a set of video stimuli and show that the main strategy is used to describe even clearly asymmetric situations, as long as more than one person acts on more than one person in a joint activity.

1.   Introduction

Savosavo is a Papuan (i.e. non-Austronesian) language spoken on Savo Island in the Solomon Islands by about 2,500 people. There are no closely related languages. Most languages spoken in the Solomon Islands belong to the Oceanic branch of the unrelated Austronesian language family (Ross 1988, Lynch et al. 2002). There are also a few other Papuan languages in the Solomon Islands, but they are structurally very different from Savosavo and indeed from each other, and it is still an open question whether any of them are related (cf. Todd 1977; Ross 2001; Dunn, Reesink & Terrill 2002; Dunn et al. 2005). The local lingua franca is Solomon Islands Pijin (SIP). Most speakers of Savosavo are bilingual in SIP and/or have some knowledge of other neighbouring languages.

Existing materials on the language are a short grammar sketch and a list of 70 vocabulary items by Codrington (1974[1885]: 559ff., 39ff.), and a comparison of Savosavo and three other Papuan languages of the Solomon Islands with respect to pre- and post-nominal particles, pronominal forms, participant marking morphology and basic vocabulary items by Todd (1977). Recent publications on

Savosavo are a paper on the major word classes (Wegener 2005), a discussion of body part terminology (Wegener 2006), and a grammatical description (Wegener 2008). This paper is based on data collected during a total of 12 months of field-work between 2002 and 2005.

Savosavo is a fairly typical SOV language, with postpositions, the possessor preceding the possessed and modifiers preceding the head. Both nominal case marking and the verbal object agreement show a nominative-accusative pattern. Subject NPs of both transitive and intransitive clauses are marked by the nominative enclitic =na, while object NPs are unmarked ((1)–(3)). There is a separate paradigm of second-position enclitic personal pronouns that can only be used for syntactic subjects (e.g., =no '2sg.NOM' in (3)). On the verb, subjects are not marked at all, whereas objects are marked by affixation or stem modification.

(1) *Pa   kaunga=na ba-i.*
     one   chief=NOM come-FIN
     'A chief came.'

(2) *Ai   lo   adaki-gha=na   pa misu ghuro-ghi-i.*
     PROX DET.PL woman-PL=NOM   one dog chase-3SG.F.OBJ-FIN
     'These women chased a (female) dog.'

(3) *Ekati=no   ghoma tuvi   l-oghoa-li   ta-i.*
     CERT=2SG.NOM   not   house 3SG.M.OBJ-own-3SG.M.OBJ   FUT-FIN
     'You won't own a house.'

Savosavo has a gender system with two classes, masculine and feminine (see e.g. the object agreement in (2) and (3)). In the pronoun paradigm as well as the object marking morphology a distinction is made between dual and plural number and, in the first person dual and plural, between inclusive and exclusive.

Verbs are intransitive, transitive or ambitransitive, depending on whether they have to show agreement with the object or not. Transitive verbs obligatorily take object marking affixes unless detransitivized, intransitive verbs cannot take object marking affixes unless transitivized, and ambitransitive verbs can occur with or without object affixes. Only when an object affix is present, can an object (i.e. unmarked) NP be used. Among those transitive verbs that indicate object marking both by a prefix and a suffix, the verb for 'give', -ame-, is the only verb that could be analysed as ditransitive. Usually the two affixes of such a verb are coreferential and therefore have to match (3). However, in the case of -ame- 'give' the suffix marks person, number and (in the third person singular) also gender of the recipient, whereas the prefix may show reduced and non-obligatory agreement with the theme, only making use of the third person singular masculine and plural forms of the prefix paradigm (4).

(4) *Pa   mi=nye   te   l-ame-pi   ta-i.*
    one fish=1SG.NOM EMPH 3SG.M.OBJ-give-2DU.OBJ FUT-FIN
    'I will give you (two) a fish.'

The recipient is therefore the primary object and the theme the secondary object. NPs referring either to recipients or themes are both treated like normal object NPs, i.e. they are unmarked and can be dropped, providing further evidence that this verb is ditransitive.

Savosavo makes frequent use of serial verb constructions. Only the last verb in such sequences is followed by markers of tense, aspect, mood and/or finiteness, but object agreement morphology is obligatory on all transitive verbs within the chain (5).

(5) *Ai=na   ekati n-eghe   sane   ta-i?*
    who=NOM   CERT   2SG.OBJ-see follow.2SG.OBJ FUT-FIN
    'Who will look after you?'

In the remainder of this paper, first the reciprocal constructions used in Savosavo will be described (Section 2), and then the data elicited with the video stimuli of the 'Reciprocal constructions and situation type' task (Evans et al. 2004) will be discussed in detail (Section 3). Numbers following the translation of examples refer to the video clips of this set.

2.   Strategies for expressing reciprocity in Savosavo

There is one main construction used to express reciprocity in Savosavo, employing the reciprocal nominal *mapamapa*. This particle can occur in three syntactic positions. The *mapamapa* construction is described in detail in Section 2.1.

A marginal strategy is to use an intransitive verb with a non-singular subject. The main function of this construction is to express participation in a joint activity, whether reciprocal or not, but it can be used to describe reciprocal situations. Therefore it is briefly described in Section 2.2.

Neither of these constructions can be used to express reflexivity, which is encoded by the nominal *ghajia* 'self'.

2.1   The *mapamapa* construction

The main reciprocal construction uses the reciprocal nominal *mapamapa*, sometimes shortened to *mamapa*. This word is probably diachronically derived from the noun *mapa* 'person'. *Mapamapa* can occur in three syntactic positions, in each of which it is distributionally equivalent to a NP:

1. taking the place of an **object** (see Section 2.1.1),
2. occurring in a postpositional phrase as an **oblique argument** (see Section 2.1.2) or
3. as a **possessor** in a possessive construction (see Section 2.1.3).

Agreement with *mapamapa* is always third person singular masculine, which is the default in Savosavo, irrespective of the number and gender of the participants. Section 2.1.4 briefly summarizes the arguments for classifying *mapamapa* as a nominal.

2.1.1 *The reciprocal nominal in object position*

When the predicate of the clause is a transitive verb, or an ambitransitive verb used transitively, i.e. when it is a verb that cross-references an object, *mapamapa* 'RECP' can take the place of the object NP (6). A noun phrase or enclitic pronoun representing the participants is used as the syntactic subject.

(6)   *Mapamapa=ze   te   lumua-li-tu.*
      RECP=3PL.NOM   EMPH   hit-3SG.M.OBJ-PRS.PROG
      'They hit each other.'   (#5)

As was mentioned above, the object marking on the verb is obligatorily third person singular masculine, even when the participants are first person ((7), (8)), or two women, as in one of the video clips (#3) that were used as stimuli to elicit data on reciprocity ((9), (10)).

(7)   *Elakati=me   mamapa   topa-li   ta-i.*
      CERT=1DU/PL.INCL   RECP   stalk-3SG.M.OBJ   FUT-FIN
      'We will stalk each other.'

(8)**Elakati=me   mamapa   topa-minyi   ta-i.*
      CERT=1DU/PL.INCL   RECP   stalk-1DU/PL.INCL.OBJ   FUT-FIN
      'We will stalk each other.'

(9)   *Mapamapa=to   te   tapori-li-i.*
      RECP=3DU.NOM   EMPH   slap-3SG.M.OBJ-FIN
      'They (two) slap each other.'   (#3)

(10)* *Mapamapa=to   te   tapori-ghi-i.*
      RECP=3DU.NOM   EMPH   slap-3SG.F.OBJ-FIN
      'They (two) slap each other.'

In the case of the verb for 'give' *mapamapa* usually appears as the recipient,[1] i.e. the primary object cross-referenced on the verb by the suffix. The order of the object NPs is free ((11), (12)), and whatever is more important at that moment of the discourse will come first.

(11) ***Mapamapa=ze*** *te*   *lo*   *kofi*   *l-ame-li-i.*
      RECP=3PL.NOM EMPH DET.SG.M coffee 3SG.M.OBJ-give-3SG.M.OBJ-FIN
      'They gave each other the coffee.'   (#34)

(12) *Pa poi=ze*   *te*   ***mapamapa*** *l-ame-li-zu.*
      one thing=3PL.NOM EMPH **RECP**   3SG.M.OBJ-give-3SG.M.OBJ-PST.PROG
      'They were giving each other a thing.'   (#34)

2.1.2 *The reciprocal nominal in a postpositional phrase*

Mapamapa is used in a postpositional phrase as an oblique argument when the verb is morphosyntactically intransitive ((13), (14)). In (13), *mapamapa* provides the patient, in (14) the goal. Such an oblique argument can also be found with a morphosyntactically transitive verb complex such as the causative construction in (15).

(13) *Ze*   [*mapamapa l-aka*]   *lupi-ghu=e.*
      3PL[GEN][2] **RECP**   **3SG.M-with** embrace-NMLZ=EMPH
      'They embrace each other (lit. with each other).'   (#29)

(14) *To-va*   *garogaro=na*[3]   *te*   [*mamapa l-omata*] *kozi-i.*
      3DU-GEN.M side.of.body=NOM EMPH **RECP**   **3SG.M-at** face-FIN
      'Their sides face each other.'

(15) *Potopoto=to*   *te*   [*mamapa l-omata*] *l-au*   *kozi-i.*
      back=3DU.NOM EMPH **RECP**   **3SG.M-at** 3SG.M-take face-FIN
      'They make (their) backs face each other.'

---

1. In theory it should be possible to use *mapamapa* as the theme as well, but such a clause (e.g. 'They gave each other to the man-eating giant', a rather unusual situation) is not found in the corpus available at present.

2. The subject of this clause is represented by a genitive pronoun because the whole verbal clause has been nominalized. This kind of syntactic nominalization is a common occurrence in Savosavo; for discussion, see Wegener (2008).

3. Number is often not marked for expressions referring to inanimates.

Postpositions agree with the NP they are heading, i.e. in the reciprocal construction they agree with *mapamapa*, and again only third person singular masculine prefixes can be used. The participants involved in the reciprocal event are usually represented by a noun phrase or an enclitic personal pronoun and occur in subject position, e.g. *tova garogaro* 'their sides' in Example (14). However, in the case of a causative construction the syntactic subject of the intransitive verb becomes the object of the causative serial verb construction. This means that in (15) the object NP *potopoto* 'back' instead of the subject enclitic pronoun *=to* '3DU.NOM' refers to the participants of the reciprocal event. Comparing it to the situation described in Example (14), it is in both cases the body parts that 'face each other', not the 'owners', although the latter are the syntactic subject in Example (15).

2.1.3 *The reciprocal nominal as a possessor*

In cases where a speaker wants to put more emphasis on which object or body part is involved she can use a possessor construction with *mapamapa* as the possessor. This possessor construction can then be used as the direct object of a transitive verb (16) or an oblique argument of an intransitive verb (17).

(16) *Ai   to=na   [mapamapa lo   gilasi]*
     this 3DU=NOM   RECP   3SG.M[GEN]   glasses
     te   oli-li-zu.
     EMPH   change-3SG.M.OBJ-PST.PROG
     'These two were exchanging each other's glasses.'   (#41)

(17) *[Mapamapa lo   mane=la]=ze   te   epi-atu.*
     RECP   3SG.M[GEN]   side=LOC=3PL.NOM   EMPH   sit-IPFV
     'They are sitting at each other's side.'   (#15)

The genitive pronoun has to be *lo* '3SG.M[GEN]' because, as discussed above, *mapamapa* always governs third person singular masculine agreement.

2.1.4 *Classification of* mapamapa *as a nominal*

The reciprocal nominal *mapamapa* always appears in syntactic positions usually filled by NPs (as object, complement of a postposition or in a possessor construction) and, like normal nouns, governs agreement on the respective targets (object marking on verbs, prefixes on postpositions and the form of the coreferential genitive pronoun in the possessor construction). *Mapamapa* is therefore analyzed as a nominal. However, it forms a distinct subclass because it differs in some respects from a typical noun: agreement with *mapamapa* always has to be third person singular masculine, it cannot be marked for non-singular number, and it cannot be modified by adjectives or other NP constituents.

2.2   The 'joint activity construction'

Sometimes an intransitive clause with a non-singular subject is used to describe a reciprocal event, although it does not contain any overt marker of reciprocity (this is cross-linguistically common, cf. Evans (2008) and other papers in this volume). Some examples are given in (18)–(21). However, speakers of Savosavo only occasionally made use of this strategy to describe the video clips used for elicitation, and when they did, alternative descriptions employing *mapamapa* were provided as well (where this was possible, see discussion below).

(18) *Abanyi-a=to.*
      argue-SIM=3DU.NOM
      'They (two) are arguing.'   (#3, two people hitting each other sequentially)

(19) *To-va   epi verevere tulola...*
      3DU-GEN.M[4] sit talk   CONJ
      'When they sat and talked...' (#26, starts with two people talking to each other, then one gives his watch to the other)

(20) *Ngutungutu   ze=to.*
      search.for.lice PA=3DU.NOM
      'They (two) searched for lice.'   (#51, one person delousing another)

(21) *Epi kolu~kolu-za   ze=ze.*
      sit RDP~put.together-DETR   PA=3PL.NOM
      'They were sitting together.'   (#8, four people sitting next to each other)

It is quite difficult even in well-studied languages to identify which verbs entering this construction **implicate** and which **entail** reciprocity. As regards Savosavo, no conclusive statement can be made at this point. Events described by means of this construction are general or culture-specific joint activities (e.g. sitting together, talking, arguing, and searching for lice). These joint activities are frequently reciprocal in their enaction. However, although the first three descriptions, (18)–(20), can be used to describe reciprocal events, a non-reciprocal interpretation is also possible, although it might be less likely in some cases. In (18) and (19) the participants could be arguing with or talking to another group of people, and (20) was indeed used to describe a video clip in which only one of the two people involved acts on the other. The reciprocal particle *mapamapa* could not be used to describe this particular scene, but because it is interpreted as a joint activity in Savosavo culture the description given in (20) is possible.

---

4. This is a subordinate adverbial clause; subordinate clauses commonly have genitive subjects (cf. fn. 2).

(21) is inherently reciprocal in the sense that if x is sitting together with y, then y is sitting together with x. A verb with the meaning 'sit together' would be a 'natural reciprocal verb', i.e. it would entail reciprocity. However, in Savosavo this meaning is expressed compositionally by a serial verb construction, and the focus is again on the joint action, not on the reciprocity of the situation. To restrict the first three descriptions to a reciprocal interpretation, or to make the reciprocity of the situation in (21) explicit, *mapamapa* could be added as an oblique argument. As is the case in Mundari (see the discussion in Evans & Osada, this volume), so far there do not seem to be verbs that have an inherent reciprocal reading.

3.   Categories encoded in the clip data

Three speakers provided data for the full set of video clips, and three for a subset of 15 clips. The sessions were recorded in June and July 2004 on Savo Island. More detailed information on the speakers is provided in Table 1. All speakers are fluent in Solomon Islands Pijin and have at least some rudimentary knowledge of English. The other local languages listed are all Austronesian and (with the exception of Marovo, which is spoken in the Western Province) direct neighbours. It is possible that the speakers have some knowledge of other neighbouring languages in addition to the ones listed.

Table 1. Information on speakers

Speaker	Age	Other languages	Full or partial set
1 (f)	~ 28	SIP, (English)	F
2 (m)	~ 28	SIP, (English)	F
3 (m)	~ 65	SIP, English, Ghari	F
4 (f)	~ 16	SIP, (English), Gela	P
5 (f)	~ 36	SIP, English, Ghari, Marovo	P
6 (m)	~ 56	SIP, English, Gela, Ghari	P

As was explained above (Section 2.2), the 'joint activity construction' can be used to describe reciprocal situations, as long as they are part of a joint activity, but it is not a dedicated reciprocal construction. It was occasionally offered as a description for clips showing joint activities such as delousing, sitting together, shaking hands, talking and chasing. It was not checked whether it would be an acceptable description when it was not offered spontaneously, but it is highly likely that it can be used for all clips featuring these activities.

The reciprocal nominal *mapamapa* was used in the description of 52 out of 64 video clips. Which syntactic position it occurred in depended on the verb used, and on how specific the speaker was with respect to objects or body parts involved. There does not seem to be an additional semantic motivation for choosing one variant over another.

Almost all clips were described using *mapamapa*, the exception being a number of clips showing asymmetric situations. In a few cases one speaker did not use *mapamapa*, but gave a more detailed description of the kind 'x does something to y, y does something to z/x'. However, this seems to be a personal preference, as the other speakers did use *mapamapa* for the same clips consistently and without any hesitation.

Within the group of clips showing asymmetric situations, all speakers agreed that *mapamapa* could not be used for the majority of clips. However, three such clips (6, 39 and 64) were consistently described using the *mapamapa* construction. Clip 6 shows two pairs of people, and within each pair one person delouses the other one; in clip 39 there are again two pairs of people involved, and within each pair one person chases the other one; finally, clip 64 shows a 'chasing' event with two people, one of whom chases the other one. Clips 39 and 64 were not part of the limited subset of 15 clips, so only three speakers provided descriptions of these clips; clip 6 was described by all six speakers. One speaker did not use the *mapamapa* construction for clip 6, but used the 'joint activity construction', which allows for both a reciprocal and a non-reciprocal interpretation (see Section 2.2). It was not checked in this case whether the speaker would have accepted a description employing *mapamapa*, but it seems very likely.

In all three clips the participants do not switch roles, and there is no participant assuming both roles, agent and patient, at the same time. However, it is noteworthy that within the group of languages that were investigated using these clips, the events of chasing, as well as events of talking, were commonly described as reciprocal when the clips in fact showed an asymmetric situation. The reason for this may be that a 'chasing' event, as well as a 'talking' event, is a joint activity where both participants are very actively involved and which is frequently reciprocal in its enaction. That 'searching for lice' is also a (culture-specific) joint activity was already discussed above in Section 2.2; because of this, both reciprocal and non-reciprocal situations of delousing could be described by the 'joint activity construction'. However, *mapamapa* could not be used to describe clip 51, showing one person delousing another (example (20) above, and the discussion following it). Therefore, the fact that clips 6, 39 and 64 showed joint activities cannot in itself explain why they could be described with *mapamapa*, although they were asymmetric.

Leaving clip 64 aside for the moment, the systematic difference between clips 6 and 39 on the one hand and the other clips showing asymmetric situations on the other hand is that clips 6 and 39 show **more than one** person acting on **two** other persons. The other asymmetric situations involve either only two people, or more than one person acting on only one other person. This suggests that the number of patients is a relevant parameter as well. Thus, based on the video clip data, the usage of *mapamapa* can be described by the following rules:

1. **If two people are involved**: *mapamapa* can be used when they are in a symmetric relation, by acting on each other, or on each other's property or body part, in a similar way, i.e. when they switch roles in an action, either simultaneously or sequential.
2. **If more than two people are involved**: *mapamapa* can be used in all situations, including situations that do not involve a switch of roles, provided that more than one person is acted upon, and that they are involved in a joint activity.

However, according to these rules the situation in clip 64 should not have been described with the reciprocal construction. It is a joint activity, and the person who is chased often looks back at the other one, there is therefore quite a bit of interaction going on between the two, but only one person is the patient. That nonetheless all three speakers of Savosavo providing descriptions for clip 64 did use the particle *mapamapa* may have been due to one or more of the following reasons:

– This was the last clip. Other clips showing 'chasing' events were shown earlier, each of which could be described with the *mapamapa* construction, in accord with the rules formulated above.
– The beginning of the clip does not correspond with the beginning of the event. The two people came around the corner, in the middle of the action – maybe an earlier change of roles was inferred.
– Furthermore the actors were still in the middle of the activity when the clip stopped. This might have facilitated a description that targeted the action as a whole (as a game of chasing one another), of which the clip only showed a part. A clip showing two people standing there, and then one starting to chase the other one until she catches her, at which both stop again, could probably not be described with the reciprocal construction.

It remains an open question for the moment why this clip evoked reciprocal descriptions. Further research, taking the points mentioned above into account, might shed some light on what the reason for this is.

Overall the reciprocal construction used in Savosavo seems to extend beyond what is normally seen as reciprocal, i.e. situations in which at least some of the participants switch roles, to include joint activities in which a number of people act upon more than one person, regardless of whether any of the participants assumes both roles or not.

4.   Conclusions

There are two interesting aspects with respect to the reciprocal construction in Savosavo. One is that whenever the reciprocal nominal *mapamapa* is used, any agreement is automatically set to the default, third person singular masculine, even where the participants are feminine or first or second person. The other is that the range of situations this construction can be used for is broader than might be expected, including even clearly asymmetric situations in which more than one person acts on more than one person in a joint activity.

As there were only a few clips in the set that showed asymmetric situations of this kind, more research would be needed to examine the limits of is broad usage. Furthermore these results need to be tested by looking at more natural data.

Orthography and abbreviations

The practical orthography used in this paper is based on, but not identical to, the two competing orthographies currently used on Savo Island. Most graphemes used correspond to the respective phonetic symbols except: *j* is used for the palatal voiced stop /ɟ/, *ny* for the palatal nasal /ɲ/, *ng* for the velar nasal /ŋ/ and *gh* for the velar approximant /ɰ/.

Abbreviations used are:

CERT	certainty marker	OBJ	object
CONJ	conjunction	PA	particle
DET	determiner	PL	plural
DETR	detransitivizer	PRS	present
DU	dual	PROG	progressive
EMPH	emphasis	PROX	proximal
F	feminine	PST	past
FIN	finite	RECP	reciprocal
FUT	future	RDP	reduplication
GEN	genitive	SG	singular
INCL	inclusive	SIM	simultaneous
IPFV	imperfective	-	morpheme boundary
M	masculine	=	clitic boundary
NOM	nominative	[ ]	non-overt element
NMLZ	nominalizer		

Acknowledgements

The research this paper is based on was financed by the Max Planck Institute for Psycholinguistics, Nijmegen, The Netherlands. I would like to thank Niclas Burenhult, Michael Dunn, Nick Evans, Sebastian Fedden, Alice Gaby, Peter Hurst, Ger Reesink, Stuart Robinson and Eva Schultze-Berndt for interesting discussions and helpful comments. Above all, I am very grateful to my host family and friends on Savo, especially to the people who participated in this study.

References

Codrington, Robert. 1974. *The Melanesian Languages*. Amsterdam: Philo Press. (Reprint, first published 1885, Oxford.)

Dunn, Michael, Reesink, Ger P. & Terrill, Angela. 2002. The East Papuan languages: A preliminary typological appraisal. *Oceanic Linguistics* 41(1): 28–62.

Dunn, Michael, Terrill, Angela, Reesink, Ger, Foley, Robert A. & Levinson, Stephen C. 2005. Structural phylogenetics and the reconstruction of ancient language history. *Science* 309(5743): 2072–2075.

Evans, Nicholas, Levinson, Stephen C., Enfield, N. J., Gaby, Alice & Majid, Asifa. 2004. Reciprocal constructions and situation type. In *Field Manual,* Vol. 9, Asifa Majid (ed.), 25–30. Nijmegen: Max Planck Institute for Psycholinguistics.

Evans, Nicholas. 2008. Reciprocal constructions: Towards a structural typology. In *Reciprocals and Reflexives: Theoretical and Typological Explorations*, Ekkehard König & Volker Gast (eds), 33–104. Berlin: Mouton de Gruyter.

Lynch, John, Ross, Malcolm D. & Crowley, Terry. 2002. *The Oceanic Languages*. Surrey: Curzon Press.

Ross, Malcolm D. 1988. *Proto Oceanic and the Austronesian languages of Western Melanesia*. Canberra: Pacific Linguistics.

Ross, Malcolm D. 2001. Is there an East Papuan phylum? Evidence from pronouns. In *The Boy from Bundaberg: Studies in Melanesian Linguistics in Honour of Tom Dutton*, Andrew Pawley, Malcolm D. Ross & Darrell Tryon (eds.), 301–321. Canberra: Pacific Linguistics.

Todd, Evelyn. 1977. The Solomon language family. In *New Guinea Area Languages and Language Study*, Vol. 1, *Papuan Languages and the New Guinea Linguistic Scene*, Stephen A. Wurm (ed.), 805–846. Canberra: Pacific Linguistics.

Wegener, Claudia. 2005. Major word classes in Savosavo. *Grazer Linguistische Studien* 64: 29–52.

Wegener, Claudia. 2006. Savosavo body part terminology. *Language Sciences* 28(2–3): 344-359.

Wegener, Claudia. 2008. *A Grammar of Savosavo, A Papuan Language of the Solomon Islands* [MPI Series in Psycholinguistics 51]. Nijmegen: Max Planck Institute for Psycholinguistics and Radboud Universiteit Nijmegen.

CHAPTER 13

To have and have not

Kilivila reciprocals

Gunter Senft
Max Planck Institute for Psycholinguistics

Kilivila is one of the languages of the world that lacks dedicated reciprocal forms. After a short introduction the paper briefly shows how reciprocity is either not expressed at all, is only implicated in an utterance, or expressed periphrastically.

1.   Introduction

When I was a young boy I was deeply impressed by a story which one of my parents' acquaintances told about his school days. The anecdote runs as follows. In primary school the teacher asked the kids one day to write an essay on the topic "My dog" as their homework. The next day the teacher asked this young boy to read out his essay and he read: "My dog – we have none!" When Nick Evans, Alice Gaby and Asifa Majid asked me to collect data on reciprocals in Kilivila, my answer was identical: "We have none". However, I was willing to use the stimuli they had devised (see Evans et al. 2004) and see what kind of data I could elicit and collect. Most of the data presented here were collected in July 2004 in the village Tauwema on Kaile'una Island, my place of residence in the Trobriand Islands. I want to point out here that Kilivila is not the only Oceanic language that has no reciprocals – Tahitian, for example, does not have them, either (see Tryon 1970: 97; Levinson 2000: 334ff); it is obviously perfectly functional for some languages to not have reciprocals[1]. In this paper I will briefly show that in Kilivila reciprocity is either not expressed at all, is only implicated in an utterance, or expressed periphrastically. However, before I do that I will provide some basic information on the language and its speakers.

---

[1]   By the way, Kilivila does not have reflexives either. Emphatic pronouns can serve some functions of reflexives (see Senft 1986: 54–59).

The Trobriand Islanders belong to the ethnic group called 'Northern Massim'. They are gardeners, doing slash and burn cultivation of the bush; their most important crop is yams. Moreover, they are also famous for being excellent canoe builders, carvers, and navigators, especially in connection with the ritualised 'Kula' trade, an exchange of shell valuables that covers a wide area of the Melanesian part of the Pacific (see Malinowski 1922). The society is matrilineal but virilocal.

Kilivila, the language of the Trobriand Islanders, is one of 40 Austronesian languages spoken in the Milne Bay Province of Papua New Guinea. It is an agglutinative language and its general word order pattern is VOS (Senft 1986). The Austronesian languages spoken in Milne Bay Province are grouped into 12 language families; one of them is labelled Kilivila. The Kilivila language family encompasses the languages Budibud (or Nada, with about 200 speakers), Muyuw (or Murua, with about 4,000 speakers) and Kilivila (or Kiriwina, Boyowa, with about 28,000 speakers); Kilivila is spoken on the islands Kiriwina, Vakuta, Kitava, Kaile'una, Kuiawa, Munuwata and Simsim. The languages Muyuw and Kilivila are split into mutually understandable local dialects. Typologically, Kilivila is classified as a Western Melanesian Oceanic language belonging to the 'Papuan-Tip-Cluster' group (Ross 1988: 25, 190ff; Senft 1986: 6).

2.   Reciprocals and Kilivila

As mentioned above, there are no reciprocal forms in Kilivila. With respect to the description of both symmetric and non-symmetric situation types where many languages use reciprocal constructions, the Trobriand Islanders fall back on the following three strategies:

- reciprocity is not expressed at all;
- reciprocity is implicated;
- reciprocity is expressed periphrastically.

In what follows I will briefly illustrate these three strategies with examples from my general corpus of Kilivila and with data that I elicited with the 64 tests clips.

2.1   Reciprocity is not expressed at all

This strategy is illustrated in Example (1) – that was produced to describe the videoclip 14 (chasing) and in Examples (2) and (3) – that are taken from my Kilivila corpus:

(1) *E-kamwau'uru-si.*
   3.-chase-PL
   'They chase [(each other)].'

(2) *Subisubi   Topwenina   e-kimapu-si.*
   Subisubi   Topwenina   3.-hit-PL
   'Subisubi (and) Topwenina they hit [(each other)] .'

(3) *Kwe-tolu   bokesi   e-takasi-si.*
   CP.general-three   box   3.-be.inside-PL
   'Three boxes are inside [(each other)] .'

This strategy was used to describe 21 of the data eliciting videoclips. With respect to six of these descriptions one can argue that reciprocity is probably implicated. However, I cannot find any sound criterion on the basis of which I could decide on whether reciprocity is simply not expressed or whether reciprocity is implicated. The Examples (4) and (5) that were produced to describe the videoclips 44 (hitting) and 51 (delousing) briefly illustrate this problem:

(4) *Beya   e-yowa'i-si.*
   Here   3.-fight-PL
   'Here they fight [(with each other)] .'

(5) *I-nene'i-si   kutu.*
   3.-look.for-PL   lice
   'They look for lice [(= they are lousing each other)] .'

If speakers of Kilivila would intend to express that 'they fight him' or 'they delouse him' they would realise the subject and the object at least in the form of full pronouns and make the situation quite explicit – as illustrated in Examples (6) and (7):

(6) *M-to-si-na   e-yowa'i-si   deli   m-to-na.*
   DEM-CP.male-PL-DEM   3.-fight-PL   with   DEM-CP.male-DEM
   'They fight with him.'

(7) *M-to-si-na   i-nene'i-si   kutu   o   kunu-la   Mota'esa.*
   DEM-CP.male-PL-DEM   3.-look.for-PL   lice   LOC   hair-his   Mota'esa
   'They look for lice in Mota'esa's hair (= they delouse Mota'esa) .'

2.2   Reciprocity is implicated[2]

This strategy is illustrated in (8) – that is taken from my Kilivila corpus – (9) – a response to clip 7 (man and woman talking) – and (10) – a response to clip 52 (hugging):

---

2.   See Levinson (2000).

(8) *Mumyepu ya-lima   e-kauvadulu-si*
     Papaya   CP.flexible-five 3.-be.in.a.row.touching-PL
     'Five papaya are in a row touching [(each other) – (but not something else!)]'.'

(9) *Vivila   tau e-bigatona-si mata-la tau mata-la vivila.*
     Girl   boy 3.-talk-PL   eye-his boy eye-her girl
     'A girl (and) a man they talk [(with each other)], the man (is) eye in eye with
     the girl.'

(10) *Beya   makala bita-kebiga   bobwelila kena avaka*
     here   like   FUT.Dual.INCL.-say love   or   what
     'Here one can say like this: showing affection or something.'

This strategy was used to describe 40 of the data eliciting videoclips. With respect
to six of these descriptions one can argue that reciprocity is probably implicated;
and with respect to another six of these descriptions one can argue that reciprocity
is either implicated or expressed periphrastically or that reciprocity is expressed
using both strategies in a more detailed description of what is going on in the
videoclip. Examples (11) and (12) that were produced to describe the videoclip 20
(three women hugging) and 10 (two women lousing) illustrate this:

(11) *E-kepapa-si asitetolu.*
     3.-hug-PL   three.of.them
     'They hug [(each other)] the three of them.'

(12) *M-to-si-na   asiteyu   e-yosa   o   kunula*
     DEM-CP.human-PL-DEM   two.of.them 3.-hold LOC hair
     so-la,   so-la   e-yosa   o   kunu-la
     friend-her friend-her 3.-hold LOC hair-her
     e   e-tota-si   e-bigatona-si.
     And 3.-stand-PL 3.-talk-PL
     'These two people, she holds (onto) the hair of her friend, her friend holds
     (onto) her hair and they stand (and) they talk.'

If we have a closer look at the examples that illustrate this strategy one could argue
that they contain what Ekkehart König (p.c.) and others have called "symmetric
predicates" or "bare reciprocal constructions". Thus, we may argue that Kilivila
uses such naturally or inherently reciprocal verbs or verbs with naturally reciprocal implicature as a lexical strategy to express reciprocity: Among these verbs –
which Payne (1997: 201) calls "lexical reciprocals" – we find, for example:

(13) *-boda-*
     'to meet'
     E-boda-si
     3.-meet-PL
     'They meet [(each other)]'.'

(14) *-katumapu-*
      'to exchange (with the implication that the counter-gift in the gift-countergift exchange can be delayed)'
      E-katumapu-si   gugua
      3.-exchange-PL   good
      'They exchange goods [(with each other)].'

(15) *-vaka'i-*
      'to quarrel'
      E-vaka'i-si
      3.-quarrel-PL
      'They quarrel [(with each other)].'

(16) *-mwasawa-*
      'to play'
      E-mwasawa-si
      3.-play-PL
      'They play [(with each other)].'

and also

(17) *-yowa'i-*
      'to fight'
      E-yowa'i-si
      3.-fight-PL
      'They fight [(with each other)].'
      (see Examples (4) and (6) above)

It may be that Kilivila – like Kuuk Thaayorre (Gaby this volume) – follows the strategy that stereotypical reciprocal events are not explicitly expressed as reciprocal; the understanding of their reciprocity is left to implicature. One could also argue that reciprocity plays such an important role in the culture of these Melanesians that it is simply taken for granted and therefore needs no explicit verbal marking – but this is just hypothetic speculation. However, whenever speakers of Kilivila want to emphasise reciprocity, they can always express it periphrastically – as illustrated in the following subsection.

2.3   Reciprocity is expressed periphrastically

Using this strategy the speakers of Kilivila describe reciprocal relations as exactly and in as much detail as possible – as Example (18) from my Kilivila corpus illustrates. Here Mokeilobu explains – in a nice chiasmus construction – to a visitor from Simsim Island that my old friend Gerubara and I can completely trust and rely on each other:

(18)   *Gerubara e-nukwali Gunter e   Gunter e-nukwali Gerubara*
    Gerubara 3.-know   Gunter and Gunter 3.-know   Gerubara
    'Gerubara knows Gunter and Gunter knows Gerubara.'

In Example (19) that was produced to describe the videoclip 41 (exchange spectacles) the speaker describes exactly who is doing what with whom. In this example the first part implicates reciprocity and the second part describes this exchange periphrastically. The second half of this utterance would alone have been sufficient to describe the exchange scene:

(19)   *Vivila tau e   si   garasi - e-katumapu-si,*
    Girl   boy and their glasses 3.-exchange-PL
    tau - la   garasi e-seki vivila,
    boy   his glasses 3.-give girl
    vivila - la   garasi e-seki   tau.
    girl   her glasses 3.-give boy
    'A girl, a boy and their glasses – they exchange (them), the boy – his glasses he gives (them to) the girl, the girl – her glasses she gives (them to) the boy.'

This strategy was used to describe 15 of the data eliciting videoclips. This is all the information on reciprocals which I can provide in connection with Kilivila.

3.   Summary

Unlike many other Oceanic languages that mark reciprocity with a fairly small set of verbal prefixes (like e.g., A'jië, Samoan, and Lenakel) or – more rarely – with a suffix to the verb (like e.g., Lusi and Anêm; see Lynch 1998: 131, 145, 216; Crowley et al. 1995: 224) Kilivila – like Tahitian – does not have any reciprocal markers or forms at all. For the description of situation types where many languages use reciprocal constructions, the Trobriand Islanders fall back on the following three strategies:

– reciprocity is not expressed at all;
– reciprocity is implicated;
– reciprocity is expressed periphrastically.

From an anthropological linguistic point of view this is a rather puzzling finding: Kilivila is a language spoken by people for whom reciprocity is one of the central, if not the central, principle of social life (see Malinowski 1922, 1935a, 1935b), yet it is not coded formally in the language! Why is this so? And if the Trobriand Islanders do not need reciprocals, why do we?[3]

---

3.   I would like to note here that Ralph Lawton – a former missionary who translated the Bible into Kilivila (Lawton 1997) – states in an e-mail to Nick Evans that Kilivila has a construction

Abbreviations

3.	third person
FUT	future
CP	classificatory particle, classifier
INCL	inclusive
DEM	demonstrative
LOC	locative
PL	plural
RDP	reduplication

References

Crowley, Terry, Lynch, John, Siegel, Jeff & Piau, Julie. 1995. *The Design of Language: An Introduction to Descriptive Linguistics*. Auckland: Longman Paul.

Evans, Nicholas, Levinson, Stephen C., Enfield, N. J., Gaby, Alice & Majid, Asifa. 2004. Reciprocal constructions and situation type. In *Field Manual,* Vol. 9, Asifa Majid (ed.), 25–30. Nijmegen: Max Planck Institute for Psycholinguistics.

Lawton, Ralph. 1997. *Buki Pilabumaboma. Kabutubogwa deli Kabutuvau.* Port Moresby: The Bible Society of Papua New Guinea.

Levinson, Stephen C. 2000. *Presumptive Meanings: The Theory of Generalized Conversational Implicature*. Cambridge MA: The MIT Press.

Lynch, John. 1998. *Pacific Languages – An Introduction*. Honolulu HI: University of Hawai'i Press.

---

to express reciprocity which consists of a "complex NP as subject" that "is usually broken so that the two (individuals or groups) appear on each side of the verb". Lawton provides examples like the following one (the morpheme-interlinear transcription is mine):

makawala	*tai-tala*	*tau*	*e-bi-bigatona-si*	*sola*	*lubai-la*	
Like	CP.male-one	man	3.-RDP-talk-PL	with	friend-his	
'just as a man and his friend talk to each other'.					(quote from Exodus 33.11)	

Lawton's work is based on the "*biga galagoki*" variety of Kilivila that is spoken in the villages Oyabia and Kavataria on Kiriwina Island. My research on Kilivila is based on the "*biga galawala*" variety of Kilivila (Senft 1986: 6–10) that is spoken on Kaile'una Island (with the exception of the village Kaduwaga where the "*biga galanani*" variety is spoken). I have never heard or documented such a construction and I could not elicit it with my consultants, either. However, I could elicit sentences in which the "complex NP" is not "broken" (see Example (2) above) and – as I have argued in this paper – I cannot detect any formal expression of reciprocity in such sentences whatsoever. I analyse the Kilivila phrase

makala	*te-tala*	*tau*	*sola*	*lube-la*	*e-bibigatona-si*
like	CP.male-one	man	with	friend-his	3.-RDP-talk-PL
'just as a man and his friend talk [(with each other)]'.					

as an utterance in which reciprocity is implicated (see also Example (9) above).

Malinowski, Bronislaw. 1922. *Argonauts of the Western Pacific: An Account of Native Enterprise and Adventure in the Archipelagoes of Melanesian New Guinea.* London: Routledge.

Malinowski, Bronislaw. 1935a. *Coral Gardens and their Magic: A Study of the Methods of Tilling the Soil and of Agricultural Rites in the Trobiand Islands,* Vol. I: *The Description of Gardening.* London: George Allen & Unwin.

Malinowski, Bronislaw. 1935b. *Coral Gardens and their Magic: A Study of the Methods of Tilling the Soil and of Agricultural Rites in the Trobiand Islands,* Vol. II: *The Language of Magic and Gardening.* London: George Allen & Unwin.

Payne, Thomas E. 1997. *Describing Morphosyntax: A Guide for Field Linguists.* Cambridge: CUP.

Ross, Malcolm D. 1988. *Proto Oceanic and the Austronesian Languages of Western Melanesia.* Canberra: Pacific Linguistics.

Senft, Gunter. 1986. *Kilivila – The Language of the Trobriand Islanders.* Berlin: Mouton de Gruyter.

Tryon, Darrell T. 1970. *Conversational Tahitian: An Introduction to the Tahitian Language of French Polynesia.* Berkeley CA: University of California Press.

CHAPTER 14

Strategies for encoding reciprocity in Mawng

Ruth Singer
The University of Melbourne

This chapter provides the first detailed description of the form and use of the three strategies for expressing reciprocity in Mawng, a non-Pama Nyungan language of the Iwaidjan language family (Australia). The only productive strategy is the reciprocal complex construction which has transparently developed from a biclausal reciprocal construction. Other strategies for encoding reciprocity include the use of a highly restricted verbal suffix -*njili* and the use of naturally reciprocal predicates in the unmarked "bare reciprocal construction". Since there is only one productive way to form reciprocals in Mawng, choice of strategy is not determined by the semantics of an event but is structurally constrained by the constructional combinatorics of the predicate most appropriate to the event.

1.   Introduction

Mawng is the main language of daily communication for around three hundred Aboriginal people living in north-west Arnhem Land, Northern Territory, Australia. Mawng people all speak English and many also speak a Bininj Gun-wok or Yolngu-matha dialect. Mawng is a member of the Iwaidjan language family, a small non-Pama Nyungan group whose only other extant member is Iwaidja (Evans 2000). Mawng and its sister language Iwaidja differ considerably but the encoding of reciprocals in the two languages is very similar[1]. Descriptive work on Mawng has been carried out since the 1950s (Capell & Hinch 1970; Evans 2004; Hinch unpublished; Hinch & Pike 1978) but this paper is the first detailed description of Mawng reciprocals.

There are three main ways to form reciprocal expressions in Mawng. The reciprocal complex construction (RC) can be used to form a reciprocal from any

---

[1].   The ways in which the Iwaidja and Mawng reciprocal constructions differ will be pointed out where relevant.

transitive or semitransitive predicate. It is a highly unusual reciprocal construction typologically (Evans 2008) as it is transparently the result of the grammaticalisation of a biclausal construction into a single clause. There are also two lexical strategies, which are restricted to a small number of verb roots. Around a dozen transitive verb roots can take the detransitivising reciprocal suffix *-njili* (see Section 3.1). There are also a small number of naturally reciprocal predicates (see Section 3.2). The formation of *-njili* verbs is formally similar to the formation of the reflexive in Mawng as both derive an intransitive verb from a transitive verb. The formal template used in the RC reciprocal construction is similar to that used for distributives. Since there is only one productive way of forming reciprocals in Mawng, choice of strategy is not determined by the semantics of the event but is structurally constrained by the constructional combinatorics of the predicate most appropriate to the event. A reciprocal strategy is almost always used when two participants act in a way that is symmetrical. If there are more participants or the event is not symmetrical a reciprocal construction is less likely to be used. Type of event is also important – delousing, chasing and following received reciprocal coding more often than other events, when other parameters are held constant.

2.   Use of the reciprocal complex to encode reciprocity

The 'reciprocal complex' is the only productive way to express reciprocity in Mawng. It is a template into which any multivalent Mawng predicate can be inserted.

2.1   The form of the reciprocal complex

Mawng verbs show agreement with up to two core arguments which are only optionally expressed as NPs. Word order is relatively free but the predicate is a fixed word order unit that will be referred to as the "verb complex". In addition to a verb, the verb complex may contain a coverb, oblique pronoun and a number of post-verbal particles and clitics. The reciprocal complex (RC) takes the form of an elaborated verb complex. The four elements of the RC are shown in the fixed order in which they occur in Table 1.

Table 1. The reciprocal complex (RC)

Verb complex	(Incorporated noun)	Conjunction	Pronoun
Subj/(Obj)-verb-TAM (coverb) (OBL)	(Noun)	*la*	Contrastive pronoun

Optional parts of the RC are shown in brackets. Note that a number of optional particles and clitics which can occur in the verb complex have been omitted from Table 1. These include preverbal negative particles, as well as postverbal directional and aspectual clitics. All elements of the verb complex have a strict word order and no elements external to the verb complex can intervene between them. The reciprocal complex is formed by the addition of the conjunction *la* and a contrastive pronoun to the end of the verb complex. A bare noun can also be incorporated into the middle of the reciprocal complex. This may encode a body part that is coreferent with a core argument or the second object (theme) of a ditransitive verb[2] (see Section 2.2). The most basic type of reciprocal clause consists simply of the obligatory elements of the RC as in (1)[3].

(1) *K-ini-lakajpu-n*   *la*   *yamin.*
     PRS-3M>3M-ask-NPST CONJ 3M.CONTR
     'They are talking to each other.'   [Reciprocals2 096[4]]

Any additional elements that occur in a sentence such as adverbs or NPs can precede or follow the RC but may not intervene between elements of the complex[5]. The RC is formed using verbs that index two arguments. These include semitransitive verbs which only show agreement with the subject but have an oblique object argument as shown in (2).

(2) *Iny-malkpa-ny ngaw*   *la*   *inyamin.*
     3F-arrive-PP 3NM.GEN[6].OBL CONJ 3F.CONTR
     'They met each other.'   [Reciprocals2 080]

The form of the RC resembles two conjoined clauses with different subjects since pairs of clauses can be conjoined with the conjunction *la* and the contrastive pronoun is frequently used to emphasise that the second clause has a new subject. Square brackets indicate these types of pairs of clauses in (3) and (4).

---

2.   Similar types of nouns can be incorporated into the Mah Meri *mōle* reciprocal construction: body part nouns and the theme of exchange verbs (Kruspe this volume).

3.   Note that verb prefixes are treated as portmanteau morphemes for the purpose of glossing. In the gloss the features of the subject prefix are given followed by the object prefix. This does not necessarily reflect the order of subject and object prefixes in analysable verb prefixes.

4.   Codes identify examples from the author's Toolbox database.

5.   Except incorporated body part nouns and second object nouns, see Section 2.2.

6.   Note that third person oblique pronouns show a two-way gender contrast, between Masculine (M) and Non-masculine (glossed 'NM.GEN').

(3) *[Inga-w-ng*   *parak] [la   yamin*
     3NM.GEN>3M-give-PP AWAY   CONJ 3M.CONTR
     inny-u-ng   parak].
     3M>3M-give-PP AWAY
     'She passed it to him and then *he* passed it to him (a second male).'
                                                    [Reciprocals3 004]

(4) *Ngarrurri arrk-puran*   *[but   ngarrurri*
     1pl.INCL   1pl.INCL-belong.to.land *English* 1pl.INCL
     k-arrpun-muy]   *[la   wemin*
     PRS-1pl.INCL>3pl-not.know   CONJ 3pl.CONTR
     k-arruntu-muy-ga].
     PRS-3pl>1pl.INCL-not.know-HITH
     'We're all countrymen but we don't know them and they don't know us.'
                                                    [Karringitpalka 062]

One possible analysis of the reciprocal construction is that it is two linked clauses in which all elements of the second clause apart from the contrastive pronoun have been ellipsed. This analysis is depicted in Table 2.

Table 2. The biclausal analysis of the reciprocal complex

Clause 1		Clause 2	
Verb complex	**(Incorporated bare noun)**	**Conjunction**	**Pronoun**
Subj/(Obj)-verb-TAM (coverb) (OBL)	(Noun)	*la*	Contrastive pronoun

Such an analysis captures the form of the RC construction. However, other properties of the RC construction support a monoclausal analysis. These properties are described in the following sections.

2.2   Position of NPs within reciprocal clauses

Mawng noun phrases often follow the verb so if the RC construction were biclausal we would expect NPs to commonly occur between the verb complex and the conjunction *la*. However NPs can only occur before or after the entire RC, with the exception of the two types of bare noun that can be incorporated (see Section 2.2). For example, in (5) the adverb *yara* 'sometimes' precedes the RC and there are two argument NPs that follow the RC.

(5) *Yara   marrik awunp-u-ni   la   wemin   [ta walij]*
     sometimes NEG   3pl>3pl-give-IRR2 CONJ 3pl.CONTR ED food
     [pata   arrarrkpi]
     PL   person
     'Sometimes people didn't give each other food.'   [Hinch unpublished: 125]

There are two types of referents which can be expressed as a bare noun between the verb complex and the conjunction *la*. The incorporation of bare nouns in the RC is quite unusual because productive incorporation of nouns into predicates is not found elsewhere in Mawng[7]. The second object of a ditransitive verb can be expressed as an independent NP outside of the RC as in (6) or it can be incorporated as a bare noun as in (7).

(6) *Awunp-u-ng   la   wemin   jurra.*
     3pl>3pl-give-pp CONJ 3pl.CONTR book
     'They gave each other a book.'   [Reciprocals2 075]

(7) *Awunp-u-ng   jurra la   wemin.*
     3pl>3pl-give-pp book CONJ 3pl.CONTR
     'They gave each other a book.'   [Reciprocals2 076]

Body part nouns which do not take a prefix for their possessor can also appear in the same position. That the RC developed historically from two clauses is supported by the fact that certain bare nouns can be incorporated into the RC in precisely the position where we would usually expect lexical NPs to appear. However, the extreme restrictions on the types of nominals that can occur in this position show that the RC is no longer truly biclausal. Instead the RC is functionally equivalent to a single verb complex within a single clause. The functioning of agreement within the RC also supports a monoclausal analysis and is discussed in the next section.

2.3   Agreement within the reciprocal construction

The indexing of participants in Mawng reciprocal constructions is quite unusual. Many languages that cross-reference two arguments in the verb encode reciprocals like intransitives – with a single agreement affix on the verb. In the RC construction the verb indexes two participants but there is evidence that verbal agreement within the RC has become grammaticalised such that it no longer encodes distinct subject and object arguments. Exactly what determines which of the participants is encoded as subject and which as object by the verb prefix is unclear. It is likely that volitionality and discourse factors are important. In addition, the contrastive pronoun no longer functions as an independent pronoun but has become grammaticalised as an extra index. The grammaticalisation of the contrastive pronoun as an index will be discussed first and then the grammaticalisation of subject and object indexing in the verb will be discussed.

---

7. Although some coverb constructions have developed through the incorporation of a bare noun into the verb complex.

2.3.1 *Grammaticalisation of the contrastive pronoun as an index*

If the RC construction was biclausal, we would expect the contrastive pronoun to encode the object of the verb because the contrastive pronoun emphasises the new subject of the second clause, which is the object of the first clause. This is largely what we find in Iwaidja except when the participants are first and second person, in which case the contrastive pronoun must be first person as in Mawng.

In Mawng we find that the contrastive pronoun shows the features of the participant which is highest on the hierarchy in Table 3.

Table 3. Participant encoded by contrastive pronoun in the reciprocal complex

$$1 > 2 > \quad \frac{3\text{M} > 3\text{F}}{3\text{pl}}$$

The hierarchy is basically a person hierarchy except that Masculine gender outranks Feminine gender. When one participant is third person singular and the other is third person plural then it is acceptable for either participant to be encoded as the contrastive pronoun. If the RC construction were really biclausal we would expect the contrastive pronoun to always encode features of the object of the first verb as in (8).

(8) *Ngani-wu-ng   la   ngapimung*
     3M>1SG-hit-PP   CONJ   1SG.CONTR
     'We (two) hit each other.'   [Reciprocals6 007]

However in (9) the argument coding of the two participants is reversed on the first verb but the contrastive pronoun still encodes the features of the first person participant even though it is also indexed as subject on the verb.

(9) *Ngi-wu-ng   la   ngapimung.*
     1SG>3M-hit-PP   CONJ   1SG.CONTR
     'We (two) hit each other.'   [Reciprocals6 009]

We would expect (10) instead of (9) if the construction was synchronically biclausal but (10) is not acceptable.

(10) **Ngi-wu-ng   la   yamin.*
      1SG>3M-hit-PP   CONJ   3M.CONTR   [Reciprocals6 010]

The fact that features of the contrastive pronoun are determined by a hierarchy shows that it no longer has a pronominal function but rather functions as a redundant index within the RC.

2.3.2 *Discrepancies between verbal agreement and argument structure*

Mawng verbal agreement usually functions to index core arguments. However, in reciprocal clauses the verbal agreement affixes do not accurately reflect the argument structure of the clause. This is because the participants in a reciprocal situation often form a homogeneous group but the form of the RC requires them to be indexed as two separate arguments. Thus we find the verb indexes two separate arguments even in RCs such as that in (11) which describes a situation in which five people interact equally.

(11) *Kayirrk   la awunp-u-ning   la   wemin.*
      [then   ]   3pl>3pl-give-PC CONJ 3pl.CONTR
      'Then they give to each other (5 people).'   [Reciprocals3 003]

Which of the five participants are indexed as subject and which as object in (11) cannot be determined. If a verb in a nonreciprocal transitive clause has plural subject and object affixes this entails that the clause has at least four participants (two objects and two subjects)[8]. However, plural subject and plural object affixes may be used in reciprocal clauses that describe situations with only three participants as in (12).

(12) *Ngarrkarrk warramumpik la   y-arakap arrarrkpi*
      two   woman   and M-one   man
      k-awuntu-ma-ø   wurlurlu la   wemin.
      PRS-3pl>3pl-GET-NPST embrace and 3pl.CONTR
      'Two women and one man hug each other (simultaneously – i.e. a group hug).'
                                                                     [Reciprocals7 049]

Presumably, the use of a singular subject and plural object prefix or vice versa in (12) would imply that a group of two was interacting with a single individual rather than all three people interacting equally.

In addition to the difference in the way plural agreement is used there is a second difference between the way that verbal agreement works in RC clauses and nonreciprocal transitive clauses. When there are more than two participants and all are first person or all second person we face a problem as there are no prefixes for first person acting on first person or second person acting on second person. In such situations there is a convention that one verbal affix encodes the relevant person feature while the other shows third person plural agreement as in (13) and (14).

---

8. Note that Mawng does not have dual forms of the verbal agreement prefixes.

(13) *Ngatpun-u-ning*   *la*   *ngarrimung.*
1pl.EXCL>3pl-give-PC CONJ 1pl.EXCL.CONTR
'We were sharing with each other.'   [Hewett et al. 1990]

(14) *Arrunp-aya-n*   *la*   *ngarrurrimung.*
3pl>1pl.INCL-see-NPST CONJ 1pl.INCL.CONTR
'We see each other (three people).'   [Reflexives1 078]

All participants are already included by the reference of the nonsingular first or second person affix in (13) and (14) so it is not clear what the reference of the 3pl agreement affix is: does it refer to part of the group or is it a dummy agreement affix? The need for conventions to deal with situations in which all participants are either all first or all second person highlights the artificiality of indexing participants as two separate arguments in RC reciprocals.[9]

The Mawng RC construction expresses in a single clause a situation which is significantly different to that prototypically encoded by a transitive or intransitive clause. There are subtle formal differences between RC construction clauses and nonreciprocal transitive clauses which parallel the semantic differences. In particular, the conventionalisation of agreement in certain contexts makes it unclear whether the verbal subject and object affixes actually index two separate arguments or whether there is really a unitary set of participants. The idea that verbal agreement does not accurately reflect argument structure in RCs is also supported by the fact that the set of participants is often expressed as a single NP – such as the NP *pata arrarrkpi* 'the people' in (5) – although indexed on the verb as separate subject and object arguments. Constructions used to encode reciprocals often combine formal features of transitive and intransitive constructions (Evans et al. 2007) which is exactly what we would expect given the difference between reciprocal situations and situations prototypically encoded as transitive or intransitive. The syntactic differences between Mawng RC clauses and nonreciprocal transitives reflects differences in the types of situations they encode.

---

9. Conventionalised third person agreement is also found in the Yélî Dnye reciprocal *numo*-construction and in the *noko* construction for 'give' (Levinson this volume). Third person agreement is lexicalised for Savosavo reciprocal nominals (Wegener this volume). Evans (2008) additionally mentions third person agreement with reciprocal nominals in Basque and Mayan languages and third person agreement on verbs in the Amele multiclausal reciprocal construction. If agreement is conventionalised in any context it is likely to be third person agreement (Singer 2006). What seems to be particular to reciprocals is the tendency for lexicalisation of third person *plural* agreement which we find in Mawng and also in the object agreement of enclitics in the Yélî Dnye transitive *numo*-construction.

3.   Lexical encoding of reciprocity

In addition to the reciprocal construction using the RC, there are two small sets of verbs that can occur in different constructions.

3.1   The *-njili* construction

There is a small set of transitive verbs that can combine with the reciprocal suffix *-njili* to form an intransitive, inherently reciprocal verb.[10] These verbs are listed in Table 4.

Table 4. Verbs which contain the *-njili* suffix

Transitive verb	Gloss	Intransitive verb with *-njili* suffix	Gloss
-arnake	'shoot, pierce with long narrow object' (probably once used for 'to spear')	*-arnaka-njili*	'fight with spears, make war'
-artpa	'boil'	*-artpa-njili*	'meet', 'marry'
-u	'give'	*-u-ku-njili*	'exchange things', 'share'
-lalke	'ask'	*-lalka-njili*	'discuss something', 'have meeting'
-wartaw	'add', 'join', 'put together'	*-wartaw-ku-njili*	'mix together', 'join together'
-aya	'see'	*-aya-njili*	'be sweethearts'
-wu	'hit'	*-wu-njili*	'fight'

Two verbs have the additional element *-ku* between the verb root and the *-njili* suffix which is probably a fossilised form of a type of reduplicative suffix used to encode iterative aspect.

Compare the nonreciprocal use of *-wu* 'hit' in (15) with use with the derived *-njili* verb in (16). Note that the verb *-wu* becomes *-pu* due to regular morphophonemic processes at the prefix-root boundary.

---

10. The *-njili* suffix is also found in Iwaidja. It seems to be slightly more productive in Iwaidja than in Mawng (Pym & Larrimore 1979). It is likely that the *-njili* suffix was once the main productive way to form reciprocals in Iwaidjan languages as it appears to be cognate with similar, fully productive reciprocal/reflexive suffixes in other Australian languages (Nick Evans pers. comm.).

(15)   *I-mi-ny*   *nuyu*   *"Nuyi werrk ngan-pu-ni."*
       3M-say-PP   3M.OBL   2SG   first   2SG>1SG-hit-IRR2
       'He said to him, "You hit me first."'   [Mayinaj1 029]

In (15) *-wu* has the transitive verb prefix *ngan-* '2SG/1SG' while in (16) *-wu* 'hit'
has the intransitive plural prefix *a-* '3pl'.

(16)   *Parang la a-wu-njili-nang   malany anny-arlukpa-n*
       [then   ]   3pl-hit-RECP-PC when   3M>3LL-MOVE.FOOT[11]-PP
       rtap ja   Yumparrparr.
       slip   M   giant
       'As they fought Yumparrparr slipped.'   [Giant1 008]

We can compare these two examples with the use of *-wu* 'hit' in the RC construction in (17).

(17)   *Wularrut kun-pu-ning   la   ngapimung.*
       before   1SG>2SG-hit-PC CONJ 1SG.CONTR
       'We had a fight before.'   [Reciprocals1 006]

The reciprocal verbs with *-njili* are similar to the reflexive form of verbs in that
they have an intransitive prefix but are derived from a transitive verb. The reflexive derivation is very simple; it does not involve the addition of a suffix or any
other type of morphology. An example of the formation of a reflexive is shown
below. Example (18) is an example of the transitive verb *-aya* 'see' in nonreflexive
form and (19) is the derived reflexive form of the verb.

(18)   **Transitive**
       Inny-aya-wng.
       3M>3M-see-PP
       'He saw him.'

(19)   **Reflexive**
       Y-aya-wng.
       3M-see-PP
       'He saw him himself.'

The meaning of most *-njili* verbs is transparently related to their transitive root.
The meaning of the predicate *-aya-njili* 'be sweethearts' parallels the meaning of

---

11. The gloss for this verb is written in caps as it is part of a coverb construction with the coverb
rtap.

the RC with verb *-aya* 'see' which can mean 'be in love' as well as 'look at each other'.[12] The only *-njili* verb whose development is difficult to explain is *-artpa-nji-li* 'meet, marry' derived from *-artpa* 'boil'.

3.2   Naturally reciprocal predicates and the bare reciprocal construction

Naturally reciprocal predicates are predicates which have an inherently reciprocal meaning (Kemmer 1993). These are intransitive in Mawng and express reciprocity without the use of any additional morphology or a special syntactic template. For this reason, when they are used to express reciprocity they are said to occur in a "bare reciprocal construction". The class of naturally reciprocal predicates in Mawng includes symmetric predicates (König & Kokutani 2006). These subcategorise for a plural subject and entail reciprocal relations between participants. Some Mawng symmetric predicates are listed in Table 5.

Table 5. Symmetric predicates

Predicate	Gloss
-liki	'back each other up (in a dispute)'
-yirtiki	'help each other'
-ngarunmi	'be similar'
-unmi	'be the same'
-wartpalmuni	'bump into'
-atpi yurnu	'shake hands'

The symmetric predicates are intransitive, like *-njili* verbs. However, they differ from *-njili* verbs in that they are not derived from a transitive verb. The predicate *-atpi yurnu* 'shake hands' is an exception. It is a coverb construction which has developed from the combination of the transitive verb *-atpi* 'hold, have' with the Edible gender noun *yurnu* 'hand, foot'. The Edible gender object agreement has become lexicalised as part of the coverb construction[13].

Another set of naturally reciprocal predicates subcategorise for a plural subject but their meanings can be interpreted as 'collective' as well as 'reciprocal'. These all predicate social relations and are listed in Table 6.

---

12. The association of sight with love/lust is common in Australian languages.

13. See Singer (2006) for more on the lexicalisation of agreement within specific predicates.

Table 6. Predicates of social relations that subcategorise for a plural subject

Predicate	Gloss
-wani	'be married'
-arra walyang	'elope together'
-ngiti	'be namesakes'
-lingan	'be siblings'
-lartparrki	'be countrymen (be from the same area)'
-lakpuntiki	'share land and resources'

There is a third set of predicates which do not subcategorise for a plural subject but have a reciprocal or collective implicature with a plural subject. These verbs are listed in Table 7 with their nonreciprocal meaning and the reciprocal meaning that they can have with plural subjects.

Table 7. Predicates which have a reciprocal or collective implicature with plural subjects

Predicate	Gloss with singular/plural subjects	Implicature with plural subject
-ngurri lintij	'play while running'	'run and play together'
-langali larr	'lean'	'lean on each other'
-lirrinymi	'be angry'	'be angry with each other'
-wani ngarlakarlak	'talk while sitting'	'sit and talk together'
-nginka	'talk'	'talk', 'fight', 'argue with each other'
-ngalkpu	'hit self on the head' (intr.) 'hit OBJ on the head' (tr.)	'fight with each other with sticks'

In (20) the predicate -nginka 'talk' is interpreted as reciprocal.

(20) *Napa*   *k-awu-nginka-ø*   *k-inyi-ma-ø*   *wurlurlu*
      DISC.DEI PRS-3pl-talk-NPST PRS-3M>3F-GET-NPST embrace
      la   *yamin.*
      CONJ 3M.CONTR
      'They're talking and hugging each other.'   [Reciprocals7 046]

The predicate -ngurri lintij 'play, running' can be interpreted as reciprocal or collective in (21).

(21) *K-awu-ngurri-n*   *lintij.*
      PRS-3pl-MOVE.FAST-NPST play
      'They're running and playing.'   [Reciprocals4 022]

The naturally reciprocal predicates in Tables 5–7 are intransitive so they cannot occur in the RC construction but only in the bare reciprocal construction. The bare reciprocal construction is a clause type that by definition lacks construction-specific morphology such as the -njili suffix or the sequence of la plus a contrastive pronoun. A bare reciprocal construction has as its predicate an intransitive verb with nonsingular subject agreement which has an inherent reciprocal meaning within that context.

4.   Summary: Three ways of encoding reciprocity in Mawng

There are three ways of encoding reciprocity in Mawng. Firstly, there are reciprocals formed by syntactic means – through the use of the RC construction. Secondly, there are those formed by morphological means – through the use of the -*njili* suffix. Lastly, there is the bare reciprocal construction which only naturally reciprocal predicates can participate in.

5.   Reciprocals and distributives

Distributives use the same formal template as the RC construction. The use of the reciprocal complex template (shown earlier in Table 1) with an intransitive verb gives a distributive reading as in (22).

(22)   *K-iny-pani-ø   la   inyamin.*
       PRS-3F-sit-NPST   CONJ   3F.CONTR
       'Two women are both sitting.'   [Reciprocals2 084]

Distributives can also involve transitive verbs so ambiguity between distributive and reciprocal readings is possible but in fact in ambiguous cases a reciprocal reading is preferred. A distributive reading is only entertained when a reciprocal reading is unlikely as in (23).

(23)   *K-inyi-la-ø   la   yamin.*
       PRS-3M>3F-eat-NPST   CONJ   3M.CONTR
       'They two (male) each eat a (crab).' (distributive reading)
       OR 'They eat each other (a male and a female).' (reciprocal reading)
                                                             [Control1 058]

There is another form for distributives which is often used to encode situations involving different groups rather than individuals. It is formally similar to the RC but differs in that it does not form a syntagmatic unit with the verb complex. This "group distributive" has a much freer position within the sentence than the RC and can co-occur with an RC or -*njili* reciprocal construction within a single clause.[14]

---

14. See Singer (2006) for more details on distributives.

6.   Categories encoded in the clip data

Responses to the elicitation videos (Evans et al. 2004) were recorded with two speakers at Martpalk, Goulburn Island. The main informant was Nita Garidjalalug, a sixty year old Mawng woman. After recording spontaneous responses to all videos, I then checked the acceptability of the use of an RC construction to describe videos which had not elicited a spontaneous RC response. Altogether around four hours of data were recorded with Nita Garidjalalug. Short responses to the videos were also recorded with Nancy Ngalmindjalmag, a forty-five year old Mawng woman. The data recorded with Nancy Ngalmindjalmag only amounted to around one hour of recording so the data from Nita Garidjalalug forms the basis for the analysis in this section. She and Nancy Ngalmindjalmag differed only slightly in their coding of the videoclips.

When a reciprocal construction was used to describe a clip, the choice of which to use was mainly influenced by whether the most appropriate predicate to describe the video was a naturally reciprocal predicate or -njili verb[15]. Handshaking was encoded using the symmetric predicate -atpi yurnu 'shake hands' so these events were encoded with a bare reciprocal construction. The direct simultaneous exchange of glasses between two people (clip 41) was encoded using the -njili verb -u-ku-njili 'exchange' so this event did not involve an RC construction either. The design of the clips distinguishes 'chasing' and 'following'. These events are both encoded using -yarru 'follow, chase' in Mawng. There does not appear to be a special predicate for 'next to' in Mawng so the 'next to' events were described in diverse ways, often not using a reciprocal construction. Only events with human actors were encoded with a reciprocal.

All symmetrical simultaneous events involving two people were encoded using reciprocal constructions so it is clear that this is the prototypical type of reciprocal situation in Mawng. Most of the sequential dual symmetrical events also elicited a reciprocal construction. There was greater variation in the encoding of asymmetrical dual events. The use of an RC was acceptable for all 'chase' and 'follow' clips. Delousing events were also usually encoded using an RC even when the activity was asymmetrical. This may be related to the prolonged close physical contact involved in delousing, or the expectation that the activity will be reciprocated at some point in the future. RCs were not used to describe other

---

15. Burenhult (this volume) also found that structural restrictions rather than semantic factors largely governed the choice of reciprocal construction used by Jahai speakers. These structural restrictions in Jahai also relate to the structure of the lexicon: certain verbs can participate in certain constructions while others cannot.

types of events if they were carried out in an asymmetrical manner. For example, the use of an RC was judged unacceptable for clip 17 in which the first actor hits a second who fails to respond in any way. Other asymmetrical videos which did not elicit a reciprocal response were videos 25 (one person looks at another who does not seem to notice), 31 (two people look at another who does not seem to notice), 47 (two people sequentially hug another who does not really respond), 59 (one person bumps into a stationary person) and 60 (three people watch a fourth walking past who does not seem to notice). This shows that it is necessary for both participants to react to each other or at least acknowledge each other in some way for an event to be encoded as reciprocal. The symmetrical events involving three or more people mostly elicited reciprocal constructions, but less frequently than the dual events.

7.   Conclusion

The Mawng RC construction is unusual because it still bears many vestiges of the biclausal construction it originated from. The incorporation of body part and theme nouns into the reciprocal complex is clearly a relict of the original biclausal reciprocal construction. Other similarities between the RC construction and a biclausal construction are superficial as the reciprocal complex is functionally equivalent to a single verb complex. The verb retains a transitive prefix in the RC construction but the conventions of agreement differ from those in transitive clauses so it is not clear whether RC construction clauses really have distinct subject and object arguments, particularly when more than two participants act as an undifferentiated group.

Reciprocals formed with the *-njili* suffix are intransitive like reflexives. However, reflexives are quite different to the RC which instead bear formal similarities to distributives. The RC construction is the only Mawng reciprocal construction that is available to any multivalent verb. The choice of which of the three constructions is used is not purely semantic but depends on what type of predicate is most appropriate for describing a particular event. Naturally reciprocal predicates and *-njili* forms tend to be available for events which can only be construed as reciprocal such as *-unjili* 'exchange', *-unmi* 'the same' and *-li-ngan* 'be siblings'. However, there was not a strong correlation between the semantic parameters along which the videos vary and the *type* of reciprocal construction used. Rather we find there is a link between the presence or absence of *any* reciprocal construction and some of the parameters. Speakers use reciprocal constructions more readily to describe events which involve two people, are simultaneous and symmetrical.

Abbreviations

1	First person
1pl.EXCL	first person plural exclusive
1pl.INCL	first person plural inclusive
2	second person
3	third person
AWAY	postverbal directional particle
CONJ	conjunction
CONTR	contrastive pronoun
DISC.DEI	Discourse deictic used to refer to previously mentioned event
ED	edible gender
F	feminine gender
HITH	hither directional suffix
IRR2	irrealis 2 suffix, used for past negative and imperative mood
LL	land gender
M	masculine gender
NEG	negative preverbal particle or prefix
NM.GEN	nonmasculine gender (used in suppletive forms: transitive subject prefix, oblique pronoun)
NPST	nonpast tense suffix
OBL	oblique pronoun
PC	past continuous suffix
PL	plural article
PP	past punctual suffix
PRS	present tense prefix
RECP	reciprocal suffix[16]
SG	singular

Acknowledgements

This research could not have been done without the support of *Warruwi Community*, Goulburn Island. Nita Garidjalalug has been my main guide through the Mawng language and I thank her for her patience. Fieldwork for the research was supported by the University of Melbourne and the Australian Research Council, through the project *Reciprocals Across Languages*. The presentation of this work at the international

---

16. Articles are glossed simply with their gender. Cardinal pronouns are glossed simply with their person and number

Reciprocals Project workshop Max Planck Institute for Psycholinguistics in Nijmegen was supported by the Max Planck Society. Thanks to Nicholas Evans for many interesting discussions about Mawng and Iwaidja reciprocals and their history. My analyses of Mawng reciprocals were also discussed with Rachel Nordlinger and Alice Gaby at the local workshops held at the University of Melbourne. The analyses also benefitted from the discussions at the international project workshop in Nijmegen and input from referees.

References

Capell, Arthur & Hinch, Heather E. 1970. *Maung Grammar*. The Hague: Mouton de Gruyter.

Evans, Nicholas. 2000. Iwaidjan: A very un-Australian language family. *Linguistic Typology* 4: 1–20.

Evans, Nicholas. 2004. Experiencer objects in Iwaidjan languages (Australia). In *Non-nominative Subjects* [Typological Studies in Language 60], Peri Bhaskararao & Karumuri Venkata (eds), 77–100. Amsterdam: John Benjamins.

Evans, Nicholas. 2008. Reciprocal constructions: Towards a structural typology. In *Reciprocals and Reflexives: Cross-linguistic and Theoretical Explorations*, Ekkehard König & Volker Gast (eds.), 169–192. Berlin: Mouton de Gruyter.

Evans, Nicholas, Gaby, Alice & Nordlinger, Rachel. 2007. Valency mismatches and the coding of reciprocity in Australian languages. *Linguistic Typology* 11.2: 543–599.

Evans, Nicholas, Levinson, Stephen C., Enfield, N. J., Gaby, Alice & Majid, Asifa. 2004. Reciprocal constructions and situation type. In *Field Manual,* Vol. 9, Asifa Majid (ed.), 25–30. Nijmegen: Max Planck Institute for Psycholinguistics.

Hewett, Heather, Dineen, Anne, Stainsby, David & Field, Robin. 1990. *Maung Dictionary*. Aboriginal Studies Electronic Data Archive: Australian Institute of Aboriginal and Torres Strait Islander Studies.

Hinch, Heather E. & Pike, Evelyn G. 1978. Speaker-addressee versus third person axes within the Maung verb. *Studies in Language* 2: 151–164.

Hinch, Heather E. Ms. Maung Clauses: United Church in North Australia.

Kemmer, Suzanne. 1993. *The Middle Voice* [Typological Studies in Language 23]. Amsterdam: John Benjamins.

König, Ekkehard & Kokutani, Shigehiro. 2006. Towards a typology of reciprocal constructions: Focus on German and Japanese. *Linguistics* 44: 271–302.

Pym, Noreen & Larrimore, Bonnie. 1979. *Papers on Iwaidja phonology and grammar*. Darwin: SIL-AAB.

Singer, Ruth. 2006. Agreement in Mawng: Productive and Lexicalised Uses of Verbal Gender Agreement in an Australian Language. PhD dissertation, The University of Melbourne.

CHAPTER 15

Reciprocal-marked and marked reciprocal events in Kuuk Thaayorre

Alice Gaby

University of California at Berkeley

Kuuk Thaayorre has a single dedicated reciprocal marker, the verbal suffix *-rr*. There are, however, a number of alternative strategies for encoding semantically reciprocal events. This chapter outlines the five constructions that may overtly signal reciprocity in an event and explores which features of reciprocal events motivate the choice between these alternative encoding strategies. It also emphasises the role of non-reciprocal clauses as a valid means of encoding reciprocal event types. I propose that event typicality is a critical factor in determining whether speakers employ a reciprocal or non-reciprocal construction in describing these events. Where the event described approaches the prototype for the verb in question, overt reciprocal coding is usually omitted. Where the event described is atypical of the events usually described by that verb, overt reciprocal coding is strongly preferred.

1.   The language and its speakers

Kuuk Thaayorre is a Pama-Nyungan language spoken on the west coast of Cape York Peninsula, Australia. Though seriously endangered, more than three hundred people currently speak Kuuk Thaayorre today, including a number of children. Its vibrant and creative use is central to daily life in the community of Pormpuraaw.

Tense, aspect, mood and voice are encoded by verbal morphology. Grammatical relations are signalled by nominal case-marking, which makes a tripartite distinction between ergative, nominative and accusative cases. It is commonplace in Kuuk Thaayorre for a single argument to be realised by multiple, apposed noun phrases. For example, the children under discussion in (1) are referred to as both *parr_r inh* 'these children' and *peln* 'they'.

(1) *parr_r*   *inh*   *yan*   *peln*   *school-thak*
     child(NOM) dem:prox go:NPST 3PL(NOM) school-DAT
     'These children (nowadays) go to school.'   [AC Conversation]

Cardinal pronouns may be either free or encliticised. These pronouns distinguish singular, dual and plural number and are the only repository for this information, nouns being unmarked for number.

Kuuk Thaayorre approaches the prototype of a nonconfigurational language (Hale 1983, Austin and Bresnan 1996). Any and all clausal constituents may be elided and the order of overtly realised constituents is pragmatically, rather than syntactically, determined.

The data discussed here were collected by the author over five field trips between 2002 and 2005. The speaker, utterance context (i.e. elicitation, conversation or narrative) and elicitation stimulus (where appropriate) are specified for all examples in a line immediately below the translation.

2.   Thaayorre reciprocal constructions

Each of the six construction types listed in Table 1 are used to describe semantically reciprocal events.

Table 1. Inventory of Thaayorre constructions used to encode reciprocal events

Construction name	Defining features	Examples
Core reciprocal construction	Presence of verbal suffix -*rr* 'RECP', single subject argument encodes both Actors and Undergoers.	(2), (17)
Asymmetric reciprocal construction	Presence of verbal suffix -*rr* 'RECP', subject encodes Actor(s) only, object encodes Undergoer(s) only.	(4)
Reflexive construction	Presence of verbal suffix -*e*.	(7), (8)
Lexical reciprocal construction	Verbal head entails reciprocity in the absence of overt reciprocal coding.	(10)
Double role marking construction	Reciprocant superset encoded as subject, subset of reciprocants dative-marked	(11), (12)
Non-reciprocal construction	No overt coding of reciprocity	(13), (16), (18)

Sections 2.1 and 2.2 detail the morphosyntax of these constructions, whilst Section 3 examines their relative distributions in the corpus of responses to the reciprocals elicitation stimuli described in Chapter 2 (cf. Evans et al. 2004).

2.1   Verb-marking strategies

2.1.1   *Core reciprocal construction*

The core reciprocal construction is defined by the presence of the reciprocal verbal suffix -*rr*, as seen in (2):

(2)   *pul   ngamal.katp-rr-ica-rr*
       3DU(NOM)   hug[1]-RECP-RUN.AND-P.PFV
       'They two went and hugged each other.'   [IC Elicitation RCP23]

In the core reciprocal construction, the reciprocal-marked verb (derived from a bivalent verb root) is paired with a single, subject argument that encodes both Actors and Undergoers. The form of this construction can be schematised as (3):

(3)   **Core reciprocal construction**: V-*rr* <SUBJ$_{non-sg}$>

2.1.2   *Asymmetric reciprocal construction*

Asymmetric reciprocal events (cf. Chapter 1) are optionally encoded by a distinct construction in which the *rr*-marked verb is paired with a transitive argument configuration: an ergative-marked subject and accusative-marked object. This construction is exemplified by (4) and can be schematised as in (5):

(4)   *pam-al   ulp   nhunh   paanth   ulp*
       man-ERG   dem:fam   3SG.ACC   woman(ACC)   dem:fam
       koorr   waak-rr-ø   nhul
       behind   follow-RECP-NPST   3SG(ERG)
       'That man is following along behind that woman.'   [FT Elicitation RCP26]

(5)   **Asymmetric reciprocal construction**: V-*rr* <SUBJ$_{ERG}$, OBJ$_{ACC}$>

2.1.3   *Reflexive construction*

Kuuk Thaayorre possesses a dedicated reflexive suffix, -*e* (seen with its canonical reflexive use in (6)). The reflexive construction defined by the presence of this morpheme is also used to encode a number of the putatively reciprocal event types represented in the stimulus clips, as seen in (7).

(6)   *kuta   ith   yiin=p   path<ath>-e*
       dog(NOM)   DEM:DIST   itch=PRAG   bite<RDP>-RFL:NPST
       'That dog keeps biting itself (because it has an itch).'

---

1.   The Thaayorre equivalent of *hug* (*ngamal katp*) is a phrasal verb composed of the adjective *ngamal* 'large' and the verb *katp* 'grasp'.

(7) *pul*   *korpn*   *nhaa<nha>th-e-ø*
    3DU(ERG)   louse(ACC)   hit<RDP>-RFL-NPST
    'They two are searching each other('s hair) for lice.'   [GJ Elicitation RCP45]

There are in fact two subtypes of reflexive construction, differing in argument structure. This variation is discussed in Gaby (2006) and is unrelated to the semantic parameters at issue here. For our purposes we need only identify a single reflexive construction (exemplified by (6)) which is defined by the presence of the verbal suffix *-e*.

To be eligible for reflexive coding, reciprocal events must satisfy two criteria:

1. There is close (physical) contact between participants
2. The actions of each participant must be coordinated

The video described in (8), for instance, satisfies these criteria in that: (1) physical contact is made between participants at the moment of collision; (2) the bumping event is dependent upon the respective movements of the two participants being coordinated – if either diverges from their path the collision will be avoided:

(8) *runc-e-r*
    bump-RFL-P.PFV
    '[They] bumped into one another.'   [IC Elicitation RCP55]

Example (9) satisfies the criteria in that: (1) the two participants are touching (each one's back against the other's); (2) they are mutually supporting – if one participant were to move the leaning event could not be sustained:

(9) *pul*   *mut-u*   *thaa.yoo<yo>ngk-e-ø*
    3DU(NOM)   back-ERG   lean<RDP>-RFL-NPST
    'They are leaning (on themselves) with their backs.'   [GJ Elicitation RCP12]

These criteria likewise hold for all the reflexive-coded descriptions of the reciprocal stimuli (see Gaby 2008 for further discussion).

2.1.4 *Lexical strategy*

I have recorded only one monomorphemic verb form that strictly entails reciprocity. This verb is *wuuthaw* 'share', which prototypically describes the communal distribution of food, but also events like the following:

(10) *kar mimp*   *wuuthaw-ø*
     like cloth(ACC)   share-NPST
     '[We] share clothes with one another, for instance.'   [YNg Conversation]

Unlike in English, a Kuuk Thaayorre speaker is unable to single out the initiator of the sharing event (as in *He shared his food with me*). Instead, *wuuthaw* 'share' subcategorises for a nonsingular subject to which it assigns both Agent and Recipient semantic roles.

There are two further *lexicalised* reciprocal verbs. These frozen forms were originally composed of a verb root + reciprocal suffix but are no longer semantically compositional.[2] Hence *wakrr* 'fight' derives historically from *wak* 'chase, follow, hunt' + *rr* 'RECP' and *pungk.ko'orr-* 'meet up' from *pungk* 'knee' + *ko'o* 'spear' + *rr* 'RECP'[3].

2.2   NP-marking strategy: Double role marking construction

In the double role marking construction reciprocity is signalled by the case marking of reciprocants in the absence of special verbal marking. The entire group of participants involved in the reciprocal event is encoded by a 'superset' pronoun (e.g. *pul* 'they two' in (11)). Additionally, though, a subset of these participants is encoded by a separate, dative-marked NP (*pam kunyangkar nhangnmun* 'with his brother'):

(11) *pul*   *pam kunyangkar nhangn-mun kuuk*   *yi\<i>k-ø*
      3DU(NOM) man   sibling   3SG.POSS-DAT WORD(ACC) say\<RDP>-NPST
      'He and his brother are talking (+> to each other).'   [MF Elicitation]

In the core reciprocal construction, it must be the direct object argument that is deleted due to its coreference with the subject. Hence alternative means must be found for encoding reciprocity where the predicate lacks an eligible direct object. This is where the double role marking construction comes in, since it allows reciprocants to be classed together as a superset participant group (by the subject pronoun), while still representing the oblique argument (and associated semantic role) via the dative-marked subset noun phrase.

---

2. Since these lexicalised reciprocal verbs both exhibit the reciprocal suffix *-rr* and entail reciprocity they were coded as examples of the core reciprocal construction for the statistical analysis reported in Majid et al. (Chapter 2).

3. It is unclear why the verb used to describe meeting events should etymologically derive from the description of reciprocal knee-spearing. At this stage I can only conjecture that this might result from the semantic broadening of a term originally describing the ritual punishing of a wrongdoer by spearing him through the knee.

In describing reciprocals stimulus clip #15 (in which two man-and-woman pairs sit next to each other), for instance, the speaker is unable to employ the core reciprocal construction (because the verb *nhiin* 'sit' is monovalent), nor the reflexive construction (because the event does not fit the criteria given above), nor is there any relevant lexical reciprocal verb or other symmetric predicate (like English *next to*). Instead, the speaker utters a double role marking construction to describe the initial subevent – encoding both man and woman as *pul* 'they two', in addition to two subset NPs *pam* 'the man' and *paanthak* 'with the woman' to mark the multiple roles of the participants – followed by a non-reciprocal clause describing the second subevent:

(12) *pam*   *ith*   *pul*   *paanth-ak*   *nhiin-nhat*   *pul*
      man(NOM) DEM:DIST 3DU(NOM) woman-DAT sit-GO.AND:P.PFV 3DU(NOM)
      'They two went and sat down, the man with the woman.'
      ngul *pul*   *ith*   *yokunmanorrp* *nhiin-nhat*
      then   3DU(NOM) DEM:DIST same.way   sit-GO.AND:P.PFV
      'Then those two went and sat in the same way.'   [GJ Elicitation RCP15]

This strategy may also be used to mark coreference between a subject and a (deleted) oblique argument of a verb that does subcategorise for a direct object. For instance *yik* 'talk, say' (seen in (11) above) subcategorises for a nominative case subject, a dative case indirect object (representing the target or Recipient of the speech), and an accusative case direct object (representing the content or language of the speech)[4]. Despite its subcategorising for a direct object, this verb may never enter into the core reciprocal construction since its direct object argument is ineligible for reciprocal binding for semantic reasons (i.e. the semantic field from which the direct object must be selected – i.e. speech – does not overlap with the semantic field from which the subject must be selected – i.e. social animals). Accordingly, reciprocal events of talking are always encoded by means of this double role-marking strategy.

The syntactic and semantic implications of this construction are elaborated upon in Gaby (2005) and Gaby (2006).

2.3   Non-reciprocal construction

Not all semantically reciprocal events are explicitly encoded as such. In (13), for instance, a reciprocal event is encoded by a simple intransitive clause ('he and his

---

4. In Gaby (2006) *yik* 'talk, say' is classified as a semiditransitive verb, as opposed to semi-transitive verbs which subcategorise for just a nominative-case subject and dative-case indirect object.

brother are talking') which nevertheless has a strong implicature of symmetry due to the absence of a specified external recipient:

(13) *pul*   *kuuk*   *yi<i>k-ø*
      3DU(NOM) WORD(ACC)   say<RDP>-NPST
      'They two are talking (+> to each other).'   [LN Elicitation]

In (14) a normally bivalent verb is paired with a single subject argument:

(14) *peln*   *ngamal.ka<a>tp-r*
      3PL(NOM=ERG) hug<RDP>-NPST
      'They're hugging (+> each other).'   [AJ Elicitation RCP2]

Evans (2008) classifies analogous clauses as examples of a 'bare conjunct' recipro-cal strategy, in which reciprocants are encoded as the single argument of a (usu-ally bivalent) predicate, thereby reducing clausal transitivity by one. But there are two key differences between the English bare reciprocal clauses (exemplified by the translation of (14), cf. Hurst and Nordlinger, this volume) and their Thaay-orre equivalents. Firstly, the English bare reciprocal differs from a standard non-reciprocal clause in the reduction of valency brought about by the omission of the direct object. So the bare reciprocal clause *they're hugging* is intransitive, despite the fact that the verb root *hug* subcategorises for two arguments. In English, it is not possible to omit arguments under normal (non-reciprocal) circumstances. Thus one cannot say **he's hugging*, because the singular subject argument rules out a bare reciprocal interpretation. In Kuuk Thaayorre, by contrast, it is always possible to omit the direct object of a clause (and any other argument). Hence (15) is perfectly grammatical, although it describes a non-reciprocal event:

(15) *nhul*   *ngamal.katpi-rr*
      3SG(ERG) hug-P.PFV
      'He hugged [the dog].'   [MF Narrative FrogStory]

The verb *ngamal katp* 'hug' likewise remains bivalent in (14) despite the ellipsis of the definite object NP[5]. A further difference between the Kuuk Thaayorre clause in (14) and its English conjunct reciprocal translation is that reciprocity is entailed by the latter but not the former, which could alternatively mean 'they are hug-ging someone else'. Not all English conjunct reciprocal clauses entail reciprocity,

---

5. It is, therefore, possible to fill both argument slots of the verb *ngamal.katp-* 'hug' (as in (i)), showing it to be a regular bivalent verb.

    (i) *pul*   *pam-al*   *paanth*   *ngamal.ka<a>tp-r*
         3DU(ERG) man-ERG woman(ACC) hug<RDP>-NPST
         'The two men hug the two women.'   [FT10/02/04 RCP2]

though. As Lakoff and Peters (1969), Kemmer (1993) and Levin (1993) have documented, there is wide variation both within and between languages as to whether reciprocity is implied or entailed in such conjunct reciprocal clauses. Thus English *they hugged* entails reciprocity, while *they talked for an hour* does not (they may have been talking to an external audience). But the fact that the English conjunct reciprocal construction does in some cases entail reciprocity – and permits an argument configuration that is otherwise impossible – justifies it as a distinct reciprocal strategy. There are no such Thaayorre clauses that can be identified as unambiguously reciprocal, however.

For these reasons, I do not distinguish a Kuuk Thaayorre 'bare reciprocal' construction from standard non-reciprocal clauses.

3.   Categorisation of reciprocal stimuli

3.1   Data

This chapter draws upon a range of elicited, narrative and spontaneous conversational data. Its focus, however, is upon data elicited by means of the set of reciprocal stimulus video clips described in Evans et al. (2004). I ran pilot version of this stimulus set (which included many of the video stimuli used in the final version) with two Kuuk Thaayorre speakers. I later ran the final (full) set of stimuli with three consultants, all aged between 40 and 60. Although the results of the pilot study were not included for statistical analysis, they proved valuable in evaluating how representative were the responses to the full stimulus set.

3.2   Distribution of constructions over event types

The reciprocals stimuli depict a range of event types manipulated for systematic variation across a number of parameters. The key variables were: (a) event type (varied for 'saturation' and 'symmetry', and classed as 'strong', 'pairwise', 'adjacent', etc. – see Chapter 1 for explication of these terms); (b) sequence (i.e. whether subevents occur simultaneously or sequentially); and (c) number of participants. Table 2 summarises the compatibility of each of the constructions outlined in Section 2 with each of these variables. The use of a particular construction (organised by column) in the description of a scene exhibiting the particular variable (organised by row) is indicated by a tick in the relevant cell. An empty cell indicates that there are no examples of the construction/variable combination in my data, but does not entail that such a combination is impossible.

Table 2. Distribution of constructions over reciprocal event types

Construction type / Event type	Core reciprocal	Asymmetric reciprocal	Lexical reciprocal	Reflexive	Double role marking	Non-reciprocal
Strong	✓		✓	✓	✓	✓
Pairwise	✓		✓	✓	✓	✓
Adjacent	✓		✓	✓	✓	✓
Chaining	✓		✓	✓		✓
Melee	✓		✓			✓
Asymmetric	✓	✓				✓

Every event type – regardless of sequence and number of participants – may be encoded by the core reciprocal construction in at least some cases. Likewise, there are no event variables that force overt reciprocal coding – the use of a non-reciprocal construction is always a grammatical alternative. The use of lexicalised reciprocal verbs is nearly as broad, applying to all event types but the asymmetric. At the other end of the scale is the asymmetric reciprocal (sub-)construction. As its name suggests, this construction is only ever found in the description of asymmetric events.

The distributions of the reflexive and the double role marking constructions were conditioned by semantics and argument structure respectively, as discussed above.

3.3   Markedness and the reciprocal prototype

Section 2 explored which of the alternative reciprocal constructions may be employed in the description of the various stimuli (also summarised in Section 3.2). Possibly more interesting, however, is the question of when and why a speaker chooses to overtly encode the reciprocity of an event rather than employing a non-reciprocal construction. We might assume there to be a reciprocal prototype[6], such that the likelihood of overt reciprocal coding correlates with the degree to which the event described approximates this reciprocal prototype. I wish to suggest that such a correlation exists, but that it is the reciprocal events that are <u>least typical</u> that are most likely to be reciprocal-marked. I thus argue that the Thaayorre reciprocal construction (like those of many other languages) primarily marks atypical reciprocal events.

---

6. Cf. Dalrymple et al. (1998) and Evans (2008) for suggestions of what this prototype might be.

Reciprocal events can be atypical in one of two ways. Firstly, they may be atypical simply by virtue of being reciprocal, where the event in question is one that is rarely reciprocated. Secondly, where the event described is frequently reciprocated, an atypical reciprocal instantiation of that event will be one where the nature of the reciprocation itself is unusual. Illustrating the first case, shaving events are usually reflexive, so a rare reciprocal shaving event will be overtly coded as such (i.e. *they shaved each other*, not *they shaved*). Likewise, the Thaayorre verb *thiik* 'break' almost never encodes a reciprocal event, since breaking events usually involve an animate agent upon an inanimate object which is unable to reciprocate. Accordingly, the non-reciprocal clause *peln thiikarr* 'they broke (something)' does not permit a reciprocal interpretation (e.g. 'they [robots] broke each other') for the speakers questioned. A reciprocal breaking event must be explicitly marked as such.

To illustrate the second kind of atypicality, let us consider events of hugging. Although a unidirectional hug is possible (and indeed depicted by stimulus clip 16, in which three people hug an unresponsive woman), hugging events usually involve simultaneous reciprocation between two people. Such typical reciprocal hugging events (i.e. where A hugs B at the same time as B hugs A, as depicted in stimulus clip 7) are rarely encoded by a reciprocal construction in my data. More usual is a non-reciprocal description, as in (16):

(16) *pul*   *ngamal.katp-ica-rr*
      3DU(NOM)   hug-GO.AND-P.PFV
      'They two went and hugged (+> each other).'   [IC Elicitation RCP7]

That such typical events are pragmatically – and consequently morphosyntactically – unmarked fits Haiman's (1983) and Kemmer's (1993) observations with respect to the iconicity of unmarked, 'naturally reciprocal' events. Conversely, less typical events (e.g. stimulus clip 20, in which three people hug simultaneously) regularly receive overt reciprocal marking:

(17) *paanth   pinalam   ith*   *ngamal.katp-rr-ø   peln*
      woman   three(NOM)   DEM:DIST   hug-RECP-NPST   3PL(NOM)
      'The three women hug each other.'   [FT10/02/04 Elicitation RCPpilot20]

How closely the event described matches the usual state of affairs described by the predicate thus seems to correlate with the presence or absence of overt reciprocal marking, with more unusual or aberrant events more likely to be encoded by the reciprocal construction. What counts as unusual must be judged on an event-by-event basis. Thus the event of washing is common in most English-speaking cultures, but it is rarely reciprocated. Accordingly, a reciprocal event of washing requires overt coding as such (e.g. *they washed each other*, not *they washed*).

Events of communication (e.g. chatting, arguing), by contrast, rarely receive overt reciprocal marking, as these are expected to involve some degree of reciprocation. Moreover, the kind of reciprocity considered typical will vary from event type to event type. Whilst it is normal for hugging events to be simultaneously and bi-directionally reciprocated (i.e. for A to hug B at the same time as B hugs A), this is impossible for events of following (i.e. A can't follow B at the same time as B follows A). Instead, the chaining reciprocal subtype is more typical for a following event (where A follows B who follows C who follows D, etc.).

The determination of where reciprocity must be overtly coded and where it can be left to inference is of course mediated by cultural knowledge. That is to say, whether a reciprocal event qualifies as sufficiently 'prototypical' to be unmarked will depend on the culture-specific frequency with which a particular event type is reciprocated, rather than unidirectional. Consider, for example, utterance (18):

(18) *parr_r*   *ith*   *peln*   *thaa-whistle*   *thunp-r*
      kid(#ERG)[7] DEM:DIST 3PL(ERG) mouth-whistle(ACC) throw-NPST
      'Those kids are whistling (+>at each other).'   [LN Conversation/Elicitation]

In English, the sentence *those kids are whistling* does not carry a reciprocal im-plicature, since the default interpretation is that the kids are whistling a tune to themselves. In Kuuk Thaayorre, reciprocation is implicated because it is common for people to whistle at one another to attract and sustain attention (especially during courtship).

Though the determination of whether reciprocity is typical for a particular event is culture-specific, the underlying principles extend beyond Kuuk Thaayor-re (and English) and beyond the reciprocal domain. These principles are founded in Grice's (1975:45) maxim of Quantity (as well as Levinson's 2000 *I heuristic*):

(19) *Do not make your contribution more informative than is required.*

Overt coding of reciprocity suggests that the event described is reciprocal in a way that the addressee would not already infer from the use of the simple verb alone. Thus in (17) the inclusion of the reciprocal suffix signals that the hugging event is reciprocal in an atypical way (i.e. because three women hug simultane-ously). In Example (16), however, the speaker does not overtly code the reciproc-ity of the event (in which two people hug each other simultaneously). Because simultaneous, pairwise reciprocity is usual for hugging events, the overt cod-ing of reciprocity here would be "more informative than is required" (see also

---

7. The ergative case assigned to this NP by the bivalent verb *thunp* 'throw' is not overtly coded because *parr_r ith* 'those kids' is both topical and a 'likely agent' (cf. Gaby [forthcoming] on the optionality of ergative marking in Kuuk Thaayorre).

Levinson's 2000: 37 *I-heuristic*). But for verbs that rarely describe reciprocal events (e.g. *shave, thiik* 'break') reciprocity of any kind is sufficient to trigger overt reciprocal coding, since the addressee is unlikely to infer that the event is reciprocal from a non-reciprocal description, requiring a higher level of "informativeness" from the speaker.

4.   Conclusion

The overt reciprocal coding of events in Kuuk Thaayorre is restricted by neither saturation, sequentiality, nor the number of participants. Excepting the symmetric reciprocal, none of the parameters systematically varied in the reciprocals field task (Evans et al. 2004) correlates with a categorical boundary between Thaayorre reciprocal constructions. Which (if any) of the reciprocal coding strategies is used in the description of the various stimulus video clips is instead determined by: (a) the existence of an applicable lexical reciprocal verb (Section 2.1.4); (b) the valency of the relevant verb root (monovalent verbs may not undergo reciprocal derivation – the double role marking strategy (Section 2.2) is employed here instead); (c) the mutual orientation of participants engaged in an asymmetric event (favouring the asymmetric reciprocal construction (Section 2.1.2)); and (d) the mutual dependence and physical closeness of reciprocants whose respective contributions are not differentiated (favouring the reflexive construction (Section 2.1.3)).

This chapter has further investigated why reciprocity was overtly coded for certain stimulus clips but left to inference for others. This appears to be determined by how closely the scene approximates the prototypical event-type associated with the predicate. Hence a simultaneous event of hugging involving two people – though close to our notional prototype of a prelinguistic reciprocal event – is less likely to be encoded by a reciprocal construction than an event in which three people hug simultaneously. The more usual it is for a particular event type to involve reciprocation, the more likely a language is to develop a lexical reciprocal verb (e.g. *share*) or to use a non-reciprocal construction (e.g. *they shook hands*) in order to describe it. I argued above that the use of non-reciprocal constructions to describe reciprocal events has its basis in Grice's maxim of Quantity, inasmuch as overt reciprocal coding on verbs that commonly describe reciprocal events is overly informative, and therefore to be avoided. The exception to this is where the event described is reciprocal in an unusual way, in which case reciprocal marking is preferred.

The general principles of conversational implicature and the association between morphosyntactic markedness and pragmatic markedness are not specific to any one language. However, the assessment of events as typical or atypical – as well as the determination of what counts as morphosyntactically 'marked' – is culture-specific. Based on their individual experiences of the world, I assume that speakers build a mental model of the norms of human behaviour, including norms of reciprocity and of individual event types. Speakers of the same cultural background build similar mental models due to their exposure to a similar range of events (cf. Clark 1996, Enfield 2000, 2002). Given these congruent mental models of event typicality, speakers are able to predict how informative they need be in order for their addressee to correctly infer the nature of the event described. Where the event is judged to be atypical of the kinds of event usually described by the verb in question, "speakers are compelled to overtly mention [the event's] markedness, in order to activate non-default cultural representations in the minds of interlocutors, ensuring convergent culturally logical solutions" (Enfield 2002: 254). Given that the majority of reciprocal events occurring in the real world are (by definition) typical, it comes as no surprise that overtly reciprocal constructions are a rarity in my Kuuk Thaayorre corpus, as well as the corpora of many other languages. Moreover, the fact that the most prototypical reciprocal events are for many languages the least likely to receive overt reciprocal coding has clear implications for cross-linguistic investigations of reciprocity, and the search for a reciprocal prototype in particular.

Abbreviations

Abbreviations employed here are:

3	Third person	PL	Plural
ACC	Accusative	POSS	possessive pronoun
DAT	Dative	P.PFV	Past perfective
DEM:DIST	distal adnominal demonstrative	PRAG	pragmatic enclitic
		RDP	reduplicated
DU	Dual	RECP	reciprocal
ERG	Ergative	RFL	reflexive
GO.AND	first associated motion verbal suffix	RUN.AND	second associated motion verbal suffix
NOM	Nominative	SG	singular
NPST	Nonpast		

In the practical orthography employed here an underscore is used to separate two adjacent rhotic segments. Hence 'rr_r' represents an alveolar tap followed by a retroflex glide, while 'r_rr' represents a retroflex glide followed by a tap.

References

Austin, Peter & Bresnan, Joan. 1996. Nonconfigurationality in Australian aboriginal languages. *Natural Language & Linguistic Theory* 14: 215–68.

Clark, Herbert H. 1996. *Using Language.* Cambridge: CUP.

Dalrymple, Mary, Kanazawa, Makoto, Kim, Yookyung, Mchombo, Sam & Peters, Stanley. 1998. Reciprocal expressions and the concept of reciprocity. *Linguistics & Philosophy* 21(2): 159–210.

Enfield, N. J. 2000. The theory of cultural logic. *Cultural Dynamics* 12(1): 35–64.

Enfield, N. J. 2002. Cultural logic and syntactic productivity: Associated posture constructions in Lao. In *Ethnosyntax: Explorations in Grammar and Culture*, N. J. Enfield (ed.), 231–258. Oxford: OUP.

Evans, Nicholas, Levinson, Stephen C., Enfield, N. J., Gaby, Alice & Majid, Asifa. 2004. Reciprocal constructions and situation type. In *Field Manual,* Vol. 9, Asifa Majid (ed.), 25–30. Nijmegen: Max Planck Institute for Psycholinguistics.

Evans, Nicholas. 2008. Reciprocals: Towards a structural typology. In *Reflexives and Reciprocals: Theoretical and Cross-linguistic Explorations*, Ekkehard König & Volker Gast (eds), Berlin: Mouton de Gruyter.

Gaby, Alice. 2005. Some participants are more equal than others: Case and the composition of arguments in Kuuk Thaayorre. In *The Case for Case: Competition and Variation in Natural Language*, Mengistu Amberber & Helen de Hoop (eds), 9–39. Amsterdam: Elsevier.

Gaby, Alice. 2006. A Grammar of Kuuk Thaayorre. PhD dissertation, University of Melbourne.

Gaby, Alice. 2008. Distinguishing reflexives from reciprocals in Kuuk Thaayorre. In *Reflexives and Reciprocals: Theoretical and Cross-linguistic Explorations*, Ekkehard König & Volker Gast (eds), Berlin: Mouton de Gruyter.

Grice, H. Paul. 1975. Logic and conversation. In *Syntax and Semantics: Speech Acts*, Peter Cole & Jerry L. Morgan (eds), 41–58. New York NY: Academic Press.

Haiman, John. 1983. Iconic and economic motivation. *Language* 59(4): 781–819.

Hale, Ken. 1983. Warlpiri and the grammar of non-configurational languages. *Natural Language and Linguistic Theory* 1: 5–59.

Kemmer, Suzanne. 1993. *The Middle Voice* [Typological Studies in Language 23]. Amsterdam: John Benjamins.

Lakoff, George & Peters, Stanley. 1969. Symmetric predicates and phrasal conjunction. In *Modern Studies in English*, David Reibel & Sanford Schane (eds), 113–42. Upper Saddle River NJ: Prentice-Hall.

Levin, Beth. 1993. *English Verb Classes and Alternations. A Preliminary Investigation.* Chicago IL: The University of Chicago Press.

Levinson, Stephen C. 2000. *Presumptive Meanings.* Cambridge MA: The MIT Press.

CHAPTER 16

Reciprocal constructions in Olutec

Roberto Zavala Maldonado
CIESAS-Sureste

Olutec exhibits three reciprocal strategies each of which convey different levels
of prominence of the second reciprocant. In the /*conjoined subject strategy*/,
both reciprocants share the same topical status. In the /*subject cum adjunct
strategy*/ the second reciprocant is treated as background information; while in
the /*subject and object strategy*/, the second reciprocant shares the same degree
of prominence with the regular primary object. The existence of these three
strategies within a language indicates that the pragmatic status of the reciprocants is a key factor to be considered in the cross-linguistic study of reciprocal
constructions.

1. Introduction

Olutec is a Mixe-Zoquean language of the Mixean branch spoken by a dozen
people in the southern part of the state of Veracruz, in Mexico. It is considered
one of the most conservative Mixe-Zoquean languages since it maintains phonological and morphological features that have been reconstructed for the common
ancestor of the Mixe-Zoquean languages, which have disappeared in other members of the family (Kaufman 1995, Wichmann 1995). For lexicographical and
grammatical information on this language see Zavala (1998, 1999, 2000, 2002a,
2002b, 2006). Olutec exhibits the following typological features: (1) it is a head-
marking and polysynthetic language with a complex verbal template that includes
affixes, incorporated nouns and adverbs, nuclear serial verbs and predicates with
depictive reading, (2) voice changing operations that include causativisation, pas-
sivisation and applicativisation are marked on the verb by affixes, (3) the pronominal proclitics on the verb follow an ergative/absolutive pattern in both simple and
complex clauses, (4) bivalent predicates exhibit a direct vs. inverse opposition,
and (5) it includes most traits of an OV language, although synchronically the
word order of the core arguments is quite flexible.

Olutec exhibits two types of clauses: independent and dependent. This distinction is overtly signaled by different paradigms of aspectual, pronominal and inverse markers attached to the verb. Independent clauses are matrix clauses, whereas dependent clauses are clauses following matrix verbs, auxiliaries, adverbs, and secondary predicates. Olutec exhibits three sets of person proclitics that will be glossed as Set A, Set B and Set C. Set A has the ergative function in independent clauses and the absolutive function in dependent clauses; it also marks possessors of nouns in all clause types. Set B functions as absolutive in independent clauses, and Set C functions as ergative in dependent clauses. Table 1 summarises the aspectual, pronominal and inverse markers that distinguish independent from dependent clauses.

Table 1. Marking patterns in independent and dependent clauses

		Independent	Dependent
Aspect	incompletive	*-pa* (intr.), *-pe* (tr.)	*-i /-e*
	completive	*-u/-w*	*-i*
	irrealis	*-am* (DIR)/ *-an...-pa* (INV)	*-ane*
Pronominal	ergative	Set A	Set C
	absolutive	Set B	Set A
Inverse	incompletive	*-ü*	*-j*
	completive	*-ü*	*-y*

All transitive verbs in Olutec show a direct/inverse opposition. In the direct construction the highest ranked participant in person or topicality aligns with the agent, whereas in the inverse, the highest ranked participant aligns with the primary object (PO). Only one pronominal appears as a proclitic in a transitive verb. In the direct pattern, the verb bears the ergative, whereas in the inverse pattern, it takes the absolutive instead. The plural suffixes for third person, *-küx*, or for first or second person, *-V:t* may cross-reference either core participant of the clause. The incompletive aspect marker for direct transitive clauses is *-pe*, whereas the equivalent aspectual marker for inverse clauses is *-pa*, which also appears with intransitive verbs. Examples (1) and (2) illustrate the direct/inverse alternation for independent clauses in incompletive aspect. The direct relation first-person acting on third-person plural is illustrated in (1), whereas the inverse relation third-person plural acting on first-person is illustrated in (2).

(1)   *tan=tze:k-küx-pe*   *jeʔtükaj*
       A1(ERG)=scold-PL3-INC.TR they
       'I am scolding them.'

(2) *ta=tze:k-küx-ü-pa*   *jeʔtükaj*
     B1(ABS)=scold-PL3-INV-INC.INTR they
     'They are scolding me.'

Example (3) illustrates an intransitive clause following the independent marking pattern.

(3) *xüw=jeʔ*   *ʔü:tz* *ta=ma:jʔ-pa*
     day=CLEFT I   B1(ABS)=sleep-INC.INTR
     'It is during the day that I sleep.'

2. Reciprocal constructions in Olutec

Olutec has three major reciprocal constructions, all involving the verbal prefix *ni-*. The most basic strategy – corresponding to Maslova's (1999) 'simple strategy' and Evans' (2008) 'predicate marking' strategy – conveys the two reciprocants in one syntactic slot, while the other two express the implicated reciprocants in two different syntactic slots. The three different types of constructions will be referred to as: (1) conjoined subject strategy, (2) subject cum adjunct strategy, and the (3) subject and object strategy. The second and third constructions did not come up in running the clips since these last two strategies are used in complex discourse contexts that manipulate the degree of topicality of the reciprocants implicated in the event, but these types of contexts were not portrayed in the clips. In the second strategy one of the reciprocants is foregrounded while the other is backgrounded. In the third strategy, both reciprocants are foregrounded but the first one is more prominent than the second one. All three strategies are only possible when the predicate involved is a transitive base that follows the inverse marking pattern.

Table 2. Reciprocal constructions and the expression of the reciprocating participants

1	*ni*-V with conjoined subject
2	*ni*-V with subject cum adjunct
3	*ni*-V with subject and object

Some Olutec intransitive verbs with plural subject may express a reciprocal reading inferred by implicature without entailing it. This type of construction will not be discussed below, since there is no overt expression of reciprocity and the construction is never used to express canonical reciprocal events like hug, shake hands, meet, make love, etc.

2.1   The conjoined subject strategy

Olutec uses the same morphological resources for coding reflexive and reciprocal constructions. There are three morphosyntactic signs that flag a reflexive/reciprocal construction in this language: (1) an explicit reflexive/reciprocal (RR) prefix *ni-* that only occurs with transitive bases, (2) an inverse marker, and (3) an absolutive pronominal affix cross-referencing the subject that refers to the coreferential participant (in the reflexive construction) or the whole reciprocant set (in the reciprocal construction). The example in (4) illustrates these features in a reflexive construction, whereas the examples in (5) and (6) illustrate the same features with reciprocal constructions. In the conjoined subject strategy, an overt plural marker is always suffixed to the verb: *-küx* for third person and *-Vt* for speech act participants. The clause in (5) has an alternative reflexive reading with plural subject.

(4)   *ta=ni-ʔawma:xantun-ü-pa*
      B1(ABS)=RR-cross-INV-INC.INTR
      'I am crossing myself.'

(5)   *ø=ni-keʔkx-küx-ü-pa=(a)ʔ*
      B3(ABS)=RR-braid-PL3-INV-INC.INTR=ANIM
      'They are braiding each other's (hair).'   (#56)
      (Also: 'They are braiding their own hair.')

(6)   *ta=ni-küʔpa:t-anüpa-:t*   *pek*
      B1(ABS)=RR-get.married-IRR_INV-PL.SAP   real
      'It is true that we are going to get married.'

There are two morphosyntactic facts that indicate that reciprocal constructions following the conjoined subject strategy are partially intransitive: (1) the subject marking with an absolutive proclitic rather than with an ergative proclitic, and (2) the selection of the incompletive aspectual marking for intransitives, the suffix *-pa*, rather that the one for transitives, *-pe*. Compare the RR constructions in (5) with the canonical transitive clause in (1) that includes an ergative person marker and the suffix *-pe* (incompletive for transitive verbs) and not *-pa* (incompletive for intransitive verbs).

In the reciprocal construction, the nominal expression (when it is present) may be a conjoined NP with a coordinate nominal conjunction, as in (7), a plural NP, as in (8), or an independent pronoun, as in (9).

(7)   *tuk=ak   yojwa mü:t=ak   tuk   majaw*
      one=ANIM   man   and=ANIM   one   woman
      ø=ni-yakke:kʔ-küx-aʔx-ü-w=aʔ   *ʔi=winʔixtük*
      B3(ABS)=RR-interchange-PL3-BEN-INV-COMPL=ANIM   A3(PSR)=glasses

'(Those who are a pair are sitting,) a man and a woman, they are interchanging each other's glasses.' (#41)

(8) *ø=ni-pa:t-küx-ü-w=ak*   **nimetzi   majaw-tük**
B3(ABS)=RR-meet-PL3-INV-COMPL=ANIM   pair   woman-PL
'A pair of women met each other (and were standing chatting).' (#9)

(9) **yaj-tük=ak**   *ø=ni-pa:t-küx-ü-w=aʔ*
this-PL=ANIM   B3(ABS)=RR-meet-PL3-INV-COMPL=ANIM
'They met each other (and slapped each other's shoulders.)' (#58)

Olutec ditransitive clauses exhibit a primary object marking pattern, i.e., the recipient argument is signaled by the absolutive proclitic in the inverse alternation and it is also the third semantic participant that becomes the subject of passive constructions (cf. Zavala 1999, 2000). In contrast, the theme of ditransitives is never expressed by the absolutive proclitic on the verb. Reciprocalised ditransitive verbs follow the same primary object pattern, since the argument coreferential with the subject is always the recipient argument, (10).

(10) *jeʔ=k*   *nitujtujko*   *ø=ni-mo:yʔ-küx-ü-pa=k*
that=ANIM   six   B3(ABS)=RR-give-PL3-INV-INC.INTR=ANIM
chaʔ=k   *ʔi=chikx-küx-pe-ʔ*   *ʔi=kü-m*
what=ANIM   A3(ERG)=have-PL3-INC.TR-NMLZ   A3(PSR)=hand-LOC
'Those six (people) are giving each other what they have in their hands.'
(#19)

The same pattern is attested with reciprocals of ditransitive external possessor constructions, in which the possessor of the theme is treated as primary object. In (11), the applicative *-aʔx* brings into primary object argument position the semantic possessor of the theme *poʔ* 'white hair', while the possessed theme stays as a clausal secondary object. The two coreferential reciprocants are the subject and the possessor / primary object.

(11) *majaw-tük ø-ni-wix-aʔx-ü-p(a)*   *ʔi=poʔ*
woman-PL B3(ABS)=RR-pull.up-BEN-INV-INC.INTR A3(PSR)=white.hair
'The women are pulling up each other's white hair.' (#6)

An additional external possessor construction attested in Olutec takes place by incorporation of the head of a possessive NP in object position. In this construction the semantic possessor is treated syntactically as the clausal object whereas the noun referring to the theme (body-part, part of a whole or kinship term) is incorporated. In the reciprocal construction with this type of external possessor construction, coreference is established between the subject and the semantic possessor of the theme functioning as clausal object.

(12)   *ø=ni-wintoj-pü?kx-küx-ü-pa=(a)?*   *je?=k*   *yojwa-tük*
       B3(ABS)=RR-face-slap-PL3-INV-INC.INTR=ANIM that=ANIM man-PL
       'Those men are slapping each other's faces.'   (#5)

Olutec reciprocal constructions are only attested with transitive verbs. The only
way that intransitive roots participate in the reciprocal construction is by modify-
ing their valence via a causative prefix or an associative applicative. Examples are:
ni-mü:-kapx (RR-ASSOC-speak) 'talk to each other', *ni-mü:-?it* (RR-ASSOC-exist) 'be
together', *ni-mü:-wit* (RR-ASSOC-walk) 'walk together', *yak-ni-?o:k* (CAUS-RR-die)
'kill each other'. The reciprocants that establish coreference in this language are
always the subject and the primary object.

2.2   The subject cum adjunct strategy

In addition to the conjoined subject strategy discussed in § 2.1, Olutec uses the
same signs that identify a reciprocal construction (RR, inverse and absolutive person marker) when one of the reciprocants is coded as an oblique phrase. In this
strategy, the entities that take part in the reciprocal event are separated and represented in two syntactic slots; one of them is the subject and the other is encoded
as a constituent with a lower structural rank headed by a comitative preposition.
The fact that the verb in (13) does not take a plural marker clearly indicates that
the two reciprocants do not form a single constituent.

(13)   *?i=ni-kü?pa:t-a?n-ej=k*   *mü:t=ak*   *?a:gila*
       A3(ABS)=RR-get.married-IRR-INV.INC.D=ANIM with=ANIM eagle
       '(the buzzard) is going to get married with the eagle.'

Examples in which the first reciprocant refers to first or second person represent
a clearer case that demonstrates that the participants involved in this reciprocal
clause type are not expressed by a single syntactic constituent. In (14), the first
reciprocant is a second-person singular subject, while the second reciprocant is a
third-person oblique comitative. Notice that the verb does not bear a plural marker. The formal signs that identify the structure in (14) as reciprocal stay intact, i.e.
the subject is coded with the absolutive and the verb follows the inverse pattern,
even though the highest ranked participant in person coincides with the logical
subject (the first reciprocant). Recall that under typical conditions, the inverse
pattern is normally attested only when the logical object outranks the logical subject in person or topicality, as in example (2) above, but in (14) the presence of the
inverse marking pattern seems to be motivated by other principles that are still
unclear. In (13) and (14) the original two slots of the transitive verb are reduced
to one, which is occupied by the first reciprocant.

(14) *ʔentonses* **mi=yak-ni-küʔ-tzi:yʔ-an-ü-pa**   **mü:t=ak**   *jeʔ*
then   B2(ABS)=CAUS-RR-hand-stick-IRR-INV-INC.INTR   with=ANIM   that
'and then you are going to shake hands with him.'

All the verbs that take part of the second reciprocal strategy can also appear in
the first type of construction. As an illustration compare the subject cum adjunct
construction in (14) with the conjoined subject construction in (15).

(15) *ø=ni-küʔ-tzi:yʔ-küx-ü-pa=(a)ʔ*
B3(ABS)=RR-hand-stick-PL3-INV-INC.INTR=ANIM
'They are shaking hands.'   (#13)

Roughly speaking, from a semantic point of view, the two strategies discussed
above imply that the entities involved in the reciprocal event share the same type
of participation in the encoded event; however, there is a noticeable pragmatic
difference between the two strategies. Unlike the conjoined subject strategy, in
which all the participants share an equivalent topical status (hence, coded as a
unique set in subject position), in the subject cum adjunct strategy, the first reciprocant is foregrounded and the second one is backgrounded and therefore coded
as an oblique noun phrase.

2.3   The subject and object strategy

Olutec exhibits a third reciprocal strategy which codes the entities included in the
reciprocal event in two syntactic slots: subject and object. The verb bears the RR
marker *ni-* and the inverse suffix, in a similar way to the two previously discussed
strategies. Unlike the conjoined subject, and the subject cum adjunct constructions, the verb in this third strategy marks its first reciprocant with an ergative
proclitic and treats the second one as an applied comitative object without being
headed by a preposition. The verb, on the other hand, bears the applicative *mü:-*
that increases the verb valence. Thus, this type of construction, unlike the two
previously discussed, is unquestionably transitive.

(16) *jeʔpi=xü=k*   *ta=mü:-ni-pa:t-i-j*
there=REP=ANIM   C3(ERG)=COM-RR-meet-INC.DEP-INV.INC.D
tan=mü:ʔku
A1(PSR)=sister
'She met with my sister.'

The transitive subject and object strategy is built on the intransitive subject cum
adjunct construction. The applicative *mü:-* increases the valence of the reciprocal
intransitive form *ni-V*, which allows the otherwise oblique comitative to become
the clausal primary object, and the otherwise absolute subject to be expressed

by the ergative. Compare the following contrast between the two strategies. In (17) the second reciprocant appears as an adjunct, whereas in (18) it is treated as an applied primary object.

(17)   *ta=ni-küʔpaːt-nü-ü-w=aʔ=koj*   *müːt=ak*
        b1(ABS)=RR-get.married-already-INV-COMPL=PERF=just with=ANIM

        yaʔ=ak   yoʔjwa
        this=ANIM   man
        'I had already been married with that man.'

(18)   *tan=müː-ni-küʔpaːt-anüpa=jaʔ*
        A1(ERG)=COM-RR-get.married-IRR_INV=3PRO
        'I am going to marry with him.'

Semantically, the two strategies convey the same situation but they show recognisable pragmatic differences. In the subject cum adjunct strategy the second reciprocant is backgrounded, while in the third strategy the same entity is foregrounded (therefore, coded as an applied object). The third strategy is the most marked of all the three already discussed, both cross-linguistically and language internally. It is the only Olutec inverse construction that bears an ergative proclitic, and it is also the only construction in the language in which the reciprocal prefix follows the applicative marker.

3.   Categories encoded in the clip data

The whole set of clips was elicited from one speaker – Antonio Asistente, around 72 years old – in December 2004 and additional information was provided by Bonifacio Canuto (70 years old) in January 2005. Both speakers have Olutec as their first language and Spanish as their second one.

Antonio Asistente used the conjoined subject reciprocal strategy 40 times in response to 64 clips. The two alternate strategies discussed in §§ 2.2 and 2.3 were never provided in his responses or in those of Bonifacio Canuto. Both speakers used the conjoined subject strategy for coding strong, pairwise, chained, adjacent and melee situations, that took place simultaneously or sequentially. Some examples that were obtained using the clips are:

(19)   *jeʔ   liːbru   ø=yak-ni-nax-küx-aʔx-ü-pa=(a)ʔ*
        that book   b3(ABS)=CAUS-RR-pass-PL3-BEN-INV-INC.INTR=ANIM

        ʔente   nituwük jeʔ-tük
        among   three   that-PL
        'They pass each others' book among the three of them.'

                                                                    (#4) [strong, sequential]

(20) *jeʔ=k   tujtujkoʔaj   ø=tünni:yʔ-küx-pa=(a)ʔ*
      that=ANIM   six   B3(ABS)=stand-PL3-INC.INTR=ANIM
      ø=ni-küʔ-wop-küx-ü-pa=(a) ʔ   ʔi=kejke-jem
      B3(ABS)=RR-hand-hit-PL3-INV-INC.INTR=ANIM   A3(PSR)=shoulder-LOC
      'Those six (people) are standing, they are hitting each other on their shoulders.'
                                             (#42) [pairwise, sequential]

(21) *ø=ni-meʔpx-kot-küx-ü-pa=(a)ʔ*   *nimakta:xko*
      B3(ABS)=RR-hug-together-PL3-INV-INC.INTR=ANIM   four
      ø=ʔit-küx-pa-ʔ   *jeʔmü*
      B3(ABS)=exist-PL3-INC.INTR-NMLZ   there
      'Four that are there are hugging one another.'
                                             (#2) [chaining, sequential]

(22) *jeʔ=k   moko:xkoʔaj   ø=ni-kejke-püʔkx-küx-ü-pa=(a)ʔ*
      that=ANIM   five   B3(ABS)=RR-shoulder-slap-PL3-INV-INC.INTR=ANIM
      mü:t=ak   ʔi=ni-wintoj-ʔe:p-küx-i-j
      and=ANIM   A3(ABS)=RR-face-see-PL3-INC.DEP-INV.INC.D
      'Those five are slapping at each other's shoulder and then they are looking at
      each other's face.'   (#57) [adjacent, simultaneous]

(23) *ø=japoyʔu:k-küx-pa*   *jaʔ   mü:t=ak*
      B3(ABS)=eat.breakfast-PL3-INC.INTR 3PRO and=ANIM
      ʔi-yak-ni-nax-küx-aʔx-e-j
      A3(ERG)=CAUS-RR-go_past-PL3-BEN-INC.DEP-INV.INC.D
      'They eat breakfast and pass (their food) to each other.'
                                             (#21) [melee, sequential]

The events that the speaker identified as portraying 'talking' situations were
always conveyed using an intransitive verb with plural subject (scenes #1, #33,
and #40) or with singular subject and a comitative adjunct (#11). Neither of
the two constructions entails a reciprocal reading. As illustration consider
(24) and (25):

(24) *ʔampiw-küx-pa   jaʔ   ti: pü:k   ʔi=num-küx-pe*
      chat-PL3-INC.INTR 3PRO what DUB   A3(ERG)=say-PL3-INC.TR
      'They are talking. Who knows what they are saying.'
                                             (#1) [asymmetrical, sequential]

(25) *ø=ʔampiw-pa=k*   *tuk   yojwa   müt=ak   tuk   majaw*
      B3(ABS)=chat-INC.INTR=ANIM   one   man   with=ANIM one   woman
      müt=ak   ʔi-küʔ   *kunuxtuni   ta=chikx-i*
      with=ANIM A3(PSR)=hand   crossed   C3(ERG)=have-INC.DEP
      'One man is chatting with a woman, he has his arms crossed.'
                                             (#11) [symmetrical, simultaneous]

The chasing situations were coded in two ways: as reciprocal with conjoined subject, or as intransitive with plural subject. The scenes #14 and #39 were described by the speaker as true chasing situations expressed by reciprocal constructions; however, the scenes #36 and #64 were described as playing and running activities expressed by intransitive verbs. For the sitting situations the intransitive verb *ju:nni:yʔ* 'sit' with plural subject showed up in scenes #15; while the alternate transitive form *mü:-ju:nni:yʔ* 'sit with', following the reciprocal marking pattern, was used in the scenes #18, and #25. Later on, the two speakers offered the alternative constructions as coding possibilities for each type of situation, i.e. the reciprocal form for scene #15, and the intransitive with plural subject for scenes #18 and #25.

4.   Conclusion

The three reciprocal constructions that Olutec exhibits are noteworthy for various reasons. They use a combination of signs to convey the reciprocal situation. The reciprocal prefix combines with the inverse marker to reduce the valence of the transitive verb by one. The semantic motivation for the presence of the inverse marker in the reciprocal construction is not at all obvious. The canonical inverse pattern takes place when the semantic patient outranks the semantic agent in person, animacy or topicality, but in none of the three reciprocal strategies found in Olutec does the patient outrank the agent in any of these features. In the conjoined subject strategy the two participants are equally prominent; while in the other two strategies the agent outranks the patient in prominence. Although this pattern is rare cross-linguistically, other languages of the world, such as Tanglapui (Donohue 1996), also mark reflexives and reciprocals as inverse.

Olutec, like other inverse languages, pays particular attention to the degree of prominence of the participants involved in a transitive clause, this being one of the most noteworthy features of this type of language. The existence of three reciprocal strategies is motivated by varying levels of prominence of the second reciprocant. In the conjoined subject strategy, the second reciprocant is as topical as the first reciprocant. In the subject cum adjunct strategy the second reciprocant is treated as background information; while in the subject and object strategy, the second reciprocant has the same prominence as a regular primary object. The existence of these three strategies within a language indicates that the pragmatic status of the reciprocants should be another of the parameters to consider in the cross-linguistic study of reciprocal constructions. For the study of this parameter in cross-linguistic perspective, it would be necessary to design a new set of stimuli in which the different degrees of pragmatic prominence of the reciprocants can be manipulated within a more complex situation.

Abbreviations

The following abbreviations are used:

=	clitic	INC.INTR	incompletive for intransitive
A	pronominal proclitic from Set A	INC.TR	incompletive for transitive
ABS	absolutive	INV	inverse
ANIM	animate	INV.INC.D	inverse for incompletive dependent
B	pronominal proclitic from Set B	IRR	irrealis
BEN	benefactive applicative	LOC	locative
C	pronominal proclitic from Set C	NMLZ	nominaliser
		PERF	perfect
CAUS	causative	PL	plural
COM	comitative applicative	PL.SAP	plural for speech act participants
COMPL	completive		
DUB	dubitative	PL3	plural for third person
ERG	ergative	PSR	possessor
INC.DEP	incompletive for dependent	REP	reportative
		RR	reflexive/reciprocal

Acknowledgements

I wish to thank the late Antonio Asistente, Bonifacio Canuto and the entire Olutec community for their generosity and ongoing support for my research. The analysis presented here benefited from the comments of the editors of this volume to whom I also give thanks. Any remaining faults are of course my own.

References

Donohue, Mark. 1996. Inverse in Tanglapui. *Language and Linguistics in Melanesia* 27: 101–118.

Evans, Nicholas. 2008. Reciprocal constructions: Towards a structural typology. In *Reciprocals: Cross-linguistic and Theoretical Explorations*, Ekkehard König & Volker Gast (eds.), 33–103. Berlin: Mouton de Gruyter.

Kaufman, Terrence S. 1995. Mije-Sokean Comparative Grammar. Ms, University of Pittsburgh.

Maslova, Elena. 1999. Reciprocals and set construal. In *Reciprocals: Forms and Functions* [Typological Studies in Language 41], Zygmunt Frajzyngier & Traci S. Curl (eds), 161–178. Amsterdam: John Benjamins.

Wichmann, Søren. 1995. *The Relationship among the Mixe-Zoquean Languages of Mexico*. Salt Lake City UT: University of Utah Press.

Zavala, Roberto. 1998. *Diccionario Trilingüe del Oluteco. Oluteco, Español, Inglés.* <www.albany. edu/anthro/maldp/olu.html>.

Zavala, Roberto. 1999. External possessor in Oluta Popoluca (Mixean). Applicatives and incorporation of relational terms. In *External Possession* [Typological Studies in Language 39], Doris Payne & Immanuel Barshi (eds), 339–372. Amsterdam: John Benjamins.

Zavala, Roberto. 2000. Inversion and Other Topics in the Grammar of Olutec (Mixean). PhD dissertation, University of Oregon at Eugene.

Zavala, Roberto. 2002a. Olutec causatives and applicatives. In *The Grammar of Causation and Interpersonal Manipulation* [Typological Studies in Language 48], Masayoshi Shibatani (ed.), 244–299. Amsterdam: John Benjamins.

Zavala, Roberto. 2002b. Verb classes, semantic roles and inverse in Olutec. In *Del cora al maya yucateco: Estudios lingüísticos recientes sobre algunas lenguas indígenas mexicanas*, Paulette Levy (ed.), 179–267. México: UNAM-IIF.

Zavala, Roberto. 2006. Serial verbs in Olutec (Mixean). In *Serial Verb Constructions. A Cross-Linguistic Typology*, Alexandra Y. Aikhenvald & R. M. W. Dixon (eds), 273–300. Oxford: OUP.

CHAPTER 17

Reciprocal constructions in Tsafiki

Connie Dickinson

University of Oregon and FLACSO, Ecuador

Tsafiki reciprocal constructions have fairly unique characteristics due to the nature of the constructions from which they arise and the overall grammatical structure of Tsafiki. Reciprocals are coded by elements that are already grammaticalised for other functions. Symmetrical positional reciprocal constructions consist of a subset of positionals that inherently code reciprocity. There are two basic types of active reciprocal constructions. The semantic distinction between the two concerns mirative notions such as the degree to which the event concurs with the speaker's expectations and general knowledge. The function of each reciprocal element is explored by examining its role in other constructions.

1. Introduction

Tsafiki is a Barbacoan language spoken by around 2,000 people, known as Tsachila (Colorados), in the western lowlands of Ecuador. Tsafiki has a variety of reciprocal constructions which are used to code symmetrical relationships. As shown clearly in utterances elicited with a series of video clips and supported by natural discourse, there are two clear categories – one for positional symmetry and another for action symmetry.

Positional notions of symmetry such as 'alongside each other', 'on top of each other' and motion verbs indicating positions such as 'follow' are coded in Tsafiki by a positional element and/or the collective enclitic =*tala*:

(1) *undi peman-ka sona **sili-ka=tala** wiru-ra-e*
    INTJ three-NCL woman **long.flexible-CL=COLL** stand-BE.POSITION-DECL
    'Umm three women are standing next to each other in a line.' (V #47)

(2) *ya unila man=lo-no tenchi mannan **bene** ji-na-e*
    3P2 man again=go.out-INF because again **behind** GO-PROG-DECL
    'After coming out again, this man is following (her) again.' (M #27)

The two most common and productive strategies for coding symmetrical actions as opposed to symmetrical positions, are differentiated by the choice of an inflecting verb in a complex predicate construction. This system most closely resembles the 'auxiliary strategy' for coding reciprocity (Evans 2006). The first construction utilises the predicating element -*a* 'RR' (reflexive/reciprocal) and the second, the verb *i* 'become'. The difference between these constructions concerns mirative notions such as spontaneity and the degree to which the event was anticipated by the speaker. In (3) the speaker provides a typical reason for why men fight. Given the circumstances the fight is expected. In (4) two groups of Tsachila, normally on friendly terms, get drunk and suddenly begin fighting. The fight was not anticipated given their normal amicable relationship.

(3) *weyan=la isa   ta   isa   ti-min=tsan*
     other=PL defend HAVE defend EXPRESS-IMPF.P=SMBL
     ti-to   ki-ka-a-la-ke-e
     EXPRESS:VCL-SR hit-INTS-**RR**-COLL-DO:VCL-DECL
     'Others, jealous ones, getting jealous (over a woman) fight each other.'
                                                    (18Jun0404.1465.198)

(4) *tsachi=la   jaa=tsan   ki-ka-i-la-i-nu-ti-e,*
     person=PL   3D2=SMBL hit-INTS-**BECOME**-COLL-BECOME:VCL-EV-REP-DECL
     winan   i-to
     intoxicate BECOME-SR
     '(They) say that apparently these guys suddenly just fought each other, getting drunk.'
                                                    (23Sep0401.2819.751)

This paper has two primary concerns. The first is to describe the Tsafiki reciprocal constructions with particular attention to action symmetry and the meaning distinctions expressed by the above examples; the second is to compare the elicited data with data found in natural Tsafiki discourse. The elicitation was done with the series of video clips described in Chapter 2 (this volume), recorded so as to portray different (a)symmetrical relationships such as simultaneous vs. sequential and notions such as strong reciprocals 'Bob and Bill hit each other', asymmetrical 'She hit her', adjacent, 'next to each other', and chains 'follow each other'. As might be expected given the types of distinctions made in Tsafiki, while the elicited data did clearly demonstrate that Tsafiki distinguishes symmetrical positions from actions it otherwise did not correlate well with the distinctions portrayed in the video clips. In particular, the elicited data was strongly biased in favor of the reciprocal construction formed with -*a* 'RR' illustrated in (3) above.

As pointed out by Frajzyngier & Curl (1999: viii) reciprocal functions are often coded by elements that have already become grammaticalised for other functions. This is certainly true in Tsafiki. Reciprocal constructions are composed of elements used in other constructions. The reciprocal constructions are not just about symmetrical or reciprocal relations but also code other meanings that are a core part of Tsafiki grammar. The constructions coding symmetrical positions comprise a subset of positional constructions in Tsafiki and hence carry aspects of this system with them into the reciprocal construction.

Active reciprocal constructions are complex predicates, as are most predicates in Tsafiki. In addition, the active reciprocal construction using the verb *i* 'become' ((2) above) has a relationship to 'middle voice' constructions and to a mirative suffix which indicates the event is non-congruent with the speaker's expectations. The relationship between mirativity and middle voice has been noted by both Maldonado (1993) and Shibatani (2006). The Tsafiki reciprocal construction falls somewhere in the middle of a grammaticalisation chain in which the function and use of *i* 'become' ranges from a simple verb coding a change of state to the non-congruent verbal suffix *-i* which has lost most of its predicating functions and serves solely as a marker of non-congruent or unexpected information. While the verb *i* in the reciprocal construction still functions as a predicate, semantically it codes a notion of unexpectedness similar to that coded by the non-congruent suffix *-i*. The coding of mirativity, or the degree to which a state or event is anticipated, is an obligatory and core aspect of Tsafiki grammar.

After examining the formation of reciprocal constructions forming (a)symmetric positional relationships, I will discuss reciprocal constructions coding active symmetry and discuss their relationship with other constructions and the grammaticalisation chain mentioned above. I will then look at the elicited data and compare this data with reciprocal constructions found in natural discourse. However, because there is little published data available on Barbacoan[1] languages in general or Tsafiki in particular, I will begin with a brief sketch of Tsafiki grammar.

2. An overview of Tsafiki grammar

Tsafiki exhibits a fairly consistent SOV word order and strong SOV traits including: postpositions, possessors precede possessed, and dependents precede heads. It has three basic patterns of case-marking for the arguments of bivalent predicates: (1) nominative/accusative (active predicates); (2) nominative/locative (stative predicates); and (3) dative/accusative or dative/nominative (a small set of complex predicates). Nominative case is unmarked. Accusative postpositions

---

1. See Curnow (1997) and (2000) for a description of the Barbacoan language Awa Pit and Dickinson (2002) for a description of complex predicates in Tsafiki.

exhibit a differential pattern in that the accusative marker almost always occurs with humans or specific objects and rarely with non-humans or non-specific objects. However Tsafiki allows rampant ellipsis and almost half of all clauses in natural discourse occur with no expression of core arguments (Dickinson 2002). The only trace of argument cross-referencing in the verb is a single optional marker which usually (but not always) indicates a collective subject.

Three grammatical subsystems in Tsafiki – the complex predicate system, the verb class system, and the mirative system – have important consequences for the encoding of reciprocity and will now be briefly discussed.

2.1   Complex predicates, verb class system and auxiliaries

Tsafiki has a system of complex predicate formation which closely resembles those found in northern Australian languages (Schultze-Berndt 2000; McGregor 2002). There are only some thirty fully inflecting verbs (generic verbs). The majority of predicates are formed by combining one of these inflecting generic verbs with an element from a large open class (coverbs), which cannot directly take finite verbal morphology. Both elements of the complex predicate can contribute semantic participants to the clause and affect the final valency. In the following Example (5) there are two complex predicates, one containing the coverb *bete* 'squeeze' and the generic verb *po* 'PUT' and the second the coverb *ku* 'breast' and *fi* 'EAT'.

(5) *na-ka   ano   bete   po-to   man=ku*
     small-NCL food   **squeeze** PUT-SR again=**breast**
     fi-nun   jo-e
     EAT-NMLZR.OBL   BE:AUX-DECL
     '(You) have to feed babies, (by) mashing up the food.' (19Sep0301.1664.378)

The predicate template is further complicated in that a subset of the generic verbs can also occur as second-order semantic verb class markers or as auxiliaries. This limited set of predicating elements can therefore occur as: (1) simple verbs (the sole predicator in a clause); (2) generic verbs (in complex predicate constructions); (3) second-order semantic verb classifiers; and (4) auxiliaries.

An example of the same element *ki* 'do' occurring as a generic verb, a verb class marker and an auxiliary is given in (6) below. In the examples, when an element functions as a simple verb or coverb it is glossed with lower case letters. Generic verbs are glossed with small capital letters. Auxiliaries and verb class markers are also written in small capital letters but are then followed by AUX or VCL respectively to indicate their function.

(6) *kuwenta* **ki**-*nin*   **ki**-*no*   **ki**-*e*   *nu*=*be*
     SP:tell DO-CONTR DO:VCL-INF DO:AUX-DECL 2=COM
     '(I) just want to talk with you.'   (10Oct0304S1.0009)

The generic verbs, verb class markers and auxiliaries can be clearly differentiated by syntactic position and function. The verbal template is quite complicated with the order of the elements varying depending on the characteristics of the individual morpheme and what other elements are present. However, the relative order of the coverb, the generic verb, the verb class marker, and the auxiliary does not vary regardless of what other elements might be present (6).

The second-order semantic verb class marker system assigns each of the thirty or so inflecting verbs to one and only one of five semantic classes exemplified in certain morphosyntactic constructions (see Appendix A for a list of verbs and the class to which they belong). The five semantic verb class markers (7) are identical in form and meaning to five of the generic verbs: *ki* 'do'; *i* 'become'; *ti* 'say/ express'; *ra* 'be in a position'; and *jo* 'be'. The verb class markers follow certain verb suffixes[2]. When a predicate suffixed with one of these elements is not followed by a verb class marker it forms a subordinate clause or nominal (Dickinson 2002). The verb class marker is necessary to form an active finite clause[3]. In the examples below the verb class markers follow the non-obligatory collective marker -*la*[4].

---

2. These suffixes include: -*la* 'collective', -*nin* 'contrastive', -*yo* 'attempt', -*n* 'stative', -*ka* 'intensive' and the enclitic =*tsan*.

3. The situation is somewhat complicated in that nouns or nominalized verbs can take the full set of finite verbal suffixes. However a noun or nominalized verb suffixed with finite verbal morphology always forms a stative rather than an active predicate. The primary morphological distinction between nouns and verbs in Tsafiki is that verbs require nominalizing morphology to function as nouns.

4. The element *la* can occur after both nouns and verbs, however both its meaning and pattern of distribution varies. With nouns or nominalized verbs *la* occurs as an enclitic, (as do the case-markers), usually cliticizing to the final element of the noun phrase. Its position is much more rigid with verbs, where it occurs immediately after the verb stem as a suffix. In addition, when =*la* occurs with nominals or nominalized verbs referring to humans it is always interpreted as a simple plural (Moore 1991). However number is not an obligatory category in Tsafiki and when *la* occurs with nominals referring to non-humans or on verbs it functions as a collective, i.e. a verb or non-human nominal suffixed with -*la* may refer to a singular referent. The -*la* indicates that this singular referent is part of a group. I cannot go into details here, so in this paper when =*la* occurs with nominals referring to humans it is glossed as PL. In all other cases it is glossed as COLL 'collective'.

(7) a.   *ya=la fi-la-**ki**-e*   (**i*, **ti*, **jo *ra*)   'They ate.'
     b.   *ya=la ji-la-**i**-e*   (**ki*, **ti*, **jo *ra*)   'They went.'
     c.   *ya=la ti-la-**ti**-e*   (**ki*, **i*, **jo *ra*)   'They spoke.'
     d.   *ya=la chu-la-**ra**-e*   (**ki*, **i*, **ti *jo*)   'They are sitting.'
     e.   *ya=la ito-la-**jo**-e*   (**ki*, **i*, **ti *ra*)   'They don't exist.'

The verb class markers are redundant in that they "copy" the argument structure of the generic verb. For example all *ki* 'do' class verbs take an actor as the nominative argument; all *i* 'become' class verbs take an undergoer as the nominative argument; *ti* 'express' class verbs take an actor nominative argument; *jo* 'be/exist' class verbs and *ra* 'be in a position' class verbs take an entity which is in a state or location. An example is given in (8) here the coverb *muna* 'desire' is followed by the generic verb *ti* 'express' which is followed by the collective suffix *-la* and then the verb class marker *-ti*. The final *ti* 'express' in the sentence is a simple verb creating the matrix clause, 'they said'. Hence *ti* occurs in this sentence as a generic verb, a verb class marker and a simple verb. The next two examples illustrate that it is the generic verb and not the coverb that determines the semantic class. *Pa* 'anger' first occurs with *i* 'BECOME' in (9) and then with *suwa* 'CAUSE.BECOME' in (10). Each generic verb is followed by a collective marker and then the verb class marker with which it invariably co-occurs (see Appendix A). Note that there can be more than one verb class marker in a single clause as in (10) where there are two. The verb phrases are delineated with brackets (8)–(10).

(8) *junni ya=la [pe=**muna ti-la-ti-na-e***]
     then   3=PL   [also=**desire SAY/EXPRESS**-COLL-**EXPRESS:VCL**-PROG-DECL]
     [ti-e],
     [**express**-DECL]
     'Then they said that they kissed (him) (lit: they expressed desire for (him)).'
                                                           (06JUN0501S1.0493.166)

(9) *junto la=ka   [pa   i-la-i-e]*
     but   1M=ACC [**anger BECOME**-COLL-**BECOME:VCL**-DECL]
     'Nonetheless they got angry at me.'   (05Dec0502.373)

(10) *ya   palu-ka   la=ka*
     3P2   two-NCL   1M=ACC
     [pa   suwa-ka-ki-la-ki-na-e]
     [**anger CAUSE.BECOME**-INTS-**DO:VCL**-COLL-**DO:VCL**-PROG-DECL]
     'The two of them are really really bothering me.'   (29Mar9701.668)

I reserve the term auxiliary for five predicating elements that occur after verbs suffixed with *-min* 'imperfective participle', *-ka* 'perfective participle', *-no* 'infinitive', or *-nun* 'oblique nominalizer'. If these verb forms are not followed by an auxiliary, they function as nominals. As with the verb class markers, the auxiliary is necessary to form an active finite clause. However these five auxiliaries – *ki* 'do', *i* 'become', *ra* 'be in a position', *jo* 'be', and *ito* 'not be/not exist' – differ from the semantic verb class markers in that they can occur with any verb that carries one of the above suffixes. In (11) below the verbs are suffixed with *-min* 'imperfective participle' followed by the auxiliary *jo* 'be', regardless of the verb's underlying semantic class. This contrasts with the examples in (7) above, where only the verb class marker appropriate for the class to which the verb belongs can be used.

(11) a. *ya fi-**min** jo-e*   'He eats.'
     b. *ya ji-**min** jo-e*   'He goes.'
     c. *ya ti-**min** jo-e*   'He talks.'
     d. *ya chu-**min** jo-e*   'He sits.'
     e. *ya ito-**min** jo-e*   'It doesn't exist.'

So in terms of both distribution and meaning these constructions behave more like what are called auxiliaries in other languages than do the generic verbs or verb class markers. Notionally, the constructions code different aspectual, realis and modality values. While the auxiliaries are not a focus of this paper, they do occur in several of the examples. I cannot go into details here, but briefly, the contrast between constructions using different auxiliaries has to do with different modality readings. All the examples in (12) have an irrealis or future reading, but differ in terms of modality.

(12) a. *ya ji-**no ki**-e*   'He wants to go.'
     b. *ya ji-**no i**-e*   'He can/has permission to go.'
     c. *ya ji-**no ra**-e*   'He is ready to go.'
     d. *ya ji-**no jo**-e*   'He has to go.'
     e. *ya ji-**no ito**-e*   'He doesn't have to go/he will never go.'

An important trait of the predicate template in Tsafiki, is that while both the coverbs and the generic verbs can contribute semantic participants to the clause and affect valency, the final predicating element determines which case-marking pattern will appear on core arguments and determines which participant will receive nominative case[5]. However while the verb class markers and auxiliaries control

---

5. In actual fact it is impossible to determine whether it is the generic verb or the verb class marker that controls case marking in that the case-marking pattern of the generic verb and the verb class marker, when it occurs as a simple or generic verb is identical. This is not the case with the auxiliaries. The case-marking pattern of the auxiliary and generic verb may differ. The case-marking pattern always follows that of the auxiliary, not the generic verb.

the case-marking pattern, they differ from the generic verbs and coverbs in that they do not affect valency and carry schematic rather than detailed semantic information concerning the event. The schematic information concerns the type of event, i.e. an act of 'doing', 'becoming', 'expressing', 'being in a position', 'being' or 'not existing', but does not include semantic detail such as path or manner of movement, or type of 'doing' or 'being' such as 'seeing', 'eating', 'putting', 'causing', 'sitting', 'lying' etc. The generic verb is the strongest predicating element in the construction in that it can affect valency, control case-marking, determine semantic class and add specific semantic detail as well as schematic information concerning the event. The coverbs, verb class markers and auxiliaries each have a subset of these properties, but only the generic verb has the potential to carry them all (Table 1).

Table 1. Characteristics of Tsafiki predicators

	Coverbs	Simple/generic verbs	Verb class markers	Auxiliaries
Can affect valency	Yes	Yes	No	No
Can control case-marking pattern	No	Yes	Yes	Yes
Can determine second-order semantic verb class	No	Yes	N/A	Yes
Can contribute detailed semantic information	Yes	Yes	No	No
Can contribute schematic semantic information	No	Yes	Yes	Yes

There are two types of macro-roles that play a role in Tsafiki argument realisation. The traditional macro-roles, actor and undergoer determined by the individual predicators, and what I call event-roles concerning the initiation and termination of the event. Nominative case is always assigned to a participant coded by the generic verb, with actors taking precedence over undergoers if both are present in the semantic structure of the generic verb. However, nominative case does not necessarily code an actor. Nominative and accusative cases in Tsafiki are essentially markers of semantic event-roles rather than grammatical relations. However these event-roles are tied to the semantics of the unfolding event rather than more traditional macro-roles such as actor or undergoer. In active clauses the nominative argument is associated with the initiating point of the event and the accusative with the focus or endpoint of the action. Regardless of the specific semantic role of the participant in terms of actor or undergoer, the nominative argument will represent the initiating phase of the event as it is presented in the discourse. This will be discussed further below in Section 4.3. There is no real passive in

Tsafiki or other constructions that 'promote' a participant to subject or nominative position over a participant positioned earlier on the event line (see Dickinson
2002). Voice distinctions, including reciprocal constructions, are coded by the use
of different generic verbs in the complex predicate construction.

2.2   Mirativity

A final characteristic of Tsafiki is its obligatory system of evidential and mirative marking. Mirative coding has to do with the degree to which the information coded in the clause is congruent with the speaker's expectations and general
knowledge concerning the event or state. Much as one could say English speakers are obsessed with espistemic modality (certainty, doubt, probability) in that
English has a large inventory of items (modals, verbs, adverbs) and a variety of
constructions for coding these distinctions, Tsafiki speakers are obsessed with
the coding of mirative distinctions. The most grammaticalised system consists
of two categories. One set of markers is used when the source of the information
is a primary participant, either socially (he is a member of the group) or physi-
cally[6]. A primary participant in an event has an epistemologically privileged position with access to information concerning the event that a non-participant does
not have. Another set of markers are used generally, i.e. either by participants
or non-participants. Both categories have independent, although notionally related, sets of markers coding mirative values. Events which are congruent with
the speaker's expectations are coded with congruent markers and events which
are not congruent with the speaker's expectations are coded with non-congruent
(DeLancey 1992[7], 1997, 2001; Dickinson 2000). The marker that is of interest in
this paper is the recently grammaticalised, non-congruent marker -*i* used in the
participant condition (Column two, Table 2). This marker has a relationship both
semantically and diachronically with the middle voice and one of the reciprocal
constructions.

---

6. Moore (1991) was the first to note the degree to which participation is formally coded in
Tsafiki, noting that the verbal suffix -*nu* indicates non-participation on the part of the speaker.

7. DeLancey uses the terms 'conjunct' and 'disjunct'. These terms correlate respectively with
what I am calling 'congruent' and 'non-congruent', with an important difference. In Tsafiki
there is a trinary rather than a binary distinction. The category congruent/conjunct is similar,
but the category 'disjunct' in Tibeto/Burman is divided into two categories 'neutral' and 'non-
congruent' in Tsafiki. These terms, conjunct/disjunct are also problematic in that they have another, completely unrelated use in linguistics. In an attempt to avoid the confusion, I am using
what I hope are the more semantically transparent terms congruent and non-congruent.

Table 2. Mirative markers

General (source of information may or may not be a participant)	Participant (source of information = participant)
∅ neutral	∅ neutral
	-*ya/i* non-congruent
	-*yo* congruent
	-*noman* congruent remote past, habitual

An important aspect of these markers is that they do not code person. There is a default pattern in which the participant markers are more likely to occur with first person subjects in both declaratives and questions and second person subjects in questions, whereas the non-participant markers most commonly occur with third person subjects. However, a speaker is free to declare himself either a primary participant or a general or non-participant at any time and hence any of the markers in either the general or the participant paradigms can occur with any person. For example, in (13) the clause has a third person subject but the congruent participant marker -*yo* is suffixed to the verb. This indicates that the speaker considers himself a Tsachi and the information in the utterance is congruent with his expectations and knowledge. A non-Tsachi could say this and the result would not be ungrammatical, simply highly presumptuous since the speaker is not a Tsachi. On the other hand in (14) the speaker uses the general congruent form -*man* '-SITU' with a first person subject in a situation where he was clearly the primary participant. This is often done when speaking about things one did in childhood. Here the mirative stance of the adult speaker contrasts with the mirative stance of the same speaker as a child, i.e. the child didn't know he couldn't comprehend. So the speaker distances himself from his childhood perspective by using a general form, coded with the mirative perspective appropriate for the adult. The suffix -*man* 'situational' indicates that given the situation, the information coded in the proposition is expected (Moore 1991), i.e. it is normal for a child to lack comprehension.

(13) *Tsachi=la   feto=ka   kasa-i-tu-min=la*
    Tsachi=PL   non-Tsachi=ACC   marry-BECOME-NEG-IMPF.P=PL
    jo-yo-e
    BE:AUX-**CNGR**-DECL
    'The Tsachila don't marry mestizos.' (appropriate for a Tsachi to say)

(14) *(la) na jo-to=ri   mi-i-nin*
      but 1M be-SR=FOC know-BECOME-CONTR
      *mi-ito-ka   i-**man**-ko*
      know-NOT.BE-PF.P BECOME:AUX-**SITU**-DUB
      'Being a child of course, (I) just couldn't comprehend.' (what it meant to
      study shamanism)'   (10Oct0303S1.1449.39)

The interpretation of the mirative markers can differ depending on the semantics
of the verb and the context. The difference between congruent and non-congruent
forms can indicate accidental actions with highly transitive verbs, i.e. verbs which
code actions with a volitional agent and an affected patient (15). However this is
not the case with other types of verbs where the difference can indicate the degree
of awareness or consciousness on the part of the participant (16), or simply a discrepancy between what the speaker thinks and what the situation indicates (17).

(15) a. *tse ya=ka   ki-**yo**-e*
          1F   3P2=ACC hit-**CNGR**-DECL
          '(I) hit (him).' (on purpose)
      b. *tse ya=ka   ki-**i**-e*
          1F   3P2=ACC hit-**NCNGR**-DECL
          '(I) hit (him).' (accidentally)

(16) a. *tse ke   ere-a-i-**yo**-e*
          1F   hit send-RR-BECOME-**CNGR**-DECL
          '(I) fell.' (expected – the ground is slippery)
      b. *tse ke   ere-a-i-**i**-e*
          1F   hit send-RR-BECOME-**NCNGR**-DECL
          '(I) fell.' (unexpectedly – for no obvious reason)

(17) a. *ten-ka   ito-**yo**-e*
          heart-NCL NOT.BE-**CNGR**-DECL
          '(I) am stupid.' (and I know it)
      b. *ten-ka   ito-**i**-e*
          heart-NCL heart-NCL NOT.BE-**NCNGR**-DECL
          '(I) must be stupid.' (although I didn't think I was)

Mirative coding is complex in that it has to do with each speaker's expectations
and knowledge not only concerning the event but also the participants, his relationship to the event, the context and the type of event and state.

The mirative, evidential and verb class markers usually do not occur with
non-finite clauses. Tsafiki has a rich inventory of clause types including: complement, purpose clauses, serial verb constructions, conditional clauses, associated

motion clauses, secondary predicates, switch reference clauses, counter-factual and several different kinds of adverbial clauses, all of which can be identified by their lack of finite verb morphology.

3. Symmetrical positions

Tsafiki has a huge number of positional coverbs that are similar to positionals in Mayan languages (Haviland 1992; Grinevald 2006). The positionals in Tsafiki code configuration and position in space as well as giving other kinds of information such as shape and texture. While the positional coverbs can code configurations concerning a single object and asymmetrical relationships, some of the coverbs that code position are inherently symmetrical. In general, Tsafiki uses positional coverbs for the conditions which Dalrymple et al. (1998) call intermediate reciprocity, (e.g. 'alongside') and intermediate alternative reciprocity (e.g. 'on top of each other') and inclusive alternate ordering (e.g. 'stacked like sardines in a can'). Tsafiki has a large number of positional coverbs which denote different configurations in space to which these 'reciprocal' coverbs belong. A few are listed below:

(18) **Positional coverbs**

nan	'two objects side by side'	*tserere*	'stand close together'
wira	'parellel lengths together w. space between'	*dekan*	'stack 3-dim. object'
papa	'lengths together touching'	*diki*	'stack flat object'
chiri	'close together, dense'	*yabu*	'randomly mixed'
tasen	'string-like objects tangled up'	*foke*	'spread apart'
chikan	'separated'	*doda*	'points together'
dolan	'flat surfaces put together vertically'	*tara*	'together in bunch'

In the data elicited with video clips, two situations were coded with *tulipa* 'lean against each other (rigid objects)'. In both situations the objects were supporting each other (19). The phrase is repeated twice to indicate that there are two pairs of sticks. In a situation in which only one of the objects is supporting the other either *tsorenre* 'lean' or *tili* 'prop up' would be used (20).

(19) *aman jun wan=bi=le*   *ya janpalu chide=ka*
now   3D1 late=in/on=in.region 3P2 four   tree:NCL=ACC
***tulipa-le tulipa-le** wiru kari-ka=la   jo-e*
lean-SUF lean-SUF stand CAUSE-PF.P=PL BE:AUX-DECL
'Now later, they have stood the four sticks up leaning against each other, leaning against each other.'   (F #34)

(20) *in=ka*   *chide=chi*   **tili**   *ke-de!*
     3P1=ACC tree=INSTR **prop.up** DO-IMP
     'Prop this (leaning fence) up with a board!'

Other positional coverbs can also be used to code notions such as 'lead', or 'follow' when they occur in conjunction with motion verbs:

(21) *koredori=se*   *man-ka*   **kake** *su*   *ji-na-min=ka*
     SP:corridor=through one-NCL **front** spring.up GO-PROG-IMPF.P=ACC
     bene=*chi*   *ne=chi*   *ka-de*
     behind=in.region foot=in.region get-ASSOC.M
     bene   *ta-n-ji-na-e*
     behind   have-ST-GO-PROG-DECL
     'He chases from behind grabbing at the other one who is running through the corridor in front (of him).'   (M #64)

A common strategy for stative relationships is to use a nominalised positional coverb and the collective =*tala*. But let's begin by considering its basic use. When combined with a nominal or demonstrative pronoun, =*tala* clearly has a collective sense as in (22).

(22) *jera ya=ka*   *ke-ka-min-e*   *ya=la=***tala**
     all   house=ACC do-PF.P-IMPF.P-DECL 3P2=PL=COLL
     'They had all been building the house together.'   (15Oct0303.1270.291)

The collective =*tala* can combine with nominalised positional coverbs, nouns or nominalised verbs. Its basic function appears to be to group a set of entities or actions together. The relationship between the grouped entities or the kind of entity grouped is then elaborated by the element to which the collective encliticises. In (23) and (24) the enclitic =*tala* occurs with a nominalised positional coverb to indicate positional symmetry.

(23) *ya=la=***tala**   *bete-n-de=***tala**
     3P2=PL=COLL behind-ST-long.rigid:NCL=COLL
     chu-la-ra-e
     sit-COLL-BE.POSITION:VCL-DECL
     'They sit together back to back.'   (V #12)

(24) *palu-ka*   *sona=la*   *palu-ka*   *unila=la* **kake-n=tala**
     two=NCL   woman=PL two-NCL   man=PL   **front-ST=COLL**
     wiru-ra-la-ra-e
     stand-BE.POSITION-COLL-BE.POSITION:VCL-DECL
     'Two men and two women are standing together face to face.'   (F #44)

When =*tala* occurs with a nouns coding kinship, it can indicate a symmetrical dyad relationship (Evans 2006). I have no evidence that it can be used to indicate asymmetrical dyad relationships. Again it groups the entities and then delineates the kind of relationship, in this case one of brotherhood (25).

(25)   *ako=**tala**   jo-min-ti-e*
       brother.of.male=COLL   be-IMPF.P-REP-DECL
       '(They) say (they) are brothers.'   (CA.1549.338)

3.1   Elicited positional reciprocal constructions

As noted above it is the specific coverb rather than the construction itself that en-codes symmetry vs. asymmetry. In the data elicited with the video clips described in Chapter Two, the same construction was used for both asymmetrical and sym-metrical positional relationships. The speakers used the positional construction in the clips which demonstrated either positions such as 'lean against each other' or 'sit next to each other' (clips 8, 12, 15, 18, 35 and 53) or notions such as 'follow' or 'chase' (clips 14, 24, 27, 36, 39 and 64). This positional construction was used regardless of whether the clip concerned simultaneous vs. sequential actions, or depicted strong, chaining, adjacent, asymmetrical or pair relationships. The elic-ited data clearly demonstrates that Tsafiki uses this construction for (a)symmetri-cal positions as opposed to the construction used for symmetrical actions which will be discussed in the following section.

4.   Active reciprocal constructions

In the following section I describe Tsafiki active reciprocal constructions in gen-eral, including the case-marking of reciprocant arguments. I will then look at oth-er constructions in which the constituent elements of the reciprocal constructions occur, namely, *-ka* 'intensive', *-la* 'collective', *i* 'become' and *-a* 'RR' occur. These constructions will then be compared with the reciprocal constructions.

4.1   General characteristics of active reciprocals

As noted above Tsafiki has two basic complex predicate constructions that code symmetrical actions. One construction is based on *i* 'become' and the other on *-a* 'RR'. These can be further divided into two categories depending on whether the construction is simple or utilizes the intensifying suffix *-ka*.

Table 3. Four predicate reciprocal constructions

	Simple reciprocal	Reciprocal with intensifier
i 'become'	(coverb) (verb)-BECOME-COLL-BECOME:VCL	(coverb) (verb)-INTS-BECOME-COLL-BECOME:VCL
-a 'RR'	(coverb) (verb)-RR-COLL-DO:VCL	(coverb) (verb)-INTS-RR-COLL-DO:VCL

The simple reciprocal construction only occurs with a limited set of predicates. Many, but not all, of these predicates fall into the category of what have been called 'natural reciprocals'. Kemmer (1993) used this term to semantically delineate events which are either necessarily symmetrical ('meet') or else very often code a symmetrical relationship ('hug', 'compete').

(26) *peman-ka feto =la*   ***aman-i-la-i-na-e***
three-NCL non.Tsachi =PL **hug-BECOME-COLL-BECOME:VCL-PROG-DECL**
'Three gringos are hugging each other.'   (Maria, #20)

(27) *unila=la=tala*   *pini*   *sona=ka*
man =PL=COM   snake   woman=ACC
isa-ta-a-la-ki-na-man-ti-e
defend-**HAVE-RR-COLL-DO:VCL**-PROG-SITU-REP-DECL
'(They) say the men were competing with each other to get the snake woman.'
         (19Mar9701S3.042).

A list of predicates which have been found to occur with the simple reciprocal construction, including some Spanish borrowings, is given below (28). Note that some of these predicates can occur with either *i* 'BECOME' or *-a* 'RR'. The meaning differences between the two forms will be discussed further below.

(28)   a.   <u>Simple reciprocal predicates with *i* 'BECOME'</u>

aya	'gather'
olon	'group'
pala	'mix'
aman	'hug'
ta	'touch/have'
muna	'desire'
o	'have sex'
kasala	'marry' (SP)
tula	'meet'
saluda	'greet' (SP)
kuwenta	'tell/converse'
isa	'defend'
nekosiya	'negotiate' (SP)
walada	'exchange'

b. <u>Simple reciprocal predicates with -a 'RR'</u>

tote	'kill'
isata	'defend jealously'
weya	'divide'
panha	'ask'
faripa	'ask a favor'

c. <u>Simple reciprocal predicates with either *i* 'BECOME' or -*a* 'RR'</u>

tensa	'play'
ika	'crash into
pata	'argue'
roka	'beg' (SP)

The second reciprocal construction, formed with the intensifier -*ka* and either *i* 'BECOME' or -*a* 'RR', is much more productive and can occur with any predicate, provided there is some kind of symmetrical relationship between participants. This construction is not dependent on the transitivity of the predicate or the grammatical roles of the reciprocants. The predicate can be intransitive as in (29), where the symmetry is between possessed locations. It can indicate symmetry between possessed objects as in (30), benefactive symmetry as in (31), or simply associative symmetry as in (32) where the participants simply grow up together. Both the reciprocals formed with -*a* 'RR' and *i* 'BECOME' conform to this pattern with the difference between the two being based on the degree to which the event was spontaneous and expected. In (29a) and (30a) below, the utterance would be appropriate in a situation in which the reciprocants were family members or friends. (29b) and (30b) would be used in a situation in which the reciprocants were strangers or known to dislike each other. In the latter case the reciprocity is unanticipated.

(29) a. *ya=la   ya=ka   ji-ka-a-la-ke-e*
        3P2=PL house=LOC **go-INTS-RECIP/REFLX**-COLL-DO:VCL-DECL
        'They went to/visited each other's houses.' (expected)

    b. *ya=la   ya=ka   ji-ka-i-la-i-e*
        3P2=PL house=LOC **go-INTS-BECOME**-COLL-BECOME:VCL-DECL
        'They went to/visited each other's houses.' (unexpected)

(30) a. *ya=la   na=la=ka   kira-ka-a-la-ke-e*
        3P2=PL small=PL=ACC **see-INTS-RECIP/REFLEX**-COLL-DO:VCL-DECL
        'They cared for each other's children.' (expected)

    b. *ya=la   na=la=ka   kira-ka-i-la-i-e*
        3P2=PL small=PL=ACC **see-INTS-BECOME**-COLL-BECOME:VCL-DECL
        'They cared for each other's children.' (unexpected)

(31) *ito-nan*   *junni*   *wa*   *ke-de*   *wa*
      not.be-INCL then   plant DO-ASSOC.M plant
      ke-de   **ji-ka-a-no-e**
      DO-ASSOC.M **go-INTS-RR-INF-DECL**
      'Not having this, (we) would have to go around planting and planting (it) for
      each other.'   (09Oct0301S1.1123)

(32) *tsan=ke*   *man=nan*   *chike=la* *man* *pare-n*
      SMBL=DO:VCL again=INCL   1F=PL   one   SP:pair-ST
      kuwenta **owa-i-ka-i-la-i-yo-e**
      like   **grow-BECOME-INTS-BECOME-COLL-BECOME:VCL-CNGR-DECL**
      'So, on the other hand, (it's) like we grew up together with each other (despite
      the fact we are not related by blood).'   (09Jun0501S1.675.735)

4.1.1 *Case-marking of core reciprocal arguments*

The subject of the reciprocal construction can be coded as a simple plural as in
Examples (29), (30) above, or each reciprocant can occur separately marked with
the enclitic comitative =*be*. A nominal marked with =*be* shares its semantic role –
actor, undergoer, locative, dative, etc. – with another participant. In all constructions when two nominals are both coded with the enclitic =*be,* the interpretation
is that both arguments share the same semantic role and are equal in terms of
prominence (33).

(33) *aman* *Martin=be*   *Samuel Loche=be*
      now   Martin=COM   Samuel Loche=COM
      pa-ka-a-la-ki-nu-e
      speak-INTS-RR-COLL-DO:VCL-EV-DECL
      'Now, Martin and Samuel Loche must have argued with each other.'
                                                  (27Oct0304.0621.971)

Alternatively only one of the participants can be marked with the comitative =*be*
and the other can be in nominative case (zero). This occurs when two arguments
share the same semantic role, but the argument with nominative case is more
prominent than that with =*be*.

(34) **Tsachi=la** **Dobe=be**   *ki-ka-i-min*
      person=PL Dobe=COM   hit-INTS-BECOME-IMPF.P
      jo-n=la-man-ti-e
      BE:AUX-ST=PL-SITU-REP-DECL
      'The Tsachila used to fight with the Dobes (another ethnic group).'
                                                  (16Nov0302.2467.021)

However the most common pattern in Tsafiki is to simply elide both arguments or just the most prominent argument and only the participant marked with =*be* remains. Clauses in which both arguments are individually expressed are fairly rare in the texts and because Tsafiki allows rampant ellipsis the more prominent argument is usually elided. In (35) I have given a second, more literal translation, awkward in English, but a closer representation of the Tsafiki construction.

(35)   *sona=be*   *pata-a-la-ki-nu-ti-e*
       woman=COM   argue-RR-COLL-DO:VCL-EV-REP-DECL
       '(He) must have argued with (his) wife.'/ '(He) with his wife must have argued with each other.'   (26Aug9601S6.093)

4.2   The collective -*la* and the intensifier -*ka*

As noted above all the elements of the reciprocal construction can occur in other constructions without coding symmetry. The collective can occur in its own to indicate group participation as seen in Example (5) above. The intensifier -*ká*[8] also occurs in other constructions. It commonly occurs followed by a verb class marker as in (36) below. The -*ka* in this construction can function as a quantifier over the temporal or path measures or to delineate the quantity of the undergoer participant in a transitive construction (36a). Or it can intensify the manner in which the event is performed.

(36)   a.   *ya ano fi-ka-ki-e*   'He ate a lot/for a long time/wolfed down his food.'
        b.   *ya su ji-ka-i-e*   'She ran hard/for a long time.'
        c.   *ya ware-ka-ti-e*   'He cried hard/loud/for a long time.'
        d.   *ya laki jo-ka-jo-e*   'She is really sad.'
        e.   *ya bare ra-ka-ra-e*   'It is really stretched tight/long/hard.'

The predicate collective suffix -*la* cross-references the most prominent argument, normally the subject (Dickinson 2002). It could be that in the reciprocal construction the intensifier serves to quantify the event itself or the object as in the intensifying construction. Either would be plausible in that the reciprocal codes the participation of both, i.e. 'he hit her and she hit him = they hit each other'. If the intensifier does quantify over the object it means that in the reciprocal

---

8.   There are several morphemes that have the same form -*ka* in Tsafiki. Each can be distinguished morphosyntactically, phonologically and by function. Some of the forms are diachronically related, others are not. The intensifier -*ka* always carries the main stress in the word. In the standard orthography used by the community, which I use here, accent is not marked. See Dickinson (2002).

construction both the subject and the object are quantified. However this issue needs to be clarified with further research.

4.3 The reflexive nature of -a 'RR'

The -a 'RR' is no longer an extant free verb in the language but it still does have predicating properties in that like the generic verbs it determines the semantic class of the predicate. For example, the normal verb class marker for the verb *ti* 'express' is -*ti* 'EXPRESS:VCL' (37a). However when the verb is followed by -*a*, the verb class marker is -*ki* 'DO:VCL' (37b). It is reasonable to assume that like all other *ki*-class verbs, -*a* codes an actor participant.

(37) a. *ti-la-ti-e*   'They spoke.'
      b. *ti-ka-a-la-ki-e* 'They spoke to each other.'

The -a 'RR' also occurs in other constructions. However it is no longer a highly productive element. There is one coverb *tere* 'step' which commonly combines with the generic verb *po* 'PUT' to depict an event of stepping on something (38). However when *tere* occurs with the generic verb *ki* 'DO', the suffix -*a* occurs after the coverb *tere* 'step' to depict 'dance'. It seems to serve a reflexive purpose here such as 'to step oneself'[9] (39). The reciprocal form of this verb occurs with two instances of the generic verb -a 'RR' (40).

(38) *ya=ri*   *pi=ka*   ***tere po-to=ri***
      3P2=FOC   water=LOC   **step PUT-SR=FOC**

      pi   *i-no*   *jo-ti-e-ti-e*
      water   BECOME-INF   BE:AUX-REP-DECL-REP-DECL
      '(They) say (they) said if she stepped in the water, she would dissolve.'

(39) *kunta*   ***tere-a-ki-man***   *jo-n?*
      thunder   **step-RR-DO-SITU**   BE:AUX-INT
      'Does the thunder dance?'   (11Dec0303.0480)

(40) *ya=la*   ***tere-a-ka-a-la-ki-e***
      3P2=PL   **step-RR-INTS-RR-COLL-DO:VCL-DECL**
      'They danced with each other.'

---

9. Tsafiki has a reflexive construction unrelated to the method represented with -*a*. The reflexive construction is a typical transitive construction with a reflexive nominal *tenkachi* or *tenkachikenan* in object position, although without the accusative suffix.

(a) *ya **tenkachikenan** kira-e*   'He saw himself.'
(b) *yala **tenkachi** to-te-la-ki-na-e*   'They are killing themselves.'

Another construction in which the *-a* appears is formed with a bivalent coverb coding two participants, an actor and an undergoer. In these constructions the bivalent coverb is suffixed with *-a* 'RR' and followed by *i* 'BECOME' to form a permissive construction. As in other Tsafiki constructions the final predicating element determines which participant receives nominative case and nominative case with active verbs always indicates the initiating point of the action. In (41) *lachi* 'peel' occurs in an ordinary transitive construction. In (42) *lachi* 'peel' occurs in the permissive construction. With an inanimate subject the interpretation of the permissive construction is that there is a quality inherent in the subject/undergoer that permits the action to be carried out. This construction can optionally contain an agentive participant cliticised with the comitative *=be*. The comitative is used here because even though the participants do not have the exact same semantic role, they are both agents of the event. The undergoer has a double role in that it denotes both the entity that instigates the action and the one that undergoes the change of state. This sense is clearer when the undergoer is animate (43). The undergoer is in the nominative, (determined by the final predicating element, in this case *i* 'BECOME'), and is interpreted as the initiator of the event or the one permitting the agent to carry out the action (see Dickinson 2002).

(41) *(ya=la)*   *kido* *jera* **lachi-la-ke-e**
     (3P2=PL)   skin   all   **peel-COLL-DO:VCL-DECL**
     '(They) peel all the bark off.'   (14Dec0302S2.191)

(42) *(ya=la=be)*   *ka*   *we*   **lachi-a-i-tu-ti-e**
     (3P2=PL=COM)   fruit   quickly   **peel-RR-BECOME-NEG-REP-DECL**
     '(They) say this fruit doesn't peel (easily) (with/for them).'
                       (09Jun0501S2.0338.377)

(43) *Maria Secundina=be*   *a*   *po-re-a-i-e*
     Maria Secundina=COM   hair   **cut-CAUSE-RR-BECOME-DECL**
     'Maria let/had Secundina cut (her) hair.'

The details of this construction are too complex to be presented here (see Dickinson 2002). What is of primary interest is that *-a* in these constructions appears to have a reflexive reading, indicating that the actor and undergoer of the coverb refer to the same entity. However because *-a* is no longer highly productive nor an extant free verb in the language it is difficult to ascertain its exact meaning.

4.4   The function of *i* 'become'

In this section, I will look at the range of uses of the verb *i* 'become', from its use as a simple verb to its most grammaticalised use as the non-congruent marker *-i*. The verb *i* 'become' is of course, the quintessential change of state verb and when used as a simple predicate in Tsafiki simply codes the change of state:

(44)   *Roberto   yuka-n   i-e*
      Roberto   evil-ST   become-DECL
      'Roberto turned into/became a devil.'

As a verb class marker it classifies primarily motion verbs, but also *puya* 'die', *piya* 'get lost', *katso* 'sleep' as well as itself (see Appendix A). In contrast to *ki* 'do' class verbs, the subject of all these verbs undergoes a change of state or location. As a generic verb *i* 'BECOME' commonly occurs in complex predicate constructions which code situations which are often called 'middle voice'. Middle voice has been described semantically in a variety of ways including: reflecting a reduction in the elaboration of the event (Kemmer 1993); or as depicting a situation where the development of an action is contained within the personal sphere of the agent such that he himself is affected by the action (Shibatani 2006). Both Maldonado (1993) and Shibatani (2006) analyse voice contrasts as concerning the evolving properties of actions as they are portrayed in discourse. Middle voice focuses on the change of state phase of an evolving event. In Tsafiki this function of middle voice is somewhat transparent since the common pattern in Tsafiki is to form it with an *i*-class verb, most commonly the generic verb *i* 'BECOME' itself or the *i*-class generic verb *ji* 'GO'. The corresponding causative construction is formed with a *ki*-class verb (see Appendix A). The subject of a *ki*-class verb is always an actor or an agent.

Some of the types of events described with this construction are: inchoative positionals (45a); spontaneous events (45b); change-of-state (45c); cognitive/emotional (45d); and translational motion (45e).

(45)

	coverb + *i*-class generic verb		coverb + *ki*-class generic verb	
a.	*wiru i*	'stand up'	*wiru kari*	'make sm. stand up'
b.	*chi i*	'get hot'	*chi suwa*	'heat sm.'
c.	*biti ji*	'snap'	*biti-le ki*	'snap sm.'
d.	*laki i*	'get sad'	*laki suwa*	'sadden'
e.	*su ji*	'go running'	*su ere*	'send running'

While a detailed description of Tsafiki complex predicates would lead us far astray here (see Dickinson 2002), it should be noted that in the majority of the middle voice constructions, the *i*-class generic verb codes a single participant that undergoes a change of location or state. The coverb also codes a single undergoer participant. The two semantic participants converge on the same nominative argument when combined in the complex predicate construction. Nominative case in Tsafiki is determined by the generic verb. Therefore the event described by the middle voice construction begins with the undergoer who is associated with the change of state phase of the event. Whether there was a causal entity or event is left unspecified in the construction itself. The change of state is the prominent phase of the event here, not the causal phase. In contrast, in the causative construction the generic *ki*-class verb codes a single actor participant which receives nominative case while the undergoer participant of the coverb receives accusative case. The description of the event begins with the actor entity that is associated with the causal phase of the event (Dickinson 2002).

Both Maldonado (1993) and Shibatani (2006) have noted that middle voice constructions often can be used to indicate that the event was unexpected, surprising or that the actor is not in control. An event beginning with the causal phase as opposed to one that begins with the change of state may naturally be less startling. If the causing sequence is expressed, the consequential change of state may be expected. While the above constructions do not explicitly code the contrast between expected vs. unexpected events, because the causal phase of the event is not explicitly portrayed, these constructions can indicate spontaneous or sudden change which can imply unexpected change.

4.4.1 *Non-translational motion constructions*

Non-translational motion verbs follow the same general pattern, but with an important difference. While in (45) above the difference between the *i*-class and *ki*-class constructions often involves an increase in transitivity – intransitive > transitive, or transitive > ditransitive – with the non-translational motion construction there is no change in transitivity, both constructions are intransitive. The notions conveyed by these constructions move closer to that of mirativity distinctions. The *i* 'BECOME' construction carries notions such as uncontrolled or unexpected motion. The uncontrolled sense is the more likely interpretation in the participant situation and the unexpected sense the more likely in the non-participant situation. The *ki* 'DO' construction simply codes an activity (46).

(46)	**coverb + *i*-class generic verb**		**coverb + *ki*-class generic verb**	
	soko i	'writhe in an unexpected or uncontrolled manner'	*soko ki*	'writhe/wiggle'
	chuda i	'move hips in an unexpected or uncontrolled manner'	*chuda ki*	'move hips'
	liblibii i	'blink eyes uncontrollably'	*libilibi ki*	'blink eyes'
	pe i	'have diarrhea'	*pe ki*	'defecate'

In these constructions the generic verb determines whether the subject will be interpreted as an actor or an undergoer. When these coverbs combine with *i* 'become', which has a single undergoer participant, there are two changes in comparison with the *ki* 'do' construction: (1) the focus is on a change from a state of not moving to one of moving – it depicts a change of state rather than an activity; (2) the participant is coded as an undergoer rather than an actor.

In a non-participant situation the difference between the two constructions concerns the degree to which the event is anticipated. In (47) below a moth has flown into a flame and as a consequence is writhing. The writhing is a predictable, expected consequence given the circumstances. (48) depicts a situation where someone suddenly just falls down and starts writhing for unknown reasons – perhaps due to an epileptic attack or spirit possession. The *i* 'become' construction is used here. If the *ki* construction were used, it would imply there was a predictable cause as in (47).

(47) *nin=bi   wi-ka   jo-n   **soko   ke-e***
     Fire=in/on go.in-PF.P BE:AUX-ST **writhe DO:VCL-DECL**
     '(The moth) that entered the flame writhed (of course).'
                                              (15Oct0304.0359.865)

(48) *junni ke-ere-a-i-na-to,   **soko***
     then   hit-send-RR-BECOME-PROG-SR **writhe**
     i-na-e   ti-e
     BECOME-PROG-DECL say-DECL
     'Then (they) say falling down, (he) was writhing (suddenly, unexpectedly and for an unknown reason).'   (17Nov0303.0967.35)

Both forms can occur with the grammaticalised mirative markers in the participant situation. Here the distinction between the two constructions often has to do with control and awareness. With a *ki*-class generic verb and the congruent suffix *-yo* the construction indicates the speaker was deliberately performing the motion (49), i.e. she is *doing* something. The congruent suffix with the *i*-class generic verb indicates the speaker cannot control the movement, i.e. something is *happening* to her, but she is fully conscious and the event makes sense given the circumstances – it is normal to blink when dust enters the eyes (50).

(49) *tse unila=ka muna i-to   duke libilibi   ki-yo-e*
     1F   man=ACC desire BECOME-SR very blink.eye DO-CNGR-DECL
     'Desiring the man, I blinked my eyes (fluttered my eyelashes at him).'

(50) *tse to   petse tenchi libilibi   i-yo-e*
     1F   earth speck because blink.eye BECOME-CNGR-DECL
     'Because of the dust, I blinked my eyes.'

The use of the non-congruent mirative suffix with the non-translational constructions indicates in both cases that the participant (usually the speaker) was unconscious during the event. Unlike a normal activity, he was not aware of his movement while it was occurring. He knows he performed the action because someone else informed him or because of some other kind of evidence, i.e. in (51) perhaps the bedclothes are completely mussed up and he knows he spent a restless night full of bad dreams. With the *ki*-class form (51) he is more likely to have some idea as what caused the action although he was unaware at the time. The *i*-class form indicates he was not only unconscious, he also has no idea what caused the motion (52). As in (48) this would be appropriately said by the victim of an epileptic attack or spirit possession.

(51) *akura=chi=nan*   *soko*   *ke-i-e*
      nightmare=INSTR=INCL writhe DO-**NCNGR**-DECL
      'Because of a nightmare, (I) must have writhed.' (while I was sleeping)

(52) *soko*   *i-i-e*
      writhe   BECOME-**NCNGR**-DECL
      'I must have writhed.' (for some unknown reason while I was unconscious)

4.4.2 *Noncongruent suffix* -i

Finally, as noted above the non-congruent mirative marker used in the participant situation is semantically and diachronically related to *i* 'become'. As noted above this is used when the source of the information is a participant in the event. The congruent form *-yo* is used when the information is congruent with the speaker's expectations; *-i/-ya* is used when the information is not. The older[10] non-congruent participant marker *-ya* is still used in the less common, more conservative dialect of Tsafiki. In this dialect, usually found with older speakers, the *-i* occurs after the non-congruent *-ya* in certain constructions (53). In the more common dialect, just the *-i* occurs, although the trace of *-ya* can still be found in the lowering of the preceding vowel (54). Tsafiki exhibits some vowel harmony, especially in rapid speech, in which a preceding vowel can either raise or lower to conform more closely to the characteristics of the following vowel – *jolajoe* > *jolojoe; kie* > *ke̠e̠*. This would not occur with a vowel sequence such as *i-i* but is predictable with the sequence *i-a*.

---

10. The majority of younger speakers do not use *-ya* and some do not even recognize it. All the older speakers I have worked with recognize *-ya*, and can use it when asked to do so, even if they do not normally utilize it in their daily speech.

(53) **Conservative dialect**

tasa	*bole*	*kilakeyain?*
tasa	*bo-le*	*ki-la-ki-ya-i-n*
sp:glass	crack-SUF	DO-COLL-DO:VCL-**NCNGR**-**NCNGR**-INT

'Did (we) accidentally break the glass?' (lit. 'Did we become unexpectedly breaking the glass?')

(54) **More common dialect**

tasa	*bole*	*kilakein?*
tasa	*bo-le*	*ki-la-ki-(ya)-i-n*
sp:glass	crack-SUF	DO-COLL-DO:VCL-(**NCNGR**)-**NCNGR**-INT

'Did (we) accidentally break the glass?'

Note that the *-i* occurs in the position for finite morphology in Tsafiki and in most constructions it is not followed by a nominaliser or verb class marker. There is however still one construction where it can be seen that this *-i* is derived from the verb 'become'. This construction uses the suffix *-n* 'be in a state' followed by the appropriate verb class marker for the generic verb. This is an evidential construction indicating that the speaker is deducing that the event occurred from his general knowledge. In (55), with a third person subject in a non-participant situation the generic verb *ki* 'DO' is followed by the *-n*, then the expected verb class marker *-ki*.

(55)

tasa	*bole*	*kinkee*
tasa	*bo-le*	*ki-n-ki-e*
sp:glass	crack-SUF	DO-ST-**DO:VCL**-DECL

'(He) must have broken the glass.'

However in (56) the generic verb is followed by *-i*, then the nominaliser and then the verb class marker *-i*, appropriate for the verb 'become' but not *ki* 'do'. While the *-i* in this construction still carries the verbal property of controlling the class of the predicate, unlike the middle voice and non-translational motion constructions above and like the non-congruent *-i* suffix, it can only indicate a situation in which the speaker was a participant. Out of context, the default interpretation is a first person subject and not third person (56).

(56)

tasa	*bole*	*keinie*
tasa	*bo-le*	*ki-(ya)-i-n-i-e*
sp:glass	crack-SUF	DO-**NCNGR**-**NCNGR**-ST-**BECOME:VCL**-DECL

'(I/*he) must have broken the glass.'

Finally, in the conservative dialect the non-congruent *-ya* is not followed by *-i* when it occurs with the evidential suffix *-nu*. This suffix indicates the speaker is inferring that the event occurred from direct, usually physical, evidence (57). In the more common dialect there are two strategies. Some speakers simply drop the -ya which again leaves a trace in the lowering of a preceding high vowel (58). However other speakers are now replacing the -ya with -i (59). This use of -i in a context where it did not previously occur provides fairly strong evidence that speakers are now interpreting it as the non-congruent marker and not the verb i 'become'. All three constructions carry the same meaning and can only be used in participant situations.

(57) *tasa*   *bole*   *keyanue*
      tasa   *bo-le*   *ki-ya-nu-e*
      SP:glass   crack-SUF   DO-NCNGR-EV-DECL
      '(I) must have broken the glass.'

(58) *tasa*   *bole*   *kenue*
      tasa   *bo-le*   *ki-(ya)-nu-e*
      SP:glass   crack-SUF   DO-(NCNGR)-EV-DECL
      '(I) must have broken the glass'

(59) *tasa*   *bole*   *keinue*
      tasa   *bo-le*   *ki-(ya)-i-nu-e*
      SP:glass   crack-SUF   DO-NCNGR-EV-DECL
      '(I) must have broken the glass.'

Semantically the use of both the -ya and the -i may have become redundant in that both can indicate non-congruency. We have already seen that the i can carry these notions, particularly when it occurs as one half of a contrasting set of constructions with the same transitivity values coding the same event. The construction with -ya-i contrasts with those in which the congruent -yo appears. (-yo can be preceded by the verb i 'become' but it is never followed by i). So speakers could drop one of the elements without losing the basic meaning distinction.

5.   Comparison of reciprocal constructions with other related constructions

In the previous section it was shown that the verb i 'become' ranges in use from a simple change-of-state verb to a non-congruent suffix used in participant situations. As a simple verb or when it occurs in middle voice constructions it does not necessarily carry mirative notions such as unexpectedness, non-control or surprise. It only begins to take on mirative notions when it occurs as a member of a contrasting set as with the non-translational motion constructions described above. Returning to the reciprocal constructions it can be seen that the same general principles hold. In situations in which either form could be used, the *i* 'BECOME' reciprocal and the *-a* 'RR' construction have meaning differences similar to the non-translational motion constructions. The *i* form often indicates non-control or unexpectedness. In (60) the two participants suddenly and unexpectedly begin hitting each other, hence the *i* form is used in the first mention of the fight. Once the fight is established the *-a* form is used. In (61) the arguing is expected given the speaker's evaluation of the mental aptitude of the participants. However in (62) the arguing is unexpected in that brothers should get along (or at least not publicly display their disagreements according to Tsachi culture).

(60) *tsan-ti-na-min=nin*   *ina*   *ki-ka-i-to*
      SMBL-SAY/EXPRESS:VCL-PROG-IMPF.P=CONTR suddenly hit-**INTS-BECOME**-SR
      ki-ka-a-la-ke-ti-e-ti-e   *Salun kela=be*
      hit-**INTS-RR**-COLL-DO:VCL-REP-DECL-REP-DECL Salun jaguar=COM
      'While (they) were talking, suddenly hitting each other, Salun and the
      jaguar were fighting each other.'   (26Aug9601.186)

(61) *kasa=le=nan*   *jaa=tsan   ten-ka   ito-n*
      first=on/at.region=INCL 3D2=SMBL heart-NCL NOT.BE-ST
      junto   pata-a-min=la   jo-e
      because.of **argue-RR**-IMPF.P=PL BE:AUX:DECL
      'From the very beginning (they) were stupid, so (they) argued (as stupid
      people will).'

(62) *ako=tala   **pata-i-na-min=la**   *jo-e*
      brother=COLL **argue-BECOME**-PROG-IMPF.P=PL BE:AUX
      'The brothers are always arguing with each other (being brothers they
      should get along).'   (26Nov9601S4.054)

However, this mirative like contrast only occurs when there are two contrasting constructions. In the simple reciprocal constructions, formed without the intensifier *-ka*, some of the coverbs only occur in the *i* 'BECOME' reciprocal construction. There is no constrastive set. These coverbs all belong to the class of what could be called 'natural reciprocals' – *aman* 'hug', *walada* 'exchange', *tula* 'meet' or the Spanish borrowing *saluda* 'greet'. In these cases, the *i* 'BECOME' simple reciprocal construction does not necessarily carry the mirative notion of unexpectedness or non-control. In (63) taken from the elicited data there is nothing surprising about the participants greeting each other as they meet. These constructions, with this specific class of coverbs, are closer to the middle voice constructions which do not necessarily carry mirative notions.

(63) *junni   ya=la=tala   saluda-i-la-i-e*
      then   3P2=PL=COLL   greet-BECOME-COLL-BECOME:VCL-DECL
      'Then they greet each other.'   (FA #5)

There is an important difference between the mirative contrasts present in the
reciprocal constructions and the more grammaticalised mirative markers. The
grammaticalised mirative markers consist of two sets that distinguish between
participant and general situations. All the reciprocal examples we have seen so far
are general situations, but these constructions can also be used in participant situations. Either the congruent *-yo* or the non-congruent *-i* can be used with some
subtle differences in meaning. In (64) the *-a* reciprocal with the non-congruent
marker indicates that the speaker, in the dark, mistook Mayra for his wife and
deliberately went up to her and hugged her. His hugging of Mayra, rather than
his wife is accidental. The non-congruent suffix with the *i* reciprocal, on the other
hand, indicates that the speaker has no idea what happened. Stumbling around
in the dark he found himself unexpectedly hugging a woman he thinks, but he's
not sure, was Mayra (65). (Note: *aman* 'hug' only occurs in the simple reciprocal
construction with *i* 'become', but it can occur with either reciprocal form in the
reciprocal with intensifier construction).

(64) *la=be   Mayra=be   duke neme jo-sa*
      1M=COM   Mayra=COM   very dark BE-DR
      aman-ka-a-la-ke-i-e
      hug-INTS-**RR**-COLL-DO:VCL-**NCNGR**-DECL
      'It being really dark, Mayra and I accidentally hugged each other.'
      (I thought she was my wife).

(65) *la=be   Mayra=be   duke neme jo-sa*
      1M=COM   Mayra=COM   very dark BE-DR
      aman-ka-i-la-i-i-e
      hug-INTS-**BECOME**-COLL-BECOME:VCL-**NCNGR**-DECL
      'It being really dark, Mayra (I think) and I suddenly and unexpectedly
      found ourselves hugging each other.'

The congruent suffix *-yo* indicates that in both reciprocal constructions the
speaker was aware and conscious that he was hugging Mayra and not his wife.
The difference is that in the *-a* reciprocal construction the speaker was in control and acted deliberately (66). In the *i* reciprocal construction, although he
is perfectly aware of what he is doing, he is not in control. He is simply over-
whelmed by the urge to hug Mayra (67). (Note that if the speaker utters either
of the following examples within hearing range of his wife, he may have some
explaining to do).

(66) *la=be*   *Mayra=be*   *duke neme jo-sa*
      1M=COM   Mayra=COM   very dark BE-DR
      *aman-ka-**a**-la-ki-**yo**-e*
      hug-INTS-**RR**-COLL-DO:VCL-**CNGR**-DECL
      'It being really dark, Mayra and I hugged each other (deliberately).'

(67) *la=be*   *Mayra=be*   *duke neme jo-sa*
      1M=COM   Mayra=COM   very dark BE-DR
      *aman-ka-**i**-la-**i**-**yo**-e*
      hug-INTS-**BECOME**-COLL-**BECOME**:VCL-**CNGR**-DECL
      'It being really dark, Mayra and I spontaneously hugged each other.'
      (we couldn't control ourselves)

So in summary, the reciprocal constructions semantically resemble the non-translational motion constructions in that the contrast in meaning involves mirative notions concerning control and expectedness. However a small set in the simple reciprocal construction pattern like the middle voice constructions. The key appears to be whether there is a contrastive set both coding the same basic event with no change in transitivity. While the reciprocal constructions exhibit mirative like notions, unlike the more grammaticalised mirative markers they can be used in either the participant or the non-participant situation.

6.   Elicited data

Data used for this chapter was elicited using the video clips outlined in Chapter 2. Four speakers, two men and two women in their thirties participated in the study. All are bilingual in Spanish and Tsafiki, with Tsafiki being their first, dominant and preferred language. All four speakers watched all sixty-four of the video clips. There was a great deal of variety between speakers. The men responded with reciprocals slightly over half the time (56% and 54%). The two women responded with reciprocals about a third of the time (34% and 28%). Hence in order to say anything conclusive, it would be necessary to elicit with more speakers.

As previously noted, the data did clearly show a difference between symmetrical positionals and symmetrical actions. In all the clips concerning positional relationships such as 'next to' or 'lean against' or in coding scenes of 'chasing' or 'following', the speakers used a positional coverb and/or the collective enclitic =*tala* regardless of the specific condition associated with the clip.

Leaving aside the video clips that were portrayed using positionals, the main factor that conditioned the use of a reciprocal construction appeared to be whether the condition included adjacent participants, paired participants, strong symmetry, a chain, a melee or asymmetrical actions (Table 4).

The only clips in which no reciprocal was used by any speaker at any time and where speakers did not accept reciprocal constructions as appropriate descriptions, all concerned asymmetrical sequential conditions. The asymmetrical sequential video clips essentially portrayed situations in which there was no symmetry or reciprocity: a woman sits on a chair while another searches her head for lice (#51); someone is hugged without hugging back (#4, #16); someone looks at someone without the other looking back (#25, #31). The single clip in the asymmetrical sequential class in which a reciprocal construction used was (#1) which portrayed one man speaking to another. However the speaker used the complex predicate *kuwenta ki* which means converse rather than *ti* 'say/express' or *pa* 'speak'. The sense may have been that this was a reciprocal communicative event even if only one man was speaking.

Table 4. Number and percentage of elicited active reciprocal vs. non-reciprocal constructions

Condition	Reciprocal construction used		Reciprocal construction not used		Total	
	#	%	#	%	#	%
Adjacent/simultaneous	04	1.00	0	0	04	.02
Pair/simultaneous	15	.94	01	.06	16	.09
Pair/sequential	07	.88	01	.12	08	.05
Strong/simultaneous	22	.81	05	.19	27	.15
Strong/sequential	23	.55	19	.45	42	.24
Chain/sequential	08	.35	15	.65	23	.13
Melee/sequential	04	.27	11	.73	15	.08
Asymmetrical/sequential	01	.02	42	.98	43	.24
Total	84	.47	94	.53	178	1.0

The other conditions in which reciprocal conditions did not tend to occur were the melee sequential conditions. In these situations not every participant has a direct reciprocal relationship with each of the other participants. For example, (#44) concerns four people who stand and hit each other sequentially, but not every person hits every other person. The speakers tended to describe these in chained sentences describing each participant's individual actions or simply describe the situation with a simple collective, *kilakinae* '(they) are hitting.' However unlike the asymmetrical sequential condition, I was able to elicit reciprocals with these constructions after the fact.

There was also a tendency for simultaneous conditions to receive reciprocal coding over sequential actions. In both the pair and strong conditions the simultaneous condition was more likely to receive reciprocal coding. This is probably due to the fact that the speakers were describing the video clips on-line, i.e. describing the event as it unfolded – "First he hits her. Then she hits him back." After the fact they were quite happy to accept reciprocals as a reasonable description for these video clips.

In general, the speakers showed a fair amount of variety in describing the clips. All of the following examples were elicited from the same video clip (#30) in which three pairs of people sequentially exchange items. The first speaker seems to focus on the sequential aspect rather than the reciprocity. He uses two instances of *man* 'one' followed by the dative enclitic =*chi* to code the sequentiality and a non-reciprocal group verb form. The reciprocity is inferred (68). The second speaker ignores the sequentiality and uses the collective =*tala* and a reciprocal verb form (69). The third speaker uses a reciprocal verb form to code the reciprocity and then two instances of *man* 'one' with the dative enclitic to code the sequentiality (70). The fourth speaker makes a finer distinction. He uses a reciprocal verb form, the ideophone *beko beko* 'back and forth', and then specifically codes the event as occurring between three pairs of participants by using the enclitic =*tala* after *peman pareja* 'three pairs' (71).

(68) *junsi* **man=chi man=chi** *kuwa-la-ki-na-e*
      and   **one=DAT one=DAT** give-COLL-DO:VCL-PROG-DECL
      'And then (they) give (things) first to one than another.'   (M #30)

(69) *junni ya=la=tala*   *kuwa-ka-a-la-ke-e*
      Then 3P2=PL=COLL   give-INTS-RR-COLL-DO:VCL-DECL
      'Then they give (things) to each other together.'   (F #30)

(70) **man=chi man=chi** *pola-ri-ka-a-la-ki-na-e*
      one=DAT one=DAT come.across-CAUSE-INTS-RR-COLL-DO:VCL-PROG-DECL
      '(They) pass (things) to each other, to first one than another.'   (V #30)

(71) *beko beko*   *kuwa-ka-a-la-ke-e*,   **peman-ka pareja=tala**
      back.and.forth give-INTS-RR-COLL-DO:VCL-DECL three-NCL SP:pair=COLL
      '(They) give (things) back and forth, between the three pairs (of people).'
                                                                                  (MC #30)

When the elicited data is compared with natural data there is a rather interesting contrast in terms of the type of reciprocal used. Again leaving out positionals and just comparing the reciprocal constructions coding symmetrical actions, in natural discourse texts the four different reciprocal constructions are fairly evenly distributed (Table 5). However in the elicited data, only one of the four possible reciprocal conditions, reciprocal with intensifier formed with -*a* 'RR' makes up well over half of the tokens. Ignoring simple reciprocal constructions where the low number of -*a* simple reciprocal constructions is probably due to a lack of these specific predicates in the elicited data, and just looking at the reciprocal with intensifier constructions, speakers chose the -*a* form 82% of the time (53/65).

Table 5. Comparison of the four reciprocal constructions in natural discourse and elicited conditions

	Texts						Elicited					
	Simple reciprocal		Reciprocal with intensifier		Total		Simple reciprocal		Reciprocal with intensifier		Total	
	#	%	#	%	#	%	#	%	#	%	#	%
i 'become'	176	.30	151	.26	327	.56	17	.20	12	.14	29	.35
-*a* 'RR'	109	.18	152	.26	261	.44	02	.02	53	.63	55	.65
Total	285	.48	303	.52	588	1.00	19	.23	65	.77	84	100

In addition out of the seventeen elicited examples that used the *i* 'become' simple reciprocal construction, all involved predicates such as *aman* 'hug', *walada* 'exchange', *tula* 'meet' or the Spanish borrowing *saluda* 'greet' in which there is no other option. Besides the 'natural' reciprocal verbs the other predicates found in the *i* reciprocal with intensifier constructions were: *tensa* 'play', *kira* 'see', *tede ka* 'shake hand/get hand', *tala* 'touch', *ka* 'get/catch', and *jala* 'pull'.

The results in the elicited examples could be simply a reflection of the types of events coded. The data had a lot of incidents of 'hitting' and 'giving' and it is possible the -*a* construction is preferred in these types of events. However looking at the verb *ki* 'hit', in both the natural texts and elicited data, there is a clear difference. In the natural texts *ki* 'hit' occurs in the reciprocal with intensifier construction slightly more often with *i* 'BECOME' (118/211 = 56%), than with -*a* 'RR' (93/211 = 44%). In contrast, all fourteen examples (100%) of reciprocal *ki* 'hit/do' in the elicited data occur with -*a* 'RR' in the reciprocal with intensifier construction. The same held for the predicate *kuwa* 'give'. In the natural discourse texts *kuwa* 'give' occurred in the reciprocal with intensifier *i* construction 66% (12/18) of the time as opposed to 33% (6/18) of the time in the reciprocal with intensifier -*a* construction. Whereas in the elicited examples *kuwa* 'give' occurred in the reciprocal with intensifier -*a* construction in all sixteen of the examples (100%).

Table 6. Comparison of the two reciprocal with intensifier constructions in natural discourse and elicited conditions with the verb *ki* 'do' and *kuwa* 'give'

	Reciprocal with intensifier constructions	Elicited data		Natural texts	
		#	%	#	%
ki 'hit'	with *i* 'BECOME'	0	0	118	56
	with *a* 'RR'	14	100	93	44
kuwa 'give'	with *i* 'BECOME'	0	0	12	66
	with *a* 'RR'	16	100	6	33

It appears that the elicitation task itself, rather than the type of event depicted biased the responses in favor of the reciprocal constructions formed with *-a*. This makes sense in light of the fact that in the elicitation task the same kinds of events are repeated again and again and the speakers were well aware that these were staged events. After seeing a few instances of reciprocal actions it might be the speakers began to anticipate that something similar was about to happen and hence used the construction which indicated that the event was expected.

7. Conclusion

In conclusion it has been shown that the different strategies used in Tsafiki to code symmetrical situations are comprised of elements that already have established uses in other constructions. There is no single element dedicated to the coding of symmetry. Positional symmetry is coded with positional coverbs that can code other types of positional configurations including asymmetrical positions and those involving the configuration in space of a single entity. The symmetrical coverbs simply comprise a subset of positional constructions. In essence this symmetry is lexically coded.

The strategies for coding active symmetry arise out of the possibilities and constraints imposed by the complex predicate constructions and the complex semantics involved in symmetrical actions. In reciprocal constructions there are of course two participants, each participant is both an actor and an undergoer. In the complex predicate constructions the speaker must not only choose from a limited set of generic verbs, but also from a very limited set of second order semantic predicate classes. Of the five classes, *i* 'become', *ki* 'do', *ti* 'say/express', *ra* 'be in a position' and *jo* 'be', only the *i* 'become' and *ki* 'do' classes are plausible categories for the coding of the reciprocal construction. If the speaker chooses the *i* class he is focusing on the undergoer aspects of the participants in that an *i* class verb always indicates that the nominative argument undergoes a change-of-state or location. In other words what is *happening* to the participants is emphasised. The opposite is true if a *ki*-class predicator such as *-a* 'RR' is used. Here the nominative argument will be an actor. In other words what the participants are *doing* will be emphasised. With the exception of a small set of coverbs in the simple reciprocal construction, the Tsafiki speaker has the option of choosing either the *i*-class or the *ki*-class construction to code the same reciprocal event.

In addition, the *i*-class verbs are also used to form middle voice constructions. As pointed out by Shibatani (2006) and Maldonado (1993) middle voice constructions often carry mirative notions such as unexpectedness. Middle voice focuses on the change of state phase of the event, leaving out the causal phase which can lead to an interpretation of spontaneous or sudden change which in turn can lead to an interpretation of unexpected change – a mirative notion. While these notions may be only incipient in the middle voice constructions, they come to the forefront in the Tsafiki reciprocal and non-translational motion constructions where the same event can be coded by either an *i*-class or *ki*-class verb without a major change in transitivity or event structure.

So while cross-linguistically the types of distinctions made by the Tsafiki reciprocal constructions may appear somewhat unusual, they are quite normal and natural in Tsafiki, also occurring in other related constructions. The reciprocal constructions can be seen to fit quite well into a scale where the verb *i* 'become' ranges from a simple verb coding a change of state, to a verbal suffix coding mirative notions.

Given the types of distinctions made by the Tsafiki reciprocal constructions it is not surprising that they did not conform well to the different criteria concerning reciprocal situations presented in the video clips. The Tsafiki reciprocal constructions have fairly unique characteristics due to the nature of the constructions from which they arise and the overall grammatical structure of Tsafiki. Finally, in comparison with the natural data, the elicited data was biased in favor of the reciprocal construction indicating expected actions, perhaps due to the fact that the speakers knew the events were staged and there was a fair amount of repetition. The type of discrepancy between the elicited and natural data found here is, of course, not particularly unusual and just serves to emphasise the need to always compare and contrast elicited data with natural data.

Orthography and abbreviations

The orthography used in this study is that used by the Tsachila community which is roughly based on the IPA with a few exceptions. The symbol 'j' represents a voiceless glottal fricative /h/ (note this differs from the Spanish voiceless velar fricative /x/). The symbol 'y' is used for the voiced palatal approximant /j/. A single apostrophe indicates a glottal stop. Tsafiki does not have diphthongs or long vowels. Each vowel in a sequence is individually pronounced with a glottal stop separating it from a following vowel. (This phonologically conditioned glottal stop is not marked in the writing system). Finally a syllable final 'n' indicates nasalization of the preceding vowel, *an* =/ã/, *en* = /ẽ/.

Glosses used in this study include:

1F	first person feminine	INCL	inclusive
1M	first person masculine	INF	infinitive
2	second person	INGR	ingressive
3P1	third person proximate one	INSTR	instrument
3P2	third person proximate two	INT	interrogative
3D1	third person distal one	INTJ	interjective
3D2	third person distal two	INTS	intensive
ACC	accusative	IRR	irrealis
ADV	adverb	LOC	locative
ASP	aspect	MIR	mirative
ASSOC.M	associated motion	NCL	nominal classifier
ATT	attemptive	NCNGR	non-congruent
AUX	auxiliary	NEG	negative
CNGR	congruent	NMLZR.OBL	nominaliser oblique
COLL	collective	PF.P	perfective participle
COM	comitative	PL	plural
CONTR	contrastive	PRO	proform
DAT	dative	PROG	progressive
DECL	declarative	QT	quotative
DESR	desirative	REP	reportative
DR	different reference	RR	reciprocal/reflexive
DUB	dubative	SITU	situational
EMPH	emphatic	SMBL	semblative
EV	evidential	SP	Spanish borrowing
FOC	focus	SR	same referent
IM	immediate	ST	stative
IMP	imperative	SUF	suffix
IMPF.P	imperfective participle	VCL	verb class marker

Acknowledgements

Research for this paper was supported by the National Science Foundation (0618887) and the Volkswagen Stiftung Foundation. I would like to thank all the members of the Tsachila organisation PIKITSA for producing the natural discourse materials used in this study and their invaluable help in the analysis with special thanks to the director, Alfonso Aguavil Calazacón as well as Jose Jacinto Aguavil Loche and Catalina Calazacón Aguavil.

References

Curnow, Timothy Jowan. 1997. A Grammar of Awa Pit (Cuaiquer): An Indigenous Language of Southwestern Colombia. PhD dissertation, Australian National University.

Curnow, Timothy Jowan. 2000. Why 'first/non-first person' is not grammaticalized mirativity. *Proceedings of ALS22, the 2000 Conference of the Australian Linguistic Society.*

Dalrymple, Mary, Kanazawa, Makoto, Kim, Yookyung, Mchombo, Sam & Peters, Stanley. 1998. Reciprocal expressions and the concept of reciprocity. *Linguistics & Philosophy* 21(2): 159–210.

DeLancey, Scott. 1992. The historical status of the conjunct/disjunct pattern in Tibeto-Burman. *Acta Linguistica Hafniensia* 25: 39–62.

DeLancey, Scott. 1997. Mirativity: The grammatical marking of unexpected information. *Linguistic Typology* 1: 33–52.

DeLancey, Scott. 2001. The mirative and evidentiality. *Journal of Pragmatics* 33(3): 369–382.

Dickinson, Connie. 2000. Mirativity in Tsafiki. *Studies in Language* 24(2): 379–401.

Dickinson, Connie. 2002. Complex Predicates in Tsafiki. PhD dissertation, University of Oregon.

Evans, Nicholas. 2008. Reciprocal constructions: Towards a structural typology. In *Reciprocals and Reflexives: Cross-linguistic and Theoretical Exploration*, Ekkehard König & Volker Gast (eds). Berlin: Mouton de Gruyter.

Evans, Nicholas. 2006. Dyad constructions. In *Encyclopaedia of Language and Linguistics*, Vol 4, Keith Brown (ed.), 24–27. Oxford: Elsevier.

Frajzyngier, Zygmunt & Curl, Traci S. (eds). 1999. *Reciprocals: Forms and Functions* [Typological Studies in Language 41]. Amsterdam: John Benjamins.

Grinevald, Colette. 2006. The expression of static location in a typological perspective. In *Space in language: Linguistic systems and Cognitive Categories* [Typological Studies in Language 66], Maya Hickmann & Stéphane Robert (eds), 29–58. Amsterdam: John Benjamins.

Haviland, John B. 1992. Seated and settled: Tzotzil verbs of the body. *Zeitschrift für Phonetik, Sprachwissenschaft und Kommunikationsforschung* 45(6): 543–561.

Kemmer, Suzanne. 1993. *The Middle Voice* [Typological Studies in Language 23]. Amsterdam: John Benjamins.

Maldonado, Ricardo. 1993. Dynamic construals in Spanish. *Studi Italiani di Linguistica Teorica e Applicata* XXII(3): 531–566.

McGregor, William B. 2002. *Verb Classification in Australian Languages*. Berlin: Mouton de Gruyter.

Moore, Bruce. 1991. *Patrones Gramticales del Colorados (Chibcha)*, Stephen H. Levinsohn (ed.). Quito: Instituto Lingüístico Verano.

Schultze-Berndt, Eva. 2000. Simple and Complex Verbs in Jaminjung: A Study of Event Categorisation in an Australian Language. PhD dissertation, Katholieke Universiteit Nijmegen.

Shibatani, Masayoshi. 2006. On the conceptual framework for voice phenomena. *Linguistics* 44(2): 217–269.

Appendix A

Classes of generic verbs and verbal suffixes

Generic verb			Generic verb		
i 'become' class		# of coverbs*	*ki* 'do/make'-class		# of coverbs
i	'become'	257	*ki*	'do/make'	269
ji	'go'	109	*suwa*	'cause to become'	156
ja	'come'	48	*kari*	'cause'	149
lo	'go out/up'	45	*ere*	'send'	50
la	'come out/up'	50	*po*	'put'	43
fe	'arrive there'	34	*ka*	'get'	35
fa	'arrive here'	33	*pa*	'talk'	10
pati	'go down'	35	*kira*	'see'	9
pata	'come down'	35	*kuwa*	'give'	4
pole	'go across'	43	*fi*	'eat'	1
pola	'come across'	35	*-le*	'direct cause'	76
wi	'go in'	37	*-ri*	'cause motion'	39
wiya	'come in'	33	*-te*	'set/place'	17
piya	'lose'	5	*-si*	'remove'	15
puya	'die'	1	*-re*	'direct cause'	5
katso	'sleep'	4	*-wo*	'indirect cause'	5
-di	'get into position'		*-miya*	'associative cause'	open
			-a	'reflexive/reciprocal'	open
ti 'say' class			*ra* 'be in position' class		
ti	'say/express'		*ra*	'be in a position'	125
			nena	'go around'	33
jo 'be' class			*ta*	'have'	11
jo	'be'		*chu*	'sit'	7
ito	'not be'		*tsu*	'lie'	5

* These numbers indicate the number of different coverbs (out of approximately 500) with which each generic verb has been found to co-occur.

CHAPTER 18

Reciprocal constructions in Hup

Patience Epps
University of Texas at Austin

This paper provides a comprehensive description of the encoding of recipro-cal relations in Hup, a language of the Nadahup or 'Makú' family of northwest Amazonia. Hup has three morphological strategies for expressing reciprocal re-lations, but only one of these – the verbal preform *ʔũh* – is fully productive. The semantic range of this primary strategy extends well beyond canonical recipro-cal interaction to include chains, melêes, and even 'converse' events, in which one participant acts non-reciprocally on another; the 'interactional' gram *ʔũh* is accordingly argued to have a unitary, underspecified semantics relating to inter-action between two or more mutually involved co-participants. Hup's secondary strategies include a marginal reciprocal extension of the reflexive preform *hup*, and the non-productive use of the preform *bab'*, restricted to a few lexical items. Typologically intriguing aspects of Hup's strategies for marking reciprocal rela-tions include the variable use of *ʔũh* and *hup* as prefixes or preverbal particles, the wide semantic range of *ʔũh*, and the apparent historical source of both *ʔũh* and *bab'* in kin terms meaning 'sibling'.

1. Introduction

The Hup language is spoken by some 1500 people in the Vaupés region of north-west Amazonia, located on the border of Brazil and Colombia. It belongs to the small Nadahup or Makú family,[1] of which all four members, including Hup, were until recently almost completely undescribed. See Epps (2008a) for a comprehen-sive grammar of Hup.

---

1. The family name 'Nadahup' is preferable to 'Makú' for two reasons. There is some confusion in the literature concerning the name 'Makú', which appears in reference to several unrelated language groups in Amazonia; also, 'Makú' (probably from Arawak *ma-áku* (NEG-talk) 'do not talk'; Koch-Grünberg (1906) is widely recognised in the Vaupés region as an ethnic slur. 'Nada-hup' combines elements of the names of the four established languages that make up the family (Nadëb, Dâw, Yuhup, Hup).

Probably as a result of intense language contact (see Epps 2007, 2008b; Aikhenvald 2002), Hup's typological profile closely resembles that of its Vaupés neighbours, the East Tukanoan and Tariana languages. Like them, Hup has basic SOV constituent order, relatively polysynthetic verbal morphology with productive compounding of multiple stems, clitics, and affixes, and is dependent-marking. Also like the East Tukanoan languages, Hup relies almost entirely on post-stem morphology (suffixes and enclitics); the few exceptions are all involved in adjusting valency (a transitiviser and markers used for reciprocal and reflexive relations). Grammatical relations in Hup are nominative-accusative; the marking of core non-subject arguments is sensitive to animacy and definiteness (Epps 2008a, 2009), and these arguments are frequently dropped when accessible within the discourse context.

Examples (1–2) illustrate basic intransitive and transitive clauses in Hup. Intransitive verbs are distinguished from transitive verbs mainly by their inability to take a direct object without additional valency-changing morphology, such as an applicative or causative (but this is not without exception; see Epps 2008a for discussion).

(1)   *tih=dóʔ*   *ʔɔ́t-ɔ́y*
      3SG=child(SBJ)   cry-DYNM
      'The child is crying.'

(2)   *tih=dóʔ-ăn*   *tih*   *tɔ́w-ɔ́y*
      3SG=child-OBJ   3SG(SBJ)   scold-DYNM
      'He is scolding the child.'

As it has grown more like the East Tukanoan languages, Hup grammar has apparently become increasingly unlike that of its sister-languages spoken outside the Vaupés contact zone – particularly Nadëb, which is ergative and mostly prefixing. This may explain why Hup's primary mechanism for encoding reciprocal relations – the verbal preform *ʔũh* – bears no resemblance to any of those reported for its sisters Dâw and Nadëb.[2] On the other hand, Hup *ʔũh* bears a close resemblance in patterning and function to the Tukano reciprocal gram *a'me* (see Ramirez 1997:6); this and the likelihood that *ʔũh* grammaticalised relatively recently in Hup, as mentioned below, suggests that its development may have been modeled on the Tukanoan form.

---

2.   In Nadëb, only a single reciprocal/reflexive construction is reported, a prefix *ka-* (Weir 1984:107). Dâw uses a pre-verbal marker *hub* as both a reflexive and a reciprocal marker (Martins 2004:379); this form is undoubtedly cognate with the Hup reflexive gram *hup*, which has a marginal reciprocal function.

2. Strategies for encoding reciprocal relations in Hup

Hup has one primary strategy for encoding reciprocity (Table 1): the verbal prefix or preform *ʔũh*. However, the functions of this 'interactional' gram are not limited to indicating reciprocity; *ʔũh* can also encode a more general interaction among mutually engaged co-participants, who need not be performing equivalent actions within the context of the broader interactive event (see Section 3). Hup also makes occasional use of a secondary strategy to indicate reciprocity via the verbal preform *hup*, which functions in most contexts as a reflexive marker, and a non-productive, essentially lexical reciprocal 'strategy' involving the preform *bab'* (from the noun 'sibling'). Other than the verbs formed with *bab'*, Hup has few natural lexical reciprocals (in the sense of a verb that entails a reciprocal interpretation); even verbs like *kay'-* 'embrace' and *tɔw-* 'scold, speak angrily to' tend to be interpreted in a neutral context as non-reciprocal (transitive with a dropped object) if not overtly marked as reciprocal/interactive, regardless of whether the subject of the clause is singular or plural. However, the marker is frequently optional if a reciprocal reading is recoverable from the discourse or pragmatic context.

Table 1. Construction types

	Grams having a reciprocal function
1	'Interactional' verbal preform *ʔũh*
2	'Reflexive' verbal preform *hup*
3	Non-productive reciprocal verbal preform *bab'*

A morphosyntactic characterisation of these construction types is provided below, followed by a discussion of how they function to encode the clip data in Section 3.

2.1 Primary strategy: The verbal preform *ʔũh*

Hup's primary strategy for encoding reciprocal relations involves prefixing the morpheme *ʔũh* to the verb stem. The verbal preform *ʔũh* is glossed here as an 'interactional' gram: it is not limited to a strictly reciprocal function, but is also used to indicate a more general interaction between two or more agentive entities who are mutually involved in an activity, as the discussion in Section 3 will illustrate.

Examples of the reciprocal use of *ʔũh* include constructions like *ʔũh-g'ɔç-* (INTRC-bite) 'fight' (animals) and *ʔũh-mæh-* (INTRC-beat/kill) 'fight (people)' (both semi-lexicalised), *ʔũh-cob-* 'point at each other', and Example (3):

(3) kaʔap=ʔắy=d'əh   ʔũh-kəmən-d'óʔ-óy³
     two=F=PL   INTRC-embrace-take-DYNM
     'Two women hug each other.'   (#7)⁴

Further examples include reciprocals formed with semi-transitive verbs like ʔũh-yú-
'wait for each other' and ditransitive verbs (Examples (4)–(5)). In ditransitive reciprocal constructions, the argument co-referential with the subject can only be interpreted as the goal (typically a recipient; Example (5)), although in a non-reciprocal
ditransitive either (animate) argument can be interpreted as goal or theme.

(4) húp=d'əh   hidnih   kəwəg-túʔ   ʔũh-kəd-ni-pǽm-ǽy
     person=PL   3pl.POSS eye-immerse INTRC-pass-be-sit-DYNM
     'The people switch their glasses with each other while seated.'   (#41)

(5) hɨd kaʔáp=d'əh   tog   ʔũh-bé-éy
     3pl two=PL   daughter   INTRC-show-DYNM
     'The two of them show each other their daughters.'
     *'The two of them show each other to their daughters.'

Interactional ʔũh usually appears as a verbal prefix, realised as a phonological
unit together with its host: it is unstressed, and is not separated from the verb
by a pause. However, in a ditransitive context, it may optionally occur as a phonologically free particle, receiving independent stress and separated from the
verb stem by the object nominal acting as the theme (6). (Note that a similar
phenomenon is attested for the reflexive preform hup, which also has a marginal
reciprocal use; see below.)

(6) húp=d'əh   ʔũ̃h   pāt   cuʔ-gʼét-éy
     person=PL   INTRC hair   grab-stand-DYNM
     'The people are standing grabbing at each others' hair.'   (#45)

This [ʔũh Obj Verb] construction appears to be semantically and pragmatically
equivalent to the alternative [Obj ʔũh-Verb] (so Example (6) is interchangeable
with pāt ʔũh-cuʔ-gʼét-éy). One important structural difference is that the object,
sandwiched between ʔũh and the verb, cannot be modified – whether by a demonstrative, adjective, inalienable possessor, number, case, etc. – even where this
would otherwise be obligatory. This fact suggests that the noun is an incorporated
object, although incorporation is not otherwise a productive phenomenon in Hup.

---

3. Hup has contrastive word-accent: rising tone is indicated by v̌, falling tone (and its allo-
phonic variant, high tone) by v́.

4. The # symbol corresponds to the number of the videoclip used to elicit these examples;
unmarked examples are from texts or (in a few cases) from other elicitation.

Morphosyntactic features of *ʔũh* include the fact that it almost always appears with a transitive verb. Where the object of the verb would otherwise be an animate patient or recipient (as with transitive and ditransitive verbs like 'hit' and 'give'), *ʔũh* normally acts to decrease valency, such that the expression of this object argument is ungrammatical (see Example (9)).[5] However, there are certain exceptions to this generalisation, as in (12) below.

Another such exception applies in the few contexts where consultants judge *ʔũh* to be grammatical with an intransitive verb. These all involve multiple participants engaging in the activity interactively (i.e. not just jointly, but by mutually influencing each other). Examples include lying in a hammock with limbs entwined or laughing uproariously face to face, as if setting one another off (Examples (7)–(8)).

(7) *ʔũhhiwíh*   *hid ʔũh-g'ǎʔ-ǎy*
     between.relatives 3pl INTRC-be.suspended-DYNM
     'They are together in the hammock.' (lit. 'They are suspended (in a single hammock) interactively'; i.e. bodies in contact, esp. if limbs entwined)

(8) *hid ʔũh-tǽʔnɔ-naʔ-yíʔ-íy*
     3pl INTRC-laugh-die-TEL-DYNM
     'They are laughing hard together.' (i.e. setting each other off in their laughter)
                                                                            (#40)

A further morphosyntactic feature of *ʔũh-* is that it normally requires a plural subject; hence a singular subject is ungrammatical. This constraint is relaxed in the few cases where the interactional marker is semi-lexicalised together with the verb stem (primarily with the fighting verbs listed above). Here, consultants accept a singular subject, although an explicit object such as *cǎp=ʔíh-an* (other=M-OBJ) 'someone else' is nevertheless not permitted:

(9) *yúp=ʔĩh (*cǎp=ʔíh-ǎn) ʔũh-mǽh-ǽy*
     that=M   (*other=M-OBJ) INTRC-hit-DYNM
     'That man is fighting (with someone).'

In keeping with the semantics of *ʔũh*, which require the mutual involvement of two or more co-participants in an event (see Section 3), the interactional construction almost always involves an animate subject; however, inanimate subjects are also grammatical:

---

5. Also compare Example (6) above, where the verb *cuʔ-gèt-* 'stand grabbing' can otherwise take either one possessed object ('stand grabbing her hair') or two objects with external possession ('stand grabbing her the hair'). With interactional *ʔũh* present, only one externally possessed object ('hair') is possible.

(10) *cug'ǽt   ʔũh-caʔ-ni-g'ét-éy*
      book   INTRC-box-be-stand-DYNM
      'The books stand together (forming a box-like structure).'   (#35)

The reciprocal relationship encoded by the *ʔũh* construction cannot in general hold between two non-actors, such that expressions equivalent to English 'he showed the boy and the girl to each other' are impossible. This normally means that non-subjects are excluded from the reciprocal relationship; however, this is not the case when actors appear as objects in a causative construction (e.g. (13) below). Subjects are non-coreferential with stated direct objects in a ditransitive construction, and where objects are understood as possessed by the participants engaging in the reciprocal interaction, as illustrated by (11) (from a traditional narrative; see also (6) above 'they are grabbing at each others' hair'):

(11) *pũʔũk   b'ɔʔ   ʔũh-nǽm'-key-yóʔ,   ʔin   ni-píd-íh*
      coca   gourd   INTRC-lick-see-SEQ   1pl   be-DISTR-DECL
      'Having tasted each others' coca, we stayed thus.'

The constraint against the presence of an overt object that is co-referential with the subject is relaxed in one realisation of the interactional construction: where the 'distributive' marker *pid* is used to indicate 'each to the next' in a chain-type reciprocal situation (see Section 3 below), as in (12) (here *ʔũh* is optional).

(12) *cāp=ʔĩh-ǎn   pid   hid   (ʔũh-)nɔʔ-tɔ́k-ɔ́h*
      other=M-OBJ   DISTR   3pl   (INTRC-)give-pass.on-DECL
      'They are passing something along, each to the next.'   (#34)

The interactional construction can interact with other valence-adjusting mechanisms in Hup. It can feed or be fed by a causative construction, which Hup creates by means of compounded verbs (13). It can be fed by an applicative, as in (14) (note that the applicative suffix is identical in form to the interactional prefix) and, in a few cases, by a reflexive (15).[6]

(13) *b'ǒy=ʔĩh   híd-ǎn   [ʔũh-biʔ-hitam]-yǽh-ǽy=mah*
      study=M   3pl-OBJ   [INTRC-work-help]-request-DYNM=REP
      'The teacher ordered / made the children help each other, it's said.'

(14) *Pěd, Mɔt   hũ-d'ǎp   hid   ʔũh-ciw-ʔũh-úy*
      Ped   Mɔt   animal-meat   3pl   INTRC-cook-APPL-DYNM
      'Ped and Mɔt cooked meat for each other.'

---

6. Reflexive *hup-* is also occasionally used to mark reciprocity; see § 2.2.

(15) ʔin ʔüh-hup-yád-óy
      1pl INTRC-RFL-hide-DYNM
      'We are hiding ourselves from each other.'

Finally, the occurrence of interactional ʔüh with non-verbal predicates is limited
to terms which are two-place predicates and their own converses; all examples
encountered to date involve kin relationships, as in constructions like (16) (in
which ʔüh is strongly preferred):

(16) ʔüh-yóh=d'əh   yi-d'óh-óh
      INTRC-affine=PL   that-PL-DECL
      'They are affinal relatives/cross-cousins.'

Other reciprocally marked nominals are nominalisations of verbal phrases or
clauses, such as ʔüh-mǽh=d'əh (INTR-hit=PL) 'those who fight'. The interactional
gram cannot appear with two-place nouns which are not self-converse, such as
'mother', 'younger sister', etc.

   To summarise, the patterns of use for interactional ʔüh are very loosely constrained, although there are clear preferences for a plural subject and a transitive
verbal predicate (frequently made intransitive by combination with ʔüh). These
preferences are in keeping with the semantics of reciprocals generally.

   It is possible to identify a likely historical source for the interactional gram.
This is the free lexical noun ʔüh 'sibling of opposite sex', as in the inalienably possessed kin expression ʔáh=ʔüh (1SG=opposite.sex.sibling) 'my opposite-sex sibling'. Evidence for a connection between these morphemes includes their shared
phonological form and a syntactic ambiguity in many constructions between the
alternative interpretations 'they did V reciprocally' and 'their opposite-sex sibling
did V', as in Example (17). That an expression like (17b) (in which the object of
'give' is dropped) might have been reanalysed as (17a) is pragmatically justified in
the context of Hup culture, where the canonical reciprocal activity is the giving of
meat and other items among close kin; likewise a close kin relationship presup-
poses such an on-going exchange.

(17) a. híd   ʔǔh   [hɔp nɔ́ʔ-ɔ́h]
          3pl   INTRC fish give-DECL
          'They gave each other fish.'
      b. hid=ʔǔh   [hɔp nɔ́ʔ-ɔ́h]
          3pl=o.s.sibling fish give-DECL
          'Their sibling gave fish (to them/someone).'

Additional language-internal parallels to a transition from the expression of
'sibling' to that of reciprocity or interaction in Hup involves the sibling term

báb' 'real or classificatory sibling (of either sex)', which has undergone a similar – though less generalised – adaptation to a reciprocal marker, as discussed
in Section 2.2 below.[7]

The grammaticalisation of the kin term 'sibling' to an interactional marker
apparently did not stop there. The bound form *ʔũh* has a remarkable number of
other functions in Hup, which correspond to an array of different morphosyntactic realisations. As a member of one class of verbal suffixes, *ʔũh* acts as an applicative marker (see Example (14) above); as a member of a second suffix class,
it indicates jussive or optative mood; and as a particle appearing with verbs and
other parts of speech, it marks epistemic modality. I have argued elsewhere (Epps
2010) that these various manifestations of *ʔũh* developed via a grammaticalisation
chain, such that the applicative marker – like the interactional gram – is historically linked to the kin term 'sibling', the jussive marker derives from the applicative, and the epistemic modality marker derives from the optative.

2.2   Additional marginal strategies: Reciprocal interpretations
of reflexive *hup* and *bab'* 'sibling'

Hup uses the verbal preform *hup* in a little-used secondary strategy for indicating reciprocal relations. The primary function of *hup* is as a reflexive marker
(which can itself feed the interactional *ʔũh* construction; see Example (15)
above). It also functions as a marker of passive voice; thus *tih hup-kít-íy*
(3SG RFL-cut-DYNM) can be interpreted alternatively as 'he cut himself' or 'he
got cut (by someone else).'[8]

Speakers virtually never prefer *hup* to *ʔũh* when indicating reciprocal relations. With the exception of Example (18), in which the two were used interchangeably in natural discourse, almost all examples of *hup*'s reciprocal use were
given in response to prompting. In the clips, this was usually after at least two
versions with *ʔũh* had already been offered (e.g. clip #7, in which two women hug
each other). Although *hup* was frequently judged acceptable with a reciprocal
reading in elicitation, speakers often found it distinctly odd.

---

7. Cross-linguistically, the noun 'brother' has taken on a reciprocal function in Biblical Hebrew (Orin Gensler p.c., Joüon 2000) and possibly in Tok Pisin (Fedden ms).

8. Like *ʔũh*, *hup* is remarkably polyfunctional. As a free lexical item, it acts as the noun 'Hup
person, human' (hence the name of the language) and as an impersonal subject pronoun
('someone'), or an adjective 'good, new'. As a nominal enclitic on nouns, =*hup* has a reflexive
intensifier function (e.g. 'I myself').

(18)   *tát   deh-ét=ʔŭy=dʼəh   ʔũh-nɔʔ-nɪ́h...*
    Ant   Water-OBL=WHO=PL   INTRC-give-NEG
    'The people of Ant Creek (place name) don't give (food) to each other...
    bahéda-át=ʔŭy=dʼəh   wæ̆d   hup-nɔʔ-nɪ́h
    Barreira-OBL=WHO=PL   food   RFL-give-NEG
    the people of Barreira don't give food to each other.'

In general, *hup* is a very marginal strategy for indicating reciprocal relations. It appears to be acceptable primarily when the subject of the clause is perceived as a group acting on itself, and is more likely to be judged ungrammatical when the difference between a reflexive and a reciprocal reading is important (and is not clear from the context). It is possible that *hup* is currently in the process of extending its primary reflexive-marking function to also cover a reciprocal function; such an extension is typologically common (e.g. Knjazev 1998) and may be occurring in parallel with a similar extension reported for Desano and other East Tukanoan languages (Aikhenvald 2002), via contact. Conversely, it is also possible that *hup* once served both reciprocal and reflexive functions, and has lost most of the former, but this seems unlikely given that *hup* appears – like *ʔũh* – to be quite recently grammaticalised from a free lexical noun to a semi-bound formative.

A similarly marginal reciprocal strategy in Hup involves the noun *babʼ* 'sibling'. This noun combines with certain verb roots to form lexically specific verbal constructions with inherently reciprocal or more generally interactive semantics; these may still be optionally preceded by the *ʔũh* interactional preform. In everyday use, verbal combinations involving *babʼ-* are limited mostly to *babʼ-ni-* [sibling-be] 'accompany', 'be consanguinally related to' and *babʼ-ʔɨd-* [sibling-speak] 'chat together'. However, responses to the clip data suggest that reciprocal use of *babʼ* may not be completely unproductive, although it is very rare. Speakers used the form *babʼ-gʼet-* [sibling-stand] 'stand reciprocally' to describe several sets of books standing propped together at the top to form an acute angle (clip #35) (and even a reduplicated variant *babʼ-babʼ-gʼet-*, presumably motivated by the presence of multiple sets); and one speaker used the construction *ʔũh-babʼ-pæm-* [INTRC-sibling-sit] interchangeably with *ʔũh-babʼ-ni-pæm-* [INTRC-sibling-be-sit] to describe two men sitting side by side (clip #25).

3.   Categories encoded in the clip data

Three full sets of responses to the 64 clips were obtained. The consultants involved were Evaldo and Imaculada Pires (a brother and sister participating together), ages approximately 15 and 19, respectively; Américo Monteiro, about 30 years old; and Jarbas Dias, about 34 years old. All of these speakers are fluent in Tukano, in addition to Hup, and Américo and Jarbas also speak a little Portuguese. Hup was used as the medium of communication in gathering these data.

Based on data from the clips and other forms of more natural discourse, the semantics of *ʔũh* can be characterised as entailing interaction among two or more co-participants, such that they are mutually engaged in the activity and with each other. In most cases, each participant can be construed in some way as an actor, involved in initiating or enabling the event; however, participants need not be equally agentive, nor does their contribution to the event need to be the same. Thus types of interaction encoded by *ʔũh* extend well beyond canonically reciprocal events in which participants perform the same action on each other.

In keeping with these broad semantics, the interactional gram *ʔũh* was used for nearly all of the clips. It was usually volunteered in the first response, although occasionally consultants offered a transitive clause first and a reciprocal construction second. Consultants considered the *ʔũh* construction to be inappropriate for only about six of the 64 clips, and even in these cases the speakers were frequently able to come up with a different way of phrasing the event, such that the interactional construction was then acceptable.

The *ʔũh* interactional construction was considered equally appropriate for situations of strict reciprocity (see (3) above), chains (19), and melees (20). Note that the compound verb in (19) (*d'əh-hi-* 'send-descend' = 'in a line') conveys part of the chain semantics by indicating a line of people extending from a reference point.

(19) *húp=d'əh   ʔũh-tab'ah-g'et-d'əh-hi-iy*
       person=PL   INTRC-slap-stand-send-descend-DYNM
       'The people hit each other down the line.'   (#57)

(20) *húp=dəh   ʔũh-mæh-hipoʔ-g'ét-éy*
       person=PL   INTRC-hit-opposite-stand-DYNM
       'The people standing facing each other hit each other.'   (#50)

In keeping with the semantics of *ʔũh*, consultants did not accept any form of the interactional construction when the event was conceived as fully non-interactive, as in clip #15 (in which four people enter the space and sit down, looking straight ahead and not at each other), clip #18 (in which two people sit side by side, looking straight ahead), and a few other similar clips. Even in these cases, however, it was occasionally possible to use *ʔũh* if the event were phrased as interactive in some way, as in one consultant's response to clip #18:

(21) *hɨd   ʔũh-bab'-ni-pæm-æy*
       3pl   INTRC-sibling-be-sit-DYNM
       'They sit accompanying each other.'   (#18)

Given that essentially any interactive event can be expressed using *ʔũh*, the interactional construction can even be used interchangeably with a straightforward transitive construction to express one participant's acting on another – i.e. a canonically **non**-reciprocal event. The *ʔũh* construction here highlights the engagement of multiple participants in an interactive event, while de-emphasising their identity – such that it is impossible to tell (from this construction alone) who does what to whom. Arguably, interactional *ʔũh* also highlights the fact that the participants are intentional agents, whose choices and actions contribute to define the event. In the clip data, the use of *ʔũh* for such events is probably motivated both by the equivalent anonymity of the participants in the decontextualised scenes, and by the fact that the task as a whole (involving the series of clips) had primed consultants to be particularly attentive to interaction. Clips in which *ʔũh* was used to describe such non-reciprocal events include #26 (Example (22)), in which one person takes off his watch and gives it to another person, who receives it; the same was true for clip #25, in which one person looks repeatedly at another, who looks straight ahead – apparently wilfully ignoring the other.

(22) *húp=d'əh   dapũh-d'ak   ʔũh-poʔ-nɔʔ-pæm-ǽy*
      person=PL   hand-attach   INTRC-open-give-sit-DYNM
      'The people are interactively taking off and giving a watch while sitting.' (#26)

In natural Hup discourse, such 'asymmetric' or 'converse' (see Lichtenberk 2000) uses of the interactional gram are rare, and appear in my corpus in only two instances. In both cases, the narrator is foreshadowing an event that will occur later in the story, so the identities of the participants are temporarily downplayed; moreover, the 'victim' of the action (pulling out of eyeballs or piercing of an anus) is complicit in that he is tricked into requesting it – in other words, the event can be conceived as symmetric in that the participants share equal willingness or responsibility, and the narrator may be exploiting this for artistic purposes. In this use of a construction that also encodes reciprocity, Hup bears a striking resemblance to Lao (Enfield, this volume).

Because of this functional flexibility of interactional *ʔũh*, its interpretation may be vague. Fixed lexical expressions can help to reinforce a particular interpretation of a predicate marked with *ʔũh*. For example, even a kind of interactive *reflexive* interpretation is possible when lexically specified, as in (23). Conversely, the reciprocal lexical form *ʔũhiwih* is used to reinforce a true reciprocal interpretation (see Example (5) above).[9]

---

9. The form *ʔũhiwih* 'reciprocally; between relatives' is probably a back-formation created from the nominalisation *ʔũh-hiwih-d'əh* (INTRC-restrain.from.trouble-PL) 'relatives; those who restrain each other from trouble'.

(23) táʔáy,   tiyǐʔ hidnǐh   cáp-át   ʔũh-nɔ́m'-ɔ́y
      woman   man   3pl.POSS body-OBL INTRC-poke-DYNM
      'The man and woman together both poke on their own bodies.'

Hup's secondary reciprocal strategies appear only rarely in the clip data. As noted in Section 2.2 above, use of *hup* to indicate reciprocal relations was strongly disfavored; it was volunteered spontaneously on only one occasion (clip #30, pair-wise giving; one consultant only), although it was accepted as grammatical (but often judged to be odd) in more cases. Reciprocal verbs formed with *bab'* were offered spontaneously by one or more speakers (both with and without preceding *ʔũh-*) for clips #1, 11, 33 (*bab'-ʔid* 'chat'), clips #18, 25 (*bab'-ni* 'accompany'), and clip #35 (*bab'-g'et* 'stand against each other'); see Section 2.2 above.

4.   Conclusion

Hup's strategies for indicating reciprocity are noteworthy on several counts. All three grams used to mark reciprocal relations have nominal origins, and two – *ʔũh* and *bab'* – derive from kin terms meaning 'sibling'. The extreme polyfunctionality of the *ʔũh* gram is particularly remarkable, representing a diachronic extension of functions ranging from a lexical kinship noun to an applicative suffix, a jussive marker, and a marker of epistemic modality – in addition to its use as an interactional preform. In addition, the interactional and reflexive markers *ʔũh* and *hup* are unusual in their morphosyntactic patterning, in that they can appear as either verbal prefixes or as a preverbal particles, separated from the verb by the object (theme) in a ditransitive construction.

As the most productive and dedicated marker of reciprocal relations, a noteworthy feature of interactional *ʔũh* is its wide semantic range. Its primary function is to mark interaction among co-participants, grouped together as the subject of the verb. In addition to reciprocity, *ʔũh* marks such interactive events as two people facing each other and laughing (Example (8) above), or even 'converse' or 'asymmetric' relations, in which one participant acts on another without the action being returned in kind (e.g. Example (22)). The Hup strategy is reminiscent of the collective construction in some Oceanic languages; in Boumaa Fijian, for example, the prefix *vei-* groups core participants together such that the subject of the resulting intransitive verb is the sum of A and O, and reciprocity is only one possible interpretation (Dixon 1988: 177–78). In cross-linguistic perspective, Lichtenberk (2000: 34) observes that languages **either** lump reciprocal + collective (and/or converse) together (such that "plurality of relations" is a common semantic denominator), **or** they lump reciprocal + reflexive, but that they do not combine these strategies. Hup appears to conform to this pattern, such that reflexive relations are encoded by one gram (*hup*) – which itself has a marginal reciprocal extension – while most reciprocal, converse, and other interactive events are handled by *ʔũh*.

Orthography and abbreviations

The orthography used here was developed during the course of my fieldwork and analysis of Hup (see Epps 2008a). The abbreviations used in glossing are the following:

APPL	applicative	OBL	oblique
DECL	declarative	PL/pl	plural
DISTR	distributive	POSS	possessive
DYNM	dynamic aspect	REP	reported evidential
F	feminine	RFL	reflexive
INTRC	interactional	SEQ	sequential
M	masculine	SG	singular
NEG	negative	SBJ	subject
OBJ	object	TEL	telic

Acknowledgements

This work is based on fieldwork conducted between 2000–2004 and supported by a Fulbright-Hays Dissertation Research Grant, National Science Foundation Grant no. 0111550, and the Max Planck Institute for Evolutionary Anthropology, Leipzig. I am grateful to my Hupd'əh hosts, the Museu Goeldi, and the Instituto Socioambiental in Brazil, and to Nick Evans, Stephen Levinson, and Claudia Wegener for their helpful comments on this paper.

References

Aikhenvald, Alexandra. 2002. *Language Contact in Amazonia*. Oxford: Oxford University Press.
Dixon, R. M. W. 1988. *A Grammar of Boumaa Fijian*. Chicago IL: University of Chicago Press.
Epps, Patience. 2007. The Vaupés melting pot: Tukanoan influence on Hup. In *Grammars in Contact: A Cross-linguistic Typology* [Explorations in Linguistic Typology 4], Alexandra Aikhenvald & R. M. W. Dixon (eds), 267–289. Oxford: Oxford University Press.
Epps, Patience. 2008a. *A Grammar of Hup* [Mouton Grammar Library 43] Berlin: Mouton de Gruyter.

Epps, Patience. 2008b. Grammatical borrowing in Hup. In *Grammatical Borrowing: A Cross-linguistic Survey*, Yaron Matras & Jeanette Sakel (eds), 551–565. Berlin: Mouton de Gruyter.

Epps, Patience. 2009. Where differential object marking and split plurality intersect: Evidence from Hup. In *New Challenges in Typology: Transcending the Borders and Refining the Distinctions*, Patience Epps & Alexandre Arkhipov (eds), 85–104. Berlin: Mouton de Gruyter.

Epps, Patience. 2010. Linking valence change and modality: Diachronic evidence from Hup. *International Journal of American Linguistics* 76(3): 335–356.

Fedden, Sebastian. Reciprocal constructions in Tok Pisin. Ms.

Joüon, Paul. 2000. *A Grammar of Biblical Hebrew*, translated and revised by T. Muraoka, Vol. II, Pt. 3: *Syntax*. Roma: Editrice Pontificio Istituto Biblico: 546f.

Koch-Grünberg, Theodor. 1906. Die Makú. *Anthropos* 1: 877–906.

Knjazev, Jurij. 1998. Towards a typology of grammatical polysemy: Reflexive markers as markers of reciprocity. In *Typology of Verbal Categories*, Leonid Kulikov & Heinz Vater (eds), 185–93. Tübingen: Niemeyer.

Lichtenberk, Frantisek. 2000. Reciprocals without reflexives. In *Reciprocals: Forms and Functions* [*Typological Studies in Language* 41], Zigmunt Frajzyngier & Traci S. Curl (eds), 31–62. Amsterdam: John Benjamins.

Martins, Silvana. 2004. Fonologia e gramática Dâw. PhD dissertation, Vrije Universiteit Amsterdam.

Ramirez, Henri. 1997. *A fala Tukano dos Ye'pa-Masa*, Vol. 2: *Dicionário*. Manaus: Inspetoria Salesiana Missionária da Amazônia, CEDEM.

Weir, E. M. Helen. 1984. A negação e outros tópicos da gramática Nadëb. MA thesis, UNICAMP, Campinas.

CHAPTER 19

Reciprocals and semantic typology

Some concluding remarks

Ekkehard König
Freie Universität Berlin

In the concluding remarks that follow the results of the preceding articles are examined and discussed in the light of concepts of reciprocity distinguished in linguistics and other disciplines. It is shown that these contributions enlarge the empirical basis for the study of reciprocity and contribute to strengthening earlier cross-linguistic generalizations. They also call some of these generalisations into question, however, thus raising interesting new questions and problems for any attempt to map out the space of variation in the relevant domain.

1. Concepts of reciprocity outside of linguistics

The approach used in the preceding analyses of the encoding of reciprocity in various languages is an onomasiological one. It is based on videoclips portraying various scenes of symmetric and non-symmetric interaction, which the informants were asked to verbalise. The relevant scenes, in turn, were based on the different meanings or use types distinguished in semantic studies of reciprocity such as Dalrymple et al. (1998), Winter (2001) and others. Interestingly enough, it is pointed out by several authors that these videoclips did not fully determine the construal of the relevant situations, which were partly fleshed out on the basis of cultural background knowledge. Given this onomasiological and conceptual basis, I will begin my discussion of the preceding papers by briefly confronting concepts of reciprocity used outside of linguistics and those generally distinguished in current linguistic discussions.

Reciprocity lies at the very root of social organisation and ethics. It is not surprising therefore that it should have preoccupied scholars from many disciplines. Major contributions to the study of reciprocal concepts and their use in different communities and cultures have been made by scholars from disciplines as diverse as philosophy, biology, economics, anthropology, sociology and history (cf. Mauss 1923–4; Field 2001; Ellis & Bjorklund 2005; Stegbauer 2002; De Waal

2005, etc.). The questions that are typically discussed include the following: Is reciprocity also found among animals? What are the origins of reciprocity in human society? Is there an essential link between reciprocity and self-interest, on the one hand, or reciprocity and morals, on the other? What is the relationship between the pure gift or love and reciprocity? Which role does reciprocity have in the interplay between parties that have similar, opposed or mixed interests? Even a brief discussion to the answers given to these questions would take me too far afield. What I will briefly summarise, however, are distinctions found between different mechanisms, forms, or concepts of reciprocity distinguished in the non-linguistic literature. One such typology can be found in biology, more specifically in studies of primate behaviour. Frans de Waal (2005) makes a distinction between three reciprocity mechanisms which are differentiated on the basis of the relations and attitudes that they involve:

i.   **symmetry-based reciprocity**
     This is probably the most common mechanism of reciprocity in nature, typical of humans and chimpanzees in close relationships. It is based on mutual affection between two parties, which prompts similar behaviour in both directions without the need to keep track of daily give-and-take, so long as the overall relationship remains satisfactory.

ii. **attitudinal reciprocity**
     In this case parties mirror one another's attitudes, exchanging favours on the spot. Instant attitudinal reciprocity occurs among monkeys, and people often rely on it with strangers.

iii. **calculated reciprocity**
     Individuals keep track of the benefits they exchange with particular partners, which helps them to decide to whom to return favours. This mechanism is typical of chimpanzees and common among people in distant and professional relationships.

The forms of reciprocity distinguished in anthropology and sociology are based on and incorporate the work done by Marcel Mauss on the gift as a total social phenomenon in archaic societies (cf. Mauss 1923–4). According to Mauss, an exchange in these societies takes the form of so-called "total social services" which do not merely involve legal and economic aspects, but also moral, spiritual, religious and aesthetic ones at the same time. The forms of reciprocity distinguished for modern societies by Stegbauer (2002) include the following ones:

a.   **direct reciprocity**
     This form of reciprocity is based on direct relationships, analysable in terms of dyadic ones no matter how many persons are involved. The essential point

is that the one who gives something to some person also receives something from the very same person. It is found in all types of exchanging goods and presents, in greeting rituals, in buying and selling and even in all forms of corruption, where something (e.g. contracts) is given that does not really belong to the giver (politician, bureaucrat) in exchange for material benefits.

b. **generalised reciprocity**
    The essential point with this form is that any exchange goes beyond a direct transaction between two people. What we find is either a generalisation over time or a generalisation over groups to which participants belong. Any system of taxation, of insurance and any pension scheme belong to this type. It is here that the notions of 'pooling' and 'solidarity' find their place.

c. **reciprocity of roles**
    As members of a family or of a society in general we have specific roles, and exchanges are often determined by our position in complementary role constellations. Roles may be either symmetric (friend – friend; colleague – colleague) or asymmetric (doctor – patient; parent – child; boss – employer). This type thus captures our interdependence in terms of social roles. Note, however, that pairs like 'doctor – patient' would not be regarded as expressing symmetric relations in linguistics, but as converse terms (A is doctor of B = B is patient of A). Only instances of auto-converseness like 'friend, mate, colleague, collaborator, relative, etc.' express genuine symmetry ('reciprocity').[1] Outside the linguistic literature the term *reciprocity* regularly includes such non-symmetric uses, though. Note also that in many languages with dyad constructions reciprocal markers are extended to such asymmetric roles.[2]

d. **reciprocity of perspectives**
    This form or aspect of reciprocity is closely related to the previous type. It is of primary importance in the genesis of cooperative communities and subsumes such phenomena as putting oneself into somebody's place ("Try to see it my way!"), mind reading, mutual knowledge, etc. This type is ultimately based on a self-reflexive perspective: How does the other perceive me, what kind of actions does s/he expect of me, etc. (Stegbauer 2002: 121–2).

---

1. Even though this is not current and established usage, I would like to reserve the term 'reciprocal' for matters of form, the term 'reciprocity' for concepts and the term 'symmetric' for the semantic relations expressed by predicates (cf. König & Kokutani 2006).

2. Cf. Evans, Nicholas. 2005. Dyad constructions. *Encyclopaedia of Language and Linguistics* (2nd edition), Keith Brown (ed.). Oxford: Elsevier.

It is a striking aspect of these differentiations that reciprocity is fundamentally seen as a positive aspect of interaction and cooperation – except for a brief digression on corruption in Stegbauer (2002). Thus, there are no antagonistic forms of reciprocity, where mutuality is not based on cooperative interaction, in the conceptual typologies summarised above.

2.   Concepts of reciprocity in linguistics

The distinctions drawn in the linguistics literature are typically based on a semasiological approach, i.e. on the variety of meanings exhibited by sentences with *each other* in English. They are neutral with regard to any evaluative dimension, thus including all antagonistic forms of symmetric interaction and differ also in other ways from the distinctions discussed above (cf. Langendoen 1978; Lichtenberk 1985; Dalrymple et al. 1998). The meanings differentiated in the studies quoted and others based on them typically include the following:

a. 'People in this house know each other.' (strong reciprocity)
b. 'The students stared at each other.' (weak reciprocity)
c. 'People at the party were married to each other.' (pairwise reciprocity)
d. 'The actors followed each other onto the stage.' (intermediate, chained reciprocity)
e. 'The dogs bit each other.' (melee)
f. 'They stacked tables on top of each other to get to the window.' (intermediate alternative reciprocity)

The most important criterion underlying these differentiations is the question: How many pairings of members of the set of reciprocants (the set denoted by the subjects in our examples) stand in the relationship expressed by the predicate? The meanings listed above can be explicated in terms of truth conditions, involving different quantifiers, or simply by drawings. Highly controversial issues in these discussions concern the number of meanings to be assumed for each reciprocal marker: Do these markers have a univocal vague meaning that is strengthened or weakened depending on the context or are there several distinct meanings the strongest of which is selected depending on the set of reciprocants, the predicate and the context (cf. Dalrymple et al. 1998; Winter 2001)?

The video clips used in the articles are based on the distinctions drawn in linguistic analyses, but the responses given by some informants are clearly influenced by culture-specific conceptualisations of the interaction portrayed on the clip. A clear example of this is the verbalisation of an asymmetric transfer of presents or an asymmetric action of delousing in terms of a sentence with a reciprocal marker, as pointed out in several of the preceding contributions. These effects show that it is somewhat problematic to simply base one's investigations on logical relations without regard to cultural notions of reciprocity. There is certainly something to be gained from paying more attention to the types of reciprocity distinguished in biology, anthropology and sociology.

The articles assembled in this volume make an important contribution both to the description of the relevant languages and to a general typology of reciprocity. While partly confirming the findings of earlier cross-linguistic studies (König & Kokutani 2006; Nedjalkov 2007; Haspelmath 2007; Evans 2008), they also raise interesting new problems for any attempt to formulate patterns and limits of variation in the relevant domain. I will discuss the preceding contributions – against the background of the cross-linguistic studies mentioned – from the perspective of two questions: (a) What kind of contribution do they make to a typology of reciprocity? and (b) What kind of problems do they raise for any attempt at integrating their findings into a comprehensive typology?

3.   Contribution to a typology of reciprocity

Since they are new and original descriptive contributions to the study of reciprocal constructions, the preceding articles greatly enhance our knowledge in this domain. Many of the assumptions made in earlier cross-linguistic work and some of the tentative universals formulated in these studies are confirmed[3] and are now supported by additional data and languages. Here is a brief summary of such corroborative evidence:

–   All languages have basic, non-derived symmetric predicates[4] such as *meet, marry, resemble, argue with* (verbs), *companion, mate, friend* (nouns), *similar, parallel, equal, different* (adjectives), *with, next to* (prepositions) and some may also derive further symmetric predicates by derivational processes. These

---

3.   A more modest assessment would simply state that these tentative universals have not been falsified by the new data.

4.   It is a well-known fact that the relevant verbs do not meet the criteria formulated for symmetric predicates in formal languages in the strict sense of the term (aRb ↔ bRa). For verbs we typically find a slight difference of perspective, initiative, control, status, etc. between converse pairs of sentences with the basic (non-reciprocal) use of these verbs. A sentence like *John married Kate* may differ slightly in terms of these notions from *Kate married John*. It is for such reasons that M. Haspelmath (2007) has proposed a new terminology, substituting *inter alia* the term *allelic* ('mutual') for *symmetric*. It will certainly take a while before such terminological innovations are generally accepted. I will therefore stick to the older terminology.

symmetric predicates manifest specific patterns of interaction with the grammar of reciprocity across languages: They allow us to describe symmetric situations or joint actions without grammatical means, or, receive parsimonious coding in reciprocal constructions (e.g. *They met. They are friends. They live together.*) and play a major role in the historical development (grammaticalisation) of reciprocal markers.

– Reciprocal markers generally have a wide range of meanings and most of the meanings or use types distinguished for *each other* in English can also be found for the relevant markers in other languages. There may, however, be special expressions for chaining situations (cf. Evans & Osada; Zeshan & Panda; Epps; Gaby; Hurst & Nordlinger, all this volume). If reciprocal markers manifest a more general polysemy the other meanings are typically 'sociative' ('together'), 'interactive' or 'reflexive'.

– Verbal reciprocals are typically, though not exclusively, intransitive, i.e. the verbal markers reduce the valency of the basic transitive or ditransitive verb. Such a valency reduction happens only very rarely in connection with the relevant reflexive markers or reflexive uses of a polysemous marker.

– Reciprocal constructions can be found in almost any language, but there are also exceptions, like Kilivila. Discontinuous reciprocals of the type (*Charles quarrelled with Diana.*) are also a wide-spread phenomenon (cf. Enfield; Epps; Zavala, all this volume).

These are just some of the generalisations that are clearly supported by the preceding articles. Many other points could be added. In addition to giving further support to reasonably well established generalisations the preceding articles also call some earlier hypotheses and assumptions into question and raise a number of basic issues that go beyond the specific goal of formulating the patterns and limits of variation in the domain under discussion. These are probably the most important results of the preceding articles.

4.   Basic issues

a.   What should be counted as (dedicated) reciprocal construction?

Like all concepts reciprocity can be encoded in many different ways. Should all of these expressions be regarded as reciprocal constructions? Here are a few problematic cases discussed in the articles (cf. Hurst & Nordlinger, this volume):

(1)   'They met at the station.'
(2)   'They have kissed.'

(3) 'They are having an argument.'
(4) 'Each of the men dislikes the others.'
(5) 'They were leaning back-to-back.'

The first two examples are instances of intransitive uses of symmetric predicates (*meet*) and of predicates typically expressing a joint action (*kiss*). There is, however, a slight difference between these two sentences: Sentence (1) can only be used for a fully symmetric situation, whereas (2) also has a distributive use ('Each person has kissed someone during a game show and therefore does not qualify for a certain price.'). Should we therefore exclude (2), since it is merely an implicit reciprocal, and keep (1) on our list? The next example can probably be treated analogously to (1) and (2), since the relevant nouns (*argument, fight, quarrel, altercation, meeting*, etc.) are nominalisations of symmetric predicates. The remaining two cases are more interesting still. Sentences like (4) are fully compositional expressions of strong reciprocity. They lack the vague (or polysemous) character of real reciprocal constructions and are used in cases where a language does not license a reciprocal marker in a certain syntactic context, as is shown by the following German translation of an English sentence, where the reciprocal anaphor occurs in the position of a possessor:

(6) 'They admire each other's houses.'
(7) 'Sie bewundern das Haus des jeweils anderen.'

Note, however, that sentences of type (4) do not necessarily have a reciprocal interpretation: The set denoted by *the men* may not include the complementary set identified in the object (cf. Maslova 2007). Even though this is an unlikely interpretation, this fact would put (a) into the same group of implicit reciprocals as (2). In other words, there is more than one reason for excluding structures of type (4) from the list of dedicated reciprocal constructions. These structures can be analysed as an intermediary step in the direction of the development of reciprocal markers like *each other* in English.

Sentence (5) is an interesting example of a half grammatical half lexical strategy of encoding reciprocity, or more specifically symmetry in space. Such examples are rarely discussed in the literature, even though they are found in a wide variety of languages.[5] It is fully compositional in the example given, but may have a number of non-literal semantic extensions:

(8) In this article we put these frameworks head-to-head, comparing each on its merits.

---

5. Cf. König & Moyse-Faurie (2009) for a first cross-linguistic discussion.

A related construction is mentioned in the article on Jahai. Here it is a symmetric predicate (Malay *sama* 'same' >) *samɛʔ* that combines with a body part noun. This construction is, moreover, quite similar to nominal reciprocals of the type *ze et ze* in Hebrew and even to *l'un à l'autre* in French.

b.   How many types?

A different, though related, question concerns the number of construction types to be distinguished. The available cross-linguistic studies differ somewhat at this point. Without going into detail I would just like to mention that there are good reasons for keeping the distinctions to a relevant minimum (cf. König & Kokutani 2006), or of organising a detailed typology into a hierarchical taxonomy (cf. Evans 2008). Tentative universals can be formulated more easily in terms of a few basic types. In his concluding discussion of the major results of the Nedjalkov (2007) volumes Haspelmath (2007) formulates 26 tentative Greenberg-style universals by drawing primarily on the distinction between verb-marked (predicational) and anaphoric (argumental) reciprocal constructions. Such parsimonious use of basic distinctions makes it also easier to assign the constructions of new data and languages to these basic types. While the bi-partite demonstrative of Khoekhoe is clearly an instance of the quantificational strategy instantiated by *each other* in English or *ze et ze* in Hebrew, provided we understand quantificational in the sense of generalised quantifiers, the *mapamapa* strategy in Savosavo cannot easily be assigned to this type. On the other hand, it can certainly be analysed as an argumental strategy. Similar problems arise with regard to the constructions with *woni .. woni* in Yélî Dnye or with *mõle verb mõle* in Mah Meri, both of which look like instances of the quantificational strategy, but cannot really be assigned to that subtype with absolute certainty.

While it is easy to assign reciprocal markers to either the predicational or the argumental type, a general, more fine-grained inventory of subtypes (clitic, pronominal, nominal, quantificational, etc.) is much more difficult to establish across languages and is probably less useful for any kind of cross-linguistic generalisation.

Even the distinction between verb-marked and anaphoric types is not always easy to draw, as is also noted in Haspelmath (2007). In the present collection of articles the data particularly interesting in this respect are structures with the prefix *ora-* in Rokotas, which may be prefixed to verbs, pronouns and body part nouns. Another interesting case is the suffix *-gu* in Khoekhoe which has been traditionally analysed as a valence-changing suffix, but functions like a pronoun according to Rapold (this volume).

c.   Counterevidence?

Finally, I will examine the universals tentatively formulated by Haspelmath (2007) in the light of the data and analyses presented in this volume.

Universal 3 excludes the existence of reciprocal constructions with two reciprocant-denoting arguments that are coded like the Agent and the Patient of a transitive clause. The *mōle verb mole* construction, which is used for many clips in Mah Mari looks like a counterexample. On the other hand, the relevant examples are always translated as 'They verbed each other' and since the participants are given on the video, their identification by a noun phrase or pronoun is probably redundant.

Universal 4 says that only verb-marked reciprocals allow a discontinuous construction. Discontinuous reciprocals with *kan3* in Lao look like a problem for this claim, since *kan3* is a free form and may also be used to reciprocalise the possessor position. On the other hand, it does not seem to have any nominal or anaphoric properties and seems to function more like an adverbial with a basic sociative meaning.

Universal 9 excludes the existence of different verbal reciprocal markers for different diathesis types, i.e. for structures where different syntactic positions are reciprocalised (i.e. left empty or replaced by an anaphor). The data from Yélî Dnye might be a problem for this generalisation, however, even though reciprocity is primarily encoded by nominal (anaphoric) markers in this language. In this language the "dedicated reciprocal pronoun" *numo* is used for basic object positions, whereas *noko* is used for basic oblique positions or possessive phrases. Levinson points out that *noko* is the dative/allative form of *numo*, but constructions with *numo* and *noko* differ in the case marking of their subjects and in their verbal inflection.

5.   Conclusion

Overall, the articles assembled in this volume make an extremely valuable contribution to the typology of reciprocal constructions. The information provided is, of course, less detailed and fine-grained than that given in the articles of the Nedjalkov (2007) volumes, which were written by native speakers or at least leading specialists for the languages in question. The regions and languages treated in the preceding articles are not easily accessible and their study required a major investment in time, energy and field methods before the focus of these investigations could even be brought up. What makes the data presented above particularly valuable is that they are all new and that they are based on exactly the same elicitation technique, i.e. the verbalisation of a set of videoclips prepared on the basis of recent insights concerning the formal and semantic distinction typically found in the domain of reciprocity. These data do not only enrich our empirical basis for mapping out the space and limits of variation in the encoding of reciprocity, they also make valuable contributions to the theoretical discussion. Among these general implications I specifically emphasised their importance for the questions of identifying reciprocal constructions, of distinguishing different types and of formulating implicational universals. With the Nedjalkov (2007) volumes, the present volume and the projects under way in Melbourne, Berlin and Utrecht reciprocity can now be considered to be one of the best studied domains of linguistic structure.

Acknowledgements

I would like to thank Nick Evans and Anneliese Kuhle for reading and criticising an earlier version of this paper.

References

Dalrymple, Mary, Kanazawa, Makato, Kim, Yookyung, Mchombo, Sam & Peters, Stanley. 1998. Reciprocal expressions and the concept of reciprocity. *Linguistics and Philosophy* 21: 159–210.

Ellis, Bruce J. & Bjorklund, David F. 2005. *Origins of the Social Mind: Evolutionary Psychology and Child Development*. New York NY: Guilford Press.

Evans, Nicholas. 2008. Reciprocal constructions: Toward a structural typology. In *Reciprocals and Reflexives: Cross-linguistic and Theoretical Explorations*, Ekkehard König & Volker Gast (eds), 33–103. Berlin: Mouton de Gruyter.

Field, Alexander J. 2001. *Altruistically Inclined? The Behavioural Sciences, Evolutionary Theory, and the Origins of Reciprocity*. Ann Arbor MI: University of Michigan Press.

Haspelmath, Martin. 2007. Further remarks on reciprocal constructions. In *Reciprocal Constructions*, Vol. 4, Vladimir P. Nedjalkov (ed.), 2087–2115. Amsterdam: John Benjamins.

König, Ekkehard & Kokutani, Shigehiro. 2006. Towards a typology of reciprocal constructions: Focus on German and Japanese. *Linguistics* 44(2): 271–302.

König, Ekkehard & Moyse-Faurie, Claire. 2009. Spatial reciprocity: Between grammar and lexis. In *Form and Function in Language Research: Papers in honour of Christian Lehmann*, Johannes Helmbrecht, Yoko Nishina, Yong-Min Shin, Stavros Skopeteas & Elisabeth Verhoeven (eds), 57–69. Berlin: Mouton de Gruyter.

König, Ekkehard & Gast, Volker (eds.). 2008. *Reciprocals and Reflexives: Cross-linguistic Explorations*. Berlin: Mouton de Gruyter.

Langendoen, Terence. 1978. The logic of reciprocity. *Linguistic Inquiry* 9: 177–197.

Lichtenberk, Frantisek. 1985. Multiple use of reciprocal situations. *Australian Journal of Linguistics* 5: 19–41.

Maslova, Elena. 2007. Reflexive encoding of reciprocity: Cross-linguistic and language-internal variation. In *Reciprocals and Reflexives: Cross-linguistic and Theoretical Explorations*, Ekkerhard König & Volker Gast (eds.), 225–257. Berlin: Mouton de Gruyter.

Mauss, Marcel. 1923/1924. Essai sur le don. Forme et raison de l'échange dans les sociétés archaïques. *L'Année Sociologique, seconde série, 1923–1924.*

Nedjalkov, Vladimir P. (ed.). 2007. *Reciprocal Constructions,* 5 Vols. [Typological Studies in Language 71]. Amsterdam: John Benjamins.

Stegbauer, Christian. 2002. *Reziprozität. Einführung in soziale Formen der Gegenseitigkeit.* Wiesbaden: Westdeutscher Verlag.

de Waal, Frans. 2005. How animals do business. *Scientific American* 292(4): 72–79.

Winter, Yoad. 2001. Plural prediction and the strongest meaning hypothesis. *Journal of Semantics* 18: 333–365.

Addresses

Nicholas Evans
Department of Linguistics,
College of Asia and the Pacific
Australian National University
CANBERRA ACT 0200
Australia
nicholas.evans@anu.edu.au

Asifa Majid
Max Planck Institute
for Psycholinguistics
PB 310
NL-6500 AH Nijmegen
The Netherlands
asifa.majid@mpi.nl

Christian J. Rapold
Leiden University Centre for Linguistics
P.O. Box 9515
NL-2300 RA Leiden
Netherlands
c.j.rapold@hum.leidenuniv.nl

Peter Hurst
School of Languages and Linguistics
5th floor, Babel Building
The University of Melbourne
Parkville, VIC 3010
Australia
peter@peterhurst.com
racheln@unimelb.edu.au

Ulrike Zeshan
Director, International Institute
for Sign Languages and Deaf Studies

Faculty of Arts, Humanities
and Social Sciences
Livesey House, LH212
University of Central Lancashire
Preston PR1 2HE, UK
uzeshan@uclan.ac.uk
spanda@uclan.ac.uk

Toshiki Osada
Research Institute for Humanity
and Nature
Kyoto, Japan
osada@chikyu.ac.jp

N. J. Enfield
Max Planck Institute for Psycholinguistics
PB 310
6500 AH Nijmegen
The Netherlands
Nick.Enfield@mpi.nl

Nicole Kruspe
School of Languages and Linguistics
The University of Melbourne.
Parkville, Vic, 3010
Australia
nicolekruspe@gmail.com

Niclas Burenhult
Max Planck Institute for Psycholinguistics
PB 310
NL-6500 AH Nijmegen, The Netherlands
Phone: +31 (0) 24 3521 172
Fax: +31 (0) 24 3521 213
Niclas.Burenhult@mpi.nl

Stephen C. Levinson
Max Planck Institute for Psycholinguistics
PB 310
NL-6500 AH Nijmegen
The Netherlands
Stephen.Levinson@mpi.nl

Stuart Robinson
Max Planck Institute for Psycholinguistics
Postbus 310
6500 AH Nijmegen
The Netherlands
stuart.robinson@mpi.nl

Claudia Wegener
Max Planck Research Group on
Comparative Population Linguistics
Max Planck Institute for Evolutionary
Anthropology
Deutscher Platz 6
04103 Leipzig
Germany
claudia_wegener@eva.mpg.de

Gunter Senft
Max Planck Institute for Psycholinguistics
PB 310
NL-6500 AH Nijmegen
The Netherlands
gunter.senft@mpi.nl

Ruth Singer
The University of Melbourne
School of Languages and Linguistics
Babel Building
The University of Melbourne
Parkville
Victoria
Australia
rsinger@unimelb.edu.au

Connie Dickinson
Adjunct Research Faculty
University of Oregon/FLACSO
Chimborazo 700 y Pampite
Cumbaya, Ecuador EC170157
csd@uoregon.edu
conniedickinson7@yahoo.com

Alice Gaby
Department of Linguistics
1203 Dwinelle Hall
University of California at Berkeley
Berkeley, CA 94720-2650
USA
agaby@berkeley.edu

Roberto Zavala Maldonado
CIESAS-Sureste
Carretera a Chamula Km. 3.5,
Barrio la Quinta San Martin
San Cristóbal de las Casas, Chiapas
México C.P 29247
rzavmal1@hotmail.com

Patience Epps
Department of Linguistics
University of Texas at Austin
1 University Station B5100
Austin, TX 78712-0198
USA
pepps@mail.utexas.edu

Ekkehard König
Freie Universität Berlin
Fachbereich Philosophie
und Geisteswissenschaften
WE 6
Goßlerstr. 2-4
14195 Berlin
phone: +49-30-83872356
koenig@zedat.fu-berlin.de

Index

A

Acceptability 12, 33, 35, 42, 54, 75–76, 78, 81–87, 115, 124, 153, 167, 170, 174, 220, 238, 246, 322–324

Adjacent 69, 72, 159, 170, 172, 174, 206, 258–259, 263, 272–273, 278, 290, 306

Adverbs 15–16, 51, 58, 59, 70, 80, 81, 138, 139, 153, 167, 200, 204, 210, 219, 235, 236, 265–266, 285, 288, 311, 337

Affiliation 34

Afrikaans 68

Agreement 14, 37–41, 50–51, 66–67, 85, 91, 93–96, 99–106, 111–112, 116, 131, 141, 178–180, 182–183, 187, 197–199, 201–202, 204, 208, 213–216, 218, 221, 223, 234–235, 237, 239–240, 243, 245, 247, 249

Agreement verb 91, 94, 96, 99–106, 111

A'jië 230

Amele 4, 16, 20, 28, 240

Anêm 230

Applicative 63–64, 115, 116, 119, 120, 122, 124, 269–272, 275, 276, 316, 320, 322, 326–327

Arawak 315

Archi 4, 13

Argument structure 33, 88, 122, 124, 130, 155, 161, 179, 209, 239–240, 254, 259, 282

Argumental strategy 336

Aslian 3, 34, 149–151, 161, 163, 165–167, 169, 174

Aspect VII, 35, 61, 74, 86–87, 92, 93, 94, 99, 125, 127, 166, 172, 177–183, 187, 192–193, 197, 209, 215, 223, 235, 241, 251, 266, 268, 279, 283, 286, 307, 310, 311, 315, 327, 330, 331–332

Asymmetrical 32, 40, 42–43, 45, 47, 53, 56–57, 66, 69, 70–72, 82–83, 87, 103, 129–130, 132, 135, 139, 140–141, 144, 154, 157, 171, 190–192, 205, 207, 209, 213, 221–223, 246–247, 252–253, 259, 262, 273, 278, 288, 290, 306, 309, 325–326, 331–332

Athabaskan 34

Atypicality 122, 251, 259, 260, 261, 262, 263

Australia 3, 27, 34, 75, 233, 249, 251

Australian VII, 1, 4, 9, 26, 29, 34, 75, 81, 88–89, 115, 126, 161–162, 241, 243, 248–249, 264, 280, 312–313, 339

Austroasiatic 3, 34, 115–116, 127, 149, 162, 176

Autobenefactive 6

Auxiliary 15, 16, 47, 58, 91, 94, 96, 99, 102–109, 111, 112, 266, 278, 280–284, 311

Awa Pit 279, 312

B

Back-to-back construction 21, 24, 58, 76, 80, 82, 87, 166–167, 335

Bahasa Melayu 157

Bahnar 116, 126

Balinese 4, 9, 26

Bantu 68, 120, 126

Barbacoan 34, 277, 279

Bare conjunct strategy 58, 62, 66–67, 71–72, 79, 149, 152, 153, 154, 156, 158, 159, 161, 257

Bare reciprocal construction 41, 58, 59, 76, 79, 82, 228, 233, 243–246, 257, 258

Barupu VII, 4, 15, 26, 34, 48, 51, 58

Basque 240

Be.next.to 32, 40

Beaver VII, 4, 16, 23–24, 34, 39, 48, 59

Benefactive 116, 119–120, 122, 172, 210, 275, 292

Biblical Hebrew 322, 328

Biclausal reciprocal construction 233, 234, 236, 237, 238, 247

Bininj Gun-wok 10, 26, 119–120, 126, 233

Binomial (quantifiers) 10, 15, 16, 18

Bipartite quantifier NPs 17, 18, 58, 62, 66, 71, 72, 76

Bivalent 253, 257, 261, 265, 279, 296

Body part adjunct 58, 163, 166, 167, 173, 174, 175

Boumaa Fijian 326–327

Bound pronoun 16, 58, 62, 64, 66–68, 72

Brazil 34, 315, 327

British national corpus 12

British Sign Language (BSL) 95, 113

Budibud 226

Bulgarian 12

Bump 32, 40, 56, 57, 83, 86–87, 135, 158, 168, 172, 173, 183, 243, 247, 254

C

Cambodian 116

Canada 34

Categorial ambiguity 168–169

Causative 7, 11, 54, 64, 73, 115, 119–120, 124–125, 198–200, 210, 217–218, 270, 275, 276, 297–298, 316, 320

Causative mutual escalation 11

Central Khoisan 34, 61–63

Ceq Wong 154, 158–159, 161–162

Chaining 5, 8, 13, 16, 19, 23, 32, 33, 40, 42–43, 45, 47, 51, 53, 56, 57, 69, 72, 77, 82, 83, 85, 86–87, 103, 115, 117, 121, 123–125, 137, 157, 159, 160, 170, 172, 185, 190, 191, 195, 207, 215, 259, 261, 272, 273, 278, 279, 290, 306, 315, 320, 322, 324, 332, 334
Chase 8, 11, 12, 21, 23, 32, 40, 56, 57, 69, 70, 71, 72, 76, 83, 103, 121, 153–154, 158, 168, 172, 180, 181, 190, 191, 192, 200–201, 214, 220, 221, 222, 226, 227, 234, 246, 255, 274, 289, 290, 305
Chicheŵa 4, 18, 26, 55, 63, 73, 88, 126, 127
Chinese 4, 150
Classifier (construction) 40, 103–107, 111–112, 151, 175, 203, 210, 231, 280, 311
Coding (mechanism/site) 1, 15, 17–18, 20, 23, 25–26, 31, 35–36, 40, 49–51, 53, 58, 69–72, 124, 126, 151, 159, 163–164, 174, 179, 182, 192–193, 234, 238, 246, 249, 251–252, 254, 259–263, 268, 272, 274, 278–279, 285, 287, 290, 294, 296, 302, 305, 307, 309–310, 334
Collaborative (marker) 129, 132, 146
Collective 29, 45, 77, 81, 83, 135, 137, 139, 153, 155, 161, 243–244, 277, 280–282, 289–290, 294, 305–307, 311, 326
Complementary action 140, 189
Complex predicate 80, 278, 279, 280, 285, 290, 297–298, 306, 309, 312
Compositionality 14, 18, 20, 25, 220, 255, 335
Concepts of reciprocity 329–330, 332
Configuration 8, 9, 11, 18, 21, 31–33, 42–43, 52, 54, 107, 129–130, 197, 253, 258, 264, 288, 309
Confucius 1
Congruent 263, 279, 285–287, 297, 299–302, 304, 311

Conjoined subject strategy 10, 122, 134, 265, 267–268, 270–272, 274
Contrastive pronoun 234–238, 245, 248
Converse 34, 65, 79, 83, 87, 115, 117, 120, 122, 130, 152–153, 193, 231–232, 252, 254, 258, 261–262, 264, 291, 306, 315, 321, 325–327, 331, 333
Cooperation 331–332
Core reciprocal (construction) 50, 191, 252, 253, 255–256, 259, 293
Country 34, 95, 140
Coverb 234, 236–237, 242–243, 280–284, 288–291, 295–299, 303, 305, 309–310, 313
Cross-linguistic 1–2, 8, 10–11, 13, 17, 19–24, 26, 28–30, 50, 52–55, 73, 80, 88, 96, 111–112, 130, 147, 162, 209, 219, 249, 263–265, 272, 274–276, 310, 312, 322, 326–329, 333, 335–336, 338–339
Cross-serial dependencies 177, 188

D

Damara 61, 73–74
Dâw 315–316, 328
Dedicated reciprocal construction 13–14, 19–21, 23, 36, 40, 41, 49–50, 91, 99, 103, 105, 117, 124, 145, 152, 154, 177, 179–180, 192, 209, 220, 225, 251, 334–335, 337
Delouse VII, 11, 22, 32, 43, 56, 57, 82–83, 123, 144–145, 154, 166, 169, 171–173, 181, 207, 220–221, 227, 234, 246, 332
Derivation, derivarational affix(ation), suffix 15, 61–63, 99–102, 108, 110, 115, 117, 150, 163–166, 168, 170–173, 178, 198–199, 201, 242, 262, 200, 210, 333
Desano 323
Diachronic 2, 16, 63, 107, 116, 147, 209, 215, 285, 294, 300, 326, 328

Dialect 26, 61, 95, 98, 109, 115, 126, 150, 162, 167, 169, 173, 195, 211, 226, 233, 300–302
Dialectal variation 169
Diathesis changes 120
Direct bilateral reciprocity 5
Direct pattern 266
Discontinuous construction/ reciprocals 334, 337
Distributive construction 16, 36, 47, 58, 149, 152, 154–155, 157–161
Ditransitive verb 64, 118, 201, 235, 237, 269, 318–319, 334
Double distributive construction 16, 47, 58, 149, 152, 154–155, 157–161
Double role marking 252, 255–256, 259, 262
Dravidian 95, 116, 150
Dual 9, 25, 32, 58, 64–66, 73, 116, 151, 171–173, 175, 178, 180–187, 189–190, 193, 197, 210, 214, 223, 228, 239, 246–247, 252, 263

E

Each-the-other construction 76–78, 84
East Tukanoan 316, 323
Ecuador 34, 277
Eivo 196, 209
English 2–3, 4, 5–18, 21, 23–24, 26–28, 34, 36, 38, 39, 40, 45, 48, 49–51, 54–55, 58, 68, 73–81, 87–89, 95, 97, 111, 119, 122–123, 126–127, 132, 141, 152, 167, 177, 180, 183, 185, 193, 220, 233, 236, 255–258, 260–261, 264, 285, 294, 320, 332, 334–336
Entailed 5, 67–68, 122, 130, 143, 189, 219–220, 239, 243, 252, 254–255, 257–258, 267, 273, 317, 324
Epistemic 193, 322, 326
Ergativity 178–181, 183–184, 186–187, 189, 193, 210, 251, 253, 261, 263, 265–266, 268, 271–272, 275, 316
Ethics 329

Event-type 9, 11, 22, 31–33, 42, 56, 57, 103, 107, 111, 140, 152, 163, 173, 251, 253, 258–259, 261–263

Evidential 178, 285, 287, 301, 311–312, 327

Evolutionary biologists 2

Exchange 2, 13, 42–43, 45, 49, 55, 67, 104, 121, 136, 152, 155, 159, 189, 191, 218, 226, 229–230, 235, 241, 246–247, 291, 303, 307–308, 321, 330–331

Expressed periphrastically 225–226, 228–230

Extensional semantics 19, 205

F

Follow 5–6, 8, 19, 22–23, 32, 36, 40, 43, 52, 56–57, 62–67, 69–70, 76–80, 83, 92, 96, 103–106, 125, 133–134, 136–137, 140, 143–144, 146, 155, 158, 161, 166, 169, 171–172, 175, 179–182, 186–188, 190–191, 207, 210, 215, 221–222, 225–226, 229–231, 234–236, 246, 253, 254–256, 261, 263, 265–270, 272, 274–275, 277–278, 280– 283, 289–290, 294–296, 298, 300–302, 304–305, 307, 311, 317, 327, 329–330, 332, 335

Frege's principle 14–15

French 4, 10, 13, 15, 17, 138, 232, 336

Frequency 12–13, 20, 48, 66, 71–72, 81, 191, 261

G

Gela 220

Generalised reciprocity 5, 331

Generic verb 157, 280–285, 295, 297–299, 301, 309, 313

Genesis 6, 26–27, 331

German 4, 14–15, 19, 27, 55, 111–112, 249, 335, 338

German Sign Language 111–112

Germanic 28, 34, 75

Ghari 220

Give 3, 5, 7, 11, 13, 20–21, 25, 30, 32, 36, 48, 52–53, 55–57, 62–63, 68–70, 85, 87, 92, 94, 99, 102,

104, 109–110, 118–121, 123–124, 130, 135–140, 142, 144–145, 147, 151, 154, 156, 160, 164–166, 169–173, 182, 187, 189, 191, 196, 201, 203, 205, 208–209, 214–215, 217, 219, 230, 235–237, 239–241, 245, 256, 263, 269, 275, 278, 280, 282, 286, 291, 294, 299, 303, 307–310, 313, 319–323, 325, 329–332, 335, 337,

Grammars 13–14, 21, 26–28, 30, 54–55, 61, 74, 88, 95, 112–113, 126–127, 129, 147, 153, 155, 162, 176–179, 188, 193–194, 211, 213, 224, 249, 264, 275–276, 279, 312, 315–316, 327–328, 334, 338

Grammaticalisation 3, 6–7, 13–15, 18, 21, 23, 25–27, 35, 50, 56, 63, 76–77, 91–97, 99, 102–103, 107–108, 111–112, 115–116, 119, 129–131, 134, 147, 149, 163, 190, 193, 196, 209, 214, 234, 237–238, 251, 257, 259, 265, 277, 278–280, 284–285, 292, 297, 299, 304, 305, 310, 312, 316, 319, 322–323, 326, 328, 334–335

Granularity 11–12

Grice 191–192, 261–262, 264

H

Haillom 68

Heavy strategy 10

Hebrew 4, 6–7, 26, 112, 322, 328, 336

Hindi 123–124

Hit VII, 5, 11–12, 32–33, 47, 56–57, 64, 66, 69, 79, 83, 85–86, 94, 110, 123, 129, 133–134, 144, 154–155, 158, 165, 168, 171–172, 179, 181–182, 191–192, 196, 203–206, 216, 219, 227, 238, 241–242, 244, 247, 254, 273, 278, 287, 293–294, 299, 303, 306–309, 319, 321, 324

Ho 115

Hottentot 61, 74

Hua 4, 16, 27

Hug 9, 11, 31–32, 56–57, 67, 79, 81, 83–84, 86–87, 123–124, 134, 143–144, 152–153, 159, 171–174,

188, 190–191, 206–207, 227–228, 239, 244, 247, 253, 257–258, 260–262, 267, 273, 291, 303–306, 308, 318, 322

Hup 4, 15, 17, 20–21, 23, 25, 34, 36, 38, 39, 40, 43–44, 47–49, 59, 315–318, 320–328

I

Iconic reciprocals 19–20

Iconicity 9, 26, 211, 260

Ideophones 16, 59, 307

Implicated 14, 28, 35, 63, 67, 104, 122, 192–193, 219, 225–229, 230, 256, 261, 263, 267, 338

Implicature 14, 122, 161, 192–193, 228–229, 231, 244, 257, 261–262, 267

Implied 50, 99, 109, 131, 152, 239, 258, 271, 298, 299

Incorporation 13, 62, 64, 132–133, 139, 155, 161, 177, 179–183, 185–186, 191–192, 199, 203–204, 234–237, 247, 265, 269, 276, 318, 330

Index finger pointing 93–94, 107–108

India 34, 91, 95, 97–98, 113, 115

Individual variation 163, 169–170

Indo-Aryan 116

Indo-European 34, 75

Indo-Pakistani Sign Language (IPSL) 16, 19, 23, 37, 39–40, 46–48, 51, 91–92, 94–99, 101–104, 106–108, 111, 113

Infixation 40, 116–118, 120–121, 124, 168

Information structure 134, 142–143

Inherent reciprocal 49, 58, 91, 99, 102, 107–110, 132, 220, 228, 241, 243, 245, 277, 323

Initiation 11, 125, 152, 255, 284, 296, 324, 333

Interaction 2, 13, 17, 20, 24–25, 32, 36, 43, 49, 52–53, 59, 73, 105, 222, 315, 317–327, 320–321, 324–326, 329, 332, 334

Interactional construction 36, 49, 319–320, 324–325

Interpersonal communication 136, 142

Intransitive verb 64, 68, 117–118, 121, 177, 181, 184, 197–199, 201–202, 208–209, 214–215, 218, 234, 241, 245, 266–268, 273–274, 316, 319, 326

Inverse pattern 154, 265–272, 274–276

Italian 4, 10, 15

Iterative 6, 22, 54, 65, 92, 111, 166, 172, 241

Iwaidja 3, 4, 16, 34, 38, 39, 48, 59, 233, 238, 241, 249

Iwaidjan 3, 34, 233, 241, 249

J

Jahai 3, 4, 20–21, 23–24, 34, 36–37, 38, 39, 45, 48, 49, 58, 115, 149–150, 161–169, 172, 174–176, 246, 336

Japanese 27, 55, 123, 249, 338

Javanese 150

Jharkand 115

Joint action 9, 20, 165, 220, 334–335

Joint activity 17, 23, 83, 122, 140, 213, 215, 219–223

Joint activity construction 213, 219–221

Juang 116

Jussive 322, 326

K

Kan3 25, 43, 48, 49, 58, 130–146, 337

Kayardild 4, 5–6, 15–16, 26, 34, 38, 39, 40, 48, 59

Kereaka 195, 209

Kharia 116, 127

Kherwari 116

Khmer 115–116, 126–127, 149–150, 154, 162–163, 176

Khoekhoe 4, 16, 34, 38, 39, 45, 48, 58, 61–64, 67, 72–74, 336

Kilivila 4, 13–14, 19–20, 24, 34, 36–37, 38, 39–41, 51, 225–231, 232, 334

Kin relationship 321

Kiriwina 226, 231

Konua 209

Korku 116

Kuuk Thaayorre 4, 15, 34, 38, 39, 40, 48, 59, 229, 251–253, 255, 257–258, 261–264

L

Lambda operators 15

Lao 4, 16–17, 20–21, 23–25, 34, 38, 39, 40, 43–44, 47–49, 51, 58, 129–132, 134, 138–139, 141, 143, 145–147, 264, 325, 337

Laos 34, 131, 147

Lean 11, 17, 24, 32, 40, 47, 52, 56, 57, 76, 80, 87, 158, 173, 244, 254, 288, 289, 290, 305, 335

Lenakel 230

Lexical reciprocals 70, 228, 252, 256, 259, 262, 317

Lexical semantics 30, 61, 209

Lexical strategy 62, 67, 70, 71, 72, 228, 234, 252, 254, 259, 317, 335

Lexicalisation 91, 99, 102, 107–108, 110, 122, 240, 243, 249, 255, 259, 317, 319

Light strategy 10, 58, 66

Locus 93–94, 100

Look 5, 8–10, 16, 32, 56, 57, 78, 82–83, 86–87, 100, 118, 136, 140, 155, 158, 166, 171–173, 178, 192, 198–199, 202–204, 206, 215, 222–223, 227–228, 243, 247, 273, 279, 290, 297, 306, 308, 324–325, 336–337

Lusi 230

M

Macro-Skou 34

Mah Meri 3, 4, 12, 15–16, 19–20, 32, 34, 37, 38, 39, 40, 46–48, 51, 58, 115, 149–163, 235, 336

Makú 315, 328

Malay 150, 152, 154, 157–158, 160, 162–163, 167–168, 176, 336

Malaysia 34, 149, 157, 161–163, 167, 175

Markedness 26, 259, 262–263

Marovo 220

Marrithiyel 4, 9, 27

Mawng 3, 4, 15–16, 24, 34, 38, 39, 40, 48, 59, 233–234, 236–241, 243, 245–249

Mayan 240, 288

Meet VII, 2, 9, 11–12, 22, 32, 56, 57, 67–68, 72, 74, 108–110, 122, 131–132, 135, 145, 152, 157, 228, 241, 243, 255, 267, 269, 271, 291, 303, 308, 333, 335

Melee 8, 32, 33, 40, 42–43, 47, 51, 56, 57, 69, 72, 78, 82, 85, 86–87, 103, 123, 125, 157, 160, 170, 172, 190–191, 195, 206, 259, 272–273, 306, 315, 324, 332

Menriq 165

Mexico 34, 265, 276

Middle voice 2, 27, 74, 126, 147, 162, 176, 249, 264, 279, 285, 297–298, 301–303, 305, 310, 312

Minor Mlabri 150, 162

Mirative 277–280, 285–287, 299–300, 302–305, 310–312

Mixe-Zoquean 34, 265, 276

Modality 3, 7, 23–24, 91–92, 111–112, 283, 285, 322, 326, 328

Modality effects 23

Mon-Khmer 115–116, 126–127, 149–150, 162–163, 176

Monovalent 256, 262

Morality 2, 5–7, 330

Movement pattern 91–92, 94, 99, 108

Multi-clausal statements 81

Multidimensional scaling 41–43, 47

Multifactorial comparison 25

Multivariate statistics 5, 31

Multi-verb constructions 135

Munda 3, 34, 115–116, 127, 149

Mundari 3, 4, 10, 15, 21, 23, 28, 34, 37, 38, 39, 40, 48, 49–50, 58, 115–118, 120–127, 163, 210, 220

Murua 226

Muyuw 226

Mwotlap 63

N

Nada 226

Nadahup 34, 315

Nadëb 315–316, 328

Na-Dene 34

Nama 61, 73–74

Namibia 34, 61, 68, 73

Natural reciprocal events 10–11

Natural reciprocal verb 220, 308
Naturally reciprocal predicate
    233, 234, 243, 244, 245, 246,
    247
Naturally reciprocal verb
    149, 152, 153, 154, 156, 158,
    159, 160, 161
Neo-behaviourist 52, 131
Nominal reciprocals 76, 79, 80,
    82, 87, 336
Non-congruent 279, 285–287,
    297, 300–302, 304, 311
Non-linguistic stimuli 3, 129
Non-reciprocal construction
    251, 252, 256, 259, 262, 306
Not expressed 153, 225–227,
    230, 270
Noun marking 200, 202, 203–
    204, 208
Noun phrase 15, 16, 50, 58,
    62, 63–64, 66, 72, 73, 76,
    118, 133–134, 142–144, 149,
    152–156, 158–159, 177, 178, 179,
    181, 183, 184–187, 196, 210,
    213–214, 215, 216, 217, 218, 231,
    234, 235, 236, 237, 240, 251,
    255, 256, 257, 261, 268–269,
    271, 281, 337
Number of participants 31–32,
    56–57, 61, 69, 71, 160, 258–
    259, 262
Number of patients 222

O
Objectivist 52, 131
Oblique pronoun 202, 234–235,
    248
Oceanic 34, 63, 127, 162, 176,
    210–211, 213, 224–226, 230,
    232, 326
Old testament 6
Olutec 4, 11, 19–20, 22, 34,
    38–40, 48, 59, 265–272,
    274–276
Onomasiology 22, 145, 329
Oriya 4, 10
Oshiwambo 68

P
Pair 8, 14–15, 32, 33, 56, 57, 69–
    70, 72, 78, 82, 84–85, 102–104,
    109–110, 157–158, 171, 181, 192,

202, 205–207, 221, 235, 253,
    256–257, 269, 288, 290, 293,
    306–307, 326, 331–333
Pairwise 8, 13, 32, 47, 50, 78,
    84, 86–87, 157, 159, 170–171,
    191–192, 206, 258–259, 261,
    272–273, 332
Paiwan 4, 9
Pakistan 34, 91, 95
Pama-Nyungan 3, 34, 251
Papua New Guinea 26, 34, 177,
    193, 195, 211, 226, 231
Papuan 16, 27, 34, 177, 193–196,
    210–211, 213, 224, 226
Parameters 11, 29, 31–33, 42, 53,
    56, 69, 129, 172–173, 175, 222,
    234, 247, 254, 258, 262, 274
Person hierarchy 238
Plural 6, 9–10, 17, 22, 25, 58,
    62–66, 73, 77, 88, 93, 116–117,
    121–122, 132–133, 137, 142, 146,
    153, 159, 171, 175, 178, 180–184,
    193, 197, 202, 210, 214, 223, 231,
    238–240, 242–244, 248, 252,
    263, 266–268, 270, 273–275,
    281, 293, 311, 317, 319, 321,
    326–328, 339
Polish 17
Polite 65, 146
Politeness 73
Portuguese 324
Positional 277, 279, 288–290,
    297, 305, 307, 309
Pragmatics 61, 65, 67, 129, 169,
    192, 252, 260, 262, 263, 265,
    271, 272, 274, 312, 317 , 318, 321
Predicate marking strategy 267
Predicational 336
Productivity 173–174, 264
Prominence 1, 131, 265, 274, 293
Pronominal index 93–94, 96,
    101, 107, 111
Pronominals, special forms for
    reciprocals 16–17, 28, 58,
    93–94, 96, 101, 107, 111, 151, 163,
    178, 195–196, 208, 210, 213, 238,
    265–266, 268, 275, 336
Pronoun marking 200, 202,
    208–209

Q
Quantificational strategy 336
Quantifiers 15–18, 58, 62, 66,
    71–72, 76, 179, 294, 332, 336
Quantifying elements 14

R
Radial 8, 32–33, 42–43, 56–57,
    82, 85
Reciprocal auxiliary 94, 101–
    103, 107–108
Reciprocal complex 233–236,
    238, 245, 247
Reciprocal mirror construction
    16, 130, 135, 144
Reciprocal nominal 213, 215–
    218, 220, 223, 240
Reciprocal obligations 2
Reciprocal pronouns 62, 63, 64,
    65, 70, 72, 76–77, 80, 88, 151,
    177, 179, 180, 181, 183, 185, 186,
    191, 192, 337
Reciprocal strategies 10, 24,
    42, 64, 67, 68–69, 70, 71, 72,
    79, 87, 99, 103, 104, 105, 234,
    257, 258, 265, 271, 272, 274,
    323, 326
Reduplication 6, 9, 15, 58, 59, 64,
    146, 163, 164, 169, 189, 202,
    204, 208, 210, 223, 231, 241,
    263, 323
Reference tracking 142–143
Reflexive 2, 6–7, 9–10, 12, 17,
    19–20, 22, 25, 26–28, 31, 53,
    54–55, 58–59, 63, 65, 73, 88,
    120, 129, 147, 151, 162–163, 179,
    186, 189, 192, 195, 198, 199,
    200, 201, 203, 204, 205, 206,
    207, 209, 210, 215, 224–225,
    234, 240, 241–242, 247, 249,
    252–254, 256, 259–260, 262–
    263, 264, 268, 274, 275, 278,
    295–296, 311, 312, 313, 315–318,
    320, 322–323, 325–328, 331,
    334, 338–339
Remo 116
Revolving switch-reference 16
Ring 8, 32–33, 57
Rotokas 4, 19–20, 24, 34, 38,
    39, 40, 48, 58, 195–201, 205,
    207–209, 211
Russian 4, 18

S

Sa 63

Samoan 230

Santali 116, 120, 126

Savosavo 4, 34, 38–40, 45, 48, 58, 213–217, 219–220, 222–224, 240, 336

Semai 154, 169, 176

Semantic typology 1, 8, 14, 17, 24–25, 28, 30, 54–56, 131, 145, 329

Semaq Beri 161

Semasiology 22, 145, 332

Semelai 150, 154, 158–159, 161–162, 176

Semnam 166

Sequential 9, 21, 32, 43, 47, 56, 57, 69–72, 81–82, 85–87, 102–103, 111, 115, 123–125, 144, 157–159, 171–172, 190–192, 219, 222, 246–247, 258, 262, 272–273, 278, 290, 306–307, 327

Serial verb construction 215, 218, 220, 265, 276, 287

Shake.hand 32, 56, 57

Shared intention 24

Sign Language 3, 4, 16, 19, 23, 24, 34, 37, 38, 39–40, 46–48, 51, 91–99, 106–107, 111–113

Sign space 91–93, 96, 99, 103–105, 111

Simultaneous 9, 16, 17, 23, 31–32, 36, 40, 56–57, 69–72, 78, 82–83, 86, 92, 99, 102–103, 111, 123–125, 138, 144, 155, 157–160, 164, 172, 188, 190–192, 210, 222, 223, 239, 246–247, 258, 260–262, 272, 273, 278, 290, 306–307

Simultaneous morphology 92, 99, 111

Situation type 9, 11, 21, 55, 69, 73, 78, 81–82, 83, 84–87, 88, 129, 130, 134, 147, 154, 156, 157, 158, 160, 162–164, 167, 170, 171, 173, 174, 176, 193, 206, 215, 224, 226, 230, 231, 249, 264

Social cognition 1, 12, 26

Social contract 2

Social reasoning 5

Sociative (meaning) 17, 53, 54, 65, 334, 337

Sociology 329–330, 333

Solomon Islands 34, 213, 220, 224

Solomon Islands Pijin 213, 220

Sora 116

Spanish 4, 10, 13, 15, 272, 291, 303, 305, 308, 311–312

Spatial inflection 96, 104

Strict reciprocal 134–135, 154, 160

Strict reciprocity 125, 129–130, 135, 143–144, 149, 152, 324

Strict sequential 123, 157

Strict simultaneous 123, 157

Strong (reciprocals) 1, 8, 18–19, 23, 29, 31–32, 33, 37, 40, 42–43, 47, 51, 56–57, 65, 69–70, 72, 78, 82–83, 85, 86–87, 92, 95, 103, 134, 157–158, 170–173, 175, 178, 191, 195, 205–206, 208–209, 247, 251, 257–259, 272, 278–279, 284, 290, 302, 306–307, 321, 326, 332, 335, 339

Structural diversity/variability 14, 15

Sub-events 157, 159, 160

Subject and object strategy 265, 267, 271, 274

Subject cum adjunct strategy 265, 267, 270–272, 274

Subject-object coreference constraint 119

Symmetric predicates 27, 126, 201, 228, 243, 246, 256, 264, 333–336

Symmetrical 8, 16, 24, 31–32, 36, 40, 56–57, 66–67, 82, 85, 130, 149, 152, 154, 156, 160, 171–172, 175, 190, 234, 246–247, 273, 277–279, 288, 290–292, 305, 307, 309

Symmetry 24, 31–32, 40, 56, 57, 67–68, 83, 144, 167, 171–172, 175, 257–258, 277–279, 289–290, 292, 294, 306, 309, 330–331, 335

T

Tahitian 225, 230, 232

Tai-Kadai 34

Talk 2, 11, 30, 32–33, 36, 56, 57, 67–68, 70, 72, 79, 83, 93, 100–101, 104, 121–122, 136, 153, 171–173, 184, 192, 208–209, 219–221, 227–228, 231, 235, 244, 255–258, 270, 273, 281, 283, 303, 313, 315

Tamil 10

Tangkic 3, 34

Tanglapui 274–275

Tariana 316

Temiar 166–167, 174, 176

Temporal organisation 31–32

Temuan 150

Tetun Dili 4, 11, 28

Thai 131–132, 147

Tibeto/Burman 285

Timing of subevents 71

Tinrin 4, 10, 28, 63

Tok Pisin 202, 205, 322, 328

Transitivity 108, 129, 147, 178, 180–181, 209, 257, 292, 298, 302, 305, 310

Translation, problems of 1, 5–7, 12, 24, 63, 97, 123, 141, 153, 200, 215, 252, 257, 294, 335

Trobriand islands 13, 225

Tsafiki 15–16, 20, 34, 39, 40, 51, 59, 277–281, 283–285, 287–288, 290, 294–298, 300–301, 305, 309–312

Tukano 316, 324, 328

Two-handed (signs) 99–100, 106, 108

U

Unidirectional configurations 11

Unidirectional construction 118, 152

V

Valency-rearranging 124

Verb class marker 280–284, 287, 294–295, 297, 301, 311

Verb complex 51, 135, 217, 234–237, 245, 247

Verb derivation 63, 101–102,
    108, 110, 170
Verb marking 200–201,
    208–209, 253
Verb serialisation 120
Verbal affixes 15, 164, 165, 239
Video stimuli VII, 3, 11, 31, 33,
    129, 140, 163, 190, 205, 207,
    213, 215, 258
Vietnamese 150

W
Wals sample/survey 19–20
Wierzbicka 17, 28–29, 38, 49,
    51–52, 56, 131, 147
Word order 96, 116, 163, 226,
    234–235, 265, 279

Y
Yélî Dnye 4, 15, 20, 34, 38, 39,
    48, 50, 58, 177, 181–183, 186–
    187, 193–194, 240, 336–337

Yolngu-matha 233
Yuhup 315

Z
Zero anaphora 131
Zipfian effects 9